D1241423

YOU WILL OWN NOTHING

ALSO BY CAROL ROTH

The War on Small Business: How the Government Used the Pandemic to Crush the Backbone of America

The Entrepreneur Equation: Evaluating the Realities, Risks, and Rewards of Having Your Own Business

YOU WILL OWN NOTHING

Your War with a New Financial World Order and How to Fight Back

CAROL ROTH

BROADSIDE
BOOKS

HarperCollins books may be purchased for educational, business, or sales promotional use. For information, please email the Special Markets Department at SPsales@harpercollins.com.

FIRST EDITION

Library of Congress Cataloging-in-Publication Data

Names: Roth, Carol (Carol J. S.), author.
Title: You will own nothing: your war with a new financial order and how to fight back / Carol Roth.
Description: First edition. | New York, NY: HarperBusiness, [2023] | Includes index.
Identifiers: LCCN 2023002246 (print) | LCCN 2023002247 (ebook) | ISBN 9780063304932 (hardcover) | ISBN 9780063304949 (ebook)
Subjects: LCSH: Wealth—United States. | Finance—United States. | Property—United States.
Classification: LCC HC110.W4 R68 2023 (print) | LCC HC110.W4 (ebook) | DDC 305.5/2340973—dc23/emg20230309
LC record available at https://lccn.loc.gov/2023002246
LC ebook record available at https://lccn.loc.gov/2023002247

23 24 25 26 27 LBC 5 4 3 2 1

This book is dedicated to my husband and best friend, Kurt.

This book is likewise dedicated to everyone fighting for individual rights, freedoms, and the pursuit of the American Dream.

CONTENTS

INTRODUCTION

THE COMING WAR

There's a war coming. A global war. You may be thinking about World War III—which, at the time of this writing, hangs in the balance with a certain probability—but I am talking about a different war. This is World War "F"—a financial world war where you are "F'd."

Historically, war has come about in a quest not just for control over another country and its people, but also to overtake their economic resources. War is always economically rooted in some manner, and World War F, in that sense, is no different.

War is also often an outgrowth of desperation. It's a last-ditch effort to cling to power or an attempt to cover up for political, social, or economic breakdowns in the land of the aggressor.

World War F, though, is a modern and unique war. It is not a quest to dominate the American government, but for the government and other related forces to dominate you.

Today there is a late-stage, empire-driven attempt to hold on to power. Multiple forces are working to that end and to set up the elite "on top" for what's ahead: the new financial world order.

These three forces are:

1. Direct government and government-related forces (think Congress and the Federal Reserve);
2. Bad actors and elite power-grabbers (think the World Economic Forum and big business); and
3. Big Tech (think Big Tech).

Individually, any one of these forces would be bad and create a challenging fight. Having them come at us all at once is an all-out major war. Sometimes these entities are working solo, and sometimes they are working together, but their goal is consistent: separating you from your property rights, money, wealth, and other freedoms.

These forces see themselves as the "founding fathers" of the new financial world order, but they are without a moral compass or a set of principles. They operate on the lowest rungs of human nature and desires: greed, power, and control.

They are working on a revolution against you in a war that uses a broad array of tactics, trying to usurp and dominate your wealth and freedom. Whether it be the government, financial powerhouses, international nongovernmental organizations (NGOs), Big Tech, or other powerful entities, they are all prepping and building their forces. They have sophisticated propaganda machines and armies of soldiers they have enlisted, often under false pretenses. They operate on a global scale, sometimes using special forces or even Trojan horses to execute their strategies.

These forces, in different but related ways, are coming for your wealth. They are coming after your livelihood, aka your path to wealth. They are coming after your social standing and access, aka the opportunities for you to create wealth. And, most directly, they are coming after your assets, which is your literal wealth, as well as your legacy and your family's future.

These three forces are bringing about and jockeying to capitalize upon a new financial world order—one with new schemes and innovative technologies that allow fewer opportunities for you. You will need to have the knowledge and the will to fight in order to hold on to the American Dream.

This is a book about what happens when the wealthy and powerful realize the financial stakes are shifting. They could sit back and see how it all plays out. Or they could proactively try to control every finite resource and who has access to such resources.

You need to get battle ready.

You Will Own Nothing

Wealth comes from ownership.

Being involved in the financial industry for nearly thirty years, and spending the past dozen-plus years in the media helping people create economic freedom and wealth for themselves and their families, I know that wealth being derived from ownership is an indisputable truth. More concretely, wealth comes from the ownership of assets that increase in value over time.

Ownership is a subject people tend to greatly misunderstand. We misconstrue where wealth comes from, and we misinterpret the benefits of hard work and taking risks. You can meet a poor construction worker putting in eighty hours a week for someone else. You can find professional athletes declaring bankruptcy as soon as their multimillion-dollar contracts end. And you can find guys sailing their boats who haven't been to an office in years. That's because it's not just how much money you make, but how you manage it and put it to work for you.

Asset ownership provides the ability for people to increase their wealth exponentially—by several multiples of the original investment. This is something that working and earning alone cannot do.

For many Americans, creating generational wealth has come from owning homes that have appreciated in value. Some individuals hold stock and other financial instruments via brokerage accounts and 401(k) plans that have largely increased in value over time. Millions of Americans have built businesses that meet the wants and needs of customers and have created wealth through that process. Others have invested in alternative scarce assets, whether they be precious metals, art, or even trading cards.

So, if there was an institutional, governmental desire for more people to become wealthy and grow that wealth, making it easier to invest and gain ownership would be a priority.

Today's reality is the polar opposite. Ownership—and the opportunities for individual wealth creation and economic freedom that come with it—is under attack.

I am known as someone with a commonsense approach to just about everything, so when I first heard that the World Economic Forum (WEF), an international organization connected to a cadre of elites that includes business, financial, and political leaders, put out a set of predictions for this decade that included the disappearance of ownership, I figured it was a conspiracy theory.

The WEF has courted, developed, and associated with business magnates and political heavyweights like Bill Gates, Salesforce

CEO and co-founder Marc Benioff, Canadian prime minister Justin Trudeau, and former chancellor of Germany Angela Merkel. The WEF hosts a fancy networking forum in Davos, Switzerland, yearly. They put out "thought leadership" around social, political, business, and economic concepts. Surely there must have been some mistake that this organization littered with the global elite would be predicting the end of private property?

It didn't take much research to find that it was right out in the open. The WEF's 2030 predictions included the stark warning, under the guise of sunshine and rainbows, "You'll own nothing. And you'll be happy." And that's just the beginning.

Yes, property rights and the ownership they convey, the cornerstone of freedom and wealth creation opportunities, have come under fire. And I am quite certain that owning nothing and being devoid of the opportunities that come with ownership makes you poor and unfree, not . . . *happy*.

What is being said by the elites aloud worldwide is playing out in real time in the US. But why?

Shifting Toward a New Financial World Order

This brings us back to the war and why you have become the enemy. Everyone, including your own government, wants what you have. More accurately, they are in desperate need of what you have—your wealth, both today and in the future.

These allied forces are on a quest to take your wealth and, by extension, your freedoms for their benefit, their prosperity, and, ultimately, their survival. Without it, their very existence is threatened.

Over the year following the March 2020 Covid lockdowns and mandates, we saw the most historic wealth transfer of all time, enabled by the US government and the Federal Reserve, alongside connected financial institutions. That multitrillion-dollar transfer went from Main Street to Wall Street. The already wealthy and well-connected saw their wealth inflated at the expense of average Americans, including savers and retirees, as well as the backbone of the US economy, small business. The coordination of the big players in the financial sector along with the government has benefited the wealthiest at your expense.

On the tail end of this giveaway, quite predictably, the highest inflation in forty years took hold. Once again, those who had the least bore the brunt of this burden. Then, two years later, the same central planning powers extracted trillions of dollars from the stock market, including from 401(k)s and other individual retirement accounts.

Some stories, facts, and injustices in this book, like the above, will be familiar to you; others will be new and shocking. Hopefully, though, you will begin to see it all in a new light.

These represent just a few battles in a much larger, coordinated, and dangerous endeavor. It is all part of a multipronged shift toward a new financial world order where they own everything and you own nothing.

As we work through the shifting pieces of the world economy and the new financial world order, we'll be looking at two underlying trends. The first is the modern drivers of wealth. The elite know where the valuable resources are in the world and where new value can be created, extracted, or conquered. They know who holds wealth today and where they can get it from in the future. And they know how they plan to take every penny of it that they can.

Debt and Desperation

When the Constitution and Bill of Rights were framed in the eighteenth century, America was primarily an agrarian society. Property rights and the wealth that you could create were heavily tied to land ownership.

Then, as industry advanced and the monetary system evolved, individuals were able to build businesses and create wealth via investment.

Americans prospered through hard work, ingenuity, thriftiness, and risk-taking, all enhanced and protected by the founding concepts of individual rights, including property rights.

As Americans leveraged their work ethic and the structure that protected their fruitfulness, they became increasingly prosperous—at levels not seen anywhere around the globe at any time in history. Credit Suisse's *Global Wealth Report 2022* estimated global wealth at around $463.6 trillion, with 31 percent of that, or around $145.8 trillion, in the hands of Americans.[1]

However, those in charge of safeguarding individual rights—the government—were derelict in their duties. They realized that to take and hold power, they had to make promises and offer "services." Services that, by the way, they weren't paying for—you were.

This led to massive increases in spending. As the government spent, given that government doesn't produce anything of intrinsic value, there were only so many ways to pay for that spending.

Of course, one source of financing government spending is taxation—the taking of a portion of your productivity and wealth.

Another financing route is debt. This leads us to the book's second, deeper issue: the shifting of the financial world order because of the natural opposition between power and too much debt. Debt isn't always bad. It can be a powerful investment tool if used to build something worth far more than the debt in the future. But, increasingly, people owe money on things that have little monetary value, and companies and governments owe money to companies and governments that owe even more money.

The US government can't afford all its spending and has turned time and again to debt as its source of financing (running upwards of $31 trillion, outpacing the GDP, and rapidly growing at the time of writing). Debt isn't a magic payment source because it eventually still needs to be paid. This is ultimately paid from—you guessed it—your productivity. It starts with more taxes to pay for the interest on the debt, making you pay additional money toward "services" you effectively have already purchased by government proxy.

When the government runs out of people who are interested in buying their debt, then they pull an accounting trick and buy (aka monetize) their own debt. By doing so, it again robs your productivity via debasing the dollars that are a proxy for that productivity.

Government could, of course, cut services, but that would threaten its power. Moreover, as everything is done on your dime, why would they choose this route?

They could also take the wealth and riches of other countries and people via invasions, something that isn't popular, for obvious reasons. It's more stealthy and genteel to rob and plunder "legally."

This works for a while, as people go along with the scheme or perhaps don't notice what is going on.

But at some point, the financial scheme starts to show cracks. Debt levels get too high. Neither investors nor other countries want to buy new debt. It becomes incredibly costly to service the substantial amount of existing debt. The monetization scheme produces noticeable damage via inflation. Everything starts to unravel—including the financial empire itself.

I will say it again: power and massive debt loads are at odds with each other.

It becomes mathematically impossible for the current trajectory to be sustained. That's where the desperation kicks in. And new and robust schemes are hatched as a way to continue this spending cycle and protect their power.

The government is desperate and in debt, and you and your fellow citizens represent a massive amount of wealth to be "legally" conquered.

As the US's financial empire is in its twilight, with the government's behaviors threatening the dollar's role as the world's reserve currency, you are at even more risk of owning nothing. The Federal Reserve's policies are greatly impacting the soundness of your money and its global financial standing. This ultimately impacts your wealth creation opportunities as well. You may hold dollars, but they are buying you less and less.

That leads us to where we are today. Many people see where we are in the broader financial cycle and where this is going. The elite and well-connected know that the economic reality isn't sustainable and that it will lead to a new financial world order, as has been the case numerous times throughout history. They have studied it and they want to capitalize upon it.

So, with this knowledge, and the power, wealth, and connections to make it happen, the elite are posturing and positioning. They want to influence, create, dictate, and, most importantly, come out on top in this new financial world order.

That's why they are working, often in alliance, together against you. To ensure that you own nothing, because that means they own as much as possible of everything as a global financial reset happens.

With that, in a postindustrial digital age, between fiat currency, technology, and elite central planning, it is becoming harder than ever to secure and maintain ownership of anything.

You work hard. You save. You invest. You do all the right things, but you still find that you aren't able to get ahead. You know that there's something wrong, but you aren't exactly sure how it all comes together and how you can fight back.

The Counter-revolution

The time is now to create a counter-revolution to these forces.

It is more clear than ever that as a new financial world order takes shape, the American Dream is under fire and may soon be unattainable. The intention is to hollow out the middle and working class and leave them with nothing. It's being done via the encroachment of government, Big Tech, big finance, and other ruling elite into all aspects of your life.

In this book I will share with you where these property rights and wealth creation opportunities are being stymied, the tactics being used to do so, and how you can fight back. You may be tempted to skip ahead and just look for the solutions, but I beg of you to read this all carefully. Understanding what is happening is a critical component of being able to secure your and your family's wealth for the future and ultimately win this war. Your rights, your privacy, and ultimately your wealth hang in the balance.

YOU WILL OWN NOTHING

CHAPTER 1

SOCIALLY UNACCEPTABLE

How Social Credit Leads to Owning You

During the spring and summer of 2020, every evening when the clock struck 7 p.m., something special happened. People across the US, especially in big cities, headed to their windows and began clapping and cheering. Some people flickered the lights in their homes on and off, and others festively hooted and hollered, all meant to show appreciation and support to frontline workers. The workers being celebrated included nurses, doctors, and other medical staff who worked in hospitals and medical facilities, many of which were at capacity because of the increase of Covid patients.[1]

Jenny was one of those frontline workers. Although not directly working with Covid patients, she worked through the pandemic performing her job with vulnerable individuals—an essential worker, as deemed by government mandate. A registered nurse for twenty-one years, during the pandemic Jenny worked as an RN in an inpatient drug rehabilitation and recovery center, as well as responding as a forensic nurse examiner in an emergency room doing evidence collection and examination related to sexual assault cases.[2]

The hospital where she was working in that latter capacity was the first of her two jobs to put in place a Covid vaccine mandate. Jenny applied for a religious exemption and appeared in front of a board that asked questions about her faith and why she didn't want to take a Covid vaccine. A short while later, she received an email that said her request for an exemption was denied. It further said that she had a week to comply and receive the vaccine or else she would be terminated from her job.[3]

Despite already having had Covid, which she was exposed to while working, making a full recovery, and having antibodies to confer what she believed to be natural immunity, this hero was no longer treated as such. She was cast aside and lost her employment.[4]

Jenny was far from the only frontline worker to lose her job. In September 2021, President Joe Biden issued a vaccine executive order related to all federal employees, as well as larger employers.[5] It required all federal employees to take the vaccine, and all employees of companies with more than one hundred workers to get vaccinated, submit to weekly Covid testing, or lose their job.[6] With that, all kinds of frontline workers went from being put on a pedestal to being knocked to the ground.

On top of that, experts said that in most cases, individuals who lost their job for refusing would not be able to claim unemployment benefits, either.[7]

In the weeks and months that followed, all kinds of businesses, with the push from government mandates, fired the "noncompliant." The Mayo Clinic fired seven hundred unvaccinated employees.[8] The city of New York fired more than 1,400 employees, including thirty-six policemen with the NYPD.[9] Individuals in a variety of private jobs, including many who had been working nonstop during the pandemic, lost their jobs.

The pressure from the White House came not only with potential job loss for individuals but also with threats to businesses. For example, with hospitals and medical facilities, if they didn't have a mandate, they would lose access to government Medicare and Medicaid funding, effectively weaponizing health care.[10]

The government pressured businesses and used virtue-signaling supporters, deciding that the very people who had been previously labeled heroic and who kept themselves and others safe for well over a year now had to be punished for noncompliance with this government mandate.

The punishment for noncompliance was taking away people's livelihoods, the ultimate bullying control tactic. And that punishment was aimed at the same people who were pushed to work while others stayed home for months on end.

If you can't earn a living, how are you supposed to live?

Even if you could find another job, government mandates were separating people from their passions and expertise. In addition to arenas already discussed like the police force, the *Military Times* reported in April 2022 on 3,400 troops who were involuntarily separated from military service.[11] In July 2022, Military.com reported, "Some 40,000 National Guard and 22,000 Reserve soldiers who refused to be vaccinated against Covid-19 are no longer allowed to participate in their military duties, also effectively cutting them off from some of their military benefits."[12] At a time when the police and military were struggling with recruitment, willing servicemen and -women, those who may have dreamed their whole lives and trained extensively for this specialized expertise, were separated from their careers and callings.

While many of Biden's private mandates were eventually shut down, with judges agreeing the government exceeded its authority (at least those for private businesses, with others remaining), the die was cast. Businesses didn't want to run afoul of other rules. Workers had already lost their livelihoods and developed animosity toward their employers.[13] Other mandates remained in place for health care workers and federal employees.

It might not have been called social credit, but if it walks like social credit and talks like social credit, it might just be the foundation of it.

Your social standing and your livelihood are the core of your opportunities and path to create wealth. If you are not aligned with the elite, you will find that social credit, whether or not formalized into a system, puts this wealth creation path and its outcomes at risk.

The Short Road from Social Acceptance to Social Credit

There's a fairly straight and certainly disturbing line that goes from social acceptance to a social credit system. It stems from the type of tribal approval mechanism that either embraces you or rejects you as part of a group. Do you support the "current thing"? If you do, you can put up an emoji in your social media biography or a ribbon on your profile picture and a sign in front of your house. You can signal that you are a virtuous and worthy moral being. You are deemed by your peers and the mainstream media as a good citizen and part of the crowd of "right think" instead of "wrongthink."

If you don't support the current thing or, worse, you speak out about it, you may be rejected by others in society. God forbid you wear a hat or a T-shirt with a slogan that identifies you as outside of "right think" or you don't wear a cloth mask to the grocery store; if so, you may be subject to a verbal haranguing in public. Worse, if a human resources manager combs your social media profile, you might lose out on a job opportunity for your lack of being part of the socially acceptable crowd.

This sort of elevated tribal social credit takes another step in its vitriol in the form of cancel culture.

Top podcaster, entrepreneur, comedian, and UFC commentator Joe Rogan received this type of treatment in 2021 and 2022. After Rogan had signed a reported $200 million deal with Spotify, a group of Spotify employees petitioned the company to have Rogan's show go through "editorial supervision" because they disagreed with some views expressed on the podcast.[14] That didn't work.

Months later, after Rogan had hosted a variety of scientists and medical experts who held views that were against mainstream groupthink, certain other academics, doctors, and influencers started to push what appeared to be a coordinated boycott of his podcast. They claimed he was spreading dangerous misinformation (none of which seemed consistent with the definition of dangerous and much of which has been validated over time).[15] Then artist Neil Young said he would pull his work from the Spotify catalog (via his record label, which held the rights to his recordings), setting off further social outrage. [16] In a town hall meeting held amid the hullaballoo, Spotify's CEO reportedly said they were not planning to edit or censor Rogan because the company operates as a distribution platform, not a publisher.[17]

When that didn't work, someone dug up a series of out-of-context clips of Rogan using offensive language, including racially charged words, and put them together in a compilation video, circulating it throughout social media. Rogan called it a "political hit job" and rightfully shamed those going after him as "judgmental, unforgiving, fu**s," which is the feature, not the bug, of this societal judgment-by-moral-superiority.[18] As his business partners mostly stuck by him, that effort didn't have the intended impact, ultimately gaining him two million podcast subscribers.[19]

Legendary comedian Dave Chappelle also faced a cancellation attempt when hundreds of Netflix employees staged a walkout in October 2021 to protest the comedian and his Netflix special *The Closer*. Bolstered by social media virtue signalers, the employees said Chappelle's content—which, by the way, is made up of jokes—was harmful, and they pushed Netflix to pull the special.[20] One of the employees had been part of a small group that also crashed a Netflix board meeting in protest of Chappelle and his work.[21]

Likely prompted by the streaming service losing more than $50 billion in market cap after reporting their Q1 2022 earnings and seeing that entangling culture wars and business wasn't good for their business, Netflix put out an employee memo. According to *Variety*, the memo included "a new section called 'Artistic Expression,' explaining that the streamer will not 'censor specific artists or voices' even if employees consider the content 'harmful,' and bluntly states, 'If you'd find it hard to support our content breadth, Netflix may not be the best place for you.'"[22]

While those movements tried to attack the livelihoods and social standings of these gentlemen and failed, likely because the targets were deemed too valuable to their respective business partners and they had strong support systems, others have succeeded. Ellen DeGeneres wound down her previously wildly successful daytime show in 2022 because of a string of "moral outrages," including being photographed at an NFL game alongside former president George W. Bush, which created a backlash that included allegations of a toxic work culture (some of her staff was "canceled" in the wake of this, as well). Kyle Kashuv, a teen who gained awareness as a survivor of the 2018 mass shooting at Marjory Stoneman Douglas High School in Parkland, Florida, had Harvard rescind his acceptance after a series of texts between him and some friends from when he was sixteen years old surfaced and included offensive racial language. Whether it results from videotaping someone having a meltdown at their worst moment, digging up an offensive tweet from a decade ago, or even retweeting a controversial joke, many individuals, including a slew who were not public figures, have found themselves with their social credit declining.

The less connected you are with a group that will support and fight for you, the more effective these tactics are.

Sometimes this social witch hunt happens even when the information is perceived incorrectly. Nick Sandmann, who in 2019 was a student at Covington Catholic High School in Kentucky, was falsely accused by various media and the social mob of aggression at a political demonstration in Washington, DC, an incorrect accusation made out of context. Eventually, more photos and videos disproved that narrative, and Sandmann settled lawsuits against CNN, the *Washington Post*, and NBCUniversal, the terms of which were undisclosed. However, had the other information not been available, who knows what long-lasting outcast treatment he would have endured?[23]

Whether or not their accusations have merit, those who levy them do so with the intent to wield power and to deliver consequences of their choosing. Those consequences typically result in poor financial outcomes.

When a social moral code replaces a legal code and gains acceptance, it is only a matter of time before those in power want to leverage that dynamic to secure more power for themselves.

That begets the foundation for social compliance and social credit at the state/government level. This is the perfect tactic for the elite in a new financial world order to ensure that the people connected to them come out on top.

But how does a true state social credit system come to be? It requires two steps. The first is information-gathering on individuals. The second is those in power using the information without being challenged. When both of those become easy to do at scale, tyranny quickly follows.

At the onset of the new financial world order, both of those components are here. Technology enables easy, scalable information collection, storage, and analytical capabilities. People voluntarily shun privacy for convenience, ego, and other purposes, and so the information is available for such collection.

The social devolution where people are widely judged not in a court of law but rather a court of public approval sets up the second part—the creep of government and other powers being able to use information for compliance and to subjugate individual rights.

And so, today, we lie just a fraction of a millimeter away from a true state social credit system, the ultimate in tyrannical control. We are remarkably close to a place where by acting outside the preferred narrative, not agreeing with the mob, having a bad day, or engaging in wrongthink like not complying with government directives, criticizing the president, or being a gun owner, the government can penalize you. Potential penalties could remove your freedoms, big and small, including your ability to earn a living and provide for your family.

If you don't comply, you can't earn a living. You will own nothing.

To understand what that means and could look like in practice, I turn to the country that currently has the most advanced social credit system, China.

Social Credit: The Chinese Communist Party Model

It is easy to dismiss the notion that the US would act in a manner similar to China when it came to your rights. Ten years ago, I may have agreed the probability was low that something like that would happen anytime soon. After 2020, I can no longer agree.

We have already seen government and societal pushes for mandatory vaccines and masking, calls for (and actual) job loss for noncompliance, vaccine passports for eating in restaurants, and the government labeling a large part of the population as "nonessential."

We have politicians who regularly attack individual citizens by name. How many times has Senator Elizabeth Warren called out specific people like Elon Musk or Jeff Bezos in an effort to push policy? The distance between what the government should be doing to ensure the protection of our rights and the government overtaking our rights has shrunk so substantially that a flea couldn't make its way through the middle.

"Yes-men" and other useful idiots from the general population are more than happy to jump on board and support these state-disseminated endeavors and propaganda. It often reaffirms their point of view. Even better, in their estimation, it creates penalties for those who don't conform, disagree with their point of view, and engage in wrongthink. The useful idiots who align with the state are happy to see penalties enacted without giving an iota of thought to principles, the precedent being set, and long-term consequences.

Given that we are so close to social credit, with the social acceptance of moral judgment outside the legal system and the technical means to collect and analyze information at scale, the Chinese system provides a frightening road map.

China's Social Credit System, often referred to as the "SCS" or "SoCS," is an emerging system of gathering information and engineering compliance for businesses, individuals, and other entities—with the exception, of course, of the Chinese Communist Party (CCP).[24]

According to Horizons, a global tech and human resources consultancy, "The term 'social credit' (社会信用体 in Chinese and *shèhuì xìnyòng tǐxì* in pinyin) doesn't have a precise meaning—rather, it is an intentionally broad and vague term allowing for maximal policy flexibility." Building in the power to change the meaning and aspects of the SCS at the CCP's whim is itself a tool of control. You will see this in other systems of control that I will cover later in the book as well, like environmental, social, and corporate governance (ESG).[25]

Certain jurisdictions throughout China do have an associated SCS scoring system; some use a scale of letter grades or numerical values, but this has not been codified and standardized throughout the country as of yet.

SCS is primarily about gathering and analyzing behavioral data of individuals, then rewarding or punishing certain actions to force individuals into compliance with the types of behaviors the CCP wants and eliminating or suppressing behaviors they don't.

The Mercator Institute for China Studies (MERICS) describes the SCS efforts as being "focused on the establishment of comprehensive digital files that track and document legal compliance."[26] I would add moral and social compliance as well.

SCS is wrapped in their perception of the concept of "trust." Trust is not a new thing for societies. Whether in China or the US or just about every country around the globe, there is a certain moral code within society. Some elements of trust are formally codified into a legal system that balances individual rights (as in the case of theft, for example), and some of it is just what others find acceptable (perhaps distasteful and offensive, but not illegal, such as using foul language in public).

Social credit takes the concept of trust in society and puts it in the hands of central planners to dictate their morals and other priorities.

This is fascism masquerading as trust. It is a tyrannical and complete centralization of powers and control over the population, with no regard for individual rights.

The History of China's SCS

The Chinese state has a history of tracking its population. Dating back to the Mao regime, they used analog (paper) files to keep track of key pieces of information on individuals called the *dang'an* (which loosely translates in English to "record"). According to the Visual Capitalist, the *dang'an* contained information such as "an individual's school reports, information on physical characteristics, employment records, and photographs. These dossiers, which were first used in the Maoist years, helped the government in maintaining control of its citizens." They nickname the SCS the "digital *dang'an*."[27]

Obviously, the CCP isn't known for its protection of individual rights (the first clue is the word *communist* in the name of the party). From the cultural flouting of intellectual property protections to systemic rights violations against the Uyghur population in the country, individual rights are substituted with "common good," which is code for what the elites in control want.

It shouldn't be a surprise that elements of social credit systems throughout history have often been associated with communist regimes.

Another item of note is how their social credit system morphed quickly from specifically financial to more broadly social, taking more liberties along the way. As Horizons explains, "The system began with a focus on financial creditworthiness, similar to credit scores used in western countries, and moved on to include compliance and legal violations. The eventual 'end-state' of the system is a unified record for people, businesses, and the government, which can be monitored in real-time."[28] This is emblematic of how swiftly a shift can occur, in this case from creditworthiness for a specific purchase or investment to control of every aspect of an individual's life.

The most relevant recent developments regarding what we think of as the Chinese SCS today happened in 2014, when, according to the Diplomat, "the Chinese State Council released the 'Guidelines of Social Credit System Construction (2014–2020),' outlining the goal of establishing a basic social credit system by 2020."[29]

Building from that guidance, according to MERICS, "43 pilot cities have launched SoCS projects since 2014, culminating in the selection of 28 model cities between 2018 and 2019 as test beds for nationwide implementation of SoCS." As one might imagine, different geographic regions have different issues and priorities, and so what and who they targeted, particularly from an industry standpoint, has some variance.[30]

It was reported that as of December 2020, more than 80 percent of China's jurisdictions (such as provinces, autonomous regions, and municipal cities) had developed or were planning to issue SCS-related regulations and laws.[31]

The system today is still evolving, a work in progress. That doesn't make it less concerning. It remains front and center, and new realities are incorporated into its design. For example, during Covid, while the pandemic put some of the program expansion on hold, the health event was itself incorporated into the system.

Currently the SCS in China is more developed around businesses than it is for individuals. This is key to understand, as it relates to the theme of this book and wealth creation. While China moved a bit more toward capitalism, the economic independence of those who have benefited from that move has been perceived as a threat by the CCP. As an example, billionaire entrepreneur Jack Ma went missing in China for several months in late 2020 after criticizing the Chinese banking industry and making other non-CCP-friendly comments.[32] He reemerged months later, and in January 2023 it was reported that he had given up control of Ant Group, taking his voting rights down to an estimated 6.2 percent. Note that "Chinese regulators pulled the plug on Ant's $37 billion IPO in November 2020 and ordered the company to restructure its business."[33]

Limiting and controlling wealth creation opportunities is a key method for controlling a society, and so it makes sense that China would focus on that first in terms of social credit, getting those with any sense of entrepreneurialism or capitalistic instincts "in line."

That doesn't mean that SCS isn't impacting individuals.

It is worth noting that when we talk about the issues around social credit, while all of the endeavors may not officially be a part of what China calls their SCS, or what any other country might, they in concept still lead to the same outcomes: centralized power and control over the individual. MERICS reports that the SCS is just a small piece of the CCP's control framework: "The Social Credit System remains the least digitized of China's tech-driven monitoring and surveillance initiatives. It relies heavily on human investigations, reports, and decisions. This also leaves room for traditional vectors of individual and political influence."[34]

As I mentioned, the path to social credit requires acceptance and technology to access and analyze data. The CCP doesn't care about acceptance, given how they rule. On the technology side, China's SCS is heavily backed by a variety of technologies. It is focused on gathering information on everything from what you look like to who your family members are to where you work. The "digital *dang'an*" is backed by "big data" algorithms and artificial intelligence (AI) to identify issues and noncompliance on an ongoing basis. Additional technology implemented involves drone monitoring and facial recognition matched to a database that has more than 1.3 billion photos.[35]

Rewards and Punishments

Some aspects of the SCS are the equivalent of the gamification of life by the government. If you do something that is deemed good, you will be rewarded. If you do something that is deemed bad, you will be punished. The "good" and "bad" are not tied to the typical infringements of others' rights, like the US legal system, but rather a variety of behaviors, some that may seem like insignificant personal choices, others that are bona fide illegal activities. All of this is dictated by the ruling party.

Depending on the scope of your behaviors, sometimes due to an individual infraction, sometimes from a cumulative result, you may be placed on "blacklists" or "redlists." As you can imagine, a blacklist bans individuals and entities from access and activities. A redlist can confer upon you perks, privileges, and other benefits for being deemed a good citizen.

The types of punishments and blacklist ramifications are still evolving. Currently, being on a blacklist may preclude you from access to jobs, access to financial accounts, prevent your kids from attending schools, and even publicly shame you in person, online, or via TV channels. It ensures that you will own nothing.

Another blacklist penalty is restricting your ability to travel. From Horizons: "Reports in 2019 indicated that 23 million people have been blacklisted from travelling by plane or train due to low social credit ratings maintained through China's National Public Credit Information Center."[36]

At the business level, being blacklisted can lead to additional audits and government oversight of your company.

The complexities of noncompliance go beyond simple penalties; they overtake your life, by design.

So, what gets you negative points or on a blacklist? Being behind in paying your debts is a big one, from all reports, as is refusing to serve in the military. But even personal, mundane actions or nonactions are judged. For example, in Shanghai, not visiting your elderly parents is an infraction.[37] Loitering, spreading "fake news" (whatever that is deemed by the powers-that-be), cheating when playing video games, taking up too much room in an airplane, making an insincere apology, jaywalking, and blocking sidewalks are all activities that can lower your social credit score and lead to punishments.[38]

A variety of behaviors and actions reportedly can get you "good points," at least in certain jurisdictions. For individuals, these include praising the government on social media, donating blood, and charity. Think about the implications of that—while perhaps seemingly innocuous, this is the government controlling speech, personal health choices, and personal finances, respectively.[39]

The CCP doesn't believe in true property rights, and so Chinese citizens already truly "own nothing." The SCS is meant for the CCP to gain further control over each person's life and uses the termination of any semblance of freedom and ownership they might enjoy as a threat.

Being on the Blacklist

NPR recounted the story of a man on the SCS "blacklist" in China. His name is Lao Duan, and he previously had a business as a physical intermediary for coal—buying, storing, and, ultimately, selling it. When the Chinese government enacted a change in its coal energy policy, the price of coal collapsed. With this massive government-enabled price change, Lao Duan found that he couldn't pay back the loans he had taken out. He was put on the blacklist by a Chinese court. They froze his credit card and financial accounts.

One day, he went to purchase a train ticket with another form of payment but was barred from making the purchase. Via an interpreter, he told NPR, "One thing that comes along with the blacklist, the untrustworthy list, is that you are barred from high-end consumption, which means that you can't take a speed train. You can't fly."[40]

Next came public shaming. In a staggering scene that could have been out of an Orwell novel, Lao Duan saw his face, name, and unique ID number projected on a giant electronic billboard highlighting various "untrustworthy" individuals. He told NPR that he recognized many faces from the billboard as former coal industry colleagues.[41] People who found themselves in a bad situation explicitly because of a government policy change were now being further penalized, as well as ostracized, by the government.

Red Light, Green Light

Social credit and technology are a dangerous combination. In terms of China's SCS, some citizens found themselves playing a different version of the kids' game "red light, green light." While not as perilous as the *Squid Game* version, it highlights the ways the already dodgy SCS can be further bastardized.

In China, the government has been using smartphones to restrict movement under the guise of Covid monitoring. If you have a clear Covid test, when your code is swiped, the code shows green. If you have tested positive for Covid, your code turns your smartphone screen red upon scanning.

The *Wall Street Journal* reports that in mid-2022, a number of individuals who found their bank accounts frozen (related to other financial issues in China, including a real estate crisis) went to the Chinese city of Zhengzhou for a protest of these financial institutions.[42]

One individual named Ye Mijian had no Covid sickness or related restrictions. He swiped his app to board the train to Zhengzhou, delivering a green light. When he exited the train, he swiped the code again. But, despite no actual change to his status, it turned red. Local officials made him quarantine in a local hotel for two days.

He was unable to protest, and when he was let out of his mandated quarantine, he swiped his phone, and his screen went back to green.

Ye's circumstances were not isolated. Many other protesters found the same thing.

After a large uproar regarding several similar situations in a couple of cities, Chinese officials denounced these actions, but actions speak louder than words.

The WEF and ACS

Money is the throughline in the quest for power and control. So, not surprisingly, that quest often not only ends with money but also begins with money. In the realm of social credit in China, the system started with financial credit assessments and branched out from there. That same foundation is being championed elsewhere as well.

Another credit scoring system with social ties is being promoted by a variety of powerful entities, including the World Economic Forum (WEF), an entity connected with the world's elites that is trying to shape the global landscape based on their vision (and of course their quest for power). They are the same group that has predicted, for 2030, "you'll own nothing." I will go into them more in Chapter 3.

This system is called Alternative Credit Scoring (ACS). As a way to sell it, it is being positioned as a mechanism to help create more financial inclusion for the underbanked (because, of course, I am sure they all truly care about the "underbanked").

ACS was part of the WEF's Davos Agenda for 2021, and details have been shared in an article on the WEF website. ACS is currently targeted at emerging economies where they don't have the same types of banking and financial data and where purchases and financial transactions tend to run through e-commerce. ACS leverages AI and other technology to build digital profiles on consumers.[43]

Some of the data collected as part of ACS includes asset ownership, utility payment records, and other bureau reports. That all sounds somewhat normal.[44]

Then, it starts to go off the rails. Also included in this profile are location data, social media data, and psychometric (aka psychological measurement) test data that go into your file, get analyzed by AI, and return your score.

A graphic included with the article explains, "ACD (alternative credit decisioning) involves the leveraging of unconventional consumer information in combination with conventional credit sources . . . to predict creditworthiness."[45]

"Unconventional consumer information" is quite the explanation, wouldn't you say? Following people's every move, using personality and behavior outside of just their capability to pay to allow access to financial products, sounds like one of those good ideas that can go horribly wrong.

The WEF goes on to say about this arena, "Consumption-related data is everywhere. Unfortunately, it is non-uniform, disorganised and scattered. In the initial phase—the consolidation process—the finding, identifying and capturing of data must be conducted. Then, we use basic data cleaning, correlating and storing technology concepts to build the unified BigData concept. Only then do we have a basis for leveraging advanced technology (AI and DS modelling) and can start correlating, experimenting and building models."[46]

What could go wrong with the WEF and other elites promoting the collection, consolidation, and analysis of more and more data about you? Just about everything.

The piece also shares an image from consumer financial services reporting bureau Experian showing all the kinds of data it hypothetically could collect and use in conjunction with ACS. From your smartphone, it shows that it can use your contact information, GPS location, and mobile and data usage. It can use your travel patterns, your spending patterns, and more.[47]

Of course, some of these types of data are already used in underwriting risk. If you have a credit card, your card company may contact you about an out-of-state purchase that was flagged in analyzing a different location versus where it believes you to generally be spending your time.

However, as we will delve into later in the book, bad outcomes often start as innocuous ideas. With the incorporation of personal data like psychometrics and social media tied to money starting in emerging markets, it may not be long before that comes to a government near you.

An article in Slate mused about a version of this future:

> we imagine a time when credit scores do indeed take into account not just our payment history, but our entire social web. . . . your credit score can be augmented by simply looking at how positive your comments are, how often you "like" posts from high- or low-risk accounts, how quickly you respond to DMs, and even how long you spend mindlessly scrolling. How often do you text your friends back? Did you call your mom on her birthday? . . . It all adds up to a nice little score at the top of a brightly colored readout: your credit score, enhanced.[48]

Again, this isn't a conspiracy or fringe set of theories. These are concepts being used and evaluated by major governments and big businesses around the world and ideas being proposed by entities with ties to the leading financial and consulting organizations in the world.

As we move into the new financial world order, and with entities from tech companies to governments looking to exert more power and control, normalizing "alternative" personality and nonfinancial behavior mechanisms to go into files and scores is fraught with issues.

A Stone's Throw from Social Credit

On April 27, 2022, in an announcement that seemed to come straight from a George Orwell novel, the Biden administration announced the formation of something called the Disinformation Governance Board, or DGB, as a part of the Department of Homeland Security.

What could possibly go wrong with the government being the arbiter of what is truth and what is not? As demonstrated by China—as well as the US in recent years—a whole lot can go wrong.

The endeavor was explained in a report from the Associated Press: "The Department of Homeland Security is stepping up an effort to counter disinformation coming from Russia as well as misleading information that human smugglers circulate to target migrants hoping to travel to the U.S.-Mexico border."

Of course, it is always fear and crisis that are used for the subjugation of rights and the theft of liberties.

The explanation and rationale might seem reasonable to some. But an op-ed in the *Wall Street Journal* nailed the issue, saying,

> The stated goal of combating mis- and disinformation is framed to seem unobjectionable. Who objects to truth and pines for falsehood? DGB experts will guide the way, separating the informational wheat from the disinformational chaff. But there's one small problem with empowering "truth experts": Experts are people. People respond to incentives. Therefore experts respond to incentives.[49]

Not only are "experts" people who sometimes make mistakes and whose behavior is motivated by a variety of incentives, but also government officials and their helpers are typically seeking more power for themselves, and that comes at your expense.

Laughably, about two weeks after the DGB announcement, the White House told a whopper so big that even the major news media couldn't ignore it. A CNN headline proclaimed, "White House tweet falsely claims 'there was no vaccine available' when Biden took office." This was an easily provable falsehood, particularly given that Joe Biden himself was first vaccinated under the Trump administration. That is one of the myriad pieces of misinformation and disinformation that have come out of the administration on topics ranging from the economy to the border. Despite their propensity to run afoul of the truth, not to mention our free speech rights, they want to be charged with monitoring misinformation—for your good, of course.[50]

The woman chosen to run this disinformation control effort was Nina Jankowicz, who had been an advisor to the Ukrainian government.[51] There were also questions about her own role in sharing disinformation. *New York* magazine said, "Critics noted Jankowicz's coziness with some liberals, her iffy comments on the Hunter Biden laptop story (whose ill-conceived censorship at the hands of Facebook and Twitter remains a hot conservative topic), and her endorsement of the largely debunked Steele dossier."[52]

There was immediate pushback to the board itself, including various references on social media and alternative media calling this new board the "Ministry of Truth," a nod to the fictional government agency in Orwell's *1984* that created its own version of reality, covered up and changed anything that didn't fit with the desired state agenda, and force-fed it to the public.

After just three weeks, the initiative was put "on pause." The phrasing was interesting because it didn't suggest it was being abandoned but rather that the heat needed to cool down.

A *New York* magazine piece said, "[P]resenting anyone from the government as an arbiter of truth in 2022—much less defining 'disinformation' in a way that more than 40 percent of the population would agree with—seemed doomed from the get-go."[53]

What the Twitterverse and certain other media were willing to acknowledge that the pro-censorship crowd wasn't was that it sounded like something that would come out of the CCP, not the USA.

That's the point. We have lived through government narratives around Covid—including those related to vaccines/therapeutics and masks—becoming items that couldn't be argued with, even when much of what was portrayed as misinformation has proven to be fact.

The government pressured tech companies to remove posts that disagreed with or contradicted their narrative.[54] Many scientists, doctors, and regular individuals saw their ability to object and speak freely censored and found themselves deplatformed.[55]

The Heritage Foundation related this behavior back to social credit:

> In the United States, the increasingly oppressive collaboration between public and private entities is not enforced at the barrel of a gun. It arises from an ideological symbiosis between tech incumbents and government officials. This has allowed governments to successfully encourage tech companies to help police the discourse of ordinary Americans. For example, then–White House press secretary Jen Psaki admitted in July that the White House works with Facebook to monitor and police speech and later insisted that other private platforms should be "doing more" of the same. . . .[56]
>
> Homeland Security Secretary Alejandro Mayorkas indicated his organization was working with tech companies to strengthen "legitimate use" of private platforms. Twitter reportedly deferred to the California Secretary of State's office when flagging and scrutinizing questions surrounding the 2020 election and criticism of President Biden.[57]

The pause of the board was short-lived and rebranded—chef's kiss perfection for a disinformation initiative. The Heritage Foundation reported, "In fact, the administration has announced that former Homeland Security Secretary Michael Chertoff and former U.S. Deputy Attorney General Jamie Gorelick will take the baton from Jankowicz and continue down the disinformation track. This plan is no better than the first one. . . . What the left and the Biden administration fail to recognize is that it cannot gain the public's trust regarding misinformation or disinformation."[58]

I would say it is deeper than that; we have free speech as the first protected right in the Bill of Rights to ensure our individual rights are protected against the government, regardless of who occupies the White House. To have any government entity as a type of arbiter of speech stands at odds with our natural rights and is a mechanism for social credit–type control.

Moreover, the government's definition of disinformation (and, by extension, that of many social media platforms) by their own actions is not "things that are factually untrue," but rather, "things that disagree with the narrative."

Information as part of social credit is not just close; it has happened. Not complying with vaccines as social credit has happened. This was done with the approval of much of the population, some of whom were willing to "rat out" others for wrongthink or noncompliance. This came about with government and Big Tech collaboration. This happened in a short period of time with no formal process. The next steps will be worse.

With the technology and tools to scale it, it's only a matter of time before it is further weaponized.

A Red Flag on Red Flags

It is not a coincidence that some of the worst genocides in history, from the Armenian genocide to the Holocaust, have begun with the disarming of the population.

With the trajectory of the government and its actions, having a well-armed population (aka a well-regulated militia) is critical for keeping the balance of power between the people and the government.

Arms are also important to help protect your property, not just from the government, but from mobs when nobody else shows up. The right to bear arms is fundamental to individual rights and intertwined with freedom and property rights.

In late June 2022, Congress passed new gun control legislation. The piece that raised eyebrows included funding for the expansion of red flag laws.[59] The concern, tied into what we have been talking about, is that, intentionally or unintentionally, people could lose their right to self-defense without due process.

Due process is the cornerstone of American justice. As Fox News host Tucker Carlson said in a monologue on his show, "In our system of justice, citizens cannot be punished without first being charged with a crime. Politicians cannot just decide to hurt you, throw you in handcuffs, lock you in jail, seize your property simply because they don't like how you think or how you vote. No. Before they punish you, they have to go through a formal process in which they describe which specific law you broke and exactly how you broke it. They have to prove it."[60]

Carlson continued, "Under red flag laws, the government doesn't have to prove you did anything wrong in order to strip you of your most basic rights. All that's required to punish you is a complaint, possibly even an anonymous complaint in which somebody says you seem dangerous. Now, that complaint doesn't come from a grand jury. It can come from anyone, including someone who hates you or someone who simply doesn't like your politics. It doesn't matter because no jury will ever see it. On the basis of that unproven complaint, you lose your freedom and your ability to defend yourself and your family."[61]

This is a frightening extension of social credit, one that undermines rights and freedoms, including property rights. The slow creep and acceptance of these unconstitutional actions cement them as such. The Constitution is just a contract. If the contract isn't enforced, it ceases to have meaning.

New York is further blending the social credit components we have been talking about with this desire to take away Second Amendment rights. The state has passed a bill requiring firearm applicants to list three years' worth of all social media accounts and provide "good moral character" references in order to exercise their constitutional rights.

Fortunately (for now), at the end of December 2022, New York State's Supreme Court ruled that New York's "red flag law" (aka the Extreme Risk Protection Order Law) was unconstitutional.[62]

Still, it is clear that your speech and good standing in society will now be used as leverage for you to exercise your most fundamental rights. That's the true red flag—in fact, it's a neon red sign of tyranny.

Having your rights infringed is all part of the new financial world order and the plan to have you own nothing. It becomes easier to enact if you can't physically fight back or defend your property.

Digital IDs

In the US, if and when you received your Covid vaccine, you received a "vaccine passport." This analog card was filled in with basic information about you and the dates and product information related to which vaccine you received. It was then updated for each subsequent dose or booster shot you received. You may have perceived it as just a piece of cardstock, but in reality it was much more: an early form factor of a social credit card. In fact, certain jurisdictions would not let you actively participate in society, such as entering a restaurant, without this card. You must show the card or you are socially unacceptable.

Some jurisdictions took this social card to the next level and digitized it. For example, New York State implemented the Excelsior Pass *Plus*. According to their website:

> Excelsior Pass *Plus* is a secure, digital copy of your COVID-19 vaccination record or negative test results. . . .[63]
>
> Your Excelsior Pass *Plus* provides safe access to your COVID-19 vaccination record or negative test results. The inclusion of health information enables you to have a verifiable record of your COVID-19 vaccination or negative test result at your fingertips. It includes the same information you would find on your CDC Vaccination Card or paper laboratory test results for record-keeping and/or usage outside of New York State.[64]

While Excelsior Pass *Plus* was an opt-in program, it reminds us how technology facilitates the collection of data and the implementation of social credit. These digital vaccination passes, also widely used in Europe, which generated a QR code that could be scanned to verify if you were approved to participate in society via your vaccination passes, are clearly a precursor to digital IDs. Using fear, safety, and virtue signaling as a way to make them acceptable, they have laid the path to more intrusive data collection.

Once the government has started a digital file on you and created the infrastructure for collection and storage, why not fill it up? Why not link it to financial information or a digital wallet? Perhaps they can link up with your other accounts—for *your* convenience, of course.

Once those who stand to profit, including the big financial service firms and the tech companies, think of ways they can monetize having access to more information, they will be all too happy to help develop, implement, and promote them.

This is all quite similar to the ACS model we talked about earlier. It is also fraught with similar risks to the red screen that would-be Chinese protesters encountered via their Covid apps that kept them from engaging in protests.

Of course, the profiteers are already figuring out how they can participate. There is a group called the ID2020 Alliance, found at ID2020.org, which "is building a new global model for the design, funding, and implementation of digital ID solutions and technologies."[65]

They are doing this, of course, for your protection and benefit—out of the goodness of their hearts, really. Their website says, "We need to get digital ID right. Identity is vital for political, economic and social opportunity. But systems of identification are archaic, insecure, lack adequate privacy protection . . ." and so on.[66]

They are already implying that your identity will allow for participation in society and they want to build something new to facilitate this. It's saying the quiet part aloud.

So, who are the partners in this ID2020 Alliance? According to the website, "No government, company or agency can solve this challenge alone. Setting the future course of digital ID and navigating the associated risks is a challenge that requires sustained collaboration and global partnership." Ah yes, the good old we are all in this together.

And the Good Samaritans who are championing this for our benefit include "founding partners" of consulting firm Accenture, technology firm Microsoft, Gavi: The Vaccine Alliance, the Rockefeller Foundation, and IDEO.org, whose website states, "We design products and services alongside organizations that are committed to creating a more just and inclusive world." General partners include other names you will recognize, such as Facebook and Mastercard.[67]

This self-appointed group, which undoubtedly has at least one entity involved that raises your eyebrow, is now working on something that could be extremely dangerous. Once there is money to be made, those with a financial incentive or who see the financial opportunity will find useful idiots to help entrench this in society. Once highly sticky technology gets rolled out and used, it is extremely difficult to remove it from use.

The Not-So-Free Freedom Convoy

Truckers are a lifeblood of any economy. They transport critical supplies, food, and other goods from one location to another so that we all can enjoy an improved quality of life. Truckers were also on the front lines during the Covid pandemic, making sure grocery store shelves were stocked and hospitals had lifesaving supplies.

In Canada, when their livelihoods were used as a hostage-negotiating tactic for vaccinations required to cross the US border, many truckers understandably became fed up. Beginning in western Canada, independent truck drivers and their supporters led protests across that country, eventually converging in the capital city of Ottawa. This became referred to as the Freedom Convoy.[68]

These protesters were fighting against infringements on their rights. They wanted mandates repealed that would force them to take a vaccine or lose the ability to work, dine out, or freely travel.[69]

After several weeks, the prime minister of Canada, Justin Trudeau, took an extreme measure by calling the convoy a national security risk and invoking temporary emergency security powers. Police began to arrest these peaceful protesters, but that was just the beginning.[70]

The Canadian government invoked authority to cut off the protesters' financial resources. The government "obligated" processors of financial transactions, including crowdfunding sites, to report any funding, including donations that "they deemed suspicious," to the government authorities.[71] The *Wall Street Journal* reported that "financial institutions froze more than 200 financial accounts belonging to individuals and an account held by a payment processor with a value of 3.8 million Canadian dollars, or the equivalent of $3 million. Police also ceased transactions involving 253 cryptocurrency addresses."[72]

Despite outrage from civil rights groups, thought leaders, and others, the Canadian government proceeded to treat protesters and dissenters as terrorists.

Not surprisingly, freedom-supporting allies in the United States took to crowdfunding sites to try to help. A GoFundMe page was put up and raised more than C$10 million from supporters. Despite its headquarters being located in California, the site bowed to political pressure from the Canadian government. GoFundMe put out a statement saying the fundraiser was a violation of their terms of service as its reason to remove it from the platform.[73]

Another US-based crowdfunding site, GiveSendGo, was used to raise close to $10 million from supporters, many of whom reportedly resided in the US. Hackers decided to align with the Canadian government, attacked the GiveSendGo website, and leaked private data on who had made the contributions.[74] The hackers posted a message intimating that the protest was an "insurrection" and alluding to the Canadian government's desire to freeze the assets of the participants. They also tried to equate the fundraising with the January 6, 2021, riot at the US Capitol.[75]

This is a perfect example of how social credit is being seeded. People wanted to live freely. But for the truckers, that wasn't aligned with Canadian government mandates, and it wasn't aligned with the "current thing." Their bank accounts were frozen. Big Tech aided the government, even when it was another country's government! While individuals tried to help, others turned not only on the people who weren't complying but also on the ones who were offering assistance.

While Canadian officials said the truckers' accounts had been unfrozen in late February, the damage had been done.

In 2017, WEF president Klaus Schwab participated in a discussion at Harvard's John F. Kennedy School of Government, where he talked about key politicians who have been featured as WEF Young Global Leaders.[76] One of the names he bragged about was Canadian prime minister Justin Trudeau. Schwab then said, "So, we penetrate the cabinets. So, yesterday I was at a reception for Prime Minister Trudeau, and I know that half of this cabinet, or even more than half of this cabinet, are . . . young global leaders of the World Economic Forum."

In the case of Canada and Trudeau's cabinet, this includes Chrystia Freeland, deputy prime minister and finance minister, and former WEF Young Global Leader.[77] Freeland was reported to be the force behind freezing the Freedom Convoy protesters' bank accounts and certainly was the public face of defending the decision.[78]

I am not saying there was or was not any direct correlation here, but it is clear that there are numerous powerful people of a similar mindset who hang out together and are happy to put you on the path to owning nothing if you don't comply with their wishes.

Will You "Own" Your Children?

As social credit seeks to make moral or power-based decisions regarding what is appropriate behavior, what is important, what you can have access to, and what you cannot if you don't comply with the narrative, that same type of power is being exerted in another sphere. This is regarding "ownership" of your children.

I hate to speak of one human being "owning" another, but kids belong to their parents or legal guardian. Parents have the rights and responsibilities for their minor children, not the state, not teachers' unions, nor any other group of elite and well-connected. So I use the phrasing of "ownership" of your children to try to convey that the powerful are trying to separate you from the influence and rights over your children, wanting to insert themselves in your place.

In Orwell's *1984*, the "Party" (aka the state) comes between parents and their children, disrupting the normal relationship and standing between parent and child. Instead of the parent being the authority figure, they are replaced by the state as the one shaping the children, to the detriment of their parents. The disruption of the family was a means for the Party to gain more power and control, and to ensure that the ideas absorbed by future generations were the ones that the Party wanted.

This has also played out in history. While I try to use references to Nazi Germany sparingly, when they are applicable they must be pointed out. In Germany, the Nazis sought to take advantage of the fact that young people are easily programmable and eager to please authority figures (plus, eventually, they make great soldiers for a cause) in establishing the Hitler Youth program. It was set up in 1933 to teach young males Nazi principles. Estimates are that by 1935, around 60 percent of all German boys were part of the program, and, according to *Britannica*, "On July 1, 1936, it became a state agency that all young 'Aryan' Germans were expected to join."[79]

These young people often spied on community members, including their parents, while they did the bidding of the state.

Today in the US, steps are being taken that illustrate how state-run schools already believe that they have some sort of ownership over children. Again, I understand how this can sound conspiratorial. You may be thinking, "Carol, *1984* is a work of fiction, not a government playbook, and we don't live in Nazi Germany." But I plead with you to keep an open mind and look at the way certain trends are connected before you dismiss this.

Over the past several years, a lengthy list of issues, including curriculum and educational materials transparency and teachers keeping information about children from parents, has been the source of parental angst and backlash during school board meetings around the US. Other parents have expressed concerns about free speech, both for the child and for the parents, discrimination based on race and other immutable characteristics, transparency of school meetings, and privacy, among other issues.[80]

As parents sought to fight back, some found themselves targeted as domestic terrorists by the FBI and Department of Justice.

In May 2022, parent activist organization Moms for Liberty announced on their website in a news release, "Moms for Liberty responds to DOJ Whistleblower Letter Confirming They Were Investigated by FBI after AG Garland Testified Under Oath Parents Were Not Being Targeted." They continued: "We now have proof of what many of us suspected and some of us knew: that the Department of Justice was using counter-terrorism authority under the PATRIOT Act to investigate parents of schoolchildren who were exercising their first amendment right to petition their local government for a redress of grievances."[81]

Parents have sought to fight back by rallying around parental bills of rights at the state level, but in many cases they have been denied. In New Hampshire, a bill where teachers were required to notify parents on several topics, including gender-identity-related issues, failed to pass the state legislature.[82]

In early 2022 in Iowa, a bill was introduced to put cameras in all classrooms. *Education Next* executive editor Michael Petrilli wrote, "Privacy isn't the only concern for teachers. Some also worry about scrutiny of what and how they're teaching."[83] That's the issue—schools should not be able to hide what they are teaching students, and there should be watchdogs and scrutiny. However, those who don't believe that you "own" your kids or who want to replace you certainly feel differently.

Tiffany Justice, one of the cofounders of Moms for Liberty, told me, "I think just what we've seen is this idea of how dare you think that you get to . . . direct the upbringing of your child? But that's a fundamental right. . . . But this piece about it being fundamental—that these are rights that the government does not give you, and they cannot take them away, and that some of these natural rights are important to be recognized at the state level and the local level, not because we need their permission to recognize them, but that everything that lawmakers do should be done through that lens, and it's important to remind them of that."[84]

This movement will only be exacerbated by social credit. If you now have an official score or rank that deems you unacceptable to society for whatever reason, that will give the state even more license to believe you are not capable of being a good parent and that they should take over increasingly more of the parental authority and moral and leadership roles for kids. Or vice versa—if you don't comply with education mandates for your kids, that will impair other aspects of your social credit.

Not having the right to make decisions for your child, not because you have violated the child's rights (which everyone should agree is a legally founded exception) but rather because of wrongthink, puts a vastly different and scary spin on the concept that you will own nothing.

At the nexus of social credit, digital IDs, and children, the FBI announced in early July 2022 that they had created their first-ever mobile application. It was . . . drumroll, please . . . the FBI Child ID app! A tweet from the FBI promoting it says that it "provides a convenient place to electronically store photos and other vital information about your children so that it's literally right at hand if you need it." They included a clarifying note on their website: "The FBI is not collecting or storing any photos or information that you enter in the app. All data resides solely on your mobile device unless you need to send it to authorities. Please read your mobile provider's terms of service for information about the security of applications stored on your device."[85]

And we have all seen just how trustworthy the FBI has been in recent years.

You can store important information about your kid without needing the FBI's help. It doesn't seem that complicated.

It starts as a free, voluntary app. The question is, where does it go next, and to what end?

Who Decides?

The continual picking of winners and losers. Deciding who is essential and who isn't. Distinguishing who is a good citizen and how they can virtue signal and gain social clout with that designation. Deciding who will be punished by having their lives and livelihoods disrupted. That is what is at stake.

The pandemic created an unbelievably dangerous precedent for the US government putting the rights of the collective above the individual and infringing on those rights, based on the weasel words "for the good of society." We saw that if you refused to get a Covid vaccine, the government would suggest that you not be able to do certain activities (travel, enter a restaurant, etc.), and ultimately, many government workers lost their job for not complying with government mandates.

Many people did comply. These mandates were accepted and embraced by a meaningful percentage of the population. The elite now know that social credit can be an effective tool for them.

As the government is spending more time deciding what is good and right, whether it be energy or car usage or food, we are on the verge of the government being able to take away rights, privileges, and the ability to create wealth for wrongthink. While this sounds like a dystopian novel, it is here, and the government's recent Disinformation Governance Board gives us no comfort that the protection of our rights is heading in a tenable direction.

Moreover, with the new financial world order, a slew of entities may be weighing in on what is right and what is wrong, and incentivizing the racketeers and useful idiots to help them police their version of "right think."

We know that this social credit framework has already been seeded, and it sets you on the path to owning nothing, particularly as a new financial world order unfolds.

CHAPTER 2

A NEW FINANCIAL WORLD ORDER, PART I

Debt Begets Desperation Begets Disorder

When I say there is a new financial world order on the horizon, it may sound like a wild conspiracy theory, but it is far from it. Rather, it is the outcome of the unavoidable combination of human nature and time. Said another way, history predicts it, and the world has been here many times before, even if we haven't personally.

As much as people innovate and advance technology and science, human nature and behavior remain remarkably constant over time. Because of that, history evolves in fairly predictable cycles, including those of "empires" or world-dominating countries.

Given that "empires" are managed, mismanaged, and interfered with by humans, money, finance, and the economy all go in cycles, too.

So, as countries shift in their overall importance in the world, ever rearranged like a massive jigsaw puzzle that is missing some pieces and is never quite finished, a variety of material events tend to bring about different financial world orders.

In each empire, prosperity leads to more people wanting to manage, direct, and benefit from that prosperity. It leads to bigger, more controlling "leadership." Those leaders inevitably take on more debt and piss off other powerful countries. Then they reach a tipping point, where their financial situation becomes too precarious, they become desperate, and they start taking action to keep their power and the empire intact.

This happened with both the Dutch and British financial empires. We have seen their relative positions as holders of the world's reserve currency begin and come to an end, the latter with the emerging global dominance of the United States.

In the US cycle, we have so far witnessed the Bretton Woods monetary system shift to the US's decoupling from the gold standard to the rise of the petrodollar, which we will dive into below. We are now seeing the US's massive debt load conflict with its power. This has weakened America's financial standing in the world. As has been the case with the financial empires that preceded it, virtually all of that weakening has been self-inflicted.

Empires, despite their privileges, fall victim to human nature, and their leaders do very stupid things. The US has had every privilege and advantage, yet has fallen victim to the same fate at the hands of very stupid and sociopathic humans. Power and debt once again remain at odds with each other.

With the US eroding its financial position and the confluence of the above factors, we are on the precipice of a new financial world order. It is more than a perfect storm—it is the perfect financial tsunami. Those with the best access, the most wealth, and the highest-level connections see this. They want to capitalize upon it, reorganize it, and benefit from it, both domestically and globally.

This reality has significant liberty and financial implications for every American.

Russian Roulette

In late February 2022, Russia invaded Ukraine, using both land and sea missile attacks, as well as ground forces.[1] The initial global reaction leaned heavily on economic sanctions. The US, along with the European Union, Australia, Britain, Canada, and Japan, coordinated a variety of sanctions meant to cut Russia off from the global banking system and restrict access to key industries.[2] This escalated to removing major Russian banks from the international settlement messaging system, SWIFT, although not sanctioning two of the largest banks, due in large part to Europe's dependence on Russia for oil.

These sanctions had very little effect in deterring Russia, which continued its campaign of bombings and aggression. The US, along with key allies, decided to take an extreme and historic measure, one that will be looked back on in history as a turning point in the US financial empire's cycle and the overall cycle of financial world orders. The US government mandated the freezing of Russia's central bank reserve assets. The European Union and Japan followed suit.[3]

To give more context to this, Russia relies on imports for a meaningful part of its economy. They import goods that range from food to clothing to everyday supplies; despite being the world's largest exporter of grain, they are still a net importer of agricultural products.[4] When they buy from foreign countries, they have to buy in that country's currency (or a currency more acceptable and stable than their ruble). Also, because of the lack of historical stability of the Russian ruble, many businesses and individuals in Russia tend to keep their accounts in foreign currencies, which are viewed as more stable.

This means that Russia needs access to other currencies so that its government and businesses can import products and so that those individuals who want to withdraw from their bank accounts can be given the appropriately denominated currency.

Given the stability of value expected in reserves (something I will address a bit later in this chapter), historically, economies like Russia have agreed to the rules of the game.

At the time of the invasion, Russia had about $650 billion worth of reserves at foreign financial institutions.

In the wake of the invasion, what the US, along with its allies, did next was unprecedented vis-à-vis a major economic player: they froze Russia's access to these reserves. I surmise that was meant to try to weaken the ruble, as the Russian Central Bank couldn't access dollars or euros or yen and sell them to buy rubles to keep the ruble's price up, as well as ensure that Russia couldn't fulfill obligations of a bank run for those Russian customers who wanted to be paid in currencies like dollars or euros, and ultimately, the economy would collapse and force Russian president Vladimir Putin's hand.

That didn't happen.

This giant gamble was a major bust, with implications not only for geopolitics but also for the United States' financial empire.

The US dollar is still considered the world's reserve currency. It has been, for almost eighty years, the center of the global financial universe.

For this "exorbitant privilege," as it is called, the US was called upon to manage its currency not only vis-à-vis the US economy but also as the stable backbone of world trade. It has been failing at both of those endeavors for quite some time, but freezing a major economy's reserve assets did something else. It fully weaponized the US dollar.

What nation wants to support the "privilege" of having to do business in dollars as an anchor if the US, at any point in time, can keep your dollars from you and try to collapse your economy?

This was a very serious action that created enormous consequences for the trustworthiness of the US and its place at the center of the financial world order (note that trust and faith in the US government is what backs today's dollar). These actions by the US were a further catalyst for a new financial world order to begin to form.

You may not like the fact that the US plays the world's "police," but the reality is that the US has been very much looked upon as a sort of referee, based on a set of universal standards and expectations for global stability. This has helped keep some semblance of peace and prosperity globally, although not perfectly and certainly at a cost. Without the US in that role, then what happens?

It bears mentioning that these actions were undertaken with the hubris of the Biden administration, the Department of Defense, and other political (and likely business and financial) elite. There was no congressional declaration of war. There were purely these actors, with a mindset that "it's not my money." They held the attitude that they could just do what they wanted without bearing much of the literal or figurative costs.

Not only did the decision to go after Russia's reserve assets have massive blowback for the United States, but also the outcome was not as intended.

Because of the world's dependence on Russia as a critical producer of oil and natural gas, including the United States' allies in Europe, as well as India and China depending on Russian energy, the sale of energy was not fully sanctioned. This allowed Russia to demand payment in rubles and cut other deals that helped support its economy.

Russia, while having that meaningful amount in foreign currency reserves, had also been lightening up on them and stockpiling gold. It is estimated that prior to the attacks, Russia had been selling

Treasurys and other central bank assets and had amassed the fifth-largest reserve of gold in the world (around $140 billion worth).[5]

In fact, four months after this historic freezing of reserve assets, CBS News reported on June 28, 2022, that "Russia's ruble is the strongest currency in the world this year" and that from January to that date, the ruble was up 45 percent versus the dollar.

This resulted because Russia was able to demand that certain nations pay for energy in rubles and implement capital controls.[6]

With sharply rising energy prices offsetting any volume declines in exports, the Centre for Research on Energy and Clean Air reported that Russia earned record-high revenues of 93 billion euros from fossil fuel exports during the first hundred days of the war.[7]

That wasn't the only blunder. The US also led a campaign to seize personal property—not government property or that of Putin and his military commanders, but the personal property of Russian billionaires called "oligarchs." These individuals found their assets seized by the US and its allies because of the oligarchs' supposed standing or ties to Putin at some point. Wherever they were in the world, mega-yachts, homes, and bank accounts belonging to individuals were taken.[8]

This was an incredible violation of property rights. The US had no information (at least that they publicly communicated) that any of these individuals had anything to do with the invasion. Some experts even surmised that the oligarchs were at odds with Putin, and vice versa. All that was communicated was that these individuals might have access to Putin, and perhaps taking their things would put pressure on them to put pressure on him.

These US government actions have three important implications in terms of your ability to generate and keep wealth.

First, these actions illustrate, in real time, the willingness of the US government to use money as a weapon, regardless of the blowback.

Second, they undermine and threaten the value of the dollars and wealth you have created.

Finally, they underscore the government's lack of protection of individual property rights when the narrative suits them.

These are all terrible developments for the future of individual rights and economic freedom.

It also represents a giant leap down the path of setting up a new financial world order.

While we don't know how long it will take or what form it will take specifically, the makings for a new financial world order are certainly under way.

To understand what may lie ahead, we need to go back to where we have been.

The Cycle of Life

Financial empires go through cycles. There is a financial ascension, a plateau, and, finally, a series of actions and events that lead to its unraveling and the emergence of a new financial empire.

In modern times, we have seen a few empires hold a reserve currency for the world on the back of free enterprise. Eventually those unraveled to see the emergence of the US as a world superpower on the back of its own financial strength.

These cycles are not coincidental. They are understood by those who research and observe history. One such perception, attributed to Mark Twain with a few small differentiations, is, "History never repeats itself, but it does often rhyme."

The "rhymes" allow students of history to see patterns, themes, behaviors, and actions that not only are similar in form but also lead to similar outcomes.

History Rhymes: The Dutch and British Financial Empires

In recent history, while many nations have built geographic empires, on the financial front there have been two major global financial empires before America—the Dutch and the British. Charting the ups and downs of the Dutch and British empires as global financial powerhouses gives us some insights into what lies ahead for the US.

The Dutch Empire

More than a century before the Americans rebelled against England and rose to power, the Dutch rebelled against Spain, winning independence for the Netherlands during what's known as the Eighty Years' War and setting up their accession.

War is one of those "rhyming" catalysts for change and new financial world orders. Not every war brings about a new financial world order, but every major new financial world order has been preceded by war.

In the late 1500s, Spain found itself at war with several powers, including France and England, which gave the Dutch an opening to be more aggressive—and successful—than they had been earlier in the war. In the 1600s, an alliance between the Dutch and the French made the Spanish fearful, and by 1648 Spain had granted the Netherlands its independence.[9]

As events are never perfectly linear, it bears noting that even before the war was over, the Dutch had taken the pole position in the global economy.

Billionaire founder of the hedge fund Bridgewater Associates, Ray Dalio, who also has written about historical cycles, talks about this "Dutch Golden Age." He describes the pinnacle of the Dutch empire, saying, "This period was one of great globalization as ships that could travel around the world to gain the riches that were out there flourished, and the Dutch, with their great shipbuilding and their economic system, were ahead of others in using ships, economic rewards, and military power to build their empire."[10]

Dalio also notes that strong education led to innovation (he estimates that the Dutch came up with around a quarter of the world's inventions during the 1600s).[11]

These innovations led to the creation of industry, particularly an advanced shipping industry that built up global trade with the Dutch at the center. With strong shipping capabilities, the Dutch could reach new parts of the globe and engage in trade, extending the reach and power of their currency.

They also had a strong military to help protect their standing, built up during the latter part of the Eighty Years' War.

During the late 1500s and early 1600s, as the Dutch increased their global commerce, they invented the stock market as a mechanism for businessmen to let others help participate in the financing of their growth and expansion, as well as share in the benefits (and losses) of the growing global trade they were spearheading.[12]

The very first publicly traded company or IPO in the world was Vereenigde Oost-Indische Compagnie, or as we know it in English, the

Dutch East India Company, whose offering was completed in August 1602.[13]

With that, the Dutch became pioneers in financial markets and in bringing wealth-creation opportunities to a broad swath of the public.

As the Dutch's strength as a financial center developed, they attracted investment from around the globe, making Amsterdam the leading global financial center.

Their currency, the Dutch guilder, was considered the first "country" global reserve currency (meaning one issued by a country versus traditional precious metals, like gold and silver).

Market-based prosperity begets even more prosperity because if other participants don't do better, it is hard to find counterparties for trade and growth. But building up counterparties creates long-term competitive risks. As Ray Dalio wrote, "As other countries became more competitive, the Dutch empire became more costly and less competitive, and it found maintaining its empire less profitable and more challenging."[14]

I share this because familiarity with the subject matter and understanding what happened in the past informs what can happen in the future.

The British started building up their economic and military strength, and the Dutch and the British began to haggle over economic issues. There were economic policies put in place that are not that dissimilar to things like tariffs or "America-first" policies that you would see today. Those economic conflicts eventually turned into full-scale military conflicts.

In addition to the external pressures from other empires becoming stronger, the Dutch themselves were experiencing the part of the cycle where they became their own worst enemy. The first issue was massive debt. Another was the division and infighting around the allocation of money; this happened between geographic provinces, political "factions," and the different classes of the people. The empire's weakening also applied to the military. As the Dutch came under attack both militarily and economically, their preeminent global financial standing was eroding.[15]

Government overspending, the cost of war, and competition from other countries ultimately put the Dutch into substantial debt. This led to a bankrupt government and a collapsed financial center and currency and signaled the end of the Dutch's position as the financial leader of the world.

The British Empire

Once again, war was a conduit for change and new financial orders. After the Napoleonic Wars, an assembly of nations meant to reorganize Europe, called the Congress of Vienna, took place.[16]

The new powerful countries (the ones that were on the winning side of the war) ironed out key factors, including changes to debt obligations and monetary systems. Dalio says, "That set the stage for Great Britain's 100-year-long 'imperial century' during which Great Britain became the unrivaled world power, the British pound became the world's dominant currency, and the world flourished."[17]

While there were interim financial cycles that created short-term issues, overall there was relative peace and prosperity.

Britain enjoyed economic strength, supported by a strong military. The British took over the helm of global trade once held by the Dutch. The Industrial Revolution took hold, and the cycle of innovation and productivity helped engender substantial prosperity. On the back of this, London became the world's financial capital, and the British pound sterling became the world's reserve currency.

The British fought hard to maintain this status against the French and ultimately won out after a French war loss.[18]

The innovation that started with the Industrial Revolution helped countries around the world become more prosperous. Inventiveness mixed with free markets improved the quality of life but also led to fighting over wealth among the classes.

Being the leading financial empire, the British expanded their government spending. Dalio notes, "As is typical at such times, the leading power, Great Britain, became more indulgent while its relative power declined, and it started to borrow excessively." These "indulgences" were tied to both domestic and international spending, all done in an attempt to maintain status and power.[19]

Again we see the rhyme: a government engages in moral hazard on the back of the productivity of its people. The government takes on massive debts, and its financial empire starts to weaken.

The cycle continues as another power starts to emerge to challenge this financial empire.

Then, as the fighting among classes about wealth continues on the perception that the proverbial economic pie is shrinking, other countries try to take more share of the global markets. Eventually this all leads to war, which, as noted, often becomes the conduit for the official changing of the guard in terms of financial empires.

Related to the British Empire coming to a close, another war, World War I, became the predecessor to another new financial world order.

You have now seen the movie and the sequel and may have an idea of how the next installment in this "trilogy of financial empires" ends.

The Rise of the US Financial Empire

After World War I, there was again a meeting of the powers on the "winning" side to map out the new global order. The Paris Peace Conference, via the Treaty of Versailles, once again reorganized debt and decided a number of other economic and geopolitical factors.

With its strength and adherence to free markets, and backed by a strong military, the US became financially significant, and New York City displaced London as the preeminent financial center. (Fun fact: in the US, Philadelphia was actually the first major financial center, boasting both the first bank and the first stock exchange in America, but eventually New York won out.)[20]

In this interim period, there was still much about the economic and overall world order that was in flux. This is important to understand, as the changing of the economic guard is neither linear nor swift. There is usually an extended period of massive chaos and disorder, which creates an abundance of pressures, including financial ones, on countries and their citizens.

The global financial order remained chaotic and in flux until World War II, which eventually cemented the United States' global standing. As the old order was on the brink, the US and other power centers stood by, ready to capitalize.

The move to the US being the world's financial leader, including having the leading financial center, the world's reserve currency, and a strong military, was very similar to the emergence of the Dutch and British.

In the US today, we face many of the same issues that are seen emerging late in the cycles of the other financial empires. Borrowing excessively. Having an economy that is becoming expensive relative to other emerging nations. Arguments over the division of wealth. The general division of the countrymen. The emergence of other competing powers. If history does indeed rhyme, our days are beginning to sound like a children's poem.

The US Financial Empire Cycle

Within historical cycles of global financial dominance, there tend to be smaller cycles as well that bridge periods of expansion and contraction. While none of this is linear in reality, the cycles help frame the causes of the internal weakening of a dominant financial empire.

While the US toyed with a variety of different monetary systems in its early history, including going on and off a gold standard and various money "printing" schemes, and had established several financial centers, the most notable development in terms of the US becoming the world's financial empire was the Bretton Woods Conference, held late in World War II.

Bretton Woods

In 1944, representatives from forty-four different countries came together at the Mount Washington Hotel in Bretton Woods, New Hampshire, to settle how trade and commerce would happen in the postwar era. The fact that the meeting took place in the United States gave a hint as to who had the leverage in the negotiations.[21]

Postwar, the United States had around 21,000 metric tons of gold. According to the Federal Reserve, in 1930 the US held around 40 percent of the gold reserves in the world (and by 1950, the US controlled nearly two-thirds of the global gold reserves).[22] This gold backed the dollar's purchasing power. The US also had strength in terms of weaponry and natural resources like oil. The United States' counterparties in Europe were all saddled with substantial amounts of war debt. This all mattered in terms of the US's leverage and ability to negotiate.

The forty-four countries hashed out a new financial world order. The website Federal Reserve History said of this get-together, "It was an unprecedented cooperative effort for nations that had been setting up barriers between their economies for more than a decade."[23]

Leading the negotiations were representatives from both the US and Britain. For the US, the chief economist at the US Treasury, Harry Dexter White, led the charge. The British Treasury advisor and economist John Maynard Keynes was the key negotiator on the British side.[24]

As you can imagine, the two individuals had different ideas on how to set about creating a new financial world order. Both meant to draw upon lessons learned from major financial events, like the Great Depression, and set forth a way to avoid similar issues.

Keynes proposed a global reserve "currency" idea called "bancor" (fun fact: it's supposed to be a portmanteau of the French terms for bank [*banque*] and gold [*or*]).

Bancor was proposed as a sort of global fiat neutral "currency," controlled and settled between an entity that functioned as a global central bank, with a mechanism to balance trade deficits and surpluses. It was meant only for international trade, not to be in the hands and accounts of individuals.

White had various concerns regarding Keynes's plan, including that, given America's financial standing at the time, much of the global trade would be going to purchase American goods and services, and the US would end up holding most of the bancor, creating a host of problems.[25]

According to the Federal Reserve, White counterproposed "a new monetary institution called the Stabilization Fund. Rather than issue a new currency, it would be funded with a finite pool of national currencies and gold of $5 million that would effectively limit the supply of reserve credit."[26]

Ultimately, with the United States' strength, the final plan leaned heavily toward White and the Americans' wishes but also addressed some of the concerns of Keynes and the British.[27]

Jim Rickards, an economist, author, and financial expert, told me that the Soviets were at Bretton Woods, and that while they didn't sign the agreement, they had some input. In actuality, they likely had a lot of input, as Rickards noted that it came out in the 1990s that White was a Stalinist agent who was given the mandate to create a system that would destroy the British Empire![28] Vox discussed this connection, noting that "a number of important records behind the mystery of White's Soviet partnership were declassified, rich with primary evidence" and mentioned his "allegiance with Soviet spies."[29] This is an incredible revelation regarding the foundation of the US empire at the center of the modern global financial system.

Out of this meeting came a monetary system known as the Bretton Woods system, where the dollar became the anchor for global trade, with all other currencies tied to the US dollar and a band where the currency peg could fluctuate. In turn, the dollar was pegged to gold at a fixed rate of $35 per ounce. This was the price gold had been set at in dollar terms for roughly the past decade, following President Franklin D. Roosevelt's devaluation of the dollar in terms of its price versus gold, resetting the previous statutory price set in the Gold Standard Act of 1900, of $20.67 per ounce.[30]

Following this agreement, with the US dollar pegged to and backed by gold at a fixed price, the dollar was perceived as "good as gold" around the globe. The agreement laid out a bunch of other mechanisms to help with a global monetary system, including creating the International Monetary Fund (IMF) and what's known today as the World Bank.

This solidified the dollar as the world's reserve currency and the United States' financial empire dominance and ushered in a new financial world order.

"King Dollar" had been born.

The Visual Capitalist, in a chart depicting currency reserves by country as a portion of total reserves over time, shows that in 1940 the British pound sterling was 68.9 percent of total reserves, and the US dollar was 27.9 percent. By 1960, the US dollar was 61.7 percent of total global reserves, and the pound sterling was down to 35.1 percent.[31]

As you can imagine, this new monetary system was quite complex to implement. Economics professor Michael Bordo wrote, "It took close to 15 years to get the Bretton Woods system fully operating. As it evolved into a gold dollar standard, the three big problems of the interwar gold exchange standard re-emerged: adjustment, confidence, and liquidity problems."[32]

With this privileged position and learnings from all the financial empires that preceded us, you would think that the US would work hard to not screw this up. Not quite.

The Triffin Dilemma

It was not only Keynes who was concerned about whether the Bretton Woods system that gave us the dollar "as good as gold" for the world would work in the long run. Robert Triffin, a noted Belgian American economist, identified weaknesses in the system in the 1960s in something known as the "Triffin Dilemma."

The Triffin Dilemma acknowledges the challenge of the country that issues the world's reserve currency between balancing the interests of policy that benefits their domestic economy with the responsibility of keeping that currency "as good as gold" for the countries around the world that depend on its stability. This in turn creates a dilemma for the country's central bank—one that the Fed has run up against many times, with different decisions and outcomes (as seen in the different outcomes under the actions of Fed chairs Paul Volcker versus Ben Bernanke versus Jerome Powell in addressing domestic versus global interests).

Additionally, Triffin believed that being the reserve currency holder and having to supply the world with ample dollars meant that the issuing country (such as the US) would be required to run trade deficits. The thought process is that demand for the dollar (or another reserve currency) makes it more expensive relative to other currencies. That is good for buying cheap imports, but from a global-competitiveness standpoint, it makes its exports more costly. This leads to a trade deficit (the value of the country's imports is more than the value of its exports).

The Downfall of Bretton Woods and Emergence of the Petrodollar

With the US now as the leading global financial empire, the country continued, as the Dutch and British before it, to leverage free market concepts. This led to innovation, productivity, and prosperity, as it had in previous cycles under the previous financial empires. The postwar period was an incredibly prosperous one for the US, with the gross national product exploding from $200 billion in 1940 to

$500 billion by 1960, making the US the wealthiest country in the world.[33]

But the US government didn't learn the lessons of the financial empires that preceded it. Politicians rapidly increased government spending, to finance both the expansion of domestic government programs as well as war abroad.

Luke Gromen, a leading global economic researcher, noted in a podcast that by the mid-1950s, both the Europeans and Japanese were emerging from their postwar malaise, becoming more productive, and starting to export and run trade surpluses.[34] The Federal Reserve explains that as these economies exported more, there was less of a need for dollars, plus the US payment imbalance, military spending, and foreign aid had built up the supply of dollars globally. This change in dollar demand versus a minimally increasing supply of gold meant that the US didn't have enough gold for all the foreign-held US dollar currency.[35]

With that backdrop, America's gold reserves started to become drained. There was a concern that there would be a full-fledged run on the US gold supply, whereby the US government wouldn't "meet its obligations, thereby threatening both the dollar's position as reserve currency and the overall Bretton Woods system."[36]

A slew of monetary Band-Aids were put in place to try to keep everything together, including using currency swaps.

With a variety of geopolitical issues converging, including a run on gold in London and a not very successful gold embargo against South Africa, gold started rising in value to $42 per ounce.[37]

By 1971, the US was reportedly down to 8,000 metric tons of gold in its reserves.[38]

President Richard Nixon was faced with a handful of options. He could have reset the price of gold in dollar terms, devaluing the dollar again. It is rumored that the Bank for International Settlements suggested that gold be repriced with the peg of $150 per ounce. Or Nixon could take dramatic and transformational action.

On August 15, 1971, Nixon addressed the nation, unveiling a slew of economic policies. None of these policies was more disruptive or historic than Nixon's announcement that "I have directed Secretary [of the Treasury John] Connally to suspend temporarily the convertibility of the dollar into gold or other reserve assets, except in amounts and conditions determined to be in the interest of monetary stability and in the best interests of the United States."[39]

As a faculty publication from Columbia Law School put it, "the United States, which had long been willing to exchange dollars for gold at the rate of $35 per ounce, would no longer do so routinely at any price." This is often referred to as Nixon closing the gold window.[40] It was a historic endeavor that, in the short term, enabled 1970s stagflation and dollar devaluation, and in the long term, changed the course and potential for longevity of the US financial empire.[41]

The US dollar, which the entire Bretton Woods system had been built around, moved to become a fiat currency.

The Petrodollar: "Good as Gold for Oil"

The years following Nixon decoupling the dollar from gold and "closing the gold window" were fraught with financial and geopolitical chaos. The US was very dependent upon the Middle East for oil, and the major oil-producing nations weren't too thrilled with the US taking the dollar off the gold standard, causing them financial losses due to their dollar-based revenue.[42] (Note that oil producers didn't have a lot of choice in the matter; the dollar was the preeminent global currency and the currency used by the wealthy countries importing oil.)[43]

In October 1973, following the Yom Kippur War, President Nixon asked the US Congress for $2.2 billion in aid for Israel. This led the major Arab oil exporters, the Organization of Arab Petroleum Exporting Countries (OAPEC), to put a retaliatory oil embargo on the US and cut production. The price of oil over the next few months jumped almost 400 percent.[44]

But the US had a plan. In 1974, negotiations took place, and on June 8, what was heralded in the media as a "milestone pact" was signed between the US and Saudi Arabia, the latter being the largest producer of oil and de facto head of OAPEC.

This "pact" enhanced the relations between the countries and included a wide variety of economic and military points.[45]

This was step one of a two step-process envisioned by the US. Just over a month later, Nixon's new Treasury secretary and deputy embarked upon a secret mission, with the backdrop of a lengthy diplomatic tour. However, their Saudi Arabian stop had a critical objective. According to Bloomberg, which found out this information forty years later with a Freedom of Information Act request, "The goal: neutralize crude oil as an economic weapon and find a way to persuade a hostile kingdom to finance America's widening deficit with its newfound petrodollar wealth . . . Failure would not only jeopardize America's financial health but could also give the Soviet Union an opening to make further inroads into the Arab world."[46]

The plan, according to the Bloomberg report and investigation, was that the US would purchase oil from the Saudis and assist them militarily (with both aid and equipment). In return, "the Saudis would plow billions of their petrodollar revenue back into Treasuries and finance America's spending."[47]

The other key term of this arrangement, supposedly asked for by the Saudis, was that it was to be kept entirely secret. The US found ways to dance around issues to keep it quiet. Bloomberg reports that one "exception was carved out for Saudi Arabia when the Treasury started releasing monthly country-by-country breakdowns of U.S. debt ownership. Instead of disclosing Saudi Arabia's holdings, the Treasury grouped them with 14 other nations, such as Kuwait, the United Arab Emirates, and Nigeria, under the generic heading 'oil exporters'—a practice that continued for 41 years." These maneuvers were all meant to hide the covert arrangement and the incredible amount of Treasurys that the Saudis held because of it.[48]

Luke Gromen, in the aforementioned podcast interview, said the outcome was that the dollar went from being pegged to gold to being pseudo-pegged to oil, and the oil market ended up serving as the "de facto reserve asset for the dollar." This underpins the concept of the petrodollar: what was previously a dollar "good as gold" was now a dollar "good as gold for oil."[49]

To boil it down, that means that oil is now basically priced only in dollars globally. So, if you are an oil-importing nation, you need dollars to buy oil, reaffirming the United States' position as holder of the world's reserve currency even after abandoning the gold standard.

Given the first part of the Triffin Dilemma, the US made sure to stabilize the dollar for the benefit of the world. Gromen said that from

1974 to 2005, oil mostly traded in a fairly narrow range because the US managed policy accordingly. When oil became high, monetary policy was tightened, and when oil slipped below the range, monetary policy was loosened.

Spot Crude Oil Price: West Texas Intermediate (WTI); Dollars per Barrel; Not Seasonally Adjusted; Monthly; 1946 to 2022

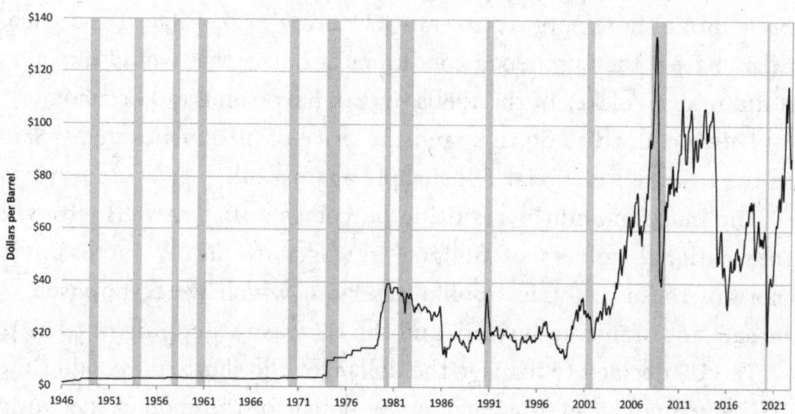

Source: Federal Reserve Bank of St. Louis, Spot Crude Oil Price: West Texas Intermediate (WTI) [WTISPLC], retrieved from FRED, Federal Reserve Bank of St. Louis; https://fred.stlouisfed.org/series/WTISPLC, November 2, 2022.

The fact that the US was beholden to many masters in terms of policy meant that they had to make some very difficult decisions that impacted the domestic economy.

To deal with the inflation that included the price of oil spiraling too high in the early 1980s, then–Fed chairman Paul Volcker made the decision to raise the Fed funds rate to nearly 20 percent, which sent the US economy into a further tailspin, including pushing unemployment to almost 11 percent. The *New York Times* illustrated some of the backlash: "Car dealers mailed the Fed keys from unsold vehicles, builders sent two-by-fours from unbuilt houses and farmers drove tractors around the Fed building in Washington in protest."[50]

A Financial Breakdown

As financial cycles go, this arrangement worked for a few decades (or, as put previously, "was tolerated"), but with the backdrop of a fiat currency and a lot of masters to please, the system eventually started to show serious cracks.

In 2004 and 2005, ramped-up energy demand coming out of China and robust demand in North America, as well as some supply and geopolitical issues, created a backdrop for oil to substantially increase in price.[51] In August 2005, oil hit another high as Hurricane Katrina took out refining capacity.[52]

Normally, the Fed would tighten economic conditions to get oil back into a more appropriate range. However, they faced the usual dilemma—if they tightened conditions at home, that would likely, as it did under Volcker in the 1980s, wreak havoc on the US economy.

They declined to do this, and the price of oil skyrocketed.[53] Said in the inverse, the dollar fell sharply against oil.

The inaction and the resulting outcomes didn't sit well with the international holders of dollars. It was now taking increasingly more of these countries' dollar reserves, which were supposed to be safe and stable, to buy oil, and the US wasn't stepping in to help.

The US decided to manage the dollar for the short-run good of the US economy instead of managing the dollar for the good of the world as a reserve currency in the long run.

Then the Great Recession financial crisis hit, and the US turned to its easy money, "quantitative easing" (QE) policies.

Instead of tightening conditions with the backdrop of skyrocketing oil prices, the US central bank dropped rates to zero and started competing in the market as a buyer of Treasury securities.

This again did not sit well with countries around the world.

Gromen helps explain that China, as a net importer of oil as well as food, was a big holder of US Treasury securities (holding just more than $900 billion worth as of October 2022, down from more than $1 trillion worth a year earlier).[54] When the same US dollar doesn't buy as much one day as it did in the past, the shift threatens China's food and energy supply. The change in the dollar's value ends up becoming a national security matter for them.

On March 23, 2009, about five days after the Fed announced another round of enhanced QE, Zhou Xiaochuan, governor of the People's Bank of China, wrote a paper for the Bank for International Settlements (BIS), the bank for global central banks, effectively calling for an end to the US dollar as the global reserve currency. The paper begins by saying, "The outbreak of the current crisis and its spillover in the world have confronted us with a long-existing but still unanswered question, i.e., what kind of international reserve currency do we need to secure global financial stability and facilitate world economic growth, which was one of the purposes for establishing the IMF?"[55]

If there weren't clear cracks in the US-dominated financial world order before, they were becoming crystal clear now.

The Aftermath

In the last couple of decades, we have seen many calls around the world to change this King Dollar–centric system.

Various economists and countries have explored whether Keynes's bancor idea or perhaps a global reserve currency backed by a basket of commodities might be better systems.

In 2009, the *Independent* ran a piece called "The demise of the dollar: In a graphic illustration of the new world order, Arab states have launched secret moves with China, Russia, and France to stop using the US currency for oil trading."[56] While some of this takes years of undoing and creates chaos along the path, many countries are actively changing strategies.

We know that Russia and China expanded cooperation, going back to at least 2014.

In recent years, we have seen many of the Middle East and North Africa (MENA) region countries and other emerging markets that export oil move away from the US dollar peg. These include Angola, Argentina, Azerbaijan, Kazakhstan, Iran, Nigeria, Russia, South Africa, and Venezuela. Gromen, in his book *The Mr. X Interviews*, explains, "Rather than burning FX [foreign exchange] reserves down and then devaluing their currency, they have shown a willingness to de-peg earlier on and take the inflationary pain to their economies."[57]

Additionally, China became the largest importer of oil in the world. Given their financial competitiveness with the US and their long-term view, they seek to pay in Chinese currency (yuan) instead of dollars. Knowing that some countries don't want to stock up on yuan reserves at this time, they have taken to offering "a credible physical gold settlement of any offshore yuan net balances created by selling oil in yuan." In looking at this, Gromen's book explains, "the easy answer is that China is now many of these nation's [*sic*] biggest customer, and these nations need Chinese goods for their people. The more nuanced answer is China is offering credible physical gold settlement, which then gives both China and these oil exporters the ability to get away from the USD that over the past fifteen years the United States has increasingly been using as a weapon against any nation that disagrees with Washington's political agenda."[58]

Many countries have reevaluated their dollar reserve holdings, ridding themselves of Treasurys and diversifying their reserve holdings, including the addition of gold.

Ultimately, as Gromen points out, "Americans have forgotten that it is oil that chose the USD as reserve, your American politicians have forgotten that if oil chose the USD as the world's oil monopoly reserve currency, there is no theoretical reason why oil could not 'un-choose' the USD."[59]

Former senior US Treasury official Juan Zarate said in his book *Treasury's War*:

> The dollar serves as the global reserve currency and the currency of choice for international trade, and New York has remained a core financial capital and hub for dollar-clearing transactions. With this concentration of financial and commercial power comes the ability to wield access to American markets, American banks, and American dollars as financial weapons. Treasury's power ultimately stems from the ability of the US to use its financial powers with global effect. This ability, in turn, stems from the centrality and stability of New York as a global financial center, the importance of the USD as a reserve currency, and the demonstration effects, regulatory or otherwise, taken by the US in the broader international system. If the US economy loses its predominance, or the USD sufficiently weakens, our ability to wage financial warfare could wane.[60]

That leads us back to where we began in this downward phase. While the US has used its financial power and waged that financial warfare in various forms in the past, it had never, vis-à-vis a meaningful economy, fully weaponized the dollar. The actions didn't do what they were intended to do, but they did destroy even more trust in the US and its reserve currency position.

End of the "Exorbitant Privilege"

The late French president and finance minister Valéry Giscard d'Estaing dubbed the US dollar's status as the world's reserve currency an "exorbitant privilege," a phrase often used to talk about the benefits extended for being the financial center of the universe.[61] Because countries around the world need to pay in dollars and therefore keep dollar-denominated assets like Treasurys in reserve, interest rates are suppressed within the US system. That gives the US an arbitrage opportunity, where Americans can use their low-cost capital to invest in higher-yielding assets, including abroad. This is particularly the case for the US government, which can use cheap debt to finance its spending.

In terms of being the world's reserve currency, the exorbitant privilege is the "pro" to the Triffin Dilemma's "con," if you will—plus the other glaring issue of enabling government moral hazard.

So, what are the implications of not having this exorbitant privilege should the dollar lose reserve currency status or at least be demoted to one of several commonly held globally?

Guggenheim Partners late chief investment officer Scott Minerd, speaking at the 2018 Milken Institute Global Conference, outlined some concerns. He said that the dollar losing reserve status would have "big implications on a defense and quality-of-life level." He also noted that "[i]f we wish to continue down that path, Americans will slowly surrender their standard of living. We will ultimately become a second-rate power, and we will cede our position of military superiority to other nations."[62]

This means that the dollar losing reserve status is a price you will ultimately pay in terms of your financial standing and quality of life.

A Quartz piece that covered these talks noted that Minerd's "argument rests on the relationship between diplomatic alliances and foreign currency reserves." Also, Quartz reported, University of California, Berkeley, economics professor Barry Eichengreen "notes that countries in military alliances with reserve-currency-issuing countries hold about 30% more of the partner's currency in their foreign-exchange reserves than countries not in an alliance. If the US retreats from the global diplomatic stage, argues Eichengreen, countries that step in to take its place—namely, China—will gain an advantage both geopolitically and in the amount of their currency held in reserve abroad. The ensuing global economic shift would hurt both the dollar's exchange rate and US borrowing costs."[63]

Those who have correctly pointed out that the dollar's position in the second half of the twentieth century as the world's reserve currency helped demolish US manufacturing (back to the original point in the Triffin Dilemma that we have to provide the world with dollars, and in doing so, it makes our exports more expensive versus other major export-based global economies, and we end up running trade deficits) have not seemed to face the reality that, given where the US stands and our very costly economy, it would be very difficult for us to fully rebuild that manufacturing capacity today competitively and cost-effectively should we lose reserve status.

It seems, at least for some time, that forfeiting global reserve currency status is a losing proposition, not a win.

What Lies Ahead

With this changing new financial world order coming from the potential weakening of the US financial system, what does that ultimately look like?

Ray Dalio, who has long been a China cheerleader, thinks it gives China an advantage. "For the first time in my life, the United States is encountering a true rival power. (The Soviet Union was only a military rival, never a significant economic one.) China has become a rival power to the United States in most ways and is becoming strong in most ways at a faster rate."[64]

Others don't necessarily see China's dominance as all-encompassing, but rather as an indicator of the US weakening.

Marc Faber, a financial and economic commentator, said, "I doubt that any empire in history was ever an 'indispensable nation' but with the rapid economic growth of China and India over the last 30 years or so, times have changed, and in the case of most countries around the world but particularly for China, India, Brazil and Russia,

US hegemony is a completely outdated concept. Paul Craig Roberts, former US assistant secretary of the Treasury for economic policy, argued, 'Neither Russia nor China will accept the vassalage status accepted by the UK, Germany, France and the rest of Europe, Canada, Japan and Australia.'"[65]

While it is clear that China doesn't want the US as a stand-alone superpower, given the Triffin Dilemma, why would China want to hold the global reserve currency?

So, who takes over? How does this tie into some of the other financial changes that are setting up a new financial world order? Moreover, do the elites entrenched in the US government even care? And how does that play into what's ahead? Jared Bernstein, who was an economic advisor in both the Obama and Biden administrations, penned an op-ed in 2014 for the *New York Times*, "Dethrone 'King Dollar,'" trying to make the argument that being the world's reserve currency has more downside than upside.[66]

Is it possible that the weaponization of the dollar is intentional, perhaps to give support to the notion that the US doesn't want a dollar reserve currency? And is that all a cover because the government knows they have mismanaged the currency? Or is removing the US's standing in the world financially in and of itself part of setting up this new financial world order? Does it tie into some of the other changes going on in terms of global finance, power, and control?

What we can project is that the US is in the twilight of its financial empire. The end of King Dollar and a US-led financial world order will lead to disorder before any stable new financial world order. This disorder will lead to chaos in all kinds of ways.

Without the US willing or, perhaps, able to step in, and given that its currency no longer holds the same threat it used to, further competition for scarce resources will happen with nobody to play referee.

This will likely lead to wars, famine, and a massive death toll around the world. The world will be turned upside down and new alliances will be formed. The world's GDP and the United States' GDP will slow and there will be a reversion to an economic mean, following the massive post–World War II expansion, turbocharged by unsustainable money printing over the last several decades.

This period of incredible abundance we have been blessed with living through will be changed. In the United States, as trade blocs shift and global supply chains realign to more regional trade, everything will become more expensive. The United States will be relatively better off than other nations, but the quality of life known to Americans for the past sixty to seventy years will deteriorate.

It will be painful, as it is when you have something special and lose it.

Some of it may happen quickly; other aspects may take a very long time to realize. But it will most likely be bumpy—much more so than we are used to.

Should certain international markets get cut off or at least have restricted access, even the biggest companies may find themselves in a handicapped position. This will make them more eager to extract more money from you, offering you more ways to run your life as a "subscription or a service."

We may find ourselves short on resources. You may not be able to access critical medicines or medical devices, technical components, and natural resources that go into producing everything from iPhones to electric vehicles.

Energy could be rationed, causing major disruptions to every facet of life, including the food supply.

Of course, the burden of these changes will rest upon the middle and the working class. The wealthy and well-connected will find a way to get access to what they need. If you aren't on the inside or among the elite, you won't have that benefit and will find your life in turmoil.

This all leads to less economic stability as well—more cycles of booms and busts, alongside a lower quality of life. There are fewer opportunities for economic mobility and to move to the middle class. The middle class may barely exist. With this, predictably, will come even more unrest.

Technical know-how will be lost, as has been the case in Germany with the shutdown of their nuclear energy plants. They couldn't bring them back online at scale if they wanted to because they no longer have the individuals who have trained for that highly specialized expertise.

The elites have put us in this situation because, in thinking they are smarter and better, they have become completely decoupled from reality. Or, perhaps, more accurately, they are setting themselves up to benefit, financially and otherwise.

In mid-2020, consultants McKinsey & Company put out a study about how the pandemic would accelerate the US reshoring of manufacturing.[67] However, that is costly and takes a long time, and the data since has shown that it has only happened at a glacial pace and certainly nowhere near what is needed. The appetite for goods and services across industries will continue to outstrip supply. Should our access to international markets decrease, that could ultimately create rationing and higher prices.

These central planning actions created other issues. The elites didn't realize that their Covid mandates, which turned off a large swath of the economy, would create supply constraints in labor, finished goods and components, and other areas. They didn't realize that any transition to green energy would take a long time, creating a situation where the US was begging other countries to produce more fossil fuels and paying record gas prices and other inflated energy costs. Or perhaps this was all part of their plan as they jockeyed to come out on top in the new financial world order.

Whether it is the natural outgrowth of economic cycles, the leaning out of being the financial center of the universe, or just great stupidity (perhaps even some of each), whatever it is and whoever is bringing it about, it is going to be a massive change. And, as usual, that change will not be to your benefit.

The elite see this and they are preparing for it.

With the backdrop of the current global financial empire nearing the end of its cycle, these well-connected people are establishing financial shifts, changes, and sometimes continuations of destructive policies that will obliterate the middle class, kill your freedoms and economic opportunities, and ensure that you will own nothing.

The new financial world disorder has barely begun.

CHAPTER 3

A NEW FINANCIAL WORLD ORDER, PART II

The Enemy Forces

> I have no reason to suppose that he, who would take away my Liberty, would not when he had me in his Power, take away everything else.
>
> —John Locke

If we were just contending with the changing global financial guard in the way that empires typically rise and fall, it would be a serious challenge. But, on top of those issues, we have several other allied forces coming at us, trying to limit our freedoms, including our economic freedoms.

There is a cadre of elite individuals who have ties to various organizations, as well as ideas, causes, and companies, that threaten your prosperity. They are working to take advantage of the broader backdrop of shifting powers. The changing global financial order brings about new opportunities to prosper, like those the US took advantage of after World War II. These elites want to effect change, shape the new reality, and capitalize upon it for their prosperity and power. It's deliberate and an outgrowth of the "rhyming" of historical cycles and human nature.

Another force is coming at you via the evolution of technology. While technology has been an enabler of broad prosperity in previous empires and for most of our lives, recent technology shifts, the scope of Big Tech, and their impacts on individual rights and property rights create a new set of challenges in parallel with the empire-level quests for financial dominance.

These forces may battle together or they may battle solo at times, but what they have in common is that they want to conquer as much of your wealth as they can.

The changing backdrop of property rights provides a great starting point for exploring how this is happening.

The Shifting of Property Rights

Property rights are fundamental to wealth creation. Studying economics and history, you can see that the advent of individual property rights brought prosperity and abundance to the world. Studying wealth creation at the individual level, you can see that the way that individuals create wealth is through ownership. Ownership is enhanced with a commitment to property rights and is threatened without such commitment.

It is not a coincidence that Marxist, communist, and other derivative regimes of control don't have property rights and ownership as tenets (other than for those in the inner circle or elite ranks). Once you as an individual own nothing, it is easy for the government or similar center of power to gain figurative ownership and control over you.

I will say this many times to hit it home: if you own nothing, they own you. "They" being any combination of government, elite power-grabbers and bad actors, and Big Tech.

We have seen time and again that a movement toward government or central ownership of property takes away prosperity, and a movement toward individual ownership of property creates prosperity. The late Tom Bethell, author of *The Noblest Triumph: Property and Prosperity Through the Ages*, wrote in a *Wall Street Journal* op-ed, "What we have only recently learned, after a sustained attempt to 'build a new society' without it, is that private property will always be with us. It is one of the most fundamental institutions of mankind and there is no workable substitute for it. It is the perennial antagonist of centralized power. Without private property there can be no prosperity, no peace and no freedom. And justice itself will be a haphazard and occasional thing. Private property is 'the guardian of every other right,' as the 18th-century Virginian Arthur Lee said."[1]

Despite the World Economic Forum predictions, detailed later in this chapter, of "You'll own nothing. And you'll be happy," it's pretty clear that people throughout history who have not had ownership or not had their personal property protected certainly have not fared well and have not been happy about it.

In *Commanding Heights: The Battle of Ideas*, famed economist Milton Friedman was asked the following: "Marxists say that property is theft. Why, in your view, is private property so central to freedom?"[2]

Friedman responded:

> Because the only way in which you can be free to bring your knowledge to bear in your particular way is by controlling your property. If you don't control your property, if somebody else controls it, they're going to decide what to do with it . . . there's a lot of knowledge in this society, but, as Friedrich Hayek emphasized so strongly, that knowledge is divided. . . . How do we bring these scattered bits of knowledge back together? And how do we make it in the self-interest of individuals to use that knowledge efficiently? The key to that is private property, because if it belongs to me, you know, there's an obvious fact. Nobody spends somebody else's money as carefully as he spends his own. Nobody uses somebody else's resources as carefully as he uses his own. So, if you want efficiency and effectiveness, if you want knowledge to be properly utilized, you have to do it through the means of private property.[3]

Friedman was not the only noted thinker to understand the linkage between property rights and prosperity. Ayn Rand said, "Without property rights, no other rights are possible. Since man has to sustain his life by his own effort, the man who has no right to the product of his effort has no means to sustain his life. The man who produces while others dispose of his product, is a slave."[4]

This is, in effect, the concept that if you own nothing, the powers that be own you.

When the US was founded, individual rights, including property rights, were core tenets, synonymous with freedom. Friedman wrote about the symbiosis between ownership rights and human rights, saying, "property rights . . . are not in conflict with human rights. On the contrary, they are themselves the most basic of human rights and an essential foundation for other human rights."[5]

And that's how the US government was set up initially, as a representative constitutional republic with the Bill of Rights enumerating individuals' natural rights and charging the government with protecting them. In a famous *Donahue* clip from 1979, Friedman discussed our country's foundation and the role of both government and property: "Government has three primary functions. It should provide for the military defense of the nation. It should enforce contracts between individuals. It should protect citizens from crimes against themselves or their property. When government—in pursuit of good intentions tries to rearrange the economy, legislate morality, or help special interests, the cost comes in inefficiency, lack of motivation, and loss of freedom. Government should be a referee, not an active player."[6]

Property rights have expanded over time with different types of property ownership. Riches once primarily took the forms of livestock, precious metals, and land. These were often gained by conquest or inheritance.

Laws to recognize and enforce property rights allowed more people to access property and build wealth. Tom Bethell said:

> The great legal innovation of this millennium was equality before the law, which first evolved in England. In the courts of common law, all men were seen to be created equal. This had momentous economic consequences. The new equality of status encouraged the freedom of contract and the rise of an exchange economy. The transmission of property became increasingly "horizontal"—from seller to buyer—and decreasingly "vertical"—from father to son. Wealth was democratized. It was acquired by those who, by virtue of their labor and ingenuity, merited it rather than inherited it. Contract superseded status.
>
> Those with small holdings became as secure in their property rights as the owners of broad estates. This is something we take for granted. Yet 18th-century German immigrants in Maryland

could marvel that "the law of the land is so constituted that every man is secure in the enjoyment of his property, [and] the meanest person is out of reach of oppression from the most powerful."

This blessed condition became the basis of American prosperity, as in Britain and other West European countries. People were willing to work hard once they knew that their property rights gave them long time horizons. Governments slowly learned to refrain from depriving people of the fruits of their labor. Alas, this forbearance has been rare in human history.[7]

From this, and with the Industrial Revolution, as well as advances in the monetary system, all kinds of innovation came forth, and with that, new forms of property ownership. Machines and the output of those machines created new circumstances for ownership and new paths to prosperity. There was more trade, and, as Bethell put it, there was even more vast "horizontal" transmission of property, expanding wealth creation opportunities to all sorts of individuals.

Building on the monetary developments of financial empires before it, in the US a more robust set of freedoms begot even more wealth-creation opportunities. The business and financial sectors grew. People started more businesses and there were more prospects to take ownership of stock in other companies that were growing as well.

Adding to that, the protection of intellectual property, from brands to the designs of important inventions in a variety of fields, created all kinds of vehicles to own things of value.

This is how people create wealth. They buy real estate. They generate and implement ideas. They build businesses. They invest in the businesses of others for diversification and growth opportunities. Wealth revolves around ownership.

Decentralization is consistent with wide ownership of various forms of property, whether physical or intellectual. The dispersion of ownership pushes back against central forces of power and control. So, it may not be a surprise that as the US cycled through its position as the leading global financial empire, it reached the part of the cycle whereby those in power wanted more for themselves and sought to gain it by removing individual ownership.

Instead of creating more opportunities for wealth and prosperity for all, the political elite have worked with special interests and big businesses to enable the "Great Consolidation" of wealth and power. They have put up more laws, rules, and regulations that make it harder for you to accumulate property and wealth.

On the land side, extensive regulations and actions post–the Great Recession have limited the supply of and access to new property. The National Association of Home Builders reported in 2021 that government regulations at all levels have added around $94,000 to the average cost of a new home.[8] Onerous property taxes mean that your home and land are never really paid for.

Business regulations have made it harder and more expensive to start and run a business. That was before taking into account the entire "Covid" slate of government policies that picked winners and losers, deeming some businesses essential and others nonessential, based not on data or science but on political clout and connections. They put mostly small businesses into financial peril, causing an estimated seven figures' worth of them to shutter forever, while transferring trillions to Wall Street, including a $3.4 trillion increase in the value of seven tech companies during 2020.

Even on the investment side, government has slanted rules and regulations in favor of the wealthy and well-connected and manipulated markets in a way that has turned off a lot of retail investors.

Property ownership was already on the decline, due to a variety of late-stage financial empire behaviors, before layering in the active efforts of governments and elites to limit all kinds of agency, freedoms, and rights and ensure that you will own nothing.

You may think it sounds insane that a wealthy country would destroy ownership in order to consolidate power, but history shows that "barbelling" a population—basically removing all midlevel and working-class wealth opportunities and leaving just the poor and the elite—is quite common. For a recent example, I direct your attention to Venezuela, which had the fourth-largest GDP in the world in the mid-twentieth century. Under the guise of creating more wealth and "equality," Hugo Chavez nationalized thousands of companies and/or the assets of companies. Nationalizing is the process of removing individual ownership and property rights; it centralizes control and ownership with the state. That didn't work out so well for the people of Venezuela, who were recently estimated to have a median net worth of zero.

The reason is always a money and power grab.

There is one final piece of the shift in property rights, which relates to technocracy, which I will explore in greater detail in Chapter 6. In our property evolution—metals, land, machines, businesses, stocks, intellectual property—the tide has turned with the latest round of technology. New, powerful technology has not enabled you to own more but, rather, has taken ownership away from you.

You may own a smartphone, a veritable supercomputer, that you carry around in your pocket. But what do you own of value? The value is in the access the phone provides. If the operating system, which you sign an agreement to license, not to own, is not available to you, you can't do anything. You own a fairly useless brick of plastic, glass, and microchips.

More people are investing time, energy, and even money in things they don't own. Kids and adults spend time buying virtual goods for their virtual avatars or even "investing" in digital lands where you don't have an asset appreciation opportunity, you can't sell it, and you have no way to build anything but the illusion of wealth. It may be called virtual wealth, but it neither pays for the rent nor leads to wealth creation in reality.

Moreover, technology has disrupted the value of intellectual property. Work done in developing brands and content is often appropriated by third parties to create derivative works, including memes, GIFs, AI output, and more. Stealing intellectual property has been normalized. While some newer technologies, including some Web3 applications, have a mechanism to compensate original creators for derivative sales or uses, overall technology has accelerated the separation of people and property rights and the normalization of such separation.

And the big technology companies that facilitate this only get more wealthy and powerful based on your money and effort. You may remember the adage that if a product is free to use, you are the product.

You own nothing and they own you—and, in many cases, your output.

Your life becomes a subscription model.

These are the battles of World War F, from the barriers to traditional wealth creation in the physical world to the lack of individual property ownership and rights in the digital realm. It's a war to decide who dominates in the new financial world order.

New World Order, Same Framework

In April 2022, I attended an event for the prelaunch of Alex Epstein's tremendous book, *Fossil Future,* where he and Peter Thiel conducted a panel on the future of energy and other forward-thinking ideas. Thiel, in case you are not familiar, is a serial entrepreneur, investor, and futurist. He was a cofounder of PayPal and Palantir, was the first outside investor in Facebook, and wrote a fantastic book about scaling businesses, *Zero to One.*

One of the ideas that Thiel shared during that panel was a framework for how good ideas turn into bad outcomes. I am paraphrasing his explanation with some additions of my own, as this model stuck with me. It illustrates how those with good intentions often don't produce good outcomes. The model is very relevant to just about every bad-in-practice idea out there today and gives some perspective on how big social and economic shifts take hold.

It also takes the "conspiracy" element out of some of the discourse, depending on how you define conspiracy. Of course, there are individuals and bad actors with nefarious intentions looking for a power grab, a money grab, or both. But many of the worst, most destructive ideas become entrenched from the starting point of someone being earnest about it.

Bad ideas often get sold with a positive or misleading wrapper. There is a famous vintage *Twilight Zone* television show episode in which aliens arrive uninvited to earth. The aliens communicate that they came to help humanity with their more advanced technology, promising to solve earth's hunger and wars. Unsure whether to trust the aliens and their supposed noble cause, the people of earth interrogate them and are comforted when the aliens' technology pans out. Then a special government agency decodes the title of a book that an alien representative has left behind. They find that in English the book's title is *To Serve Man.*

To serve man seems like a noble and worthy intention. Based on that and the aliens' stated vision, people line up to visit the aliens' planet and expand cooperation with them.

Ultimately, the woman who helped break the code of the book's title figures out the rest of the book's text, screaming to her boss as he boards a spaceship—*To Serve Man* is a cookbook.[9]

There are lots of people looking to serve man these days. With that in mind, let's explore the framework of ideas going south and see how the propaganda arm of the economic war machine takes hold.

The "good-idea-to-bad-outcome" framework looks something like this:

Believers ➡ Racketeers ➡ Useful Idiots

I think of it in the following terms:

Idea ➡ ROI ➡ ROE (where ROI is return on investment and ROE is return on ego)

The model starts with an idea. There is a problem that an individual or a group somewhere decides needs to be solved or a cause that needs to be pushed, and individuals become passionate about the concept. They are the believers. This is sometimes in earnest, and other times because bad actors have planted a propaganda seed. From there the believers usually latch on to a solution (at least for a time), either through naïveté or deliberate factors. Think of the "green" believers. The concept is a good one. People want to ensure that we are not destroying the planet we inhabit and are being respectful to nature. I think we can all agree this is a noble idea in principle.

As people go around spreading the idea, it eventually morphs into a moneymaking opportunity. This is what I call ROI, or return on investment, and Thiel playfully calls "racketeers" (I will also use "profiteers" to encapsulate this behavior); either way, it's about cashing in. There are activists who need to spread the word. There are studies to be made. There are speeches to be given. This is where the racketeers or other profit seekers come to play and they secure the idea in place because there is a big payday and clout to be gained from doing so. Sophisticated propaganda is profitable. The profiteers cannot produce information that contradicts the idea and associated solution, because if they do, the money stops. If you are being funded by "climate justice activists," your findings are likely to be biased in that direction. Otherwise you are out of a job.

This is why rational progress is often thwarted. We can generally agree that making sure the planet is well cared for is a worthy cause. As that relates to energy, in a rational scenario, we should be able to evaluate different options that make sense to produce abundant but clean energy. This would likely include a mix of "green" initiatives like wind and solar, but also account for their limitations and evaluate how to use fossil fuels and nuclear energy in the mix.

But this is not the case, ostensibly because the believers and cheerleaders for nuclear weren't that good at creating a profiteering ecosystem around nuclear energy. Moreover, the acknowledgment that fossil fuels need to be in the mix might put many racketeers out of a job—or at least take away their current paychecks. This is ROI-driven and is very "sticky" (in a business sense).

Moreover, the racketeering part of the model is a conduit for transferring wealth, which makes it doubly attractive to those in power.

Sometimes the main thesis becomes hard for the profiteers to continue to support. Then it shifts, but the participants still know which masters they are serving: the ones giving them money, access, and power.

Think about all of the shifts we have seen in terms of climate predictions. In my lifetime, we have gone from paper bags to plastic bags and back again to paper bags because of all kinds of environmentally based mental gymnastics. Mark J. Perry, from the American Enterprise Institute, details a list of "50 Years of Failed Doomsday, Eco-pocalyptic Predictions" from "experts," which include a slew of ice age predictions, then predictions calling for the melting of all the ice, oil to be gone by the mid-1970s, then oil to be depleted by the early 1990s, and even Manhattan being underwater by 2015, among dozens of other climate and eco-predictions that have all been wrong.[10] Despite the changes in theses, failed predictions, and data to the contrary, the propaganda around saving the planet continues.

The other thing about the racketeers is that their actions often don't match their advocacy. The Biden administration's special presidential envoy for climate, John Kerry, flies around the world in a private jet. Other climate pushers have built waterfront properties, signaling that they might not be as concerned about water levels rising as their rhetoric suggests.

Despite their hypocritical actions, their overpropagandized hysteria still sticks because the racketeering infrastructure is strong.

The racketeering part of the model is incredibly important. If there is no money to be made, an idea or movement has a hard time gaining traction. The late comedy icon George Carlin made this observation as it relates to homelessness. Homelessness is an important cause you would think many people would get behind and want to solve. But, as he said in a famous bit (paraphrasing, but it's worthwhile to check out online), we have wars on just about everything except homelessness because corporations and politicians don't stand to make any money off solving homelessness.[11]

There is one final component of our model that adds to the racketeering and locks it all in place, and that is the useful idiots. Again, these people may have good intentions (in some cases, in other cases maybe not), but often they are seeking validation, clout, tribal belonging, or some other set of benefits that comes from supporting the cause and its propaganda that they really don't understand. They can share on social media, add flags, emojis, and slogans to their bios and posts, and get some sort of ROE (return on ego). ROE is also quite sticky, and while these individuals usually couldn't tell you why nuclear energy is not a viable option, for example, their support lends popularity to the given cause. A formal social credit system may even give incentives for more support of specific narratives and causes.

Ideas get invaded by those desiring money and clout. This turns dreams into nightmares.

You can see this model in play widely. Take Black Lives Matter. On its surface, it's a worthy cause. People shouldn't be treated differently by institutions because of their skin color. Pretty much everybody agrees with that. However, this idea was co-opted by a radical group with Marxist ties and whose profiteers made a fortune (donated funds were used to purchase a $5.8 million home, which a former BLM leader denies was improper in any way, and another member of its leadership had a consulting firm that was paid $2 million, which said member has noted was paid legally per contracts in place, among other alleged issues).[12] The profiteers were supported by a bunch of suburban moms who gained ROE for being justice warriors.

ESG (which I will discuss in Chapter 7) and a whole host of other alphabet soup concepts all fit this model as well. Take a concept where you can't figure out how it has become a "thing" and look for the racketeers and the useful idiots spreading highly coordinated messaging.

Of course, there are other instances where the power grab is blatant, and the suppression of wealth-creation opportunities and individual rights has no good seed to start. Knowing the difference can inform a different plan of action to fight back and preserve your opportunity to thrive.

Additionally, those who do have nefarious intentions prey on this model being set in motion (or work to set this model in motion) for their own benefit—and to your detriment. It is an effective tool of war.

The Hollywoodification of Crisis

The elite know that the new financial world order creates a huge profiteering opportunity. They also know that the right propaganda can enhance this new financial world order profiteering and enable a massive transfer of wealth.

Here's how they are effective in putting this in place. Have you ever noticed in sci-fi dramas how there is always a crisis against all of humanity that threatens their existence? This is a powerful storytelling structure. Think of *The War of the Worlds* by H. G. Wells, which was published in book form for the first time in 1898 and has never been out of print. A crisis of survival plays well for the masses.

It provides a template for the Hollywoodification of crisis as a means to extract and transfer wealth. Imagine sitting with Jon Hamm as Don Draper in his *Mad Men* office, smoking a cigarette (because hypocrisy doesn't matter here and it sets the mood), and asking him to come up with a campaign that will help you extract fees from the biggest companies in the world.

He tells you that he needs to build drama and stakes. He needs to create a hero. He needs all other issues to become secondary. He needs a mechanism for wealth transfer.

He has the idea—climate change!

He pours himself a glass of whisky, leans back in his chair, and puts his well-polished black shoes up on the conference table.

"Picture this," he says.

"Our threat against all humanity will be the changing of the temperature of earth. It will cause the ice caps to melt, water to rise, and countries to fall into the seas! It threatens all of humanity and the earth itself!" (High drama and stakes—check and check.)

"Our hero," he continues, "will be a liberal politician. A nice-looking, clean-cut authority figure. How about . . . Al Gore? He can be supplemented with other politicians and bolstered by selected people from science and academia." (Don't worry, we can cast them later, Draper assures the room.)

"The entire focus must be on climate change. Our campaign will make everything else shrivel in comparison because if you don't focus on climate change, nothing else matters! Everyone who disagrees must be ridiculed and focus needs to be drawn back to our cause for the good of humanity." (Full focus with everything else secondary—check.)

"What our campaign will do is use this backdrop to help you establish new rules, regulations, taxes, and incentives." (Wealth transfer mechanism, part one—check.)

"Then, industries can expand to help everyone, especially the business class, navigate these new rules. This will help you move more money from industry to the consultant class, including lawyers, consultants, and financial services businesses and professionals." (Wealth transfer mechanism, part two—check.)

"As a benefit, you and your cronies in the political class can gain more power, 'wet your beak,' and benefit from this change campaign."

He puts his feet back on the ground, pushes away from the table, and looks around the room. Then he claps his hands together and asks, "When do we start?"

This Hollywoodesque production template has been used for all sorts of green initiatives around the concept we now know as climate change to go after the big energy companies and their money. This template was used with Covid to go after Main Street and transfer money to Wall Street. And it will likely be used against Big Tech in the near future. Because the bigger and better-funded the target, the more profiteering and fees there are to be extracted and transferred. The more power there is to be gained. And in the emergence of the new financial world order, money grabs become more and more common.

The Big, Bad Globalizers

The "special forces" of World War F are the elite, wealthy, and well-connected. They are using tactics from our good-ideas-to-bad-outcomes and Hollywoodification-of-crisis models to both shape the future of the world and profit in terms of dollars and power along the way.

Who are these organizations? Well, frankly, there are a lot of powerful individuals and organizations that have deservedly received scrutiny for their role in trying to shape a new financial world order in their vision—one that undoubtedly benefits them.

There is probably no organization that has received more scrutiny in recent years, based on their own associates, words, and actions, than the World Economic Forum (WEF).

Though they have already been referenced a few times in this book, let me give you some additional background.

The WEF was founded by a German engineer and professor named Klaus Schwab in 1971.[13] It was started first as the "European Management Forum," with a two-week symposium attended by European company executives, the European Commission, and various academic types.[14] The marketing of this symposium coincided with Schwab's book *Modern Enterprise Management in Mechanical Engineering.* This is a book that, according to his Amazon biography, argues "that a company must serve not only shareholders but all stakeholders to achieve long-term growth and prosperity."[15]

There was a natural symbiosis whereby the forum served as an outlet to push Schwab's often radical ideas (dressed up, of course, as noble intentions), usually incorporating government and "society" as business "stakeholders."

Major geopolitical and economic events that were happening during the first few years of the forum provided a catalyst for it to broaden its focus. The United States' decoupling from the gold standard and ultimate collapse of the Bretton Woods global monetary system, the Yom Kippur War, and the resulting oil embargoes that we discussed in the previous chapter provided the backdrop for the WEF to move into economic and political issues. Political leaders were added to the roster for the 1974 meeting.[16]

As it grew, the forum became more economic and political in nature, and ultimately changed its name to the World Economic Forum in 1987.[17]

To the casual observer, the WEF seems like a snotty boondoggle where the elites come together to signal how smart they are and how much they care about humanity.

But these elite individuals have actually convinced themselves that they know what's best for everyone, or perhaps, for some of these elite, they just want the cover for their power grab. Their ideas are the embodiment of central planning: a handful of people making decisions for the masses, usually done with opacity, based on their objectives and not the desires of the masses. This impacts every aspect of individual freedom and, by extension, prosperity.

This is all very much by design.

The WEF's 2020–21 annual report boasts its logo with the tagline "Committed to Improving the State of the World." That sounds quite "good-idea-to-bad-outcome" model-ish; even similar to *To Serve Man*.

The people involved with the WEF are a who's who of power and influence. Politicians, business leaders, and other influential and connected figures have become associated with the WEF, whether casually or deeply.

The WEF tries to get notable individuals involved early in their endeavors through a program called the Young Global Leaders.

Search firm Heidrick & Struggles International Inc. put out a press release upon being selected to help identify candidates for this program. It sounds prestigious, they get a payday—what could go wrong? Their 2009 list included Facebook (now Meta) CEO Mark Zuckerberg, Digg founder Kevin Rose, Boris Nikolic of the Bill and Melinda Gates Foundation, and golfer Tiger Woods.[18]

This is not meant as an indictment of any specific person, including those mentioned above. While some of these people probably just see the WEF as an opportunity to network, raise their profile, rack up another accolade, or get help with their pet projects and nothing more (that happened to me about a decade ago, when I didn't know much about the group and was invited to a WEF event in New York to blog about some of the speeches—yes, I was a useful idiot briefly myself), others are more entrenched.

Whether they act as racketeers, useful idiots, or a bit of both, some of these influential elites have carried ideas from the WEF into the mainstream, including into the organizations they represent.

At the WEF level, it is hard to believe this is not all well thought out and executed. I mentioned previously how, in 2017, at Harvard's Kennedy School, Schwab explained, "This notion to integrate young leaders has been part of WEF for many years, I have to say when I mention some names like Ms. Angela Merkel, even Vladimir Putin and so on, they all have been Young Global Leaders of the World Economic Forum." He continued to talk about penetrating the cabinets of governments globally, as mentioned in Chapter 1.

That sounds like a very cozy relationship at a minimum, and more likely an attempt to get Schwab's and the WEF's ideas installed in governments around the world. Using a phrase like "penetrate the cabinets" sounds like what it sounds like.[19]

In recent years, with some of the ideas that have been espoused both by Schwab in his books and in information to come out of the WEF—both their meetings and their "thought leadership" pieces—more attention has turned to its influence in setting and pushing various agendas globally. This is especially the case given the elite people connected to the WEF and their access to the highest levels of business, politics, and influence worldwide.

Among these ideas, laid out in painstaking detail in many of Schwab's books, and in many cases nuttier than a jar of peanut butter, are a slew of very concerning agendas, proposals, and predictions.

One that has received some attention, but not enough, is the Great Reset, a plan first launched by Schwab in a book and then propagated by the WEF to leverage the Covid pandemic crisis to reshape the world—for the "good of humanity," of course. Maybe even "to serve man"?

I will refer you to Glenn Beck with Justin Haskins's tremendous book, *The Great Reset,* for a deep dive into this topic and themes that complement what we are uncovering.

What you will find is that many of these ideas are ones that Schwab has been pushing, rehashing, and repackaging for a long time. And they are downright frightening.

Related to the Great Reset is the concept of "you will own nothing," the core theme of this book. This has gotten some attention because of the interest in the Great Reset, but the WEF has been pushing this for much longer.

A video uploaded in January 2017 to the WEF's official YouTube channel is titled "Can You Rent Everything You Need in Life?"[20] In the video, they try to normalize socialized "ownership," comparing a library for books to possible ownership models for other goods. While it is presented with the notions of saving money and preventing waste, it also has major implications for wealth creation, and economic freedom and prosperity.

This preceded the widely shared video from the WEF, "8 Predictions for the World in 2030," posted by the WEF on Twitter in 2018 and created from an article they published in 2016.[21] Now, 2030 is not that far off, so how radical could these ideas be?

Well, the number one prediction was, "You'll own nothing. And you'll be happy." That is further expanded upon by stating that "whatever you want you'll rent and it'll be delivered by drone."

The number two prediction: "The US won't be the world's leading superpower. A handful of countries will dominate."

Number four is "You'll eat much less meat . . . an occasional treat, not a staple—for the good of the environment, and our health."

And after talking about better incorporating refugees, number eight is, "Western values will have been tested to the breaking point."

These aren't light, fun, futuristic predictions of having robots that fold laundry. These are transformational economic and social concepts that move us further away from freedom and agency and more toward planning and control. They frankly sound more like a dystopian novel than a *Jetsons*-esque fantasy.

These elites want you as an indentured servant. They want to take your life, or at least take your life and rent it back to you.

In August 2021, the WEF published on its website an article about a recent study they found enlightening enough to highlight. The article was titled, "Psychologists Say a Good Life Doesn't Have to Be Happy, or Even Meaningful."[22] Either the WEF employs the best clickbait trolls on the planet, they really can't read the room, or something is seriously wrong with them (you can choose your favorite theory; I have mine).

The WEF has their hands in—oh, I mean "ideas" and "proposals" for—just about every aspect of your life and freedom. From social and health to political and economic changes, if there's an idea to be had, they are probably on it. They are weighing in on everything from cybersecurity (aka surveillance), via their Cyber Polygon event, to digital currencies and cryptocurrencies.[23]

And, of course, given that they predict "you'll own nothing" by the end of this decade, a lot of their proposals put you directly on that path.

If these were just some fringe lunatics off by themselves, it wouldn't cause any alarm. But given the political, business, academic, and other powerful individuals who are aligned with this organization and who, by the organization's own admission, carry the ideas back to their countries and companies, this is concerning. Add on the changing cycles of the new financial world order and the technology to implement ideas at scale, and it is downright terrifying.

The WEF website lists a slew of "Partners" under categories like Strategic Partnership, Platform Partnership, New Champions, and others. There are so many that they have to divide them up by alphabetical letter, but it includes the who's who of organizations from A to Z, Amazon to Zoom.

The WEF's site in 2017 listed the cost of being affiliated with them in this way, "Membership and partnership fees range from CHF60,000 to CHF600,000 depending on the level of engagement. Most types of membership include the opportunity to participate in the Annual Meeting for the CEO of the company, although Davos participation incurs a fee over and above membership or partnership fees."[24] At the time of writing, the Swiss franc (CHF) was about at parity with the dollar.

The Davos World Economic Forum event also is a costly one, with funding coming from participant tickets and sponsors. Forum tickets reportedly are five figures each for those who don't have it included with their membership, as described above.[25]

This all helped the WEF generate revenue north of $300 million for their 2020–21 fiscal year.[26]

Worse yet is the fact that not only are corporations that you patronize funding the WEF, but so are you. A report by Open the Books found that, from US taxpayer funds, the WEF received $26 million under Obama's second term and $33 million under the Trump administration![27] (Note: call your representative immediately and ask them to withdraw funding support from this unelected, non-American organization.)

Even some of the Swiss are getting sick of the WEF. Despite constant criticism of CEO pay and focus on inequality by the WEF, Schwab himself takes a salary of one million Swiss francs per year. SRF, a Swiss media company, also has reported that the WEF pays no federal taxes (ostensibly because of the way its entity is organized), yet leans on the Swiss taxpayers to help subsidize security for the Davos forum.[28]

Well-funded, well-aligned, and well-executed organizations that are espousing ideas and strategies for the minimizing of your rights and freedoms, including wealth-creation and wealth-preservation opportunities, are effectively creating an economic war plan.

The World Health Organization

A specialized agency of the United Nations, headquartered in Geneva, Switzerland, the World Health Organization (WHO) has "a broad mandate to act as a coordinating authority on international health issues."[29] It is made up of 194 member states. According to its website, "WHO leads global efforts to expand universal health coverage. We direct and coordinate the world's response to health emergencies. And we promote healthier lives."[30]

In May 2022, the WHO put forth a proposal for a pandemic treaty among nations, which would give this organization incredible influence and power over sovereign nations and their people. The WHO already has a bad reputation in my book—quite literally. I researched them extensively and covered some of their insane and highly politicized decisions and nondecisions relating to the Covid debacle for my last book, *The War on Small Business*.

More importantly, even if they had a stellar track record, none of us elected them, so why would we cede power to them?

An investigative researcher going by the handle @CriticalSway on Twitter did a deep dive into the pandemic treaty proposal and found a slew of disturbing information that consolidated more power within the organization. He found mentions of "vaccines" in some form 33 times, "surveillance" 30 times, and "misinformation" 7 times. It brought up, per his analysis, many questions about free speech, privacy, and freedom, with more money and power going to the WHO.[31]

In addition to trying to take power, the WHO is trying to get more funding (a complete shock, I know). The WHO has pushed back against the critics because, you know, it's only trying to help (serve man, perhaps?).[32]

KFF, an independent organization for health information, has reported that the WHO's two-year budget is more than $6 billion. In terms of funding, the US is typically the biggest funder (aka, your taxpayer dollars). KFF said, "The U.S. has historically been the single largest contributor to WHO, though in the 2020–2021 period (when President Trump withheld some U.S. funding during the COVID-19 pandemic) it was the second largest as other donors, notably Germany, increased their contributions." In FY 2020, the US contribution was down to a mere $163 million (sarcasm noted), but in FY 2021 and 2022, it was $581 million and $434 million, respectively.[33]

This organization falls into our model. We want to have a healthy worldwide population, but you can bet with a $6 billion two-year operating budget there is a lot of profiteering going on. It benefits them to do what they can to make themselves more powerful, and that is gaining more control and money at your expense.

Bad Actors and Profiteers and Useful Idiots, Oh My!

It's not that any one of these organizations is going to change the world alone, but all of the forces coming together at the same time, looking for more control at your expense, creates a battle plan that impacts every aspect of your life and wealth.

There is a slew of other organizations that all have come under scrutiny, whether fairly or not, for coming up with big ideas that sound like central planning instead of free markets.

The United Nations, the international, intergovernmental organization of "cooperation," is certainly one of those. They have had a range of issues (such as human rights–violating countries like China and others on their Human Rights Council, causing the US to leave the council under President Trump and return under President Biden) and a broad range of connections and affiliated agencies (like the WHO, discussed above).[34] They are involved in financial areas, directly and indirectly, as well. For example, the World Bank Group notes their cooperation with the UN, saying, "In addition to a shared agenda, the Bank Group and the United Nations have almost the same membership."[35]

While less known, the Bilderberg Group and its Bilderberg Meeting, which features a rotating list of American and European business magnates, politicians, and other notables, also get a raised eyebrow or two from time to time. The *Independent* reports that the late Labour MP Denis Healey was interviewed for a book in 2001 and said, "To say we were striving for a one-world government is exaggerated, but not wholly unfair. Those of us in Bilderberg felt we couldn't go on forever fighting one another for nothing and killing people and rendering millions homeless. So we felt that a single community throughout the world would be a good thing."[36]

In several media appearances, I have been asked why so many major corporations and powerful executives are members of groups like these and the WEF that have garnered so much recent controversy. I honestly believe that many businesspeople get involved for the anticipated ROI (return on investment) and ROE (return on ego), and they haven't heard much of the other information that we have been discussing.

In organizations, CEOs are so overwhelmed with their own businesses that they do things operating only with surface-level information. To them, the WEF is nothing more than a way to get to Switzerland, hobnob with celebrities and other CEOs, and make some deals and networking connections. There are others who may derive some kind of benefit or patronage by being connected and are completely blind to the WEF's full slate of positions.

I know from discussions that many C-level executives, including CEOs of publicly traded companies, either don't know much about the ideas they are pushing or don't really care about them. They may have ESG all over their websites (which we will discuss later), but they can't explain it to you. They take on other alphabet soup initiatives because the ideas are foisted upon them. Their job is, in part, to mitigate risk, and so they figure it is easier to just say they are part of the current thing and maybe throw some dollars at training sessions and marketing materials than have to deal with a huge PR crisis or disgruntled employees.

The CEOs and other executives are, at the highest levels, often the useful idiots.

While the propaganda is planned among the elite, it is spread by some active collaborators as well as by unknowing or misinformed participants. A lot of racketeers and useful idiots, some working together, some working in parallel, and some all on their own, are all doing the things that humans do in cycles. This helps entrench the message and lay the foundation for wealth transfers.

The elite and well-connected find ways to direct more power to them at the expense of everyone else, even if they have talked themselves into believing they are being noble. To serve man, the tenet, becomes *To Serve Man*, the cookbook.

Plus, in addition to the NGO and intergovernmental groups mentioned above, Big Tech may play the most important and disruptive role in the new financial world order. It is so important that I have dedicated an entire chapter (Chapter 6) to technocracy (society, in effect, run by the tech elite). We know that while not a one-to-one comparison, the market capitalizations of Microsoft and Apple were larger than the GDPs of Italy and Canada, even after the market and their respective stocks lost substantial value in 2022. Companies like Netflix and company products like Amazon Prime Video have more customers than the entire populations of countries like Japan and Mexico. Facebook, at the time of writing, had two times more monthly active users than the population of China.[37]

These firms are incredibly large, powerful, and savvy and often work with governments to enact policy, whether it be social platforms controlling the Covid narrative or Apple and Alphabet (parent company of Google) disabling Apple Pay and Google Pay in Russia in 2022 at the behest of the US government.

The tech companies are large and encompassing, and while often as big in scope as a major country, they aren't concerned with protecting individual rights.

Each one of these actors and their actions, separately and collectively, brings us closer to the new financial world order. Because of the structure of where we are in the world, the types of powers that have emerged, and the tools they have to enact their ideas at scale, there will be fewer, not more, opportunities for you and me if we don't take swift action.

The New World Order

In a speech before the Business Roundtable in March 2022, a group made up of the CEOs of the biggest corporations in America—the elite of the US business elite—President Biden remarked that he believed there would be a new world order coming soon.

He said, "You know, we are at an inflection point, I believe, in the world economy—not just the world economy, in the world. It occurs every three or four generations. As one of—as one of the top military people said to me in a secure meeting the other day, 60—60 million people died between 1900 and 1946. And since then, we've established a liberal world order, and that hadn't happened in a long while. A lot of people dying, but nowhere near the chaos. And now is a time when things are shifting. We're going to—there's going to be a new world order out there, and we've got to lead it. And we've got to unite the rest of the free world in doing it."[38]

He mentioned the cycles we have been exploring, he mentioned the economy and that it plays a role in this change, and he acknowledged that things are shifting.

Where the question mark comes from is, will the US truly be "leading" it? And if so, are American ideals, from freedom to wealth-creation opportunities, going to be destroyed from the inside, from the outside, or both?

What does this new financial world order look like? Another superpower taking control? A bipolar financial regime? More de-globalization and independent blocs with their own financial interests? More globalization and fusion, with a centralized body making financial decisions that benefit "the world"? Shadow tech governments that act as de facto financial superpowers?

The new financial world order could be one or more of the above. But, regardless of what emerges, none of the ultimate orders and outcomes have the inherent benefits and structure of what America's founders created and which let the United States lead the world and bring prosperity and freedom to ourselves and global economies.

Americans did not take care of the unique structure that we were given to support our freedoms, including our economic freedom. We let it morph, and it has moved its way through many of the same cycles of the financial empires that preceded it.

I can't tell you exactly which form it takes, but I can tell you that for your individual interests, it isn't going to be pretty. As with the downward spirals of other financial empires, the final act could come swiftly or could take time. It may even require another parallel war to finalize it.

What can we do to stop it, or at least slow it and preserve as much financial freedom as possible? How do we stand up, fight, and take back our rights? We still have time, but the clock is ticking, and we need to understand the battle in order to fight in it and win.

CHAPTER 4

THE INCREDIBLE SHRINKING DOLLAR

Killing Your Wealth by Debasing the Currency

For as long as there have been riches and power to be had, there has always been someone trying to get more of both for themselves. As noted French economist Frédéric Bastiat said, "When plunder becomes a way of life for a group of men living together in society, they create for themselves, in the course of time, a legal system that authorizes it and a moral code that glorifies it."[1]

Eventually, this brings down financial empires, as we saw in the previous chapter.

The stability—or lack thereof—of the US dollar is at the center of the new financial world order and your financial opportunities. As we discussed, in being the center of the financial universe, the US was faced with a dilemma on whether to manage the dollar for the benefit of the world or the benefit of Americans. Incredibly, over time, the government and the US central bank, the Federal Reserve, have managed to do neither.

This utter mismanagement by the Fed creates a foundation for destroying your wealth. It comes from the confluence of cycles, events, institutions, and people all working to gather power. Ultimately, the weakening of the United States' financial standing ends the exorbitant privilege, as well as all the financial benefits conferred from such privilege. It also erodes the purchasing power of the dollars you have earned and invested. This one-two punch is a critical part of the story.

But, again, it's not an entirely new story. If you sometimes feel like you are in the second coming of the Roman Empire and watching it crumble from the inside, you would not be that far off.

Nero's Greed

We have covered the undoing of two modern financial empires, but one of the most relevant parallels to America's situation today is also one of the all-time most powerful—the Roman Empire. Many scholars link money to that empire's downfall. In the documentary *In Money We Trust*, anthropologist Jack Weatherford noted that you can follow the decline of Rome with the decline of its money and that the two were very closely associated.[2]

Concerning the Roman Empire's downfall, a large expansion in government spending (for both bureaucracy and war) and currency debasement set them on the path to destruction.

Stable money is critical to a stable society. Stable money was valued as such by the Roman Empire and monetary stability was considered central to their economy.

In terms of creating a stable form of money, the Romans began with a silver coin (the denarius, which was the "unit of account"). They also had a copper or bronze coin (the sesterce) and added a gold coin (the aureus). For almost three hundred years, different leaders kept the denarius coin stable, with a consistent weight and purity (around 95 percent silver).[3]

This shifted under the rule of the emperor Nero. Nero would call in the coins in circulation. Those would be melted down and reissued, but with a catch—he would change their makeup. In some instances he would reduce the amount of the precious metal and replace it with a less valuable material; in other instances he made the coins smaller, keeping some of the extra percentages of precious metals for himself. By doing this he became richer at the expense of everyone else. He also used some of the valuable metals siphoned off the previously issued coins to help finance the empire's growing expenditures.[4]

Following Nero's example, future Roman leaders continued to extract wealth from the public to pay for varied expenses using currency debasement. The various leaders had different ways of spinning it and different methods of enacting it, but the endgame was the same—less real value in the previously stable money.

Over the span of the Roman Empire, we can quantify the currency debasement. Historian and professor Joseph R. Peden noted that by the middle of the third century, the denarius contained only 0.5 percent silver and inflation had run rampant, destroying the value of and confidence in the currency, and increasing prices by nearly 1,000 percent! While the gold aureus started out being worth 25 denarii, within a few hundred years it was worth thousands of denarii.[5]

This created a downward spiral for the Roman Empire. Twenty different emperors came and went, the currency became basically worthless, and the average Roman citizen saw their wealth dissipate. This predictably led to the poverty of the masses and civil unrest.

History rhymes, and that again sounds an awful lot like a familiar tune.

When your currency is debased, no matter the time or the place, it ultimately leads to inflation, unrest, and the collapse of financial empires.

This is the trajectory that the US is on that will ensure, like the former holders of Roman wealth, that you will eventually own nothing.

How Much Is a Dollar Worth?

My friend Steve Forbes often talks about money as a measure of value, the way that a scale measures weight or a clock measures time. Similarly, he says, money measures the value of goods, services, and investments.[6]

To be able to measure something, the measuring device needs to be fixed in value.

As Forbes said in his documentary *In Money We Trust*, "Time is a fixed measure. Sixty minutes in an hour; sixty seconds in a minute. Imagine if that floated each day; fifty minutes in an hour one day, eighty minutes the next. We know intrinsically that would make life chaotic. . . . [C]hanging the value of money destroys trust between buyer and seller, lender and borrower because it changes the values that were agreed upon. One party got an undeserved gain, and the other got an undeserved loss." And when it comes to undeserved losses, it is usually those without the wealth and connections who get that side of the coin (no pun intended).

Money as a unit of account or measure is a critical concept that has global implications. As discussed in Chapter 2, oil-producing countries agreed to allow oil to be priced in dollars because they believed the US would take measures to keep the dollar stable and the measurement of value would remain fairly constant—at least bound by a tight range.

Perception becomes the problem when the unit of measure isn't constant.

As the dollar has become fiat currency, its value has been manipulated and debased by policy. As opposed to the precious metal–based currency of Rome, the US dollar currency didn't have its value in its makeup. After Bretton Woods, the dollar was a representative currency that had its value tied to the backing of a certain amount of gold. This meant that instead of having to carry around gold, you could carry a Federal Reserve note (aka dollar), which was at any point redeemable for a specific amount of gold. When that standard was thrown by the wayside upon Nixon closing the gold window and the dollar became "backed" by the "faith in the government" (aka fiat currency, which doesn't have intrinsic value and doesn't represent stable assets held in reserves), it became easier for the Federal Reserve and government to continue to decrease the value of the currency through policy.

But the psychological trick of changing the measurement keeps people from fully comprehending what has happened. You may think that a certain amount of money—whether that be $100,000 or $1 million—affords you a certain lifestyle, but the $100,000 of today purchases far less than it did twenty years ago.

This leads too many people to focus on the headline numbers and ignore what central bankers have done to the value of our currency.

In a 1978 *Saturday Night Live* skit that is just as appropriate today as it was then, Dan Aykroyd plays President Jimmy Carter dealing with rampant inflation. He smirks as he delivers satire about inflation being great because everyone can be a millionaire and own "expensive" clothes and cars.[7]

Then the skit does something that hasn't been done in pop culture for far too long—it talks about money printing! Aykroyd says: "What about people on fixed incomes? They have always been the true victims of inflation. That's why I will present to Congress the inflation maintenance program, whereby the US Treasury will make up any inflation cost losses through direct tax rebates to the public—in cash. Now you may say, 'Won't that cost a lot of money? Won't that increase the deficit?' Sure it will! But so what? We'll just print more money! We have the papers, we have the mints. I can just call up the Bureau of Engraving and say, 'Hi. This is Jimmy. Roll off some of them $20s. Print up a couple of thousands sheets of those century notes.' Sure, the glut of dollars will cause even more inflation, but who cares? Everybody will be a millionaire!"[8]

That's more or less what has happened. While cost-of-living adjustments (COLAs) are tied to CPI-W inflation increases, CPI measures have seen their formulas changed by the government to understate inflation. That way the government doesn't have to increase the benefits they give out by as much as they would have in the 1980s, before such changes.[9]

As the government and Fed have debased the dollar, much like the Romans did with their denarius about two thousand years ago, the warped perception of money has allowed the debasement to continue. People can identify the symptoms—they know that they can buy less today and that it is harder to purchase a home, for example—but they don't necessarily realize why.

This is an easy and deceptive way for the government and central planners to steal wealth.

You can see it in the following chart, showing how the purchasing power of your dollars has been eroded since the creation of the Federal Reserve.

The dollar's role as a medium of exchange has stayed fairly constant, although much more so digitally than physically, as the use of physical

Consumer Price Index for All Urban Consumers: Purchasing Power of the Consumer Dollar in US City Average; Index 1982–1984=100; Not Seasonally Adjusted; Monthly; January 1913 to September 2022

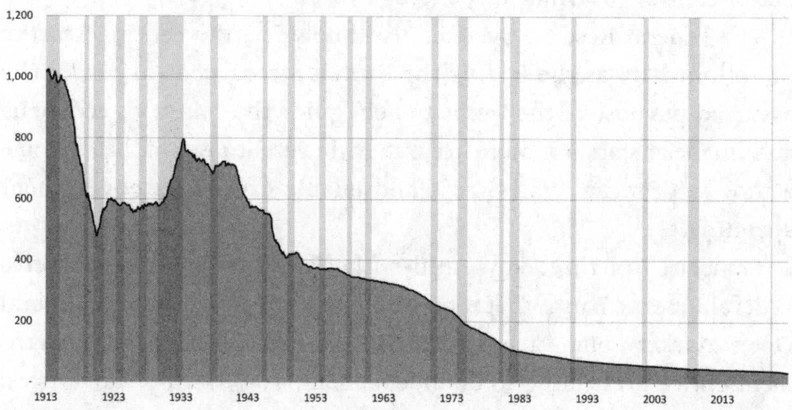

Source: US Bureau of Labor Statistics, Consumer Price Index for All Urban Consumers: Purchasing Power of the Consumer Dollar in US City Average [CUUR0000SA0R], retrieved from FRED, Federal Reserve Bank of St. Louis, https://fred.stlouisfed.org/series/CUUR0000SA0R, October 29, 2022.

money over time has substantially been replaced by digital transactions. In October 2021, a piece in *Harvard Business Review* said that more than 97 percent of the money in circulation is via digitized transactions (including checking transactions), versus using physical money.[10]

The dollar is amazingly still considered a store of value, even though it has lost almost 97 percent of its purchasing power since 1913, the year the Federal Reserve Act was passed, and 86 percent since 1971, when we came off the gold standard.[11]

The St. Louis Fed says as much, without getting into scope: "Although it is an efficient store of value, money is not a perfect store of value. Inflation slowly erodes the purchasing power of money over time."[12] They also leave out the fact that money isn't eroded naturally by inflation; inflation is caused by fiscal and monetary policy.

It's incredible that people around the world still consider the US dollar a safe haven, which is a testament to both the strength and productivity of Americans and their economic output today, as well as the relative economic and financial issues (including central bank money printing) around the rest of the globe.

It Was the Fed, It Was the Fed . . .

One of the biggest factors in the dollar's debasement has been the actions of the Federal Reserve, both directly and indirectly via enabling out-of-control government spending.

The Federal Reserve System, also known as the Federal Reserve or colloquially as the Fed, is the United States' central bank. The assumed purpose of the Fed is to help guide the country's economic and financial stability. More accurately, in recent years, it has become a tool to prop up Wall Street and enable capricious government spending.

Comprised of three key entities (the Board of Governors, twelve Federal Reserve Banks that represent twelve districts, and the Federal Open Market Committee, or FOMC), the Fed is basically a government entity pretending to be independent. The Board of Governors, which is an agency of the federal government that reports to and—in its words but not in reality—is directly accountable to the United States Congress, oversees the twelve Federal Reserve Banks, and provides input and guidance for the entire system.

While the Fed derives its power and mandates from Congress, it is not truly accountable to anyone. That is intentional and by design. It may be the only entity in America not owned by or accountable to anybody else, yet it has control over the country's monetary policy!

Moreover, its independent status and guise of decentralization mean that it operates without the checks and balances essential to the rest of the government system. It is not audited. Though it releases "recaps" of its meetings, it doesn't release the full content of its discussions. It doesn't tell congressional representatives or committees about its behind-the-scenes undertakings, and it has little in the way of oversight.

The Fed uses a few "tools" to set monetary policy, which is really a manipulation of our economy and the markets by their directive. For example, lowering the Fed funds rate is associated with expansionary monetary policy, as it is supposed to spur more demand for credit by making it "inexpensive" to borrow, thus stimulating economic activity. (In layman's terms, the lower the interest rate, the more an individual or business can borrow while keeping the cost of each debt payment—and their overall cost of debt—lower.)

The Fed also uses open market operations, or, more simply, the buying and selling of government securities from banks and other investors in the market, to make adjustments to the supply of money and influence economic activity. As the Fed buys more securities and replaces them with "credit" in the selling banks' accounts, there is more "money" or credit available for lending, and interest rates are also pushed downward (this is aligned with expansionary policy; contractionary policy would have the Fed selling securities and have the opposite effect).

In layman's terms, if you or I found a mechanism that let us go into our online bank account and change the balance to whatever we wanted, and we then used that money to buy things, it would be called fraud. When the Federal Reserve does the same thing, we call it monetary policy.

This Fed intervention has had a huge impact on the debasement of the dollar over time, particularly in the recent past.

The people who run the Fed have changed their tenor and their focus, despite their stated mandate being generally consistent. This ranges from the actions of Fed chair Paul Volcker, who, as noted in Chapter 2, took interest rates up to north of 19 percent in 1981 in an attempt to tame inflation and keep the petrodollar "good as gold for oil"—a move that wreaked havoc upon the US economy—to those of Jerome Powell, who, beginning in 2020, held on to an "emergency measure" to save the stock market for so long that the Fed's balance sheet blew up to $9 trillion and helped create inflation at a rate that the US hadn't seen in forty years. (Note that the government's fiscal and other policy decisions played a substantial role here, too.)

But there are a few recent decisions that reflect the Fed's manipulation of our money, markets, and economy.

From Nero to Powell

Take a look at the charts of the Fed funds effective rate history (first), blown up to highlight just the last two decades (second).

Federal Funds Effective Rate; Percent, Not Seasonally Adjusted; Monthly; July 1954 to September 2022

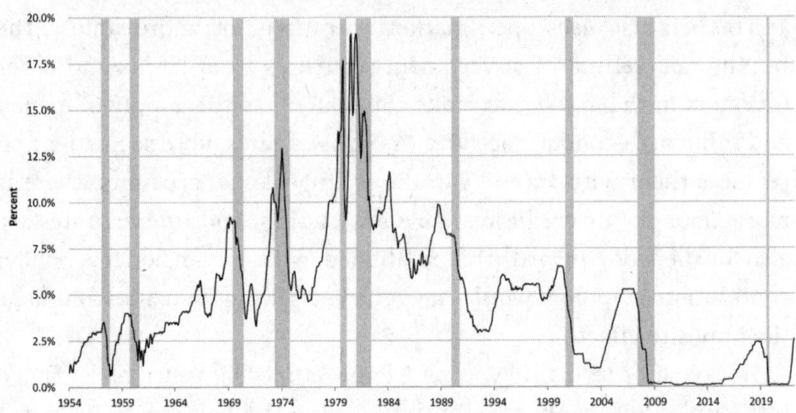

Source: Board of Governors of the Federal Reserve System (US), Federal Funds Effective Rate [FEDFUNDS], retrieved from FRED, Federal Reserve Bank of St. Louis, https://fred.stlouisfed.org/series/FEDFUNDS, October 29, 2022.

Federal Funds Effective Rate; Percent, Not Seasonally Adjusted; Monthly; September 2002 to September 2022

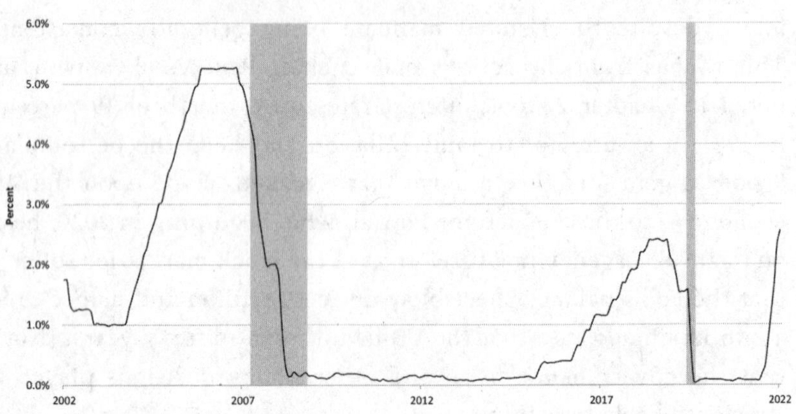

Source: Board of Governors of the Federal Reserve System (US), Federal Funds Effective Rate [FEDFUNDS], retrieved from FRED, Federal Reserve Bank of St. Louis, https://fred.stlouisfed.org/series/FEDFUNDS, October 29, 2022.

You can see that while the Fed has enacted a lot of different policies with a range of outcomes, their interference in the markets and the economy, and with our money, has accelerated over the last fifteen or so years. In the case of the Fed funds rate, it has been substantially artificially depressed.

The most substantial intervention first happened, as you may recall, with the Fed's policies during the Great Recession (aka the 2007–2009 financial crisis) under Fed chair Ben Bernanke (Alan Greenspan officially opened the door in 1987 with his actions around Black Monday, but Bernanke burst through it with reckless abandon). Historically, the Fed's balance sheet wasn't a tool that was substantially used in a way that made anyone other than policy wonks take notice.

The Fed's actions during the Great Recession changed that. Prior to the crisis, the Fed's balance sheet had been less than $1 trillion to accommodate monetary policy. During the Great Recession, when the Fed had already brought the target rate down and believed it needed more tools to enact its policy, it engaged in large, coordinated purchasing of securities in the open market to expand its balance sheet. This series of actions goes by the financial term *quantitative easing*, or QE, mentioned earlier. As you can guess, QE was not a traditional activity of the Fed historically and introduced a significant amount of artificial intervention into the markets.

Starting with a 50-basis-point cut in September 2007, where the Fed funds target rate stood at 5.25 percent, the Fed lowered the target rate all the way to 0.00 to 0.25 percent by December 2008.[13] What happened was unprecedented in both absolute numbers and duration. You'd have to go back around sixty years to find a Fed funds target rate as low as 0.50 percent. However, under the stewardship of Fed chairs Ben Bernanke and then Janet Yellen, the Fed kept the unprecedentedly low 0.00 to 0.25 percent rates for seven years!

In addition to the interest rate maneuvering, the Fed's balance sheet was leveraged as both a financial and political tool, or, more accurately, a financial and political weapon. By the end of 2009, the Fed's balance sheet stood at close to $2.25 trillion, more than two and a half times what it had been just sixteen months earlier.

It's important to remember in this discussion that the Fed had bought those assets with money it had generated from an accounting entry. This is the equivalent of Nero melting down coins and issuing less valuable ones to make purchases, but is much easier to do.

Though people may argue that this Fed action was required to provide needed financial system liquidity during the crisis, and even if you agree, the level and duration of interference remain unprecedented and dangerous. It is very reminiscent of the good ideas to bad outcomes model. As with so many other "good intentions," once you give up a principle, it is too easy for the ensuing actions to be abusive.

There were a lot of folks to blame during this time and a bunch of bad behaviors converged at once. However, as the late J. Paul Getty famously said, "If you owe the bank $100, that's your problem. If you owe the bank $100 million, that's the bank's problem."[14]

That played out here with a giant step toward ensuring that you will own nothing. Despite the big financial institutions playing the largest role in this financial disaster, they were deemed "too big to fail." They received bailouts, and the government spent hundreds of billions of dollars, yet millions of average Americans lost their homes and did not receive a bailout. This picking of winners and losers took away people's homes and wealth, instead of bailing them out or at least having some sharing of the pain. The economy tanked. People were angry and had been bankrupted. And, with a couple of exceptions, the financial services sector came out of this more powerful than ever.

The long-tail impacts of this are still being felt and it set the foundation of wealth transfer by crisis and normalized emergency support, extending it far past any actual emergencies.

The Fed continued to hold down interest rates, print money, and buy securities. They set up a decade and a half of savers and retirees getting no return on their money while giving cheap and easy money for big corporations to go out and become more powerful. This, along with an explosion in government spending and deficits, continued to debase the dollar.

These actions have accelerated the destruction of wealth for Main Street Americans in a variety of ways and set up a benchmark that was used to further wealth destruction.

The Magic Money Tree

While all of this has been going on, the progressive wing of the Democratic Party put forth an insane concept called Modern Monetary Theory, or MMT (I've adopted calling it by a term I heard somewhere along the way, "Magic Money Tree," because that's a more appropriate moniker for this unicorns-and-rainbows idea). While not a new idea, the packaging tried to make it so. The basic premise is that if you have the means to print money, you can always print more, and so the government can keep spending more.

The concept was extrapolated from a quote by none other than former Federal Reserve chairman Alan Greenspan: "The United States can pay any debt it has because we can always print money to do that. So there is zero probability of default." That's one of those things that is true as worded but not really in principle. When my mom had leukemia a quarter century ago, she was treated with harsh radiation procedures. This killed off the leukemia, but also her organs and, by default, her. The doctors patted themselves on the back that they had triumphed against leukemia. They said that the leukemia didn't kill her. Still, their actions to combat it did—an infuriatingly stupid perspective. So, yes, we can technically fulfill any debt, but not without eradicating the value of the dollar in the process—another infuriatingly stupid perspective.

MMT is an outgrowth of too much debt leading to desperation.

The MMT folks say that if you are in control of your currency (spend, tax, or borrow in that fiat), you don't have to worry about deficits. You can print whatever you need and you shouldn't be worried about rising debt. It's the equivalent of saying that because you have a checkbook, you can write an unlimited amount of checks. While there are some other nuances and factors in their argument, like taxing the rich more to regulate the inflation induced by spending, the guts of it remain the same.

You don't have to be an economist to know this is idiotic, but the proponents of it, including some economists, will say that a government is not like a household and continue to talk in circles.

Even as this concept has been disproven throughout time and history, and any basic economic understanding lets you understand that just manufacturing more "notes" with no associated improvement in productivity will make each note less valuable, this gained traction from people who presented themselves as serious, who taught economics at universities, who advised presidential candidates, and who infiltrated the government.

The MMT pushers ignored that the fiat money itself wasn't valuable, but rather it represented value in terms of your productivity. If they print more money without a corresponding increase in productive value, you must work harder because each unit of money is worth proportionately less.

MMT throws a lifeline to the government at your expense. Embracing MMT in the US has expanded capricious government spending, thrown financial responsibility and discipline by the wayside, and caused our national debt to explode.

While we have had plenty of examples throughout history, after the printing and spending of recent years, the United States now had concrete real-time evidence of how MMT doesn't work and how money printing and government overspending cause inflation.

It debases the currency and makes it harder for you to thrive, survive, invest, and own. MMT is a key driver of "you will own nothing."

Of course, the Magic Money Tree contingency, who have been lying low lately and yet not receiving nearly the amount of public ridicule that they should, will likely say, "But that wasn't *real* MMT!" as they do with everything else.

And of course the Biden administration, as I write this, is still looking for more ways to spend money that they don't have.

The Cozy Relationship Between Money and Power

Understanding how the elite have been orchestrating a power and money grab requires a deeper look at the ties between Wall Street and their most powerful financial players, and the Federal Reserve and the Treasury (as a representative of the government). The musical chairs between individuals in these roles and the people they have been connected to paint a very interesting picture. And in this game of musical chairs, when the music stops, it is you, the average American, who is left without a chair.

Looking at pairings of Fed chairs, Treasury secretaries, and related personnel in recent administrations, you will note they come from power centers and return to them after their tenure. Remember, the Fed and the financiers are the ones with the real power and always have been. They created the central banking system, not the government. The government politicians are the useful idiots (and, more recently, useful co-profiteers) that work together to secure money and power for themselves via this interdependent, symbiotic relationship.

The Fed chairs and Treasury secretaries going back to Alan Greenspan have come from politically connected backgrounds, Wall Street powerhouses, big businesses, and elite universities like Harvard and Princeton. After their tenures, they go back into positions at Wall Street powerhouses, big businesses, and elite universities.

If you look at the people who have in recent times been put into the Fed chair and Treasury secretary positions, they are extremely well-connected with Wall Street and other elite institutions and individuals before heading into office. Think of a powerful financial firm, and they are represented or are one connection away.

For example, Treasury secretary Robert Rubin became a director and senior counselor at Citigroup and had a stint as their temporary chairman.[15] Treasury secretary Larry Summers became president of Harvard University and in 2006 was one of five cochairs of the World Economic Forum. He also served as director of the National Economic Council under President Barack Obama. He has served on boards including Square, the Brookings Institution, and the Broad Foundation, among others.[16] Treasury secretary Tim Geithner became president of the major private equity firm Warburg Pincus.[17]

Fed chair Ben Bernanke, postretirement, was hired as an advisor to both PIMCO (a top investment management firm with around $2 trillion in assets under management) and the hedge fund Citadel.[18]

Between her stints as Fed chair and Treasury secretary, Janet Yellen pulled in $7.2 million in speeches from large financial and business institutions, including "Citi, Goldman Sachs, Google, City National Bank, UBS, Citadel LLC, Barclays, Credit Suisse, Salesforce and more."[19] And after leaving office, Treasury secretary Steve Mnuchin started a new private equity firm, Liberty Strategic Capital, with a reported $2.5 billion in assets under management, with "most of the money . . . from sovereign wealth funds in the Middle East, including Saudi Arabia's Public Investment Fund."[20]

One thing that has become clear as time has gone by is that in the powerful alliance between Wall Street, the Federal Reserve, and the government, a well-connected Fed chair and Treasury secretary combination can facilitate a lot of influence, perks, and wealth accumulation for the money class, asset accumulators, and fee hounds.

You may think these may just be the best people for the job. That may also explain how, after office, they often land extremely plum, well-paid roles at some of the most prestigious firms in the country. It may be because of their pedigrees—or it may be for other reasons. Rubin, for example, was awarded $126 million in cash and stock by Citigroup during his time there, which overlapped the Treasury's bailout of Citigroup. He ultimately resigned among criticism of his performance, but with that nine-figure compensation to console him.[21]

Also, individuals who have contradicted the cash bonanza wealth transfers facilitated by the Fed and Treasury have found themselves out of a job quickly, such as former Treasury secretary Paul O'Neill, who lasted less than two years before being fired by President George W. Bush, despite his business savvy. He was against another round of tax cuts, worrying they would lead to greater deficits and hurt the economy (he was also an Iraq War critic).[22]

Wall Street, the Federal Reserve, and the government, with strong Treasury secretaries, have been the ultimate enablers of profiteering and wealth transfers. The money class, asset accumulators, and fee hounds have accumulated more and more wealth for themselves. Whether it was Rubin's role in setting up the ultimate repeal of key provisions of the Glass-Steagall Act, a move that changed the face of the banking industry; the "Greenspan put," which is often attributed to enabling the dot-com bubble and the subprime mortgage crisis; Paulson, Bernanke, and Geithner's well-rewarded bailout of the financial services sector; or Mnuchin and Powell's hiring of BlackRock to work with the Fed during the "Covid era," it's hard not to see these collaborations as enabling a well-connected cash grab.[23]

You can go back to the Troubled Assets Relief Program (TARP) bailout recipients for some confirmation. Not only was no individual ever convicted of any crimes, but look at the bonuses of the recipients for 2008, including bonuses that were in excess of one million, two million, and three million dollars:

TARP Recipients' 2008 Bonus Chart

Institution	TARP Received	Bonus Pool	Bonuses at or > $3 million	Bonuses at or > $2 million	Bonuses at or > $1 million
Bank of America	$45,000,000,000	$3,300,000,000	28	65	172
Bank of New York Mellon	$3,000,000,000	$945,000,000	12	22	74
Citigroup, Inc.	$45,000,000,000	$5,330,000,000	124	176	738
Goldman Sachs Group	$10,000,000,000	$4,823,358,763	212	391	953
JPMorgan Chase & Co.	$25,000,000,000	$8,693,000,000	>200	--	1626
Merrill Lynch	$10,000,000,000	$3,600,000,000	149	--	696
Morgan Stanley	$10,000,000,000	$4,475,000,000	101	189	428
State Street Corp.	$2,000,000,000	$469,970,000	3	8	44
Wells Fargo & Co.	$25,000,000,000	$977,500,000	7	22	62

Source: Attorney General Andrew M. Cuomo, "No Rhyme or Reason: The 'Heads I Win, Tails You Lose' Bank Bonus Culture," report, State of New York, July 2009, Appendix A.

Millions of Americans lost their homes and the TARP recipients made millions of dollars.

It may seem counterintuitive, but boom-and-bust cycles are good for those with long-term outlooks and staying power and are a conduit to transferring wealth. The well-capitalized reap the rewards during the booms, and during the busts they have the financial wherewithal to remain patient and take advantage of the bust cycles, picking up assets in distress and waiting for the cycle to inflate them all over again.

It appears that going back to Paul Volcker under the Carter and Reagan administrations, his actions make him an outlier—not so much because of what he did, but rather because he was playing by a different set of rules and intentions.

It is this group that sits at the center, making sure that they and their cronies are well compensated, even if that means you end up owning little to nothing in the process.

The Covid Multitrillion-Dollar Inferno

Returning to the Fed, coming out of the Great Recession they never normalized their "emergency" policy. The US was in a state of emergency with Fed intervention and policy for more than a decade and a half.

This likely resulted from what I call the "not-so-secret other dual mandate" for the Fed, in conjunction with the Treasury Department. While the stated Federal Reserve mandate from Congress is full employment and stable prices (aka not letting inflation take hold), it seems as though the Fed has been operating to prop up Wall Street and give the government cover for overspending (aka government expansion).

Wall Street, the Treasury, and the Federal Reserve have a very interdependent, symbiotic relationship, as explained above.

Take the interest rate the US government pays on its debt. The Fed funds rate influences the rates the government pays when it issues its Treasury notes and bonds (indirectly, not on a one-to-one basis). As the Fed funds rate goes higher (or is anticipated to move higher), other interest rates, including the rates on Treasurys, also typically move higher.

At the time of writing, the average duration of Treasury debt was about five to six years, and the interest rate was a mere 1.4 percent, but the ten-year Treasury note yield had moved above 4.0 percent. With more than $31 trillion in national debt and growing, as the government retires Treasury securities and issues new ones, they now have to do so at higher interest rates. Over time, a 1 percent increase in the cost of their financing will translate to more than $300 billion in additional interest expense that needs to be paid on today's debt—not for new spending but paying for things the government already bought. It's like an adjustable rate on a credit card, and you know that increasing costs make it harder to keep your finances sound.

The Congressional Budget Office (CBO), in their "Budget and Economic Outlook: 2022 to 2032" report, expects the national debt held by the public to surpass $40 trillion in the next decade and expects net interest paid on that debt to almost triple, to over $1 trillion by 2030. There is no real plan for government spending or debt reduction, and the current path shows more debt expansion. With the government's unfunded liabilities and obligations, the projected amount is estimated at tens of trillions of dollars more; plus, CBO estimates tend to be conservative (especially if interest rates remain elevated).[24]

To address this, it is likely that more money will be "printed," which will further devalue the dollar.

Over the next thirty years, the CBO estimates, interest payments on the debt will total more than $60 trillion—nearly three times our current GDP.[25]

Michael Burry, the famed investor from *The Big Short* who was an early predictor of the 2008–2009 Great Recession, tweeted, When you see mention of the strong dollar, the almighty dollar, please remember this is only in relation to other fiat currencies. The dollar is not at all strong, and it is not getting stronger. We all see it every single day in prices of everything.

As my friend and market strategist Jim Iuorio put it in layman's terms, the dollar may be strong against the euro but it isn't strong against a bag of groceries.

The ridiculously large national debt load that the US government carries (the US public debt was estimated at around 120 percent of GDP as of Q3 2022) has undoubtedly been a major influence on the Fed's monetary policy. Given the fact that rising interest rates mean more interest expense, it will likely influence Fed policy for years to come.

With that backdrop, the Fed helped enable the most historic transfer of wealth we have ever seen during the Covid years.

As a side note, which Burry alludes to, money printing and currency debasement is an issue not just in the US, but also for major central banks around the world. Central banks like the European Central Bank and the Bank of Japan have, combined, printed trillions of dollars' worth of their own currencies in recent years.[26] Countries including Japan, Italy, France, Spain, Greece, Portugal, and Belgium, among others, have public debt that is near or exceeds their GDP. They will all be contending with the same issues the US is facing, but in many cases with less underlying economic strength, which could materially impact the global economy.

The Big Lie: Inflation Is Transitory

As I recounted in *The War on Small Business*, in Q1 2020, the very first financial measures that were taken related to the Covid pandemic were to save the stock market. In March 2020, the Fed undertook two emergency rate cuts, bringing the Fed funds target rate down to 0.00 to 0.25 percent. They also announced a QE program, which ultimately went on for two full years and swelled their balance sheet to nearly $9 trillion.

This was clearly meant to help Wall Street. The lower interest rates and securities purchases inflated assets at the expense of retirees and savers, who were not able to earn anything on their savings and had to either take on more risk to generate any sort of return or just forgo it. It also wasn't a benefit to Main Street—in fact, it just made their larger competitors stronger.

The strengthening of the corporate Goliaths took place not just with monetary policy, but via government policy as well. The shuttering of small businesses by mandate meant that larger competitors who could remain open received more of consumers' dollars. The financial support from the Fed was the second piece of this one-two punch.

Had Wall Street had to suffer the same pain that everyone else was suffering, the overly strict Covid policies would probably have lasted fewer than the target fifteen days to slow the spread, and we would have moved directly to a mitigation stance. This would have reduced the long-tail impact of these bad ideas, from the disruption of the labor market to the potential for worldwide mass starvation (a talk for another time).

After President Biden took office, he had an opportunity to normalize the economy and help stop the percolating inflationary environment. Despite trillions of dollars in stimulus added to the economy, vaccines being widely rolled out, and the economy reopening across the board, the administration decided to add more fuel to the fire. They passed the $1.9 trillion American Rescue Plan, which, of course, the Fed was on standby with their asset purchasing program to help absorb. That, along with other bad economic decisions from the administration, including canceling oil and gas leases, was all the supply-constrained economy could handle.

The stimulus further stimulated the economy, something that should be apparent from the word *stimulus* but clearly caught some people by surprise.

Inflation very predictably took off like a rocket ship. By June 2021, inflation had reached its fastest pace in thirteen years.[27] But Americans were told, by the Fed and by the Biden administration, the big lie—that percolating inflation was "transitory." While it was clear to everyone with a basic economic degree that the historic level of spending and Fed intervention would put pressure on the dollar's value, making everything more expensive for everyday Americans, they continued to push the lie.

Treasury secretary Janet Yellen, at an early June 2021 meeting of the G7 in London, said, "We're seeing some inflation but I don't believe it's permanent," later adding, "I personally believe this represents transitory factors."[28] In October 2021, she reiterated the transitory view in an interview with the *CBS Evening News*.[29]

The media kept running cover and the Fed and Biden administration kept pretending reality didn't exist.

In January 2022, inflation, despite our being told that it would not be an issue, reached a forty-year high and continued to hit highs over the following months, reaching 9.1 percent for the CPI in June 2022, and 11.6 percent and 11.3 percent for the Producer Price Index (PPI) in March and June 2022, respectively.[30] It was still a couple of months after reaching historic inflation levels that the Fed stopped buying securities and decided they would have to start raising interest rates to quell the inflation that they and the government together had caused.

Everyone who caused this epic dollar debasement or was a cheerleader for the actions that enabled it blamed everyone and everything except themselves.

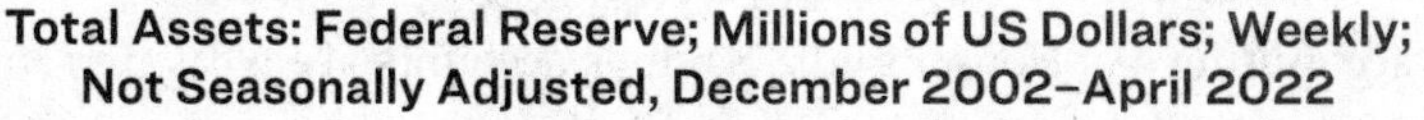

Total Assets: Federal Reserve; Millions of US Dollars; Weekly; Not Seasonally Adjusted, December 2002–April 2022

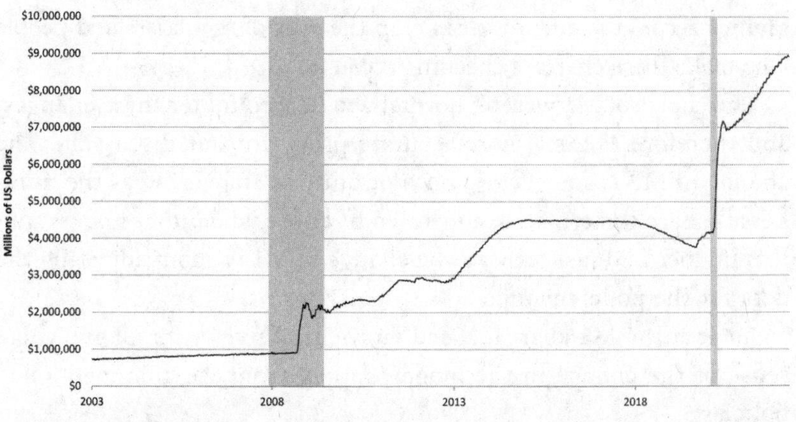

Source: Board of Governors of the Federal Reserve System (US), Assets: Total Assets: Total Assets (Less Eliminations from Consolidation): Wednesday Level [WALCL], retrieved from FRED, Federal Reserve Bank of St. Louis, https://fred.stlouisfed.org/series/WALCL, October 29, 2022.

For a sense of the scope of what was done, first take a look at the Federal Reserve balance sheet over the past twenty years, from before the Great Recession financial crisis through April 2022, when they were first starting to "normalize" their policy.

Alongside that, take a look at the money supply. The money supply is a proxy for money in circulation that consumers can easily access to make purchases (and differentiated from their investments). M1 includes cash and checking deposits as a proxy for cash equivalents, and M2 includes all the elements of M1, plus money in savings accounts, money market accounts, and other "time deposits" that are under $100,000 in value, which represents cash equivalents and money easily converted into cash.[31]

While in the past I would have shown you M1 in relation to the change in the money supply, today I am using M2 because of an accounting change that happened alongside the extraordinary financial measures taken over the past couple of years. Morgan Housel, author and partner at the Collaborative Fund, helped to break this down. He explained that, historically, due to banking regulations, savings accounts differed from checking accounts because savings accounts had a limit of six withdrawals per month.[32]

But in April 2020, when people lost their jobs because of government closure mandates, the six-withdrawal rule on savings was eliminated to allow them to more readily access their savings if needed. That changed the accounting. As Housel said, "Savings accounts are measured in M2 and left out of M1. But once the six-withdrawal rule was removed, every savings account suddenly became, in the eyes of regulators and people who make these charts, a checking account."

The charts of M1 weren't normalized to account for these changes, and therefore M2 is a more accurate proxy for our discussion. The change in M2 is staggering, but not quite as staggering as the numbers that are sometimes exaggerated by those who didn't understand this nuance and just showed the change in M1 without adjusting the data for the policy change.

Look at the M2 chart focused on the past five years to give you a sense of the change in the money supply from the aforementioned policies.

Even if you are not a chart aficionado, hopefully you can still ascertain the scope of the monetary, fiscal, and other government policy

M2; Billions of Dollars; Seasonally Adjusted; Monthly; May 2017–May 2022

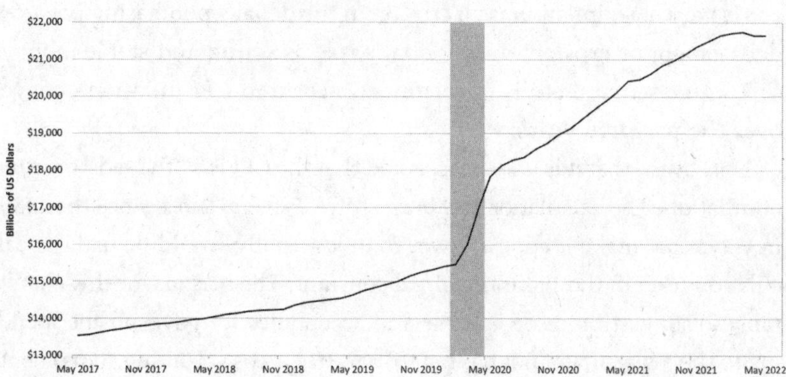

Source: Board of Governors of the Federal Reserve System (US), M2 [M2SL], retrieved from FRED, Federal Reserve Bank of St. Louis, https://fred.stlouisfed.org/series/M2SL, October 29, 2022.

Consumer Price Index for All Urban Consumers: All Items in US City Average vs. Consumer Price Index for All Urban Consumers: All Items Less Food and Energy in US. City Average; Percent Change from a Year Ago; Seasonally Adjusted; Monthly; May 2017–May 2022

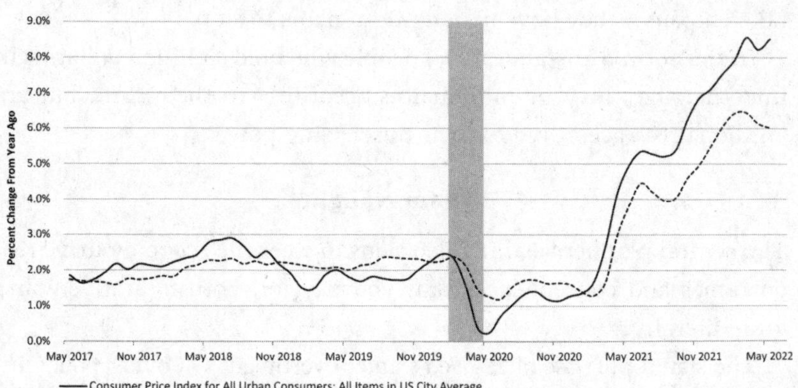

Source: US Bureau of Labor Statistics, Consumer Price Index for All Urban Consumers: All Items in US City Average [CPIAUCSL], retrieved from FRED, Federal Reserve Bank of St. Louis, https://fred.stlouisfed.org/series/CPIAUCSL, October 30, 2022; US Bureau of Labor Statistics, Consumer Price Index for All Urban Consumers: All Items Less Food and Energy in US City Average [CPILFESL], retrieved from FRED, Federal Reserve Bank of St. Louis, https://fred.stlouisfed.org/series/CPILFESL, October 30, 2022.

and now connect the dots as to what that has done to your purchasing power and wealth creation opportunities.

As we know, inflation is an erosion in the dollar's purchasing power—debasement or erosion of the dollar's role as sound and stable money.

To give scope, here is government-measured CPI inflation changes over the past five years:

Note again that it is widely accepted that the CPI is a "fudged" measure of inflation. The calculation has been shifted several times since the 1980s in ways that make it appear lower than it actually would be had the calculation used in the 1980s remained constant. The reasons for this change range from getting more latitude and acceptance for government spending to the government not having to make their cost-of-living adjustments for programs by the same amount of money. They are shortchanging you on money on both sides, marching you further toward owning nothing.

The bottom line is that all of this intervention and policy stole wealth from Americans, as well as holders of dollars around the world. The Fed and US government's actions rhyme with the Roman, Dutch, and British empires before it.

These actions march us closer to a change in the financial world order, all while devaluing the earnings and wealth of the people who worked hard for them. And while the government and Fed may have taken a pause, they have no long-term plans to stop.

In the not-too-distant future, people who hold a million dollars will find that they may be millionaires according to their bank but are "nillionaires" according to their purchasing power.

All for Naught

The central planners making decisions to steer the economy drive real outcomes and consequences that you pay for, both figuratively and quite literally.

The stated purpose of the Fed's and government's "Covid" policy intervention back in 2020 was to save the economy. It, however, transferred wealth to Wall Street, drove up inflation, and then, upon changing course due to the policy outcomes, induced the stock market to give much of its gains back. Overall, the Fed and government policy wreaked havoc on the economy via stagflation and a two-quarter technical recession.

If the purpose was to stabilize the economy, they failed miserably.

But they transferred a ton of wealth. And shortly thereafter, much of that was drained from the stock market ($8.5 trillion drained out from January 1, 2022, to June 30, 2022, with $3.4 trillion of that coming from 401(k) and IRA retirement funds.)[33] Plus, they caused massive inflation and still ended up with a damaged economy. Wages didn't come anywhere near keeping pace with inflation, and average Americans found themselves struggling to cover the basics of food, housing, and gas.

The historic printing of money by the Federal Reserve enabled the biggest wealth transfer in history. It has also enabled the highest level of inflation in forty years, further widening the wealth gap in the US and creating hardship for average Americans.

Net-net, this intervention did nothing to save the economy and created a slew of problems and a worse outcome.

The US would have endured short-term pain without their intervention, but that could have ended quickly. Instead, their meddling caused nothing but long-term destruction.

Whether you think it was incompetence, intentional destruction, or a combination of both, it doesn't matter. The outcome is the same as it has been in all the financial empires that have fallen before.

The unwillingness to respect the sanctity of money and support a stable currency, the unwillingness to preserve it as a store of value and an unwavering unit of account, means that every dollar you work so hard for is worth less and less over time.

Take a look at what was done at the expense of consumers. The personal saving rate, which shows savings as a percentage of disposable personal income, demonstrates the depletion of individual savings as this policy worked its way through the economy. With government stimulus benefits and staying at home, Americans brought up their savings to historic levels (reaching 33.8 percent, the highest level since tracking began).[34] As their lives normalized and inflation began to take hold, individuals depleted their savings. This was an abnormal time, so we would want to look at where the saving rate was before the pandemic for comparison, and it was on the rise. It was up to 8.3 percent in February 2020.

After the inflationary pressures, by October 2022 it was down to 2.2 percent, the lowest rate since mid-2005, and the second-lowest rate on record (government data released from 1959).[35]

Personal Saving Rate; Percent; Seasonally Adjusted Annual Rate; September 2012–September 2022

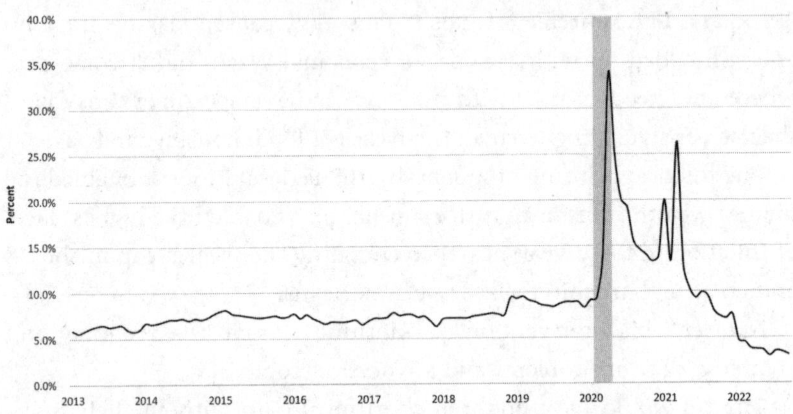

Source: US Bureau of Economic Analysis, Personal Saving Rate [PSAVERT], retrieved from FRED, Federal Reserve Bank of St. Louis, https://fred.stlouisfed.org/series/PSAVERT, October 29, 2022.

Debt spending also went through the roof, as consumers had to worsen their financial standing to cover their expenses. By the end of Q2 2022, household debt surpassed $16 trillion, an increase of about $2 trillion over 2019, according to the New York Fed. The same report showed that credit cards' "13% year-over-year increase marked the largest in more than 20 years."[36]

So, the central planners wanted to keep the consumer spending to avoid a recession, but they also wanted to cool demand to stop inflation. Those objectives are completely at odds with each other, and the economy ended up in stagflation.

The individual American's financial position needed to be sacrificed to prop up the economy based on the actions of the central planners.

They destroyed the dollar, destroyed the economy, and then expected you to destroy whatever wealth you had left to save the long-term outcome.

They don't care because they will still get their power positions, speaking fees, and other perks. You, on the other hand, will own nothing.

The Retail Revolution Roadblock

As the Fed was manipulating the market, in late 2020 and early 2021, a retail investor revolution started to take hold. Beginning on message boards and spilling over across social media, retail investors formed different tribes to take on the elite and Wall Street.

One investor told me during that time that their focus was a digital version of Occupy Wall Street. This time the protesters weren't holding signs in the streets. They were using their balance sheets to fight back.

Given the manipulations in the market since the Great Recession and the first Occupy Wall Street protests, retail investors believed the markets were tilted in favor of the large, institutional Wall Street traders and investment houses, and wanted to participate in the wealth creation that was going on.

They were on to something. The US economy has been rigged as it has been moved further away from free market capitalism to a cronyist nightmare wherein central planners and big companies work together to consolidate power. They scratch each other's backs and ultimately attack barriers that get in their way of rolling up money and control. Small businesses and small individuals, which make up the backbone of the economy and stand for economic freedom, have been both passively and intentionally targeted.

The retail investors were fighting for free market capitalism. They wanted a fair game. They sought transparency and a level playing field. They, in large part, didn't have a problem with the rich; they had a problem with the rich getting to play by a different set of rules.

Insiders get to trade in dark pools, which mask the free flow of information. Bad actors often get small fines for running afoul of rules. Inside information, which is supposedly not legal, moves markets before the news hits the media.

While Wall Street insiders (such as institutional investors and business media) often refer to retail investors as dumb money, they are not. The retail investors are just not on the inside. They don't have a VIP pass. And, when retail investors do well, they are viewed as a threat.

One of the main practices upsetting retail investors was naked shorting. While illegal, this practice of selling shares short that a seller has not borrowed (or perhaps even located) has a loophole for market makers. The concern was that the same share could be sold time and time again, basically creating the existence of the shares from nothing.

While their concern is valid, the biggest perpetrator of the creating something from nothing that has slanted the market in favor of the big guys and insiders at the expense of small businesses, retail investors, and individuals wasn't short sellers or prime brokers; it was the Federal Reserve.

As discussed, the Federal Reserve has created not synthetic shares but synthetic money, in effect, and instead of the amounts being in millions, they are in the trillions.

There was a backlash from the government against this movement, wanting to regulate the retail investor. First the government was concerned with retail investors potentially manipulating the market. Then the government, of course, wanted to "protect" the little guy. Well, the biggest market manipulator that the retail investor needed protection from was the Federal Reserve. Once again, the call was coming from inside the house.

See, the government doesn't mind when consumers waste money on all kinds of stupid things—lavish vacations, gold toilets, whatever—you can buy as much as you want. That's because spending depletes your ability to create wealth for yourself but often transfers it to those closer to the inside. But try to invest to build wealth? Well, you are just too dumb for that.[37]

It's all code for you will own nothing.

Of course, those on the inside took advantage of this overinflation in the market.

If you were to purchase stocks in advance of learning about non-public information or making decisions that influence the stocks' outcomes, it would be called insider trading. When Congress does that, as then–Speaker of the House Nancy Pelosi put it, it's part of "a free market economy."

As is the case with many other government and Fed officials, owning and trading stocks has netted Pelosi and her family millions of dollars.

In addition to dozens of members of Congress from both major political parties not fully complying with reporting requirements around trading, during this period members of the Federal Reserve and many members of Congress traded under circumstances that, if not outright insider trading, certainly created the perception of substantial conflicts of interest.

Two regional Fed presidents, Robert Kaplan and Eric Rosengren, disclosed active stock trading in 2020 while the Fed made decisions on historical intervention in the markets, including major asset purchases, raising some moral questions. After these disclosures came to light, these two gentlemen announced their retirements (Kaplan noting the distraction of the issue and Rosengren citing health issues). In October 2021 the Federal Reserve introduced "a broad set of new rules that will prohibit the purchase of individual securities, restrict active trading, and increase the timeliness of reporting and public disclosure by Federal Reserve policymakers and senior staff."

In January 2022, Federal Reserve vice chair Richard Clarida announced his early resignation as well, following scrutiny of his trading activity and disclosures.

Members of Congress also traded actively during that time, as well as many other times. Senators Dianne Feinstein, Kelly Loeffler, James Inhofe, and Richard Burr were actively investigated by the Justice Department, but no criminal charges were filed. The Securities and Exchange Commission closed an investigation into Burr and his brother-in-law on trades made after Q1 2020 congressional coronavirus briefings without action in January 2023.

The Pelosis' track record of making millions in the market is so strong that retail investors have taken to tracking and mimicking their trades. The unusualwhales.com website has been disclosing the millions that the Pelosis and other members of Congress have made via individual stocks, including showing the Pelosis and other members of Congress with returns beating the performance of the S&P 500 for 2021.

Even federal judges are in on the action. A *Wall Street Journal* report found that between 2010 and 2018, 131 federal judges failed to recuse themselves from 685 lawsuits in which they or their family members had a financial interest via stock ownership.[38]

On the back of the Federal Reserve and government enabling a historic wealth transfer from Main Street to Wall Street, this trading by true insiders and influencers furthers concerns that wealth creation is rigged. How does the average American participate in wealth creation when all the elites are doing is looking out for themselves?

Ultimately, while the Federal Reserve's unscrupulous and damaging policy lured many investors into the market, it also left them holding the bag. As discussed, trillions of dollars in value evaporated from the markets, with trillions more bleeding from crypto and other asset classes, and retail investors lost a great deal of tangible wealth.[39]

By the time the Federal Reserve runs to prop up the market again, many of these smaller investors will be disenfranchised and sit out of the market, missing out on the next run-up.

The Fed transferred money to the wealthy, lured in the small guys, and then popped the bubble. The retail revolution had met the ultimate in market manipulation.

Credere: What Are We Trusting?

The word *credit* comes from the Latin word *credere*, which means trust. But when it comes down to it, what exactly are we trusting?

The Federal Reserve, in conjunction with the government, has managed to do just about everything wrong. They have taken advantage of fiat money, overspent, and eroded the dollar's value. They failed to hold the dollar to be as "good as gold for oil," leading the rest of the world to rethink pricing oil in dollars.

They have failed to create an environment at home that created a prosperous economy for all to participate in and generate wealth. Instead they have helped transfer more wealth from the average American to the already wealthy and well-connected.

And they allowed the reserves they were holding on behalf of a sovereign nation to be weaponized, effectively signaling to the entire world that the United States' financial system is a weapon, not a source of stability.

All of this comes together in a complex web with you, your freedoms, and your wealth at the center. Their actions accelerate the new financial world order. They allow bad actors to profit at your expense. They create a position whereby what you own will be worth less, and then it will be worth nothing. And you will own nothing.

But they want you to trust them again, further centralizing their control over money with what's called a Central Bank Digital Currency. This is another tool of control that in no way will make you better off and in every way will make you worse off.

CHAPTER 5

DIGITAL DOLLAR DESTITUTION

How Central Bank Digital Currencies Control You and Your Wealth

Show me the incentive and I will show you the outcome.

—legendary investor Charlie Munger

If a government wanted to control how you acted and interacted, push an agenda for "the good of society," or exert some other control, the easiest way to do that is through money.

In fact, governments already do this. Behaviors they want less of, they tax. In the United States, products that are seen as immoral and harmful "to society," like tobacco, alcohol, and even soft drinks, may receive punitive taxes (they are literally called "sin taxes"). On the other hand, when certain behaviors are desired, the government will often provide tax credits to encourage their desired behaviors. We have seen this with the "green" energy push via the US government issuing tax credits for electric vehicles, solar panels, and other green-associated purchases and behaviors.

Cities and states that want to attract more business often provide monetary incentives to lure new businesses to their localities.

To entice citizens to take the Covid vaccinations, many states resorted to cash lotteries for compliance. A variety of states pushed vaccines for a chance at cash, some using names like "Shot of a Lifetime" and "Vax for the Win." States including California, Colorado, Kentucky, Louisiana, Maryland, Nevada, New Mexico, North Carolina, Ohio, Oregon, Washington, and West Virginia all offered up a chance at seven figures for you to do what they wanted—put a drug into your body.[1]

If you didn't take the vaccine, you could lose your job and source of income.

The bottom line is that money incentivizes behaviors, which is why the more centralized the control of money is, the more opportunities for abuse that arise.

Combine this truth with the recent activities of the Federal Reserve, covered in the previous chapter, and the emergence of a new financial world order, and it is easy to see how more centralization of wealth could engender a massive disaster for individuals. This is why the discussions around Central Bank Digital Currency (or CBDCs) are so frightening, particularly as it pertains to the realm of economic freedom and wealth creation.

What Is a CBDC?

As we discussed in Chapter 2, the monetary system both worldwide and in the US has gone through many evolutions.

You may think of money in its physical form. In the US, that would be Federal Reserve notes (you know them colloquially as dollars or dollar bills) and minted coins of varying denominations. These are, in the words of the Federal Reserve, "obligations of the United States and shall be receivable by all national and member banks and Federal reserve banks and for all taxes, customs, and other public dues. They shall be redeemed in lawful money on demand at the Treasury Department of the United States, in the city of Washington, District of Columbia, or at any Federal Reserve bank."[2] Today, as fiat money, these dollars exist backed by merely the "full faith and credit" of the US government, which really means the faith in the strength and productivity of the American economy, plus the US military to protect it.

Both the form that money takes and the means to exchange money have shifted and evolved over time. As technology has progressed, more of the exchange of money has shifted to digital formats. Most of us are more likely to pay for goods and services with a debit or credit card than via cash. New technologies, whether they be Apple Pay or PayPal, facilitate substantial money transfers each day all over the globe.

Even at the Federal Reserve, when they take the action referred to in the press as "printing money" and expanding the money supply, it's not via physical dollar notes. It's merely a digital entry in the accounts of the financial institutions (who have accounts with the Federal Reserve). This trend, notably, has made governments (and, arguably, consumers) more irresponsible with their money management. There's a psychology behind spending when you have to fork over a dollar versus use a proxy for it (as casinos know all too well when they have you change your money into chips or slot machine credits).

The same goes for the Federal Reserve, which was once bound by the gold backing of the dollar and no longer has those constraints.

A CBDC is a further step in this digital evolution of money, but with even more centralization of control and power than what you might think of in the digital realm for money.

A CBDC is merely a digital version of whatever currency the government is already backing with its "full faith." It is issued and regulated by the same monetary authority or central bank that issues the country's fiat money.[3]

For the US, what is currently being considered is replacing or supplementing some of the Federal Reserve notes with digital US dollars. Instead of a dollar that you keep in your physical wallet, under a mattress, or in a cereal box, you would have a digital-equivalent place of storage, since those dollars' forms are digital-only. That digital holder for money is a digital wallet.

A digital wallet is meant as a digital replacement for a physical wallet. The digital wallet is a software application, today generally accessed via smartphone, that securely (or, in truth, somewhat securely, as no technology is entirely secure) stores the types of things you would in a regular wallet. This could be not only digital dollars and credit card information, but also cryptocurrency and personal information (like the information on your driver's license, again in digital form).

The software application assists with the transfer of money, enabling you to pay for goods and services or to transfer money to friends and family. If you have an iPhone or an Android-operated phone, you may already use well-known digital wallets like Apple Pay and Google Pay. PayPal, while itself a robust payment transfer system, also has a digital wallet you can access. And many banks are starting to offer their own digital wallets.

You do not need to have a bank account to have a digital wallet, but many digital wallets can connect to bank accounts. Digital wallets facilitate payment but do not provide—at least currently—any other banking products or services.

One of the key aspects of digital currency is that it can be programmable. Because of this, each dollar could have a unique identifier. Think about when someone draws a picture on a dollar bill to see if it ever circulates back to them in the future. Now think of that at scale, using technology, with the government tracing it. Each digital dollar could have a unique code so that it can be traced as it circulates from person to person to business to business, giving the government a treasure trove of information about what you are doing, where you are doing it, and who you are doing it with.

Wholesale and Retail CBDCs

A key question for all CBDCs, but particularly for a US dollar CBDC, is how the flow of funds will work. And related to the implementation of the digital central bank currency, the question is whether it is implemented at the "wholesale" level, meaning between the Federal Reserve and the financial institutions it interacts with, or rather at the public or "retail" level, which means directly to individuals. Or perhaps a hybrid of both.

A wholesale CBDC sounds an awful lot like what the Federal Reserve already does. The idea for the wholesale CBDC is that when a bank or other financial institution opens an account at the central bank, digital dollars are used in deposits and settlements. Just like today, monetary policy allows changes to reserve requirements, interest on reserves, and bank-to-bank lending to create desired outcomes in the market (as an editorial note, I would qualify that as "desired by the central bank," because, as we have seen, those outcomes have severe implications, such as asset bubbles and inflation).[4]

The question then becomes whether the digital currency is used only between the Fed and the intermediaries, or if the public also uses the Central Bank Digital Currency.

Public-facing "retail" CBDCs are ones given to the public to replace your physical dollars with digital ones for transactions. How this is accomplished is critical. It can be done via intermediaries (banks, online financial companies, etc.) in a public-private type partnership, or it can be done directly by disrupting the banking system and removing intermediaries. This would mean that businesses and individuals would have to open accounts at the Federal Reserve (or the relevant country's central bank). This would effectively eliminate the middleman of the banking system and fully centralize finance within the Fed and government's purview.[5]

While the current Federal Reserve chairman, Jerome Powell, has said that the consideration of a direct-to-public CBDC is off the table, as I will discuss in more detail below, once we take even a baby step in that direction, it's unlikely the government will stop moving over time, especially when it gives them so much power. If you give the government an inch, they take a mile, and then they don't stop taking (and probably eventually charge a toll for use).

As a reminder, when the government has worked to take things away from the private sector and further centralize them, it typically comes with disastrous results. Take student lending, which, as the government has nationalized it in large part, has caused college costs to increase exponentially above the inflation rate and has saddled young people with substantial debts.

Money is already politicized and centrally planned more than enough in the US; we do not need further centralization of the financial system.

On the technology side, different technology architectures and systems exist for CBDCs. As they will likely evolve as blockchain and other fintech evolves, I won't spend a lot of time on those here.

Your wealth creation opportunities are already substantially under threat today from the government. The threat of more constraints on wealth creation increases exponentially if the government has a digital, programmable, trackable currency that it fully and effectively controls and can tie into social credit, formally or informally.

So, Is This Cryptocurrency?

Interest in cryptocurrency (or "crypto") and blockchain technology has exploded around the world.

In June 2022, the value of cryptocurrency was less than $1 trillion, down from a peak of almost $3 trillion in late 2021.[6] While there are estimated to be more than 18,000 different cryptocurrencies in existence, the most popular and valuable include Bitcoin and Ethereum, each of which operates differently, with a variety of characteristics.

A basic explanation of cryptocurrency is they are digitally native tokens (colloquially known as "coins") that are accounted for via a decentralized network (also known as peer-to-peer network) using a distributed and decentralized ledger called the "blockchain."[7]

According to Investopedia, "The 'crypto' in cryptocurrencies refers to complicated cryptography that allows for the creation and processing of digital currencies and their transactions across decentralized systems. Alongside this important 'crypto' feature is a common commitment to decentralization."[8]

One of the reasons many people cite for interest in blockchain-based cryptocurrencies is the abuse by central banks of their respective currencies.

Cryptocurrency like Bitcoin does not have a central authority directing it (or manipulating it for political purposes), and its decentralized nature is an intentional pushback against such control, which is why many individuals find it attractive. The desire from individuals for monetary decentralization and not having currency dependent upon any one government or consortium of governments is exactly why governments and central banks consider it a threat.

A digital currency is not a cryptocurrency. You will find some intentional confusion and even conflation around them, including by the governments considering them. This is intentional as central planners seek to piggyback on the interest in cryptocurrency without decentralization.[9]

Digital currencies, particularly those being proposed as CBDCs, are the opposite of cryptos. While CBDCs are digitally native and may share some technical architecture and design or even use blockchain technology, they are entirely centrally planned and controlled, taking away a key benefit that individuals are seeking from cryptocurrencies.

The central planners are using the confusion about what a digital currency versus a cryptocurrency is to try to capitalize on the enthusiasm for crypto and drive interest in something incredibly different.

For example, in March 2022, the Biden administration put out an "Executive Order on Ensuring Responsible Development of Digital Assets," which started talking about cryptocurrency broadly and then switched to cover "Policy and Actions Related to United States Central Bank Digital Currencies."[10]

CBDCs could use blockchain and distributed ledger technology or other technology systems. Governments could program the currency (similar to the functionality that certain cryptos have), but none of those elements are required for it to be considered a CBDC.

Despite some possible benefits, the risks of going down the CBDC path, particularly in the US and in other developed nations, are far too great.

What Is at Stake?

Imagine this.

You wake up and are excited about your big day. Today you are going to close a major deal that will change the trajectory of your company. The financial implications of this new transaction will save your business, which has been struggling because of onerous government regulation and government- and Fed-induced inflation. You meticulously get ready, putting on your best suit. You eat breakfast, then open Uber to digitally hail an electric car, as you no longer have your own car; the government long ago instituted a crippling tax on car ownership, particularly non-electric vehicles.

Uber informs you that it cannot offer you a ride because the government has limited access to your CBDC digital wallet. You rack your brain—what could have happened? You realize the culprit was probably that Facebook post you made criticizing the government's decision to reduce fossil fuels, a move that created energy rationing throughout the country.

You panic, as you now have no way to get to your potential big customers' office, sixty miles away. If you blow this deal, your company will be in financial peril.

You are at the whim of the government, its CBDC, and its control over your day, and ultimately your livelihood.

This hypothetical scenario can easily become reality with a CBDC-enabled monetary system.

CBDCs and Individual Rights

The biggest concerns around a CBDC, particularly in the United States, relate to individual rights. A US CBDC (aka a "digital dollar") threatens your rights and freedoms on many accounts. It would mean that a government-sanctioned entity could have complete access to everything that you do that involves a monetary transaction, and could even freeze your access to money and transactions altogether.

CBDCs threaten your privacy, as well as enable the government to tie your access to your money to behaviors. As I covered in the opening to this chapter, money incentivizes behavior. If we further centralize money, the government could weaponize it as a tool to implement more social policy and even a formal social credit system. As we have seen in many instances, the government in the US, as well as governments abroad, is not hesitating when it comes to weaponizing money.

A CBDC converges the new financial world order with social credit, backed by a tangible way to enforce it. Digital dollars could impact just about everything you do and certainly everything you own.

Imagine that the government, in its push for green initiatives, wants to reduce the consumption of beef (academics have already been suggesting that less red meat would be consistent with their agenda).[11] A digital dollar would grant them the direct capability to turn off your payments in a restaurant where you order a burger if you have exceeded your beef quota for the month (which they know, of course, because they are tracking it).

You may be inclined to say that this would never happen in the US or other developed nations. But you would have said the same thing about many government mandates and actions over the past few years before they happened.

Or what if the government wanted to stimulate the economy? They could give you currency that disappears if you don't spend it right away, perhaps incentivizing you to shop at the businesses of cronies by only making it spendable at certain retailers. Again, this is not a stretch; China is already exploring a "use it or lose it" feature with its e-CNY digital currency.[12]

The power inherent in how a CBDC can be used is unlimited and unjust, and that is why so many people who understand what a CBDC could lead to are pushing back now before it is too late.

Of course, privacy invasions will be sold under the guise of security, as they always are. The government will say they are just trying to monitor for terrorism. Or they need to ensure that financial crimes, such as money laundering, aren't being committed. It will be in the "public interest" for them to have access to your information—it just won't be in your interest.

If you think that level of access, power, and control won't be weaponized, I have a few bridges to sell you as well.

The US government is consistently trying to find ways to get more and more of your financial information already, and it's not for your benefit or to help you create wealth.

In March 2021, under the American Rescue Plan, the Biden administration snuck in a tax-reporting requirement that went into effect January 1, 2022, that targets not megacorporations but hobbyists, side-giggers, and small online sellers.

This change focused on 1099-K reporting to the IRS. It used to be that reporting related to transactions via third-party settlement processors or their electronic payment facilitators (in layman's terms, e-commerce sites and marketplaces like eBay, Etsy, home rental sites, etc., and the companies that process their payments, including goods and services processed through apps like Venmo or PayPal) was only done if your activity exceeded a threshold of more than $20,000 in gross payments and more than two hundred transactions in any given year. President Biden's American Rescue Plan lowered that threshold for reporting to a mere $600.

You are always responsible for reporting any income you make to the government, regardless of the amount. However, lowering this threshold to hundreds of dollars puts additional burdens on taxpayers. Not every marketplace transaction may be taxable or a given transaction may have relevant deductions, but this reporting change creates additional IRS scrutiny for everyone from moms who resell items from around the house to kids making some extra cash from side jobs to hobbyists who frequently change the items in their collections. If you are flagged for not reporting something that you didn't need to report, the burden is still on you to prove that.

This means that, as an individual, you need to keep extensive records, from how much you paid to relevant deductible fees and expenses, much like a business would. Ultimately this rule change brings about more stress, costs, and time for middle- and working-class Americans for something that may be underreported by just a few dollars or even something that wasn't misreported at all.

In terms of money the IRS can make versus the effort and cost put into reviewing this additional information, it doesn't seem like a huge payday for the IRS. It is a substantial burden for Americans who find that the paperwork and risk and headache of being audited for doing nothing wrong aren't worth it.

While there has been a delay in the implementation of the reporting because of its inherent complexity, the IRS certainly hasn't abandoned it.

One thing is certain: a $600 reporting threshold isn't meant for the wealthy to pay their "fair share" of taxes.

The same goes for the Inflation Reduction Act, which granted Biden's "Build Back Better" wish for an additional $80 billion for the IRS, which reportedly is going to go toward hiring 87,000 new staff, with more than half earmarked for "tax enforcement." With only somewhere in the neighborhood of 800 US billionaires, certainly 87,000 new IRS staffers won't be spending their time solely on the megawealthy.

And that's the ruse: while headlines talk about going after billionaires, the details always make it harder for you. The wealthiest will get loopholes to preserve their wealth while you will be forced to give up yours.

Also in 2021, a cadre of government officials tried to enhance bank account reporting for small-value accounts and transactions. The proposals, which received backlash and were tabled, included financial accounts that either had $600 in them at any point or completed $600 worth of transactions during the year having to report aggregate inflows and outflows to the IRS.[13] While this was not (at least at the beginning) a line-item report of every transaction, it could easily lead to that from the IRS's scrutiny.

In October 2021, Secretary of the Treasury Janet Yellen went on the *CBS Evening News with Norah O'Donnell* to say, "There's a lot of tax fraud and cheating that's going on." She then laughably said the $600 reporting requirement was not meant to invade privacy but to hold accountable . . . high-income earners, many who have opaque sources of income. Because, you know, there are so many $600 accounts held by shady multimillionaires and billionaires.[14]

The government seeks to use financial envy to sow discord and gain acceptance of laws that restrict wealth. They do this with billionaires as the carrot. But billionaires have already made their money, and they will certainly lobby for and figure out the loopholes to any new proposals. Ultimately the government will come after the middle and working classes. You guessed it—you will own nothing.

On the weaponization front, giving government access to payment information can enable activist government workers to leak your information. If a US Supreme Court draft can be leaked, as one was in May 2022, what would stop an activist government worker from dropping some information if they had a beef with you? You can just imagine a nemesis leaking on social media that you spent money at OnlyFans, as a means to try to ruin your job or relationships.

The methods and amounts of potential abuses are endless. The bottom line is that you should be able to transact privately and anonymously in a country that protects rights and freedoms.

You will likely hear pushback from the elite CBDC activists, racketeers, and useful idiots. One possible argument is that transacting digitally (whether through online banks, credit cards, PayPal, digital wallets, or otherwise) already creates the potential for breaches of privacy. In addition to these companies not being able to send you to jail or use the information for political control and gain, the main difference lies with choice. You can choose to transact in cash. You can choose your digital payment intermediary with some level of competition. There are still many concerns related to tech companies and payments (covered more in Chapter 6), but covering a different set of issues than that of complete, centralized government control.

Again, a CBDC enables giving more power and giving up privacy to an entity that can force behaviors through control of money at the highest level.

Changing the Banking System

Another big question that needs to be addressed is how the entire banking ecosystem might be shifted with a CBDC.

The Bank Policy Institute (BPI) has identified some issues in a recent piece. For example, as noted above, banks and other financial institutions make money in discrete ways that are priced into how they do business. If those are removed, yet they remain an intermediary between the public and the Federal Reserve, how do they get compensated and by whom, and how does that shift or add costs to the system?

The BPI piece notes:

> With an intermediated model, no one has identified who would pay the intermediators . . . for services attendant to holding and transferring CBDC. Those services would include customer service, dispute resolution, AML compliance . . . fixed and variable technology expense, and more. The risk of a cyber-attack would be massive, and the intermediator, not the Fed, would likely be liable for any loss. So, intermediating a CBDC would be a very expensive and very risky proposition. . . .[15]
>
> Currently, banks make money on payment systems predominantly by lending out deposits and earning net interest income, but, because a CBDC held in a digital wallet cannot be lent out to borrowers, it would come with zero net interest income for a bank or other intermediator . . . companies that set up a digital wallet to hold and transfer CBDC seemingly would have to charge consumers a considerable fee for that service.[16]

What about consumer interest payments? When individuals and businesses deposit their money in the bank, they expect some level of interest for the use of their money, which comes from the bank using that money to make loans to other customers. With a Fed-held CBDC, how and from what fees would they pay interest? It is likely they wouldn't pay interest at all.

If they did not, that would be another barrier to making your money work for you and building up wealth—or even trying to partially keep pace with inflation via your deposits at financial institutions. Certainly the Federal Reserve has already disrupted this with its zero-interest rate policy for the larger part of a decade and a half. Some fintech companies also do not pay money on balances. There is a trend to not have your money work for you without a fairly substantial amount of risk, and CBDCs would add another significant layer. That trend is aligned with you owning nothing.

The Bank Policy Institute also expresses other banking concerns around the impact on credit. "The Fed's discussion paper explains that paying interest on a riskless CBDC 'could reduce the aggregate amount of deposits in the banking system, which could in turn increase bank funding expenses, and reduce credit availability or raise credit costs for households and businesses.' It also describes at length how payment of interest would disrupt monetary policy."[17]

Harvard Business Review brings up other issues, saying, "Other concerns revolve around the role of a central bank as a wholesale lender of first resort. State-controlled credit could potentially be susceptible to political pressure for sector-focused lending. Would there be formal criteria for determining which banks would qualify for central bank funding? How easy would these be to manipulate in some way?"[18]

While again, the government promises that they are not looking to remove the banks and financial institutions as intermediaries, it is critical to think ahead.

CBDCs and Cybersecurity Risks

CBDCs engender a great number of cybersecurity risks. These exist at the individual or public/retail level, the intermediary level (should there be one), and certainly at the Federal Reserve/government level.

Cybercrime cost an estimated $6 trillion in 2021.[19] Crypto itself saw $3.2 billion stolen in 2021, a sixfold increase over the previous year.[20]

We know that the US government doesn't do a great job in ensuring that fraud and theft don't take hold and that their technology in many areas substantially lags behind the private sector. Now imagine making the main currency fully digital.

The more centralized the currency, the more epic the scale of systemic risk. As currency becomes less centralized, there may be more attacks, but they are likely to be smaller in nature and unlikely to collapse an economy. Once you fully centralize the currency, as with a CBDC, you have now created "too big to fail" on a level that makes the Great Recession financial crisis look like child's play. A sophisticated hacker could theoretically bring an entire economy to a halt. As fintech entrepreneur and expert Ajay S. Mookerjee said in a recent *Harvard Business Review* piece, "Essentially, the trade-off would be between recurring but manageable breaches and highly infrequent but catastrophic ones. A central bank would definitely be too big to fail."[21]

In addition to risks related to the currency itself, you are trusting a government agency—which will be a massive target—with myriad private, sensitive data. If you already don't trust the US government with your data, one would extrapolate that you also would not want it in the hands of hostile foreign entities that might hack the government and access it. CBDCs and their associated data could compromise individual security and privacy, as well as national security.

Others have noted that quantum computing, which is currently being developed and adds exponential power to existing computing capabilities, will throw a major security wrench into all the main methods that are used today to protect data. Government will have to plan ahead for a complex emerging technology. Cybersecurity expert Amnon Samid wrote, "CBDCs are vulnerable to hacking and the powers of quantum computing. . . . Central banks must heed the warning." In a note, even the WEF warns that "quantum computers in the future might be able to break the cryptography in the CBDC system without detection."[22]

If nations with bones to pick with the United States, either at the government level or just the individual level, want to disrupt the entire US economy, centralizing the currency through a digital dollar does nothing but exacerbate that problem. In 2021, the US saw Russian-connected cyberattacks on the Colonial Pipeline and JBS, the largest supplier of beef in the world. [23] Wouldn't the ultimate in retaliation or even just trying to get a leg up in the global economy make a CBDC system an ongoing target?

A Solution in Search of a Problem

Much like a product advertised on late-night television infomercials, for developed economies like the United States that have many private, easy-to-use payment transfer solutions, a CBDC looks much like a solution searching for a problem, as opposed to the other way around. Simply put, we don't need it.

Despite that, according to the IMF, today around one hundred countries are considering CBDCs at different stages. Some are doing exploratory research, while others are in test phases. Countries like Jamaica and Nigeria are already "circulating" CBDCs.[24] And, in October 2021, G7 finance officials assembled and endorsed thirteen principles for "for retail central bank digital currencies."[25]

So, why the big push? While the data points in most cases to cryptocurrency threatening central banks' power and central banks not wanting to be left behind, CBDCs will also play an important role in consolidating power and wealth in a new financial world order.

Even if done in phases, remember that small, seemingly innocuous shifts in a system can enable wholesale, monumental, and undesirable changes over time.

The law firm Skadden, Arps, Slate, Meagher & Flom LLP and Affiliates (Skadden Arps) weighed in on this in a recent piece, saying, "The advent of distributed ledger technology . . . has prompted central banks around the world to assess their roles in the digital asset economy—in particular, by examining the pros and cons of offering a central bank digital currency (CBDC) to the public."[26]

The key phrase is "assess their roles in the digital economy." Governments and their central bank counterparts don't want to give up the thing that gives them the most power in the world: control over money. No doubt they will fight to keep that, and potentially be willing to do a lot of damage to keep their power intact.

Yes, the reason that central banks in countries with advanced economies seem to be pursuing this is not to solve a need, but rather for control in the new financial world order.

Despite the inherent arguments against them or even lack of need for them, CBDCs and the control they offer in terms of access and regulation are tempting for central planners.

Entrepreneur and writer Colin Brightfield echoes the point that more choice and independence are real concerns of central planners and that the central banks want a monopoly, not competition. He writes, "One concern of many governments is that cryptocurrencies offer populations a choice to opt out of the traditional financial system into decentralized finance which exists beyond the typical oversight of government regulation. CBDCs are a way for governments to offer a digital payment competitor to cryptocurrency and decentralized financial systems being built outside of most current government regulation infrastructure."[27]

Regardless of the reason, a CBDC allows those who have the intention of pushing social credit and marrying that concept to money an easy path forward. This is a path that does not bode well for your property rights.

It also allows those who may have—shall we say—"questionable" intentions to add fuel to the fire. The WEF, for example, has positioned itself to provide "guidance" to governments on CBDCs via its Digital Currency Governance Consortium and related resource center.[28]

China FOMO

As the US, at the hands of the Federal Reserve, has made many questionable choices in terms of the soundness of its currency and its economic standing worldwide, many prominent investors and entities have been suggesting that China is the United States' main competition on the global economic front.

In January 2021, asset management giant BlackRock's Investment Institute touted "a rewiring of globalization, with a bipolar U.S.-China world order at its center."[29] Billionaire Ray Dalio has "predicted a new global order that has China ascending and the United States diminishing."[30]

While I question China's ability to be the long-term top global economic superpower, at least by choice, for a variety of reasons, ranging from "who wants to trust communists?" to the notion expressed in the Triffin Dilemma that to be a reserve currency you need to run trade deficits, among others, there is no doubt the idea of another superpower weighs on those in power positions in the US.

It is not a coincidence that the people in similar positions to the ones who enabled China's dominance—including normalizing trade relations with them, which lifted up their populace while outsourcing US jobs and creating an intellectual property (IP) infringement nightmare—and whose decisions have weakened trust in US money here and abroad, are the ones now looking to make similar mistakes by trying to beat China at the digital currency game.

So, what is the concern of these central planners?

China has been working on a CBDC launch since 2014. It's no coincidence that this aligns with the date of their major social credit road map, given the direct link between social credit and monetary control.[31] The Chinese CBDC goes by several different names, including the digital yuan, e-Renminbi (e-RMB), and the one most widely used, e-CNY.[32] The e-CNY is a work in progress. China is ahead of most developed nations in the central bank currency endeavor, but behind some smaller nations that have fully operational ones.[33]

(A quick note: The currency discussion in China can be confusing between the yuan and renminbi. While colloquially they are often used interchangeably, technically the renminbi is the broad name for the currency, while the yuan is the unit of account [what items are priced in]. This would be like the Federal Reserve notes that you use being called by their unit of account, dollars [$1, $20]. Yuan is like dollars, whereas renminbi is like Federal Reserve notes.[34])

The drive for the CBDC in China is threefold. Externally, China's currency is substantially behind other countries in its use for international payments, estimated at around 3 percent.[35] This is a tiny amount given the relative size of China's economy. However, the fact that other countries don't want to use the Chinese renminbi likely has more to do with distrust of the Chinese government as a steward of money than with concerns over its form.

The other two drivers for China's CBDC focus are domestic issues. Currently, a handful of Chinese companies have taken over digital payments in China, including Ant Group's (an affiliate of e-commerce giant Alibaba) Alipay and Tencent's WeChat Pay, which together in Q2 2020 accounted for around 95 percent of all Chinese mobile payment transactions.[36] This gives these companies enormous power in the country, not to mention access to valuable data.

Finally, the Chinese government has said that it wants to create a digital currency and platform to ensure "greater resilience in their payments ecosystem."[37] But the reality is that the government is in competition with these "private" platforms and wants neither to cede them power nor give up the opportunity to integrate social credit and their currency.

Of course, all of these drivers are about power and control in some way, shape, or form.

This digital currency is not a cryptocurrency. It is a centralized, highly controlled endeavor that may incorporate similar technology used by some cryptocurrencies.

The current choices with e-CNY for the consumer relate to the type of wallet (individual or corporate) and limits on transaction amounts (smaller transactions can be done with just a phone number, while larger ones require more associated identification data). From a user-interface perspective, the wallets can be traditional app-based digital wallets, or users can choose a card format (like a credit card).[38] In terms of providers, the e-CNY wallet can be accessed via an app or can use "private" intermediaries that are already widely accessed, like Alipay and WeChat Pay/Tenpay, or one of the other authorized banks, like Bank of China, Bank of Communications, or a half dozen others.[39]

The challenges for the Chinese in rolling out the CBDC are twofold. On the technology side, they are behind. The number of transactions per second at the time of writing that this new currency platform could handle has substantially lagged that of "private" digital payment systems like Alipay, as well as those of other test digital payment systems in progress.[40]

Second, on the user side, nobody wants to use it. While the CCP touted in October 2021 that 261 million digital wallets have been opened up to support the e-CNY, upon scrutiny of the data, researchers found that the average balance held in these wallets was around RMB 3 for individuals, less than the equivalent of US 50 cents, and the average balance in corporate wallets was about US$4.90.[41]

As for the attempt to get more foreign payments, there was a big push during the Beijing Winter Olympics in 2022. The adoption numbers doubled ahead of the Games, as the e-CNY and Visa, an official Olympics sponsor, were the only accepted forms of payment. Visa won gold in that battle, according to the *Wall Street Journal*.[42] Mu Changchun, the People's Bank of China's digital currency research institute head, said, without providing a specific breakdown, that it "seems all the foreign users are using hardware wallets."[43] Other reports said that most foreign visitors used cash or Visa.

Bank Policy Institute posited that the potential for surveillance issues would drive any foreign visitor using the e-CNY to "convert their digital yuan back to their local currency at the earliest possible moment, lest their transactions be tracked by the Ministry of State Security."[44]

This means that the Chinese government may be compelled to force the use of it. A report in Bloomberg said that the Chinese government "has already started taking steps to assert more control over the data gathered by financial and tech companies, including Ant and Tencent." Also in that piece, consultant Zennon Kapron said of the lackluster early rollout, "At the end of the day, I think it's going to have to be the government saying: 'You have to use this.'"

There is no doubt that the Chinese will continue to push their centrally planned and controlled digital currency. It will be a conduit to marry surveillance and control through the combination of social credit and e-CNY. Communists don't believe in property rights, so this plan fits in with the enslavement of the people by moving them further away from anything that resembles ownership without CCP approval.

Despite all this, the prospect of being behind China in the financial realm is a material part of what is luring lawmakers, Fed officials, and other politicians and elite to follow suit with Central Bank Digital Currencies. And those who see the Chinese road map as a tool for control in a new financial world order will leverage that desire to ensure it comes to fruition if Americans don't vehemently oppose it.

Power Is the Purpose

Given the United States' robust private payment system, why would consumers or financial institutions need anything that looks like a CBDC?

Dante Disparte, chief strategy officer and head of global policy at Circle, a digital financial services firm and architect of USDC, a dollar-pegged digital currency, agreed that the need for a CBDC in the US wasn't there, saying that arguments for it "miss the larger point, which is that by today's hypercompetitive digital currency and blockchain standards, the U.S. may not be a laggard at all, but rather is already winning the race for the future of money and payments."[45]

He continues: "In trying to 'out-China China' on these important issues, we miss that the future of money and payments should be about enhancing domestic financial optionality. Upgrading payment and banking systems, enhancing interoperability and open banking standards, requires a major upgrade in the technology stack that supports value transfer and more open financial services innovation."[46]

Given what we know about where China stands on a CBDC and the lack of interest from their citizens and noncitizens in using it, that should be a red light for the US, not a green light.

Skadden Arps, the law firm cited above, agrees, saying, "In the U.S., there is a fundamental question of whether a general-purpose CBDC is needed, given the variety of private electronic payment options available within the existing payment system, including online bill payments through banks and payment methods such as PayPal, Zelle, and Venmo. They already offer speed and accessibility and are low cost."

Writer Derek Andersen broke down key takeaways from a podcast interview on *Banking with Interest* with Randal Quarles, former vice chair of the Fed, writing, "a close analysis of CBDCs would show that their advantages are 'extremely marginal, if they exist at all.' He did not see the potential for CBDCs in promoting financial inclusion, commenting: 'You're going to need an account at the bank, the way you need to use money now, and in addition . . . a cellphone and wireless access, and all that is making inclusion harder.'" The piece added, "Using a CBDC to exclude the role of the bank would be 'pathological.'"[47]

In that interview, Quarles also worried that the fear of missing out, aka FOMO, and pressure to keep up with China were driving a decision that otherwise lacked a lot of sense. The piece continued, "'we tend to win' when U.S. private sector innovation competes with state-run entities," and Quarles thought that a US CBDC could thwart innovation, saying, "Why are you going to invest a whole lot of effort to developing a . . . stablecoin payment system if the Fed is just going to bigfoot you out of existence?"[48]

The reality, as I noted previously, is that particularly where fiat currency is concerned, the form factor doesn't matter; the faith in what backs the currency matters. Federal Reserve chairman Jerome Powell concurred, saying the dollar has global reserve status "because of our rule of law; our democratic institutions, which are the best in the world; our economy; our industrious people; all the things that make the United States the United States."[49] I would add to the top of that list a well-funded and powerful military (a notion to which BPI also agreed in its piece).

There are real threats to the dollar's reserve currency status, all of which have to do with the Fed and the US government. The Bank Policy Institute's case against a US CBDC posited, "While highly unlikely to supersede these considerable benefits, there are a few current threats to the dollar's status: (1) $30 trillion in government debt; (2) persistently high inflation; and (3) over-leveraging of the dollar in economic sanctions. The first two phenomena have been the death of other reserve currencies in the past. . . . Converting commercial bank money to CBDC would not reduce the federal deficit."[50]

Coming to a Digital Wallet Near You

Several Federal Reserve officials have made statements that lend credence to the idea that a CBDC is unnecessary. Fed chair Powell has talked about the strength of the US payments system. Fed governor Christopher Waller said in a virtual speech for the American Enterprise Institute, "After careful consideration, I am not convinced as of yet that a CBDC would solve any existing problem that is not being addressed more promptly and efficiently by other initiatives."[51]

However, the Federal Reserve continues to evaluate a CBDC. It asked for public comments in 2022 and closed that commenting period in the spring of that year.[52]

Several officials, including Powell and Vice Chair Lael Brainard, have reiterated that they are not considering at this time a retail CBDC. However, an April 2022 paper from the Federal Reserve called "Retail CBDC and U.S. Monetary Policy. Implementation: A Stylized Balance Sheet Analysis" seems to suggest that it is not as off the table as some Fed officials have indicated.[53]

Several legal scholars and firms, including Skadden Arps, have noted that a retail CBDC would require congressional action. But given the political power that comes from a CBDC and the actions of Congress over decades, that doesn't seem to be a huge barrier. Plus, with recent woes in the cryptocurrency industry, lawmakers may try to slide approval into a broader crypto regulation bill.

Skadden Arps also noted that a retail CBDC made little sense, saying it is "highly unlikely that we will see a retail CBDC in the U.S. in the next few years."[54]

I ask you to focus on the words "in the next few years" because that is the issue. A few years go by quickly. Once any type of CBDC is set in motion, even if it wasn't intended to go retail from the start, with the new financial world order and the prototype in China, it's too great a risk to bear. Think of all the temporary or small government programs that have been extended.

As noted, in October 2022, finance officials from the US and the other G7 countries put out a set of thirteen policy principles for retail CBDCs. That means that retail CBDCs are closer and a more coordinated effort than has previously been communicated.[55]

The Federal Reserve has been happy to destroy your wealth to hold on to and expand its power. The CBDC is a next-level tool in its power grab.

Own Your Money, Own You

Most of the benefits of a digital dollar seem to have counter-costs that greatly outweigh them. The soundness of money doesn't come from its format; it comes from policy and treating the stability of money with intention and respect. The latter, not the former, is where we have the issues.

Moreover, how can we expect that the same people who didn't see historic inflation coming and the impacts of their ginormous money-printing efforts would be able to identify all of the risks of a digital currency? These are the same people who have consistently debased the dollar; now they want to be entrusted with more centralized control over the monetary system.

The CBDC plays a key role in the future devolution of property rights. We saw rights infringements like vaccines and vax passports become a gateway to digital IDs and the foundations of social credit. A CBDC gives the government a mechanism for enforcement, and the one enforcing it is an entity that has done nothing but steal money from the American people.

They say they are trying to protect us, but we need protection from them.

Transacting freely and privately is critical in maintaining property rights and wealth creation. Any movement against that moves you closer to owning nothing.

CHAPTER 6

THE TECHNOCRACY AND DIGITAL RIGHTS

In a Digital World, You Are the Product

We shape our tools and, thereafter, our tools shape us.

—John Culkin

Imagine saving up for a luxury car—perhaps it is your first? You decide to go for a BMW. The car is all decked out with amazing gadgets and capabilities. Some are newer features, and others have been around forever. Then the salesman at the dealership asks you if you would like a subscription for heated seats.

You are entirely confused. A subscription? You ask if the car comes with heated seats, as many cars have for decades.

The salesman says that while the hardware to heat the seats is installed, you can't turn the seats on without your subscription. But, good news, it only costs $18 a month! Or you can opt for a yearlong or multiyear subscription.

"That's insane!" you think to yourself. "I am paying for a car that has a heated seat mechanism in it. I own this. Why do I have to pay for the ability to use it? And what if I sell the car—the next person has to then pay? If I own the car for ten years, that's more than $2,000 worth of additional, ongoing expense to heat the seats that I own!"

This may sound ridiculous, but it is happening right now in South Korea, where BMW is offering different subscription products, some of which can be added via an app.[1] One would imagine it won't be too long before this happens in America, too.

While the government may be trying to keep you from ownership in a variety of ways, technology firms and applications are ensuring your lack of ownership with subscription models, making you a lifetime renter. This is what the WEF predictions meant when they talked about products being turned into services.

You will own nothing, and the tech firms will collect a fee and get richer.

This is just the beginning. The impact of technology on every aspect of our lives is shaping up for rule by an unelected, powerful set of companies that have no constitution or checks and balances on their power, yet wield increasing power and control over just about everything you do.

The Technocracy

In the past, when someone said "technocracy" they were likely referring to political governance by domain experts, often in technology-adjacent arenas, such as science and engineering. As Investopedia says, "A technocracy is a model of governance wherein decision-makers are chosen for office based on their technical expertise and background. A technocracy differs from a traditional democracy in that individuals selected to a leadership role are chosen through a process that emphasizes their relevant skills and proven performance."[2]

Technocrats are not only chosen because of their supposed domain expertise, but also are often appointed by those in power to fulfill agendas.

Because these technocrats are often nonelected and make specific domain decisions, technocracy is often associated with various forms of central planning.

As the new financial world order takes shape, a new kind of technocracy has also emerged. This is one where technology firms have become so powerful and entrenched in our lives that they have overtaken large parts of traditional governing to become shadow or alternate governments themselves.

They may be structured as private entities, but singularly, and certainly together, they represent a threat to your freedoms, privacy, and agency, with a terms-of-service agreement replacing any sort of normal moral code or constitution.

Big Tech is centralized power with the illusion of choice (in some ways similar to the illusion of choice we have related to government today). I say illusion because there isn't much in the way of competition for you to make opt-in decisions. And, whether you opt out by choice or are forced out, you may have few options regarding where you can turn to participate in society in a meaningful or free manner.

This is the new technocracy—ruled by Big Tech—a powerful component of the new financial world order. If left in its current form, it will destroy your rights, including your property rights.

Digital Gatekeepers

Thinking about the rights you have that are supposed to be protected by the government, whether it be free speech, the right to assemble and protest, property rights, a justice process, or otherwise, none of that is present with the technocracy.

Big Tech companies, which provide platforms that are creeping into almost everything you do, have their own set of rules that they can enact at any time, at their discretion, in basically any manner of their choosing. In a free market environment with ample competition, this wouldn't be such an issue. But when large swaths of your activity are tied to just a handful of major platforms with few alternatives, we have moved away from a free market.

Moreover, when there's no path to redemption, once you are kicked off a platform or banned from a service, there's no reentry point to that part of society.

Big Tech has the ability to censor speech, making themselves the sole or final arbiters of what information and behaviors are good and right, regardless of whether their decisions have merit. In addition to setting their own rules about what is acceptable and what isn't, they have taken to monitoring misinformation on their own behalf and on behalf of other powerful entities, including the US government. Moreover, they often censor speech that is proven true, decline to censor speech that is proven false, and push narratives that often turn out to be false, at least in part.

The execution of their speech censorship is dangerous—and ridiculous. In the summer of 2022, amid gas prices that exceeded $5 per gallon on average nationally, I shared a meme on Instagram. It was a photo still of Michael Douglas in his iconic role as defense contractor William Foster, or "D-FENS," in the 1993 film *Falling Down* (a must-watch movie if you haven't seen it). In the film, during a series of "having a bad day" issues, Douglas's character has a meltdown in a fast food restaurant. He orders breakfast, but they won't serve it to him, since they switch to the lunch menu at 11:30 a.m., and it was a couple of minutes after that. The meme showed a still of his face during this exchange with the following words plastered over the image: "That look on your face when someone tells you gas went from $2.00 to $5.00 in a year because the economy is doing better."

The meme was poking fun at the gaslighting by those trying to spin the state of the 2022 economy as "the best ever!" among very serious economic issues. This is pretty straightforward humor that everybody understands.

Except for Instagram. They slapped a misinformation label on the meme post, saying it was "Missing Context" and "The same information was reviewed by independent fact-checkers in another post."

What? They were fact-checking a joke meme? You have to be kidding me!

Nope. Not only was I warned that I could lose my account for misinformation (of which there was none), but the attributed fact check made no sense, either. It was fact-checked by a group called "Lead Stories," and it said, "Gas prices did NOT reach national average of $1.87 per gallon in February 2021."[3] Again . . . huh? That had nothing to do with anything, yet I was getting a social black mark.

Of course, I left it up. People thought it was hilarious and that the fact check was bizarre. So, in a matter of days, after it had received a ton of interactions, Instagram suggested that I use advertising dollars to promote this post labeled by them as "misinformation" on their site so it could reach a wider audience. (Yes, you can facepalm now.)[4]

The issue comes down to wrongthink, narratives, and control. If tech companies find your speech not aligned with their preferred narrative, for whatever reason, they, in their sole discretion, can boot you from their platforms. YouTube (owned by Alphabet/Google),

Facebook and Instagram (both owned by Meta), Twitter, and other platforms have permanently banned high-profile politicians, doctors, and scientists for engaging in wrongthink, as well as countless random individuals, without a path to get back on.

Given the financial heft of Big Tech and the stickiness of their platform models (such as you building a following), it's hard for other platforms to compete, and it is costly, in dollars, time, and effort, for you to start somewhere else—if such an option even exists.

If you break the law in the real world, you may be required to serve time or have another penalty before your life normalizes. This is not meant to downplay the fact that former felons often have a hard time reentering society, but in the tech world you can break a term of service that is very vague and doesn't violate anyone's rights and still not have any chance to come back on the platform for the rest of your natural life.

The penalties for any perception of breaking terms of service have no path to redemption.

Further, it's another tie into a form of social credit with specific consequences. Not only does it impact your speech, but also potentially your livelihood, relationships, access to information, and the general ability to participate in society with millions of other people.

A few people have fought back successfully. Journalist Alex Berenson, who was critical about Covid responses, vaccines, and other information, had a nearly eleven-month "permanent ban" from Twitter. He sued the company, ultimately reaching a settlement. As he wrote on his Substack, "The parties have come to a mutually acceptable resolution. I have been reinstated. Twitter has acknowledged that my tweets should have not led to my suspension at that time."[5]

Not everyone has been successful. Prior to Elon Musk's purchase of Twitter, even the former president of the United States was banned from the platform.

It's not just speech that is at risk. A few Big Tech players have the only mobile operating systems that power your ability to communicate (two players, Alphabet's Android and Apple's iOS, account for more than 99 percent of the market).[6] A few Big Tech players control the major servers that allow you to conduct commerce. Slightly more, but still a relatively small number of players, control your ability to access money, and send and receive payments. As you invest your time in various platforms, you aren't granted property rights or ownership—you are merely engaging in a license or subscription.

Technology companies are becoming elite gatekeepers and shadow governments in a digitally enabled and digitally immersed world.

And they have a lot of control and power. The market capitalizations of Microsoft and Apple were in recent years larger than the GDPs of Italy and Canada. Facebook has two times more monthly active users than the population of China.[7]

If you think about your rights, particularly if you are an American, you can see where technology does nothing to protect them and, frankly, compromises them.

Censorship impacts the right to independent thought and self-expression. The lack of any rigorous adjudication process compromises you and everyone else being treated equally or fairly, or even having a path to redemption or recourse for any indiscretions, real or perceived. Such indiscretions are not tied to violating others' natural rights.

Privacy is compromised. Free will and choice are compromised. Socialization and relationships are compromised. Property rights, whether they be the ability to own and protect your property or to keep it from unlawful search or seizure, are compromised—as often what you think of as your property, in reality you don't own: you license or subscribe to it.

All of this impacts your rights to pursue life, liberty, happiness, and wealth.

Tech Creep

There's no doubt that technology has enabled many improvements in our standard of living and often made our lives better. It has democratized access to information and tools for people around the globe. But the geeks and nerds who have given us positive transformative tools have also bestowed upon us many tools of destruction, whether they be nuclear, biological, or other weapons.

Perhaps less obvious, in recent decades technology has also produced tools, and people wielding such tools, that are destroying individual freedoms, forcing us as individuals to give up our rights, our sovereignty, our agency, our privacy, and our wealth. They are also enabling a new era of cyber warfare.

Of course, a lot of this fits our good-ideas-to-bad-outcomes model. Ideas start out nobly, but as money is to be made and power is to be consolidated, what starts as innovation can become a tool of destruction.

So, what enabled this shift that has allowed technology to be so dominant and, ultimately, so potentially destructive? The answer is the most recent digital revolution, often known as the Third Industrial Revolution, with the power of the World Wide Web.

Techopedia describes the Third Industrial Revolution as "the advancement of technology from analog electronic and mechanical devices to the digital technology available today. The era started to [*sic*] during the 1980s and is ongoing. The Digital Revolution also marks the beginning of the Information Era."[8]

This massive change in how technology works enabled full-scale changes in human behavior and made a different set of companies powerful and treated as indispensable.

If you look back to see which companies dominated our landscape as we headed into the year 2000, aka Y2K, it was not technology. In 1997, for example, the Dow Jones Industrial Average had just a handful of tech companies, including Hewlett-Packard and IBM.

But, in the last fifteen years, technology has become pervasive, powerful, and megacapitalized.

In 2007, only one technology company, Microsoft, was among the ten largest companies around the globe.[9] At the time of writing, five of the top ten companies, by market cap, in the world were technology companies (the figure was six earlier in 2022, but Meta's own issues dropped its market cap, moving it from the #9 spot to #26), with many more of the top one hundred solidifying their place by being technology companies or tech-enabled. Four tech companies had market capitalizations of more than a trillion dollars, even after a tech rout in the stock market over the preceding months.

Coincidentally or not, five of the top ten are also listed as partners of the World Economic Forum at the time of writing.[10]

Tech companies have become massive, which has granted them great power. As the *New York Times* noted in 2021, "The 10 largest

Dow Jones Industrial Average as of March 17, 1997

AlliedSignal Incorporated	Exxon Corporation	Merck & Co., Inc.
Aluminum Company of America	General Electric Company	Minnesota Mining & Manufacturing Company (3M)
American Express Company	General Motors Corporation	Philip Morris Companies Inc.
AT&T Corporation	Goodyear Tire and Rubber Company	Procter & Gamble Co.
The Boeing Company	Hewlett-Packard Company*	Sears Roebuck & Company
Caterpillar Inc.	International Business Machines Corporation	Travelers Inc.*
Chevron Corporation	International Paper Company	Union Carbide Corporation
The Coca-Cola Company	Johnson & Johnson*	United Technologies Corporation
E. I. du Pont de Nemours & Company	J.P. Morgan & Company	Wal-Mart Stores, Inc.*
Eastman Kodak Company	McDonald's Corporation	The Walt Disney Company

*Company added to DJIA

Source: "The Ins and Outs of the Dow Jones Industrial Average," *Wall Street Journal,* January 25, 2017, https://www.wsj.com/graphics/djia-components-history/; "Historical Components of the Dow Jones Industrial Average" for March 17, 1997, Wikipedia, https://en.wikipedia.org/wiki/Historical_components_of_the_Dow_Jones_Industrial_Average.

The World's Largest Companies by Market Capitalization, End of October 2022

Rank	Name	Market Cap	Country
1	Apple	$2.5 trillion	US
2	Saudi Aramco	$2.0 trillion	Saudi Arabia
3	Microsoft	$1.8 trillion	US
4	Google	$1.3 trillion	US
5	Amazon	$1.0 trillion	US
6	Tesla	$711 billion	US
7	Berkshire Hathaway	$661 billion	US
8	UnitedHealth	$516 billion	US
9	Exxon Mobil	$461 billion	US
10	Johnson & Johnson	$460 billion	US

Source: CompaniesMarketCap.com, https://companiesmarketcap.com/.

tech firms, which have become gatekeepers in commerce, finance, entertainment and communications, now have a combined market capitalization of more than $10 trillion. In gross domestic product terms, that would rank them as the world's third-largest economy."[11]

These companies are so large and have so much capital that they dominate the landscape. They have created deep moats around their businesses, and they keep purchasing competitors and businesses in new verticals. For example, Amazon, which morphed from bookseller to seller of everything, has scaled its Amazon Web Services (AWS) server business to be a critical part of the web's infrastructure, and has an AI assistant named "Alexa" that has infiltrated homes around the world, but decided that wasn't enough. Amazon has also been on a buying spree in all kinds of industries. They have purchased Whole Foods (groceries), Zappos (e-commerce), MGM (film studio and production company), Twitch (livestreaming), Zoox (autonomous driving), Ring (home/on-location security and in-home technology), Kiva Systems (robotic fulfillment), PillPack (online pharmacy), and One Medical (primary care), as well as more than one hundred other businesses.[12]

That's clearly the blueprint of a company that wants to be entrenched in every facet of your life.

The scale and pervasiveness of these Big Tech firms have impacts on competition, choice, rent-seeking, and your rights. Writer Farhad Manjoo discussed this evolution with NPR. He first discussed how in today's consolidated tech world "there's now kind of a ceiling on how successful your idea can be, and the ceiling is kind of determined by these five companies," and how those handful of companies win when others win. He continues:

> [A]ll app makers have to put their apps in the Apple app store or the Google app store. And when they sell in those apps, 30 percent of that money goes to Apple or Google. They all have to advertise on Facebook or Google to get customers . . . And so any new app—Uber, Airbnb, Netflix, all the other sort of smaller companies online—have to go through these five to get to their customers. And what ends up happening is that other companies succeed, but always these five benefit off of that success.[13]

With their power, during this Third Industrial Revolution, technology companies have given you very sticky tools and, in doing so, entrenched them in your everyday life. Email. Social media. Online payments. Content. Business infrastructure. Even the way you now license instead of buy and own music is a shift.

And from all of this, what do you own? If your email provider wanted to shut down your email communication, what could you do about it? You own a cell phone's hardware, but not the mechanism to make it operate.

In 2022, we watched real-time as the US government asked Apple and Alphabet to shut down Apple Pay and Google Pay in Russia.

It's pretty hard for you to operate as a modern human without interacting with some or all of these companies or their limited competitors.

They are owning more and, in the process, you are owning less. They are generating more control over you, and you have few options and little recourse.

Writer Edwin Black has commented on this technology creep, which even predates the most recent tech takeover. He said, "Mankind barely noticed when the concept of massively organized information quietly emerged to become a means of social control, a weapon of war, and a roadmap for group destruction." In another observation, he said, "Not only can I count you as a member of the crowd, but I can individualize the information I have about you—where you live, what your profession is, and where your bank accounts are."[14]

The pace of their takeover is a fast one, with tech adoption and scalability at exponential rates of technology of yesteryear. It took sixty-eight years for the airlines to be adopted by 50 million users. It was sixty-two years for cars. Cell phones took twelve years. Twitter took two years. The Pokémon Go game took nineteen days.

With that scalability and their fortified balance sheets, these Big Tech firms are marching us toward dystopian realities where Big Brother may in fact be Big Tech.

Big Tech and the De Facto Government

Today Big Tech is incredibly powerful, and in many ways these companies resemble a shadow government.

Many of the big technology companies boast more users than we have citizens of the United States. The businesses are well capitalized, with solid balance sheets and more productive capacity than the US government. They are able to control the flow of information. They have access to myriad personal data and insights and can access them more elegantly than many government agencies. In some cases, Big Tech controls the servers and software used widely by the government, charged with serving up data from the mundane to the top secret.

Should the government need tools and technologies to further control the public, there's no doubt they will be turning to these tech behemoths rather than trying to develop that capability internally.

As an article in the *Conversation* put it, "Already today, the private sector is deploying cutting-edge technology as soon as practicable while the public sector struggles to implement turn-of-the-century solutions to seemingly straightforward tasks. . . . The private sector's capacity and ability to work with IT is already higher than the government's. As salaries and opportunities continue to draw talent to the private sector, we'll likely see a corresponding increase in the capability gap between the two." They further said that we have an "industrial age government" and an "information age world."[15]

The only thing these Big Tech companies seem to be missing is a military (although I am keeping an eye on Tesla's AI robots and what those could be programmed to do). Also, the wars of the future may be largely cyberwars, putting Big Tech and their experts squarely on the digital battlefield.

A group of writers published in the British magazine the *Tribune* noted the emerging parallels between Big Tech and the big state, saying, "A handful of Big Tech corporations now wield more power than most national governments. . . . Today, a handful of Big Tech monopolies form the infrastructural core of an ever-expanding tech universe, operating as obligatory digital interfaces for social exchange—colonising professional life and private consumption, monopolising flows of information and communication."[16]

Tech has taken over more of our infrastructure. Amazon has become a competitor to the US Postal Service. Uber and Lyft have displaced public transportation for some people. And the rights and freedoms that government is supposed to uphold have a digital barrier between them.

The *Conversation* noted how government competition now comes from technology instead of other states: "The challenge for constitutional democracies no longer comes from state authorities. Rather, the biggest concerns come from formally private entities but which control things traditionally governed by public authorities—without any safeguards. The capacity of tech firms to set and enforce rights and freedoms on a global scale is an expression of their growing power over the public."[17]

With this Big Tech takeover, the Constitution is supplanted by terms of service. From the *Conversation*: "For example, when Facebook or Google moderate online content, they are making decisions on freedom of expression and other individual rights or public interest based on private standards that do not necessarily reflect constitutional safeguards. And these decisions are enforced directly by the company, not a court."[18]

Because government overreach has become so pervasive, and politicians are often not the sharpest crayons in the box, individuals are preferring rule-by-tech to rule-by-unsharp-crayons.

In Europe, a poll by researchers at the IE Center for the Governance of Change found that the majority of respondents would prefer to replace government with technology, specifically AI. As was reported by the Next Web, respondents preferred getting rid of politicians and replacing them with algorithms.[19]

However, trading one type of tyranny for another isn't a great option, either. It's likely some individuals haven't recognized the full potential implications yet.

As tech companies are morphing into something that resembles the state, some state entities are taking notice. In China, as we discussed in Chapter 5, more Chinese citizens are using private digital wallets than government-issued digital wallets and digital currency. As these types of challenges occur, the CCP has been cutting down the power of the tech companies and their executives as they start to take on too much of it.

In April 2021, the *New York Times* reported that "China fined the internet giant Alibaba a record $2.8 billion this month for anticompetitive practices, ordered an overhaul of its sister financial company and warned other technology firms to obey Beijing's rules."[20]

It's not just the Chinese. In Europe, according to the *Times*, "the European Commission plans to unveil far-reaching regulations to limit technologies powered by artificial intelligence."[21]

The *Times* also reported, "Around the world, governments are moving simultaneously to limit the power of tech companies with an urgency and breadth that no single industry had experienced before." They note that reasons vary by country, from threats to competition to privacy concerns to wanting political control.[22]

This all stems from technology challenging government. According to *MIT Technology Review*,

> Technology companies have taken many aspects of tech governance from democratically elected leaders. . . . There's a long list of ways in which technology companies govern our lives without much regulation. In areas from building critical infrastructure and defending it—or even producing offensive cyber tools—to designing artificial intelligence systems and government databases, decisions made in the interests of business set norms and standards for billions of people. [23]

The piece continues to discuss companies usurping government roles and creating "products that affect fundamental rights," citing examples that invade privacy, "often without consent."[24]

It is easy to draw some parallels between the technocracy's and the Chinese Communist Party's way of "doing business." The CCP does not believe in individual rights, and with that, it means it does not believe in property rights.

For example, in China nobody owns land other than the government. The government then leases it out to individuals and developers via leases that range in duration from twenty to seventy years. This gives an illusion of ownership (we can perhaps draw a similar line to US property taxes, but with nuanced distinctions).

At any rate, getting people used to the benefits of leasing and comfortable with non-ownership is telling, like the tech companies have done with their products and the CCP has with their land leases rather than deeds.[25]

Like with the CCP, Big Tech is not bound by the protection of our rights. As the *MIT Technology Review* piece says, "decisions that companies make about digital systems may not adhere to essential democratic principles such as freedom of choice, fair competition, nondiscrimination, justice, and accountability. Unintended consequences . . . could create serious risks for public safety and national security. And power that is not subject to systematic checks and balances is at odds with the founding principles of most democracies."[26]

Big Tech is already limiting rights and has few constraints to keep them from doing more damage. They, as private entities, are unchecked in many ways, even when their purview surpasses that of a traditional business entity.

The Culprits

Technology companies emerging from the Third Industrial Revolution—and headed into the Fourth Industrial Revolution—are different than the companies of yesteryear. There has never been a time when companies had so much information about you, were so entrenched in your daily routine, and had the scale and capital of Big Tech today.

When it comes to the information you see, Google has a ton of control over that. Sure, there are a few other options. Bing, owned by fellow tech behemoth Microsoft, and DuckDuckGo don't give you much choice in finding what you are looking for, and of course their algorithms pick what is most relevant in an ever-changing and opaque manner. The same goes for Google's sister company, YouTube, owned by Google's parent company, Alphabet.

Of course, if you are an individual or business trying to get found, you also have to pay Alphabet in some way to improve your chances. Whether this is done directly via advertising or from spending the right amount of time or indirect dollars to improve your ranking, the information flow is heavily controlled by Google's search engine.

Other types of information are also controlled by the main social media platforms, including Facebook, Twitter, Instagram, and, for video, YouTube and TikTok (the latter has been widely reported to be a Chinese data-harvesting and surveillance tool).[27]

If you have a business, particularly a small business, you may be paying a toll to advertise on Google or Facebook so your business can be found. You may also be paying Amazon, Microsoft, or a competitor to host your website. Or maybe you are hosting your business on a bigger marketplace site, like Amazon, Shopify, or Etsy. While they don't own your business, the arrangement seems to resemble a protection racket, as you don't make money without them collecting fees.

You can keep your accounts with Google, Meta, Shopify, etc., as long as you are a good person, whatever that means and according to whomever in Big Tech's ranks (or the ranks of their cronies) decides. There have been many people who have found themselves stripped of access from various sites, many times for perceived infringements (or bad social credit, perhaps?) that didn't even occur on their own site. Sometimes it even comes without an explanation at all.

For example, journalist Ian Miles Cheong said that his account had been permanently banned from PayPal without an explicit reason and that he couldn't withdraw the money he had in the account for 180 days.[28]

In response, venture capitalist David Sacks said, "This banning could be non-political but I don't trust that to be the case given PayPal's recent history. Big Tech companies should be required to provide reasons when they deplatform users and there should be grounds for appeal."[29]

PayPal came under fire in October 2022 for what, ironically, they said was "misinformation" about a misinformation policy—one that was reported to fine PayPal users up to $2,500 for sharing information they deemed incorrect. They quickly said the release was an error and that it wasn't a policy, but many users weren't buying it and some took to deleting their accounts.[30]

On top of all this, you must consider privacy and information. While I was doing my research for this book, I couldn't pay to see certain articles without handing over my email address. All kinds of tech sites have several of my email addresses. Almost all of them have had some kind of hack or breach that has subjected my personal information to people I don't want to have it. This has caused me to waste a bunch of time with a flood of spam in my email boxes, as well as have to contend with fixing things like stolen credit card data from my privacy being breached by third parties. Of course, there was no compensation for this on my end and no real penalty on theirs.

On sites like Twitter and Facebook, I had to put forth personal information to be verified as an "important internet person"—again, whatever that means at their discretion. Some people have been denied such verification, even though they have a larger public footprint than others who have received verification because the guidelines are loose and discretionary. Of course, it was my choice to become verified, but not doing so would impact my livelihood as I seek to promote my work and content.

Paying and receiving payment also walks you into a web of well-connected companies (literally and figuratively). PayPal requires bank account and other information; Apple Pay links to your Apple account. Of course, should you be deemed socially unacceptable, then a payment provider may no longer welcome your business, and that word gets around quickly. So much so that you may have a hard time finding a payment option that is widely used by your potential customers, impacting your livelihood.

As noted, the government had Apple and Alphabet shut down payment system access in Russia. I will note that Apple has otherwise been generally good on privacy (such as refusing an FBI request to unlock a suspect's iPhone), but that's based on current management and personnel.[31] What's to stop them from changing course in the future? You may say choice and competition, but they are one of two mobile operating systems used by 99 percent of the planet, and the other is owned by Alphabet.

You may say, well, that's capitalism, but it isn't. Private business doesn't equal capitalism. Capitalism has competition and choice. Big Tech has become an "everything cartel," and you seemingly run into them at every turn of your life.

Payment systems are also at the center of collecting more invasive personal information. Some companies are looking at using all sorts of biometrics to allow you to pay (or access other technology). Apple has used a fingerprint, Amazon has used a palm reader (a technical reader, not one of the Psychic Friends Network variety), and Mastercard has piloted facial recognition.[32] They will, of course, say it's for safety and to keep fraud at bay, but at what ultimate costs to you and your rights?

As Big Tech has taken over, what rights do you have? We know that most people don't read user agreements before signing up to use technology. Even if you did, should you decline to agree to those terms, then what? You certainly aren't entitled to any specific technology, but when it becomes the infrastructure that runs society, it would be like keeping you off the roads, or not allowing you to have a TV connection, phone line, or bank account. None of this is for breaching someone else's rights or for nonpayment of services; it's for breaching the desires of Big Tech.

Think about telephone service historically. Not only did phone carriers not just randomly decide to stop doing business with people, there existed a legal requirement that carriers provide services. The Communications Act of 1934 guaranteed phone service for all and even required providers to serve any customer requested, even when they were in a location where it wasn't profitable to do so. This "provider of last resort status" meant that carriers could not discriminate or refuse service—certainly not for what someone said over the phone lines or because they were a person they didn't like or agree with on one or a variety of topics.[33]

This legislation became unnecessary when there were other phone communications options, but the idea was that where there wasn't competition, and communications infrastructure was concentrated in the hands of a few, the companies couldn't use their heft to discriminate in providing services.

A lack of access to service providers and their platforms is just the tip of the iceberg when it comes to tech and rights issues.

If It's Free, You Are the Product

We all know that we may invest in our social media accounts. Many of us create content that is shared by others on the platform, who then may consume, curate, comment on, or reshare that content. Doing so brings great value to these platforms, which are worth tens of billions of dollars or more on the back of our investments of time and effort.

As the saying goes, if the product or service is free, you are the product. Sometimes, that's the case even when you pay for products and services!

Our investment, though, doesn't lead to us owning our account. We can't take the followers we earn with us to another platform or directly communicate with them outside the platform at scale. We are subject to having the account seized from us for violating rules or terms of service, pretty much at the company's sole discretion. Whatever a tech company deems is against the rules (and it is very easy for them to deem thus), they can seize and appropriate the value you have created—for yourself and them—with no recourse and no compensation.

What about the content you create? Do you own that?

Twitter is my favorite social platform to participate in and one where I have created and curated tens of thousands of pieces of content, so I decided to check their terms of service. The Twitter User Agreement as of June 10, 2022 (pre–Elon Musk's takeover) included the following:

> You retain your rights to any Content you submit, post or display on or through the Services. What's yours is yours—you own your Content (and your incorporated audio, photos and videos are considered part of the Content).[34]

Okay, that sounds good. At least they are acknowledging you own your content. However, the very next paragraph contained the "catch."

> By submitting, posting or displaying Content on or through the Services, you grant us a worldwide, non-exclusive, royalty-free license (with the right to sublicense) to use, copy, reproduce, process, adapt, modify, publish, transmit, display and distribute such Content in any and all media or distribution methods now known or later developed (for clarity, these rights include, for example, curating, transforming, and translating). This license authorizes us to make your Content available to the rest of the world and to let others do the same. You agree that this license includes the right for Twitter to provide, promote, and improve the Services and to make Content submitted to or through the Services available to other companies, organizations or individuals for the syndication, broadcast, distribution, Retweet, promotion or publication of such Content on other media and services, subject to our terms and conditions for such Content use. Such additional uses by Twitter,

> or other companies, organizations or individuals, is made with no compensation paid to you with respect to the Content that you submit, post, transmit or otherwise make available through the Services as the use of the Services by you is hereby agreed as being sufficient compensation for the Content and grant of rights herein.[35]

To break some key pieces down for those of you who aren't lawyers (or don't play one on TV), the "you grant us a worldwide, non-exclusive, royalty-free license" means Twitter can use the content without paying you.

Where can they do that? Well, "to use, copy, reproduce, process, adapt, modify, publish, transmit, display and distribute such Content in any and all media or distribution methods now known or later developed" means they can use the content you create and put on Twitter for free anywhere they want, not just on the Twitter platform.

The "right to sublicense" means they can, for free or for compensation to them, grant anyone else the right to use your content anywhere.

And "such additional uses by Twitter, or other companies, organizations or individuals, is made with no compensation paid to you with respect to the Content that you submit, post, transmit or otherwise make available through the Services as the use of the Services by you is hereby agreed as being sufficient compensation for the Content and grant of rights herein" means that even if they get paid by letting someone else use your content, you get nothing, and your ability to use the platform is compensation enough for you.

So, what do you really own when others can earn compensation from your content without compensating you?

Technology is continually training you for non-ownership, via licenses and subscriptions. When I was growing up, I cherished my collections of music (in three different form factors), books, toys, and more. Each item might not have had a ton of value, but it was concrete and tangible. It was something that you could hold and even trade with a friend. Once you paid for it, as long as you took care to protect it, it was yours.

Now, more things exist only in theory and are being rented or licensed. Your records, cassette tapes, and CDs are replaced by digital files. Many people don't even own the files; they own a subscription to a service like Spotify or Apple Music, where you can listen on demand to what you want for as long as you pay for the privilege to do so.

While there are certainly benefits associated with more access, it is also important to be cognizant of the downsides.

You may be one of the millions of gamers who buy things within video games and virtual worlds. You outfit your avatar with fresh sneakers, buy it a digital car, and invest money in a virtual mansion. You may spend hundreds to thousands of dollars for pixels. However, you can't take any of it with you. You can't sell it or trade it to a friend. You really own nothing.

The training of generations to accept a lack of ownership and privacy does not bode well for rights or creating wealth and prosperity for individuals—just for the technology companies.

When it comes to tech's usurpation of your rights and your property, it goes beyond the obvious arenas you may consider. Think about companies like 23andMe, which, in a very real sense, own information about your DNA and have created "DNA databases." Even if you don't want to be traced, unwitting family members could breach your privacy.

As a piece in Slate said, "While 23andMe has resisted snooping from law enforcement, the courts may eventually force the company to provide access to its customers' data. Given 23andMe's reach, even people who have not signed up for the service would be forfeiting their genetic privacy in such an event. . . . Families delight in gifting each other these genetic tests and comparing their results. Meanwhile, the company is quickly building a huge genetic database, and in some cases, sharing that data with partners like GlaxoSmithKline for studies; in coming years, there's no telling how individuals' genetic data might be used, or worse yet, what could happen if that database is ever compromised."[36]

While they are infringing on your rights, the tech companies and their management assume you will just acquiesce your rights given enough time or perks.

Slate quoted 23andMe CEO Anne Wojcicki on DNA privacy: "The

reality is that, with a new technology, it just takes time for people to become comfortable with it." Said Slate, "The statement made headlines because it precisely articulated the gradual social acceptance of genetic genealogy that privacy advocates have been warning against."[37]

It's not just any one of the tech companies. All of them envision a future that gives them more control and you less ownership.

Controlling Freedom

Tech platforms like Airbnb are enabling the turning of homes into short-term rentals. And at the Bloomberg New Economy Gateway Latin America conference, Uber's vice president and head of Latin America, George Gordon, addressed the audience as part of a panel with a vision for the future: "What we want to do with our platform is replace the need for people to own a personal vehicle."[38]

His rationale was a seemingly innocuous and sympathetic one, as they often are. He explained that most personal vehicles are not utilized, by his estimation, 95 percent of the time. We know that cars generally, outside of times of supply and chip shortages and, of course, some classic collectible models, are depreciating assets and major expenses.

Wouldn't a world be great where you didn't have to have a car and you could just depend on Uber? That may sound utopian, but it is truly dystopian.

There's a reason why in many areas outside of very densely populated urban areas, public transportation is used by those with less in the way of economic means, and those with economic means choose to drive, at least some of the time, despite the costs and other downsides. Having a car (or other mode of transport) at your disposal gives you freedom. If you need or want to go somewhere, you can. You don't need to depend on the schedule of a bus or a train. Your time has value, as does your liberty.

Now imagine that you must—no matter where you are—depend on Uber (and maybe a couple of other competitors, like Lyft and a taxi company). What happens if you need to go somewhere, even work, and there aren't enough cars available? Or there are, but the costs are too high? This scenario is not giving you choice and freedom; it is making you dependent.

Moreover, as previously discussed, once you have removed this object that can give you liberty and you have dependence on the infrastructure, there is more leverage by the powers that be—whether that be tech, government, or a combination of the two—to make you compliant. Don't criticize "x" initiative because if you do, you are risking your access to transportation and, in turn, your economic freedom.

If you choose not to have a vehicle, for whatever reason, that is very different than not being able to own a vehicle because of central planning directives or a lack of appropriate social credit. It's the difference between choice and control.

As we see where technology is already, and its implications today, there is more coming down the road, fast and furiously.

An Intentional Addiction

As even the founders and management of some tech platforms have admitted, a large amount of social engineering has gone into training people to derive gratification from a fantasy world.[39] Taking a cue from casinos, everything has become gamified. Look at the video game industry. While a small percentage of players play for free, there's not much they can do in many of these gaming universes until they pay fees. There is a mid-tier of individuals who spend on an occasional to frequent basis. Then there are the addicts, or "whales," who spend a virtually (no pun intended) unlimited amount on their tech addictions.[40]

But it's not just games. Gamification has come into a variety of aspects of the tech universe, even financial services. Retail stock-trading app Robinhood used to use confetti to "celebrate" after you placed a trade, but dropped it, perhaps feeling pressure after it received a lawsuit from the state of Massachusetts over its alleged gamification strategy.[41]

Often, you don't realize what you are spending on these tech platforms. Just like when you turn your money into credits in a slot machine, you keep going and don't realize the cost. In the digital world, you may not realize your total spend until you get your credit card or bank statement—if you even take the time to review that.

It's an endeavor that is meant to get more people to trade short-term pleasure at the expense of long-term consumption or wealth. They want you to be addicted to owning nothing.

China has realized the addictive impact of gamification and put out moderations in their own country in an attempt to curb that. In relation to video games, the *Wall Street Journal* reported that China's National Press and Publication Administration banned minors from playing online games four days a week (Monday to Thursday) and are allowing play for only an hour maximum (between 8 and 9 p.m.) on holidays and Friday through Sunday.[42]

This, by the way, is not an argument against video games (or for CCP-style rule); it's just pointing out the intentions, power, and evolution of the tech companies and their weaponization of dopamine.

Consistent with the CCP's style, China required, according to the *Journal*, "all users to register using their real names and government-issued identification documents," and partnered with companies to leverage technology to do their bidding. The *Journal* reported, "Tencent Holdings Ltd., the world's largest videogame company by revenue, has used a combination of technologies that, for example, automatically boot off players after a certain period and use facial-recognition technology to ensure that registered users are using their proper credentials."

If it's not the government, it's tech, and if it's not tech, it's the government. And sometimes it's both working together.

Of course, given the addictive nature of many of these products and platforms, China is happy to push that addiction elsewhere, such as using the highly addictive TikTok app to engross kids in the US and globally (and using it to reportedly spy on users, as well).[43]

As technology continues to evolve, such as with the metaverse, the push for the addiction to owning nothing will intensify.

The Metaverse

If shadow governments weren't enough cause for concern, what about parallel worlds? Not necessarily just in the physical world, as some have hypothesized, but complete, immersive, *Ready Player One*–style worlds where you can live, work, and play digitally.

This is the plan behind one of the new investment areas for Big Tech, the metaverse. It's an important enough endeavor that one of the biggest tech companies in the world changed its name from Facebook to Meta to reflect this renewed focus, and other large companies, tech and otherwise, have been ramping up their investments in this arena, to the tune of hundreds of billions of dollars.[44]

While this potential next digital evolution may represent a tremendous moneymaking opportunity for corporate America, where does it leave you?

As currently defined, the metaverse can be thought of as a series of immersive, digital worlds, or the next step in digital connectivity. The idea is that instead of the more two-dimensional interactions you currently have on the internet, you will be interacting in three-dimensional worlds, likely with the assistance of hardware, such as a virtual reality (VR) headset or something similar.

Big businesses are seeing this as a way to transform interactions and get more money from you. For example, you may enter a world built by one of the Big Tech companies and have an off-the-shelf avatar to represent you as you move through the world. Where the opportunity comes is, not unlike current video and interactive games where you can make in-game purchases, these companies will want to sell you digital goods and services that supposedly enhance your digital life. Perhaps you buy your avatar designer digital sneakers to replace the off-the-shelf ones that come standard with every avatar. Or you buy a digital high-end car to help your avatar move between digital worlds in style. Each one of those comes with a cost, and the biggest brands want to be there first to sell to you.

As the *Economist* noted, "The MAAMAs' [Microsoft, Alphabet, Amazon, Meta, Apple] other priority is creating software platforms that will allow them to extract rents, by drawing in users, and then relying on network effects to draw in even more."[45]

This may seem far away, but it is consistent with the way many people are already interacting in games and online. According to ironSource, in 2021, in-game purchases for iPhone and Android alone amounted to $79.5 billion.[46] This opportunity was likely a rationale for Microsoft's offer to acquire gaming company Activision Blizzard as well.

It's not just about a money grab, though. This issue is about your access as an individual to opportunity and property rights. How does the average person participate in these new, parallel worlds? How do they retain ownership, and how do they build and retain wealth?

If the worlds are owned by Big Tech, then they control the platform, its access, and its rules, becoming an even more entrenched de facto digital government, with more control than those we have already been discussing.

Will you, as an individual, be able to buy digital property and resell for a profit, or open a small boutique and offer goods and services (with Big Tech, of course, taking a cut)? Or will that opportunity be reserved for big brands and partners with significant money and clout?

Once you "own" something digital, do you actually own it? Can you port it to another digital world? If you get kicked off a platform for any perceived violation by its Big Tech ownership, will you be forced to sell or even forfeit your digital goods? Do you really own anything or are you living in a licensable world where you, once again, are the product?

Or perhaps you are not invited to even participate at all, and since a private enterprise is the gateway, there is nothing you can do.

If this becomes the norm, with no additional focus on protecting property rights and technology companies' desire to make your life into a subscription model, it is pretty clear that you will own nothing.

Certainly, there are decentralization efforts that underlie the Web3 evolution, including various cryptocurrencies and open-sourced digital platforms. There are "public" metaverses where you can buy virtual land and storefronts today. However, it remains to be seen if those efforts will be able to be a force against Big Tech companies and their allies that have a lot of cash and a lot of clout and if there will be a commitment to property rights if and when the bigger players come to dominate. Given the trajectory of other tech, it is a substantial concern, in concert with the concern of trading real life for a digital one and what that means for wealth and freedom long-term.

If we don't each start demanding to be a part of what's coming, you may end up being a subject of a Big Tech kingdom or find yourself a digital outcast.

Tech and Politics

Technology is not only in pseudo-competition with governments, but is also impacting politics itself. What about when tech impacts elections? Having technology companies and platforms decide what speech can run prior to elections and what is shown to you can have a material impact on elections.

This has manifested itself in many ways. In the 2020 presidential election, major platforms suppressed the *New York Post*'s exposé on Hunter Biden's laptop. Twitter locked the *Post*'s account for more than two weeks and barred users from sharing the story. Not allowing this information to be widely disseminated or examined may have had an impact on the election itself. It was even acknowledged as problematic by then-CEO of Twitter, Jack Dorsey, at a congressional hearing in 2021. He called it a "total mistake."[47]

Big Tech has even censored candidates, their supporters, and their critics in a way that tilts the playing field.

Having another country interfere in an election is a huge issue. What about a shadow government that has an incentive in what the outcome is?

Certainly, media companies have always had some ability to pick and choose narratives. At least in legacy broadcast media, such as TV and radio, there is an equal-time rule. It is far from perfect, but it at least gives the illusion that there's some attempt at fairness.

In terms of tech and political manipulation, there is also the Cambridge Analytica and Facebook scandal, wherein a British consulting firm was allowed to collect and analyze personal data on millions of Facebook users without their consent. This data was ultimately passed on and used for political advertising purposes.[48] CNBC reported that data was harvested without permission from up to 87 million Facebook profiles and turned into "psychographic profiles" before ultimately serving them political ads.[49]

It seems like big data is a fancy way of saying privacy breach.

It wasn't that long ago that NSA contractor Edward Snowden exposed the ties between the agency and tech firms. As Reuters said in 2020, "The NSA has long sought agreements with technology companies under which they would build special access for the spy agency into their products, according to disclosures by former NSA contractor Edward Snowden and reporting by Reuters and others. These so-called back doors enable the NSA and other agencies to scan large amounts of traffic without a warrant."[50]

Regardless of who is doing the giving and who is doing the taking, and even if they are in some competition, the government and Big Tech have a history together.

With tech and politics becoming more intertwined, it will only become a bigger issue.

Digitalizing the New Financial World Order and Consent

As tech gains more scale and the new financial world order seeks more control and power, the coming together of the two will lead to even more technology that supplants and suppresses rights. Digital IDs and digital currencies and their ties to social credit (not unlike the digital *dang'an* we discussed in Chapter 5) create more mechanisms to gather and store information. And with that comes the opportunity to leverage that information.

Think about the control over your information. Of course, for decades, companies have had access to, used, and even sold certain pieces of data. They may have known your name, address, and maybe your phone number and marital status. They may have asked for some demographic information as well, which was optional when you registered for a warranty, for example.

Then companies started asking for your email address. Nowadays, what don't they know about you?

Moreover, the illusion of choice and the illusion of consent are allowing Big Tech to keep you from freedoms, rights, and prosperity.

Does having few choices and you clicking "yes" on a terms-of-service policy, with the option of forgoing participation in speech, commerce, or other aspects of society, truly mean consent? Do you have agency when you are limited in your choices or by freedoms?

The journal *Frontiers in Communication* shared an interview with writer Aldous Huxley that was conducted by Mike Wallace, along with some relevant commentary on consent and technocracy. They said, "Aldous Huxley had forewarned the world 4 years before President Dwight D. Eisenhower's famous farewell message that alerted citizens to a new threat to peace. Huxley's interview with journalist Mike Wallace foretells a time when public relations messaging controlled by the power elite would threaten to undermine man's capacity to reason and, thus, like a Trojan Horse opens the way for attacks on human rights and sovereignty. Huxley begins with the presupposition, elaborated earlier by Walter Lippmann, that leaders must 'manufacture [the] consent' of the people they govern."[51]

This is relevant, whether the domain is the state or Big Tech as a de facto state.

The piece continues with Huxley's interview. "'They will do it,' notes Huxley, 'by bypassing the sort of rational side of man and appealing to his subconscious and his deeper emotions, and his physiology even, and so making him actually love his slavery.'"[52]

You will own nothing. You will have chosen it. You will be happy—or so they will tell you—to be free of responsibility and the burdens of ownership and having to care for anything or anyone.

The story will be sold as an ideal world. But you must ask, ideal for whom?

CHAPTER 7

SOCIALLY UNACCEPTABLE, THE BUSINESS EDITION

How ESG Is a Power and Money Grab via Business Social Credit

> To rob the public, it is necessary to deceive them. To deceive them, it is necessary to persuade them that they are robbed for their own advantage, and to induce them to accept in exchange for their property, imaginary services, and often worse.
>
> —Frédéric Bastiat

From the pot of alphabet soup, you may have heard of another three-letter acronym being pushed by the World Economic Forum, United Nations, governments, big business, investors, and other global elites: ESG.

ESG, which stands for environmental, social, and corporate governance, and is also referred to in concept with terms like "stakeholder capitalism" and "sustainable investing," encompasses various nonfinancial criteria for companies and their investors. ESG is based on some elites' own decisions around morality and "what is good for society" (that always ends well, doesn't it?).

It is somewhat difficult to explain what ESG is because it shifts and changes around a moral code dictated by a relatively small number of people without specificity. This shifting is deliberate so ESG can serve the elites' whims as their ideas and priorities shift.

We likely broadly agree regarding concepts related to ESG. Most people would concur that we want to be good environmental stewards. On the social and governance side, it makes sense to treat employees well and incorporate diversity in many forms.

Where ESG goes sideways is in its actions. Basic free market economic tenets largely solve many social, governance, and even environmental issues. People don't want to do business with companies that don't treat employees well. As a business, your employees are stewards of your brand; unhappy employees become unhappy brand stewards who often engender negative customer responses. Self-regulating and reaching equilibrium is all built into the model.

The same goes for diversity. Those who seek out diverse perspectives and experiences and incorporate them in an authentic manner often see better business results.

So, ESG concepts make general sense. However, once they have been co-opted by a profiteer class and enabled by useful idiots, the free market concepts become bastardized and guided to central planning outcomes. As we have learned throughout history, and paid the price for in recent years, this is never to anyone's benefit other than the central planners and their cronies.

Imagine a bunch of entitled elites and bad actors sitting around a conference table and asking, "How can we give businesses a social credit score so that they do what *we* want them to do instead of what's in the best interests of their shareholders, customers, and business model?" That's ESG at its core.

What started with perhaps good intentions has now become a hybrid scam and capital diverter.

A whole class of rent extractors found that they could make a ton of money by exploiting ESG. For those in the exchange-traded fund (ETF) and mutual fund businesses, which are often low-margin, by slapping an ESG label on their funds they can charge a higher fee and have a new, virtuous marketing campaign.

Pension advisors, accountants, board consultants, speakers, and other subsets of the professional class have found a new place to assert expertise and charge fees, regardless of whether this work actually helps companies.

The ESG ecosystem has created an extremely valuable industry. Dan Katz, a former senior advisor at the Treasury Department, wrote in *Barron's*, "ESG has become a dominant force in recent years, attracting more than $40 trillion in assets, driving profound impact on capital markets and through them the entire U.S. economy."[1]

Forty trillion dollars! That's almost two times the US GDP. And that's just the direct asset implications and value, not the entire ecosystem built around it. No wonder the elites are pushing it so hard.

Brian Moynihan, CEO of Bank of America, called the transition to ESG a "big business opportunity" for banks. *Financial News* reported, "Bank of America has invested in ESG dealmakers in recent years, as banks including Citigroup, Deutsche Bank, Goldman Sachs, and JPMorgan have all created dedicated teams of bankers to help finance the clean energy transition that is estimated to be worth $7tn every year, according to an OECD [Organisation for Economic Cooperation and Development] report cited by the Sustainable Finance Initiative in October." That's a lot of green up for grabs, if you catch my drift.[2]

But we must ask, "Who gets to set these criteria that everyone in the world has to adhere to? Should it be the World Economic Forum? The World Bank? BlackRock and Vanguard? Professional accountants and consultants who are seeking to extract fees? Why should any of these entities get to dictate social mores and why would anyone think that any of these groups—or any other groups or individuals—have the best interests of the environment or society in mind over their own self-interests?"

They certainly don't have your best interests in mind and you will find that ESG presents a windfall for those connected to it, but not one for you.

Between a BlackRock and a Hard Place

ESG is a way to not only extract fees but also exert influence.

BlackRock is the largest asset manager in the world, with a reported $10 trillion in assets under management (AUM) as of 2021, a figure that came down a bit in 2022 in concert with overall declines in the market.[3] Given the amount of capital they have to deploy, BlackRock, or one of a handful of other mega-investors like Vanguard and State Street, is usually a top investor in just about every substantive publicly traded company. And with this great power, BlackRock's chairman and CEO,

Larry Fink, has been very vocal about how ESG is an opportunity to shape the world according to his and his cronies' visions.

In early 2020, after laying the groundwork for several years by talking about companies needing to have a purpose beyond profits (very similar to ideas from Klaus Schwab and the WEF), BlackRock started to talk about reshaping finance via ESG. Fink wrote in the firm's yearly shareholder letter, "I believe we are on the edge of a fundamental reshaping of finance." When you manage $10 trillion in assets, there's not much guessing; "believe" means you are planning to lead the charge via your actions.[4]

In BlackRock's 2020 letter to clients, "Sustainability as BlackRock's New Standard for Investing," Fink had this to say (bold is BlackRock's emphasis in the online printed letter).[5]

Fink first introduces the ESG platform they intend to push, saying, **"We believe that sustainability should be our new standard for investing."**

Additional language included:

> This year we will begin to offer sustainable versions of our flagship model portfolios, including our Target Allocation range of models. These models will use environmental, social, and governance (ESG)–optimized index exposures in place of traditional market cap–weighted index exposures. Over time, we expect these sustainability-focused models to become the flagships themselves.
>
> **Strengthening Sustainability Integration into the Active Investment Processes**—Currently, every active investment team at BlackRock considers ESG factors in its investment process and has articulated how it integrates ESG in its investment processes. By the end of 2020, all active portfolios and advisory strategies will be fully ESG integrated—meaning that, at the portfolio level, our portfolio managers will be accountable for appropriately managing exposure to ESG risks and documenting how those considerations have affected investment decisions. BlackRock's Risk and Quantitative Analysis Group (RQA), which is responsible for evaluating all investment, counterparty, and operational risk at the firm, will be evaluating ESG risk during

its regular monthly reviews with portfolio managers to provide oversight of portfolio managers' consideration of ESG risk in their investment processes. This integration will mean that RQA—and BlackRock as a whole—considers ESG risk with the same rigor that it analyzes traditional measures such as credit and liquidity risk.

That's a lot of ESG focus.

In BlackRock's 2020 letter to CEOs, titled "A Fundamental Reshaping of Finance," Fink had this to say about these new initiatives (bold is BlackRock's emphasis in the online printed letter):[6]

> . . . we will see changes in capital allocation more quickly than we see changes to the climate itself. **In the near future—and sooner than most anticipate—there will be a significant reallocation of capital.**
>
> . . . And with the impact of sustainability on investment returns increasing, we believe that sustainable investing is the strongest foundation for client portfolios going forward.
>
> While government must lead the way in this transition, companies and investors also have a meaningful role to play. As part of this responsibility, BlackRock was a founding member of the Task Force on Climate-related Financial Disclosures (TCFD). We are a signatory to the UN's Principles for Responsible Investment, and we signed the Vatican's 2019 statement advocating carbon pricing regimes, which we believe are essential to combating climate change.
>
> BlackRock has joined with France, Germany, and global foundations to establish the Climate Finance Partnership, which is one of several public-private efforts to improve financing mechanisms for infrastructure investment . . . we are facing the ultimate long-term problem. We don't yet know which predictions about the climate will be most accurate, nor what effects we have failed to consider. But there is no denying the direction we are heading. **Every government, company, and shareholder must confront climate change.**

The message is, in my interpretation, that if you don't follow what we (BlackRock) want you to do, we will allocate capital away from you. Given that we control a heck of a lot of capital and are connected with all sorts of powerful people, entities, and governments, you may want to be with us, not against us.

The clarity of their mafia-esque muscle is apparent in the following paragraph from the letter:

> We believe that when a company is not effectively addressing a material issue, its directors should be held accountable. Last year BlackRock voted against or withheld votes from 4,800 directors at 2,700 different companies. Where we feel companies and boards are not producing effective sustainability disclosures or implementing frameworks for managing these issues, we will hold board members accountable. . . . **we will be increasingly disposed to vote against management and board directors when companies are not making sufficient progress on sustainability-related disclosures and the business practices and plans underlying them.**[7]

The message again is clear—you will not succeed if you are not aligned with us. That is not capitalism; that is a corporate version of fascism.

This maneuvering benefited the cause of ESG, which in turn benefited BlackRock and its cronies. On the last day of 2021, Bloomberg ran a piece called "How BlackRock Made ESG the Hottest Ticket on Wall Street," looking back on the nearly two years since "Larry Fink, the chief executive officer of BlackRock Inc., declared that a fundamental reshaping of global capitalism was underway and that his firm would help lead it by making it easier to invest in companies with favorable environmental and social practices."

Bloomberg called out the heft that BlackRock used in making this happen by force instead of choice:

> . . . BlackRock drove a significant part of that shift by inserting its primary ESG fund into popular and influential model portfolios offered to investment adviser who use them with clients

> across North America. The huge flows from such models mean many investors got into an ESG vehicle without necessarily choosing one as a specific investment strategy, or even knowing that their money has gone into one.
>
> In short, an apparent BlackRock–led rush of investors into ESG in the past two years has been something of a self-fulfilling prophecy.

In addition to shoving ESG down everyone's throats and reaping financial rewards, very little of this has anything to do with benefiting any broad set of social impact goals.

The Bloomberg piece further said, "A *Bloomberg Businessweek* investigation published earlier this month revealed that the ratings BlackRock cites to justify the fund's sustainable label have almost nothing to do with the environmental and social impact companies in the fund have on the world."[8]

Tariq Fancy, who previously was the chief investment officer for sustainable investing at BlackRock, left because he felt it was primarily impacting power and fees for Wall Street. Bloomberg reported, "Even for investors who make a conscious decision to go into ESG, be they institutions or individuals, the funds are doing little other than benefiting Wall Street, according to Fancy." He said to Bloomberg, "There's no reason to believe it achieves anything beyond sort of giving them more fees. . . ."[9]

Fancy, who believes strongly in environmental issues, also critiqued the initiative in a *Wall Street Journal* article in November 2021.

> Is ESG good for the industry? Undoubtedly yes. It presents a lucrative new opportunity to raise funds and fees. And as an added bonus, it keeps government regulation to address the climate crisis at bay through feeding us yet another narrative in which our answers are solved by the "free market" magically self-correcting.
>
> But good for the planet? . . . [T]here is no compelling empirical evidence that ESG investing mitigates climate change.[10]

It's no wonder that even those who consider themselves environmental advocates think that ESG is, well, a scam. Now, they might argue for a different version of ESG, but that would just end up with the same set of problems.

Below see the top holdings, reported by *Barron's*, of the Northern US Quality ESG Fund, as of the end of March 2022.[11] The top ten holdings, accounting for almost a third of the entire fund as a percentage of assets, look like a normal large-cap fund. But no, it's ESG, because . . . fees, I guess.

Northern U.S. Quality ESG, Holdings as of March 31, 2022. Returns through April 25; Three-Year Returns Are Annualized

	Total Return		
	YTD	**1-Year**	**3-Year**
NUESX	(10.1)%	3.4%	16.7%
Morningstar Large Blend Category	(9.4)%	2.0%	13.7%

Top Ten Holdings

Company/Ticker	% of Assets
Apple/AAPL	6.9%
Microsoft/MSFT	5.9%
Alphabet/GOOGL	5.8%
Tesla/TSLA	2.1%
Coca-Cola/KO	2.1%
Mastercard/MA	2.0%
Nvidia/NVDA	1.8%
Amazon/AMZN	1.8%
Intel/INTC	1.7%
Home Depot/HD	1.7%
Total:	31.8%

Source: Morningstar via *Barron's*.

It is entirely unclear what it is about this portfolio that makes it ESG compliant, but people are extracting special fees in the process.

It all appears quite scammy.

Bloomberg featured an article headlined "ESG Funds Managing $1 Trillion Are Stripped of Sustainable Tag by Morningstar. Over 1,200 funds no longer merit ESG label, analysis find. Move feeds into fears fund industry is rife with greenwashing." The article referenced a forensic analysis by Morningstar, saying, "The findings feed into concerns that asset managers are still making misleading claims on the extent to which their allocations are doing the planet or its inhabitants any good."[12]

I'm shocked, I tell you!

Of course, the designation is also up to whatever Morningstar deems to be "ESG."

ESG creates a bevy of profiteering possibilities, which means there are lots of people who are going to work very hard to make sure they can still feed at the ESG trough.

The Real Toll of ESG

While nobody likes enabling a profiteering racket, the consequences of the ESG push are much more dire.

ESG adoption has had real cost and supply ramifications for energy production and commodities, which is materially affecting your wallet today and is likely to do so in the future. ESG pressures have kept many capital providers from lending and investing capital across an entire vital industry for years for fear of losing their own ESG accreditation or potentially their own capital.

This financial pressure campaign has led to massive underinvestment in the traditional energy sector, which hit consumers' pockets in 2021 and particularly in 2022. Gas prices and overall inflation, which hit the highest level in forty-plus years during 2022, were heavily influenced by the underinvestment in the sector and the corresponding decrease in energy supply.

Lewis Davey, a recruiter and service provider in cleantech and related industries, talked about this intentional shift in capital, particularly around fossil fuels and energy.

They said, "Bloomberg Intelligence has reported that oil businesses find it more challenging to raise finance amid the increasing ESG concerns, while banks are under added pressure from their investors to reduce or remove fossil fuel financing. According to Goldman Sachs, the cost of developing fossil fuels now exceeds renewable energy projects. This change is generating an unprecedented shift in capital allocation. This year represents the first time renewable energy will represent the highest part of energy investment."[13]

ESG creates intentional pressure to move capital based not on market demands but on the objectives and directives of the elite. ESG is effectively their bullying mechanism.

Forbes contributor and energy specialist Jude Clemente wrote, "Despite rising oil prices, we're not seeing the investments in new supply that we would've seen in previous cycles before the pandemic . . . There has been: 1) a lack of access to financing because of climate concerns, 2) investor demands to decarbonize, and 3) a shortage of sufficient investments in new supply for many years."[14]

Forbes also referenced an Evercore ISI report showing that private oil and gas exploration and production firms, which are not subject to the same level of ESG pressures as publicly traded firms, were planning to increase their capital expenditures for 2022 at double the growth rate of their publicly traded peers.[15]

Clemente further laments the hypocrisy of the ESG anti-oil agenda and how it is merely transferring production to OPEC and Russia. He says, "As we're seeing today, these rogue nations, with, contradicting the purported goals of ESG, horrific records on human rights are now controlling the market after ceding it to American shale over a decade ago." [16]

That's the rub. America can produce energy more cleanly than these other countries. If being "green" were truly the most important thing, ESG advocates would not only be all-in on nuclear energy, but also they wouldn't act as if handing off production to these rogue countries is an appropriate or "green" action. It's like believing that having an open smoking section in a restaurant works.

The Biden administration's focus on the *E* in ESG has been fierce. In a CNN primary debate in March 2020, Biden campaigned on ESG and energy initiatives. He said, "Number one, no more subsidies for fossil fuel industry. No more drilling on federal lands. No more drilling, including offshore. No ability for the oil industry to continue to drill, period, ends, number one." He also said he would not allow new fracking.

In the US, the ESG initiatives led to more expensive energy, a stoking of record inflation, and ultimately an economic recession. Gas alone hit a record of more than $5 a gallon on a national average in June 2022.[17]

Moreover, ESG activism led to less economic and national security, both in the present and the future, for the United States and its allies. It prompted President Biden to beg bad actors around the world to produce more oil (instead of just changing his policy stance).[18] The biggest global oil production alliance, OPEC+, responded "no, thanks" in October 2022 and cut production by 2 million barrels per day instead.[19]

It also led to less food security and cost surges in thousands of derivative products, both in the US and around the globe.

This had significant impacts on Europe, too.

By July 2022, electricity prices in France and Germany hit record highs. Energy prices also impacted German inflation, pushing the country to the brink of a recession.[20]

The European Union, which both moved away from traditional energy sources but also reportedly gets around 40 percent of its gas supply from Russia—because it's more green for the planet if Russia sends it to you or something—started to ration energy in July 2022 for fears that there wouldn't be enough.[21]

An *Insider* piece noted that in Germany, hot water and heating were starting to be rationed by landlords, schools, and other entities.[22] Then the Nord Stream pipelines, which transported natural gas from Russia to Europe, were sabotaged.

These crises had Europe rushing to redefine ESG to suit its current needs.

The *Financial Times* reported, "Energy crisis prompts ESG rethink on oil and gas. Investors are starting to look more favourably on energy companies because of their role in the transition to a decarbonised economy." When it serves them, they can change around what ESG means.[23]

The *Financial Times* also said, "European funds that employ environmental, social and governance (ESG) metrics as a group are heavily 'underweight' in oil and gas stocks but some tentative signs of a shift in positioning have appeared. Six per cent of European ESG funds now own Shell, compared to zero per cent at the end of last year, according to Bank of America. Holdings have also risen modestly this year in other energy companies, including Galp Energy, Repsol, Aker BP and

Neste, across the 1,200 European ESG active and passive funds monitored by BofA."[24]

This change even got into the European Union Parliament, which voted in July 2022 to allow nuclear- and gas-powered plants to be labeled as sustainable investments in financial markets. *Politico* reported, "Under the new rules—known as the taxonomy—new gas-fired plants built through 2030 will be recognized as a transitional energy source as long as they replace a coal- or fuel oil-fired plant, switch to a low-carbon gas like hydrogen by 2035 and stay under a maximum emissions cap over 20 years. Existing nuclear plants will receive a green label if they pledge to switch to so-called accident-tolerant fuels beginning in 2025 and detail plans for final storage of radioactive waste in 2050."[25]

That's very convenient timing. But it doesn't fix the risk of underinvestment in traditional energy, given the whims and changes of the political class vis-à-vis ESG.

ESG has the potential to kill human flourishing, denying reasonable energy solutions and thus keeping people worldwide from participating in wealth creation, and in some cases a decent standard of living.

Decisions on ESG will lead to starvation around the globe and may set back the US and its productivity and GDP via energy rationing. We will be moving backward, not forward.

How Did This ESG Stuff Start?

Much of what ESG is today can be traced to the United Nations. Preqin, a data and analytics company focused on alternative assets, notes that "[i]n 1992, The United Nations Framework Convention on Climate Change (UNFCCC) is established, signed by 154 states at Rio de Janeiro, coming into effect in March 1994. The overall goal of the UNFCCC is the 'stabilization of greenhouse gas concentrations in the atmosphere, at a level that would prevent dangerous anthropogenic human-induced interference with the climate system.'"[26]

The UN's ESG pressure became more robust at the end of the 1990s and into the early aughts. Kofi Annan, UN secretary-general, spoke for the third time in two years at the World Economic Forum in February 1999.[27]

In his remarks, Annan said, "Our challenge today is to devise a similar compact on the global scale, to underpin the new global economy. . . . I call on you—individually through your firms, and collectively through your business associations—to embrace, support, and enact a set of core values in the areas of human rights, labour standards, and environmental practices. Why those three? In the first place, because they are all areas where you, as businessmen and women, can make a real difference."[28]

A year later, the UN launched its United Nations Global Compact. Preqin describes it as "both a principles-based policy platform and a practical framework for companies committed to sustainability and responsible business practices."[29]

The Global Compact morphed into a gathering, coordinated by the UN. In 2004, leading financial companies, worldwide organizations, and other experts began working on ways to integrate certain principles into the financial markets. A white paper coming out of this in 2005 called "Who Cares Wins" is regarded as the first use of the term "ESG."[30]

In April 2006, the UN—which now has a Global Compact Office—launched their principles for responsible investment, or "PRI."[31]

Key takeaways from the release include that institutions "representing more than $2 trillion in assets owned, officially signed the Principles at a special launch event at the New York Stock Exchange." It also talks about the "[m]ore than 20 pension funds, foundations and special government funds, backed by a group of 70 experts from around the world," that were involved in crafting the principles.

The release says, "These Principles grew out of the understanding that while finance fuels the global economy, investment decision-making does not sufficiently reflect environmental, social and corporate governance considerations—or put another way, the tenets of sustainable development."

This is the backbone of ESG, and more and more investors sign up to them every year, estimated at more than 5,300 signatories worldwide today.[32]

What are these principles? Well, according to the UN's PRI (which became so large, it now has its own annual report),

> The six Principles for Responsible Investment offer a menu of possible actions for incorporating ESG issues into investment practice. The Principles were developed by investors,

for investors. In implementing them, signatories contribute to developing a more sustainable global financial system. They have attracted a global signatory base representing a majority of the world's professionally managed investments.[33]

The commitments that these firms are signing on to are as follows.

As institutional investors, we have a duty to act in the best long-term interests of our beneficiaries. In this fiduciary role, we believe that environmental, social, and corporate governance (ESG) issues can affect the performance of investment portfolios (to varying degrees across companies, sectors, regions, asset classes and through time).

We also recognise that applying these Principles may better align investors with broader objectives of society. Therefore, where consistent with our fiduciary responsibilities, we commit to the following:

Principle 1: We will incorporate ESG issues into investment analysis and decision-making processes.

Principle 2: We will be active owners and incorporate ESG issues into our ownership policies and practices.

Principle 3: We will seek appropriate disclosure on ESG issues by the entities in which we invest.

Principle 4: We will promote acceptance and implementation of the Principles within the investment industry.

Principle 5: We will work together to enhance our effectiveness in implementing the Principles.

Principle 6: We will each report on our activities and progress towards implementing the Principles.

The Principles for Responsible Investment were developed by an international group of institutional investors reflecting the increasing relevance of environmental, social and corporate

> governance issues to investment practices. The process was convened by the United Nations Secretary-General.
>
> In signing the Principles, we as investors publicly commit to adopt and implement them, where consistent with our fiduciary responsibilities. We also commit to evaluate the effectiveness and improve the content of the Principles over time. We believe this will improve our ability to meet commitments to beneficiaries as well as better align our investment activities with the broader interests of society.
>
> We encourage other investors to adopt the Principles.[34]

The PRI website notes that this is voluntary, but heavily extols the virtues of ESG.

As time went by, the Great Recession financial crisis pushed a number of financial firms to rehabilitate their image and, in doing so, they publicly embraced more "social" ideals.

The UN's fingerprints continue to be on ESG, particularly around 2015, with the establishment of Sustainable Development Goals (SDGs) and, of course, the Paris agreement on climate change.[35]

ESG-related searches on Google, the most broadly used search engine, were very low for a very long time, even after its introduction by the UN in the early aughts. Searches for the term "ESG" didn't begin to really move until 2019, with ESG investing searches picking up a little earlier in 2017.

You can tie some of this back to the WEF holding the Sustainable Development Impact Summit in 2017 and BlackRock talking more about ESG a couple of years later, among other factors.[36]

A 2020 report from the World Economic Forum, in collaboration with Boston Consulting Group, was titled "Embracing the New Age of Materiality: Harnessing the Pace of Change in ESG." It states, "In September 2019, we began a process of building an effective ecosystem for ESG aimed at advancing the state of ESG reporting."[37]

The article linked to in that particular sentence in the report disappeared from the WEF website, but, using the Wayback Machine on the Internet Archive, I was able to pull up a snapshot of it.[38]

Google Searches for "ESG"; Interest Over Time; January 2004 to October 2022

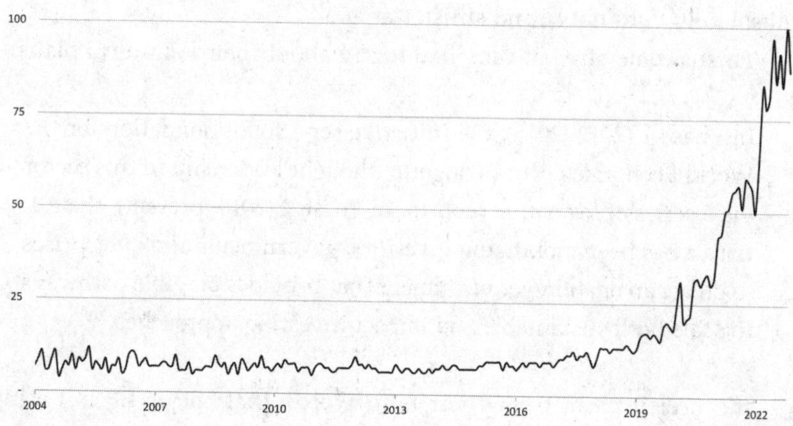

Source: Google Trends, https://trends.google.com/trends/explore?date=all&geo=US&q=ESG. Numbers represent search interest relative to the highest point on the chart for the given region and time. A value of 100 is the peak popularity for the term. A value of 50 means that the term is half as popular. A score of 0 means there was not enough data for this term.

Google Searches for "ESG Investing"; Interest Over Time; January 2004 to October 2022

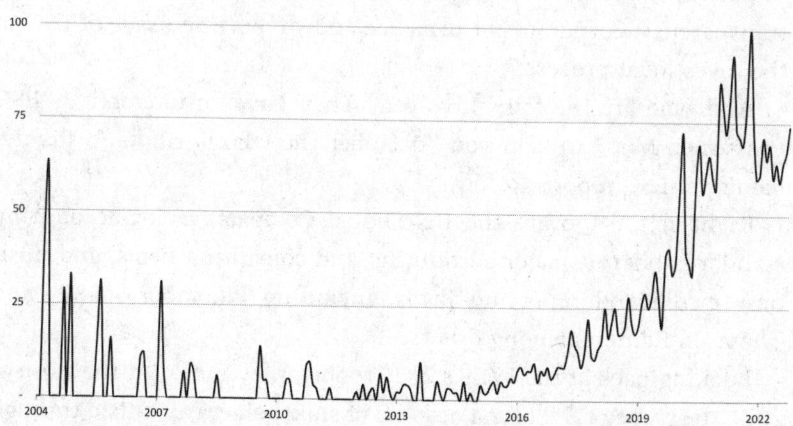

Source: Google Trends, https://trends.google.com/trends/explore?q=esg%20investing&date=all&geo=US. Numbers represent search interest relative to the highest point on the chart for the given region and time. A value of 100 is the peak popularity for the term. A value of 50 means that the term is half as popular. A score of 0 means there was not enough data for this term.

The first thing on the page said, "This project is part of the World Economic Forum's Shaping the Future of Investing Platform," which absolutely does not sound sinister at all.

This is some of what they had to say about their long-term plans:

> In Phase 1 (2012–2015), the initiative set a solid foundation for the World Economic Forum's ongoing thought leadership in this sector via a series of formative reports. In Phase 2 (2016–present), the initiative has been mobilizing investors, governments and enterprises to create an enabling environment that provides tangible pathways to scale both sustainable and impact investing approaches.

It's pretty clear from their own words that the WEF is taking a large amount of credit for the ESG push and has plans to stay centrally involved. They write, "The Forum network is uniquely positioned to provide influence and direction for the traditional investing community, governments, and enterprises with the desire to see positive systems change."

Under the title Active Workstreams, they touted the following: "Building an Effective Ecosystem for ESG (Environmental, Social and Governance): A multi-stakeholder effort to increase the coherence of initiatives within the ESG reporting ecosystem—ultimately boosting transparency, corporate performance and supporting usage of ESG in the investment process."

And who are the folks involved? They have an interactive "ESG Ecosystem Map" to help you "decipher the who is who and the dynamics of ESG reporting."

Right at the top are the UN Global Compact, major accounting standards boards, major accounting and consulting firms, and business media and reporting firms, including Bloomberg, S&P, and Thomson Reuters, among others.

Looking back at the WEF's 2020 report, they note, "At the close of 2019, the scene was set for a new era of stakeholder capitalism through the reinvigorated '2020 Davos Manifesto.' Nearly five decades after the original was released in 1973, articulating that the purpose of business is to serve more than shareholders alone, the updated manifesto expands on this idea by stating, 'A company is more than an economic unit generating wealth. . . . Performance must be measured not only on the return to shareholders, but also on how it achieves its environmental, social and good governance objectives.'"[39]

They also quote the then–global head of sustainable investing at BlackRock as saying, "We cannot wait for corporate reporting to become perfect; we need to become more forward-looking now and push for better corporate reporting at the same time." Who was this gentleman? His name is Brian Deese. If that sounds familiar, it is because Brian Deese was a senior advisor to President Obama prior to his BlackRock stint and now is director of the National Economic Council of the United States, under President Biden.[40]

The same names—BlackRock, the WEF, the UN—seem to pop up repeatedly. It may all be a coincidence, but I fall back on the theory that a few instances can still be coincidental, and after that, it's not.

Section 3.2 of the report talks about escalating stakeholder activism. They mention that "NGOs and activists are more frequently focusing their efforts on investors," and that "[a]dvocacy groups and activists are deploying highly professional campaigns and media strategies." They even expose funding sources, saying, "Large funders and the general public are giving greater support to environmental advocacy campaigns. For example, the European Climate Foundation is financing a number of environmental NGOs and initiatives, and amplifying the financial support of foundations."[41]

They are putting it all in print for everyone to see—they are engineering a massive, well-funded strategy to push their and their cronies' objectives.

In his book *The Great Reset*, Glenn Beck shares that while there are various ESG metrics, the ones promoted by the World Economic Forum and the International Business Council (a group that Beck mentions was created by the WEF) were put forth in conjunction with experts from the "Big Four accounting firms." These are not only powerful entities, but entities that stand to make a fortune advising and consulting on the very metrics they helped to craft.[42]

All of this activity, laid out by the UN and the WEF, and pushed by mega-investors like BlackRock, begets the Business Roundtable, an association made up of CEOs of major US companies (their website as of January 2023 says the companies of their CEO members support

37 million American jobs and $10 trillion in annual revenue, accounting for 24 percent of the US GDP, ostensibly plus international revenue as well), getting involved in ESG, signing a statement of corporate purpose.[43]

The Business Roundtable statement on corporate purpose, as laid out in *IR Magazine*, "supercharged the ESG movement: companies began competing for high ESG ratings and inclusion in ESG-targeted investment funds, and selling products based on their corporate ESG commitment. Simply put, since August 19, 2019, almost every public company—and many a private company—has sought to fortify its reputation by making statements of commitment to environmental stewardship, social justice, and responsible governance."[44]

Today, nearly every publicly traded corporate website has "ESG" plastered somewhere on it, even if their management can't really explain it.

As a reminder, you are funding this crap. In addition to the WEF funding disclosed earlier, in 2020 the United States gave $11.6 billion of taxpayer money to the UN, which is about 20 percent of its budget, so that a bunch of elite and global decision-makers can figure out different ways to push their agendas at your expense and ensure you will own nothing.[45]

All of these organizations seem to be tied together. While, as discussed, their ties go back further, in 2019 the WEF announced that it had signed a "strategic partnership framework" with the UN "to accelerate the implementation of the 2030 Agenda for Sustainable Development."[46] Coincidentally, I am sure, 2030 is the same year as WEF's slate of predictions that include "you'll own nothing and you'll be happy." We also know that BlackRock is a WEF partner.[47] And we know that all of these entities have played a significant role in making ESG a mainstream initiative.

The elite are driving the bus and have a complete map charting where they want to go.

Sri Lanka and the Almost Perfect ESG Score

Sri Lanka was, not that long ago, a nation on the rise. Between 2008 and 2018, their overall GDP and GDP per capita had nearly doubled. They had, according to a Bangladesh-based newspaper, the *Daily*

Star, a thriving economy that was "bringing in more jobs and billions of dollars, and middle class comforts: high-end eateries and cafes, imported cars, and upscale malls." The country was capturing the attention of investors around the globe.[48]

By 2022, just a few years later, their citizens couldn't access food or fuel, protesters overtook the president's palace and ran him out of the country, and Sri Lankans faced their worst economic crisis in seventy-plus years.

What happened?

The answer has a lot to do with ESG.

As ESG was being formulated, refined, and mobilized, a very familiar cast of characters was creating the groundwork for Sri Lanka to become the ultimate ESG prototype country.

Dating back to 2014, BlackRock's investment team started to champion the country. *Daily FT*, Sri Lanka's daily business newspaper, ran an excerpt from Gordon Fraser, fund manager and member of the BlackRock Emerging Markets Specialists Team. Fraser said, "I would say now is an excellent time to invest in Sri Lanka. I am very positive about the outlook of the Sri Lankan economy; in my opinion the best economic growth stories are very supply side-led, here Sri Lanka can excel, adding infrastructure where it did not exist before."[49]

On the back of their various connections and likely capital commitments, Sri Lanka embraced a commitment to ESG.

In 2016, WEF member and then–prime minister of Sri Lanka Ranil Wickremesinghe wrote the first of several articles about his green vision for the country's future.

> Sri Lanka is committed to achieving 20% renewable energy usage by 2030, over and above the current 35% of hydropower. Environmental sustainability is central to the country's development plans. At the same time, Sri Lanka is ready to be a constructive partner in global climate negotiations.[50]

In 2018, the World Economic Forum ran another Wickremesinghe article headlined "Sri Lanka PM: This Is How I Will Make My Country Rich by 2025." He wrote:

> Our economic policy, Vision 2025, is firmly embedded in several principles, including a social market economy that delivers economic dividends to all.
>
> We have also played a constructive role in promoting international and regional initiatives in many areas, ranging from the environment and climate change to maritime security and migration.
>
> The upcoming 27th World Economic Forum on ASEAN in Ha Noi, Viet Nam, provides me with the opportunity to showcase the landmark changes in Sri Lanka. . . . [51]

The Vision 2025 policy referenced and linked to in the WEF op-ed is hosted not on the official Sri Lankan website, but on the website of the World Bank. The World Bank, which provides financial assistance to developing countries around the world, happens to also be affiliated with the UN.[52]

It should be noted that as policy was implemented in Sri Lanka, like many emerging economies the country went on a borrowing spree, using debt to finance all kinds of projects and infrastructure.

During the 2019 Sri Lankan election cycle, President Gotabaya Rajapaksa touted green initiatives, including an election promise to transition Sri Lankan farming to organic within a decade.[53]

The climate agenda was one promise the Sri Lanka leaders intended to make good on. To comply with "green" initiatives, the Sri Lankan government tried unsuccessfully to commercialize farmland and weaken the farming community to implement their initiatives. When that didn't work, they returned to their organic farming promises, implementing in 2021 bans on foreign-made and nonorganic fertilizers and pesticides.

World Economics, a division of Information Sciences that provides data to financial institutions, governments, and corporations, gave Sri Lanka in 2022 an "Environmental Factors Emissions Index" score of 98.1, with 100 being perfect. In comparison, the United States was given a score of 58.7.[54]

On the "Social Factors Index," Sri Lanka ranked at 69.7, a hair under France (the United States was given 77.7, with the high score being Israel at 82.5).[55] On the "Governance Index," Sri Lanka received a 42.9 (the

US was given a 69 and Norway a perfect 100). Regardless, with climate change being front and center, Sri Lanka's green efforts were lauded.

With its ESG embrace, green initiatives, and WEF ties, Sri Lanka was well on its way to being a model of the future world.

Or was it?

Covid shutdowns and natural disasters had crippled travel and tourism. Without traditional fertilizers, those farmers who didn't abandon farming in protest altogether realized tiny yields, barely enough to feed their own families, let alone sell their overages for income as they had done in the past.[56] One farmer interviewed by Reuters reported harvesting just one-sixth of his usual yield. In the Agbopura region, the yields of five hundred farmers were estimated to have been cut in half overall.[57]

In 2022, Sri Lanka faced a food crisis for the first time in modern history.

With all of this, plus a ton of government-incurred debt denominated in dollars (which gained in strength relative to other global currencies by midyear), Sri Lanka started to unravel economically.[58]

In March 2022, propelled by food insecurity, fuel shortages, rationing, and rampant inflation, significant protests from the Sri Lankan people picked up steam. By the beginning of April, President Rajapaksa declared a national public emergency.[59]

Niluka Dilrukshi, a Sri Lankan rice paddy farmer, told the *Guardian* in April 2022, "If things go on like this, in the future it will be hard to find a farmer left in Sri Lanka."[60]

The *Guardian* reports:

> For the farmers of Sri Lanka, their problems began in April last year when President Gotabaya Rajapaksa, who now stands accused of pushing the country into financial ruin, implemented a sudden ban on chemical fertilisers.
>
> The full implications of the ill-advised policy—which has now been reversed—are only just being realised. Farmers say their livelihoods are under threat and for the first time in its modern history, Sri Lanka, which usually grows rice and vegetables in abundance, could run out of food as harvests drop and the government can no longer afford the food imports the country has become overdependent on in recent years. The rice yield

> dropped to 2.92m tonnes in 2021–22, down from the previous year's 3.39m, and the speaker in parliament last week warned of imminent starvation among the island's 22 million people.[61]

Rajith Keerthi Tennakoon, former governor of Sri Lanka's Southern and Central Provinces, said, "We are a tropical country full of rice paddies and banana plantations, but because of this stupid fertiliser ban, now we don't even have enough food to feed ourselves. . . . We have had past economic crises, security crises but never in Sri Lanka's history have we had a food crisis."[62]

An article in *Foreign Policy* put the cost of the green blunders for just tea production alone as an expected economic loss of $425 million. For rice production, the country went from being self-sufficient to importing around $450 million in rice.[63]

By late June, Prime Minister Wickremesinghe told his parliament, "Our economy has faced a complete collapse."[64]

In early July 2022, protesters occupied President Rajapaksa's house in Colombo, and shortly thereafter, Rajapaksa fled the country. Despite his role in this unraveling, the Sri Lankan parliament elected Prime Minister Wickremesinghe as the new president.[65]

CNN described the scene: "For Sri Lankans, the crisis has turned their daily lives into an endless cycle of waiting in lines for basic goods, many of which are being rationed. In recent weeks, shops have been forced to close because they can't run fridges, air conditioners or fans. Soldiers are stationed at gas stations to calm customers, who line up for hours in the searing heat to fill their tanks. Some people have even died waiting."[66]

CNN noted that the economic collapse was widespread: "Even members of the middle class with savings are frustrated, fearing they could run out of essentials like medicine or gas. And life is made more difficult by frequent power cuts that plunge Colombo into darkness, sometimes for more than 10 hours at a time."[67]

People couldn't find food. People died waiting in line for fuel. Energy was rationed. But, hey, they had a great environmental score!

The fertilizer ban was eventually overturned, but not without substantial consequences, for which the country and its people will be paying for decades to come.

The Sri Lankan outcome is a centrally planned disaster from the masterminds who want to be in charge of ideas and capital allocation. Guided by these masterminds, the government and ESG led the people of Sri Lanka and the country from a road to prosperity to owning nothing.

Other high environmental and ESG-scoring nations have also seen recent problems that threaten their standard of living and, in some cases, their lives. Ghana, which has an Environmental Index score from World Economics of 97.7 in 2022, faced nationwide power outages that year. I guess living with blackouts is great for the environment (although not so great for living).[68]

The Netherlands, whose ESG components included an Environmental Index score of 90.7, a Social Index score of 74.9, and a Governance Index score of 88.5, making it an ESG model country, faced protests from farmers in 2022.

The protests, which have been on and off since 2019, escalated in 2022 with backlash against ESG and green legal proposals that threatened the farmers' livelihoods by putting them out of work or cutting their livestock (including pigs, cattle, and chicken) in the name of reducing emissions and pollutants. A government statement said, "The honest message . . . is that not all farmers can continue their business."[69]

These proposals impact the farmers' livelihoods, and are relevant in terms of feeding the planet. The Netherlands is a robust agricultural country and the second-largest exporter of food in the world, behind only the United States. A farm lobbying group called LTO reportedly estimated the number of agricultural businesses in the Netherlands at 54,000.[70]

If you control the food supply, you control the people.

It may be just another coincidence, but the prime minister of the Netherlands, Mark Rutte, is a member of a big global organization that weighs in on things like ESG. Would you like to guess which one? If you guessed the World Economic Forum, you would be correct![71]

If you go down the World Economic Forum rabbit hole, you will find something called the "Food Action Alliance."[72] According to a January 2020 release on the WEF website, "The World Economic Forum, the International Fund for Agricultural Development (IFAD) and Rabobank, together with a growing roster of private and public sector partners have come together to launch the Food Action Alliance (FAA). The FAA brings together the international community to tackle an urgent historic challenge: to reshape the way we think, produce, supply and consume food."[73]

Why do we need to reshape how we think, produce, supply, or consume food? It was working quite well until the ESG folks got involved!

According to the WEF, this initiative "mobilizes a next generation of multistakeholder partnerships that build on existing synergies and complementary capacities to deliver food systems that are efficient, sustainable, inclusive, nutritious and healthy in line with the United Nations' Sustainable Development Goals (SDGs)."[74] Sustainable Development Goals is sister alphabet soup to ESG. Now the bad actors want to mess with the food supply.

In 2021, the WEF announced, "The World Economic Forum, the government of Netherlands and several public and private sector partners are launching Food Innovations Hub to help transform the food ecosystem."[75]

The press release continued: "Mark Rutte, Prime Minister of the Netherlands, said: 'Global food insecurity has been rising again. This stresses the need to redesign how we produce and consume food. The Netherlands is committed to forming partnerships that will catalyze the innovations that are needed to address the food system challenges. I am therefore proud to announce that the Netherlands will host the Global Coordinating Secretariat of the Food Innovation Hubs.'"[76]

So, the WEF, with the prime minister of the Netherlands, announced the need to redesign the production and consumption of food.

Whatever the intentions are, the actions are deliberate and will impact farmers' livelihoods, what you eat, and if you have food to eat. It worked out very well for Sri Lanka, don't you think?

When Electric Cars Aren't ESG

In mid-May 2022, after billionaire serial entrepreneur Elon Musk, whose tweets have garnered him almost as much attention as his business endeavors, announced a takeover bid for Twitter to fix its widely perceived censorship issues, he found that another one of his businesses had been impacted. Tesla, the world's leading electric vehicle manufacturer, was removed from the S&P ESG 500 index.

Maggie Dorn, head of ESG Indices North America at S&P Dow Jones Indices, who decides which companies are put in and removed from the index, wrote in a post about Tesla's removal, "A few of the factors contributing to its 2021 [ESG] Score were a decline in criteria level scores related to Tesla's low carbon strategy and codes of business conduct."[77] The "codes of business conduct" part sounds an awful lot like they disapproved of Elon's recent stances and affirms the notion that ESG is a corporate social credit score.

Musk responded in a tweet, Exxon is rated top ten best in world for environment, social & governance (ESG) by S&P 500, while Tesla didn't make the list! ESG is a scam. It has been weaponized by phony social justice warriors. He also said that the ratings firm had lost its integrity and warned that political attacks on him would escalate in the coming months.[78]

One of Tesla's investors responded, "Ridiculous. Not worthy of any other response."

Musk wasn't the only outspoken businessperson to find that he had personally negatively impacted the company's social credit, I mean, ESG score.

CSRHub's Consensus ESG Ratings deals in ESG reporting and other tools. They have a badge on their website indicating they are or have been a part of the GRI community, which says about itself, "GRI (Global Reporting Initiative) is the independent, international organization that helps businesses and other organizations take responsibility for their impacts, by providing them with the global common language to communicate those impacts. We provide the world's most widely used standards for sustainability reporting."[79]

The CSRHub tool on its website lets you type in a company and see what the "consensus" ESG rating is. If you typed in Home Depot at the time of writing, they came out with an 89, which puts them in the best category, called "high." However, the dashboard calls out one "special issue" associated with the company. A special issue is described further as "things you feel especially strongly about that don't fall into a simple category structure." These can be positive or negative, per the explanation, but it is unclear whether that impacts the scoring or is just called out as a "gold star" or "black mark," depending on the issue.

On Home Depot's dashboard, at the time of writing, there was one "special issue"; it was denoted with a Trump logo, which, when you hover over it, says "Trump involved." It doesn't take much insight to guess that it is a black mark and not a gold star issue.

I can find no particular links between Home Depot and Trump other than that one of its cofounders, Bernie Marcus, had supported President Trump's election campaign. Marcus retired from the company in 2002. Yet, in 2022, twenty years after his retirement, his use of free speech is impacting the business social credit of his former company.[80]

Not only is ESG a great tool to handicap enemies, but it is also completely malleable when it doesn't serve a purpose. According to Bloomberg, the EU proposed to tax commercial flights, but not private jets, to discourage fossil fuel use. Also exempt in the proposal were cargo flights that carried packages for businesses like Amazon.[81]

Of course, that is nothing compared to the aforementioned change of heart on gas and nuclear power plants, labeling certain ones green in the wake of Europe's energy crisis.

Also, in February 2022, after Russia's invasion of Ukraine, Bloomberg reported, "Europe now finds itself discussing whether weapons should be listed as ESG assets, to grant them more favorable access to financing."[82]

They are all admitting that they control financing and prosperity based on their objectives, and their objectives change based on what they deem is best at any given time. It's no wonder they believe you will own nothing.

The Continuing ESG Push

Despite the significant issues associated with ESG, it is being entrenched through the US government.

Under President Biden, the Department of Labor's Employee Benefits Security Administration proposed a rule that threatens the fiduciary duty standard that employee benefit plans must follow in terms of picking investments that maximize shareholder value. The rule allows nonfinancial criteria, such as, you guessed it, ESG, including climate change, to be considered.[83]

An op-ed in the *Wall Street Journal* said of this rule when proposed, "This would encourage America's perpetually underfunded pension plans to invest in politically correct but unproven ESG strategies. It would also violate retirees' basic right to have their money invested solely to advance their financial interests."[84]

The rule was codified quietly in late November 2022, effectively saying benefit plan managers no longer have to invest in your best financial interest; now they can favor ESG and economically targeted investments (ETIs). This codifies business social credit at your expense.[85]

This shouldn't be a surprise. In addition to his campaign promises and actions in the first days of his presidency to cancel oil and gas leases and the Keystone XL pipeline, President Biden has ESG-pushers all around his administration. This includes, as noted earlier, Brian Deese, who was formerly BlackRock's global head of sustainable investing and now leads the National Economic Council.

The Securities and Exchange Commission's (SEC) mission is described on their website: "The mission of the SEC is to protect investors; maintain fair, orderly, and efficient markets; and facilitate capital formation. The SEC strives to promote a market environment that is worthy of the public's trust." In February 2021, shortly after Biden's inauguration, the SEC announced the addition of Satyam Khanna as senior policy advisor for climate and ESG. According to Glenn Beck's *The Great Reset*, "Mr. Khanna is the first-ever senior policy advisor for ESG issues at the SEC."[86]

What exactly does ESG have to do with maintaining orderly and fair capital markets? Nothing. Installing ESG in the SEC was a political takeover of the capital markets.

Meanwhile, the Federal Reserve, whose explicit dual mandate from Congress is full employment and stable prices, also added ESG and climate initiatives. One was the Supervision Climate Committee, announced in January 2021.[87] The other was the Financial Stability Climate Committee, announced in March 2021. The Federal Reserve said of this initiative, "The new FSCC is a Systemwide committee charged with developing and implementing a program to assess and address climate-related risks to financial stability."[88] That sure doesn't sound like part of the Fed's mandate.

Biden's ESG commitment accelerated in 2021. *National Law Review* noted that "President Biden announced an Executive Order to help 'tackle the climate emergency,' a top priority for his Administration. The Executive Order builds upon the Securities and Exchange Commission's (SEC or Commission) on-going efforts to develop a disclosure framework for environmental, social, and governance (ESG) risks, particularly climate change–related financial risk."[89]

In May 2022, the SEC announced a proposal to enhance reporting and disclosures around ESG. Cloaked under the guise of making things more transparent, it is a backdoor way to entrench ESG further. It also could create additional administrative headaches for businesses that should be focusing on generating value for their shareholders and serving their customers and employees.[90]

Some people don't think ESG goes far enough. Two Harvard-associated and Reform for Resilience Commission members wrote an op-ed arguing that ESG should include *H* for health and that it should be prioritized and led by institutional investors. Those same investors who manage your money and have a fiduciary duty to you now have another group that wants the investors' attention and preferential treatment.[91]

Cars are already an area where ESG and technology are leading to behavioral changes. According to a report by Lang Marketing, in the US more than 48 percent of sixteen- to eighteen-year-olds do not drive at all, and by age nineteen, more than 40 percent don't even have a driver's license. The report attributes this shift to environmental, social, and technological factors (many of the same factors that are broadly keeping you from ownership).[92] If you don't drive, you don't need a car.

The World Economic Forum caused a stir in July 2022 when it published an article suggesting that private vehicle ownership should be reduced in favor of shared usage of cars and other vehicles. Of course, the reason was to keep "materials at their highest value." In the WEF's eyes, their highest value does not include personal property and freedom for you.[93]

However, just like most WEF ideas, this one has been recycled and rebranded; I guess they find recycling ideas to be a "green" initiative. A 2016 article from the WEF's website was titled "Goodbye Car

Ownership, Hello Clean Air: Welcome to the Future of Transport." In this, it solved the world's problems through something it branded as "FAVES"—*f*leets of *a*utonomous *v*ehicles that are *e*lectric and *s*hared (how surprising that moniker never caught on). The article reads like a manifesto to combine technology and socialism. The conclusion is the same as other initiatives—taking ownership from you.[94]

ESG Backlash

As more people have become aware of ESG and its implications, particularly with many high-level participants changing the application at their whim, the backlash is growing.

In a March 2022 op-ed in the *Wall Street Journal*, Arizona attorney general Mark Brnovich announced, "ESG May Be an Antitrust Violation. I'm investigating a coordinated effort to allocate markets." He calls out the coordinated efforts of large financial services institutions, working together to stop energy investments and implement a political agenda.[95]

After calling out the role of well-funded activists like Climate Action 100+ as part of this effort, he says, "As attorney general of Arizona, I have a responsibility to protect consumers from artificial restrictions on production. That's why I've launched an investigation into this potentially unlawful market manipulation. The resources of hard-working Arizonans should never be compromised in the name of spurious political activism, especially if that activism is a coordinated conspiracy that allocates markets in violation of the law."[96]

In July 2022, Florida governor Ron DeSantis took action against financial institutions using ESG as part of their criteria. A report from *Florida's Voice* said, "Florida will prohibit the State Board of Administration fund managers from using political factors to determine where to invest the state's money. This board includes the fund managers that manage the state of Florida's pension funds."[97]

The *Voice* added, "The governor said SBA fund managers will be required to only consider maximizing the return on investment on behalf of Florida retirees." You know, actual investment criteria.[98]

That same month, West Virginia state treasurer Riley Moore sent a warning to six major financial services institutions, saying that "boycotting" fossil fuels would result in them being banned from state business.[99] One institution, U.S. Bancorp, presented follow-up materials that it had removed restrictions against financing coal mining, coal power, and pipeline construction from its ESG Policy. It was not given any sort of ban.

However, five financial institutions—BlackRock, Goldman Sachs, JPMorgan Chase, Morgan Stanley, and Wells Fargo—found themselves on the state's restricted financial institutions list.[100]

Of course, that created counteraction from activist politicians. Brad Lander, the comptroller of New York City, whose Twitter bio included at the time, "For a more just, more equal, and more sustainable future" (I am not sure what any of that has to do with being a comptroller, so I will let it speak for itself), held a web call. Environmentalist Bill McKibben reported that Lander "made it clear" that "if @BlackRock and other financial partners don't start meeting their commitments to climate action, NYC won't be able to meet its own pledges."[101]

The backlash against ESG in concept is also being met with the backlash that ESG is smoke and mirrors.

Without admitting any wrongdoing, BNY Mellon found itself settling charges, including a penalty of $1.5 million, with the SEC, which accused the firm of making misleading statements related to ESG. Basically, the SEC alleged that the funds weren't considering ESG criteria in some stock holdings. Deutsche Bank and its asset management arm DWS were "raided" by German police for allegedly overstating their ESG focus (aka "greenwashing").[102]

One financial services executive at HSBC, Stuart Kirk, pushed back and was ultimately suspended for doing so. At the time he was serving as HSBC's global head of responsible investing, he gave a presentation titled "Why Investors Need Not Worry about Climate Risk."[103]

As an op-ed in the *Wall Street Journal* noted, Kirk made salient points about how asset prices had been increasing as climate warnings increased and that the focus had been diverting resources from its core lending function.[104]

The piece cheekily noted the issue with Kirk, saying, "We understand why banking regulators and businesses that hope to make money off the coming tidal wave of climate regulation might be offended by his truth-telling."[105]

The *Economist*'s July 23–29, 2022, issue featured a cover with a hand holding scissors, cutting through a paper with "ESG" written on it. Underneath it said, "Three letters that won't save the planet." A tweet from the *Economist*'s Twitter account on July 21 featured the cover and said, "ESG is often well-meaning but it is deeply flawed. The industry is a mess and needs to be ruthlessly streamlined." Again, they seemed to be more focused on the flaws with the implementation than on the concept.[106]

ESG Equals Money for Them, Not for You

Whether ESG is a scam or a mechanism for fee extractions, it isn't helpful and likely won't go away easily.

Remember that business social credit scoring predated the ESG moniker and is likely to survive or be rebranded if ESG gets enough of a bad name. I am already seeing language tweaks, such as words like *impact*, in the financial services community as a replacement.[107]

ESG works to consolidate wealth with the elite and keep wealth-creation opportunities from you, whether directly, by weakening the investment output and productivity of companies, or by hampering the ability of important companies to improve your life and ability to transact and create wealth.

One Twitter user, an architect named René Girard, put it quite eloquently: "ESG is a way for politicians to force ideology on the public without having to go through the electoral process and gaining public support. This power is exercised through the proxy of corporations. It is anything but democratic. It is totalitarian."[108]

CHAPTER 8

RENTING THE AMERICAN DREAM

Putting Housing Out of Reach for the Masses

He is not a full man who does not own a piece of land.

—Hebrew proverb

Owning a house has been the defining symbol of the American Dream. There's good reason for that—it has been a substantial mechanism for wealth creation. If you want people to create more wealth, you make it easier for them to own a home.

Even in Communist China, housing accounts for a reported 70 percent of household wealth, making it, according to the *New York Times*, "the most important investment for most Chinese people."[1]

So, it is alarming, as noted previously, that the very first prediction in the World Economic Forum's "8 Predictions for the World in 2030" was "You'll own nothing. And you'll be happy. Whatever you want you'll rent. . . ."

Whether that prediction follows the expectations of the new financial world order or is a directive to help create one, it doesn't matter much. Being a perpetual renter, rather than a homeowner, is a substantial affront to creating individual and generational wealth.

Housing and Wealth, by the Numbers

The Federal Reserve Board's 2019 Survey of Consumer Finances (SCF) illustrated the link between home ownership and individual wealth in the United States.[2]

In terms of dollar value, the home (aka primary residence) was the largest asset:

- Across households;
- Across ethnic groups; and
- By age, with the exception of the 55–64 year age bracket, where business interests equaled the primary residence value, and 65–74 where it was behind "other financial assets."

Major Assets on Household Balance Sheets, 2019

Primary Residence	26.0%
Other Financial Assets	20.0%
Business Interests	20.0%
Retirement Accounts	15.0%
Stocks and Bonds	7.0%
Vehicles and Other Non-Financial Assets	6.0%
Other Residential Real Estate	6.0%

Source: "Homeownership Remains Primary Driver of Household Wealth," National Association of Home Builders' Eye on Housing, Figure 1, February 16, 2021, via The 2019 Survey of Consumer Finances, https://eyeonhousing.org/2021/02/homeownership-remains-primary-driver-of-household-wealth/.

In terms of breadth of assets owned, the latest US Census Bureau Wealth of Households report (2017) showed that "equity in own home" was the third most commonly owned asset type in the US, behind assets held in financial institutions and vehicles (which mostly aren't investment assets, but rather depreciating assets). More households had home equity than they did stocks and mutual funds or retirement accounts (including IRAs, Keogh plans, Thrift Savings Plans, and 401(k) accounts)![3]

There is also a correlation between home ownership and overall wealth. The median net worth across homeowners was almost $255,000. The National Association of Home Builders (NAHB) estimated this at more than forty times the net worth of those who rent (reported at just shy of $6,300).[4]

NAHB economist Fan-Yu Kuo, based on the information from the Fed's survey, said, "households that owned primary residences also had holdings among the majority of other asset classes, such as other forms of residential real estate, vehicles, other non-financial assets, business interests, retirement accounts, stocks and bonds and other financial assets." She also noted that the survey results indicated "that owner-occupied households are able to build their wealth gains into other categories."[5]

This is multifaceted. Those who have more money can afford a house and eventually other investments, but also those who face increasing rents are often priced out of investing, creating a cycle of non-ownership and lack of participation in wealth creation. NAHB's Kuo surmised that there were "impacts of homeownership itself (attaining homeownership leads to higher wealth)."[6]

A report from the National Association of Realtors showed that most homeowners had benefited in some way from the increase in housing prices. From 2010 to 2020, the report said, the value of homes as primary residences increased by around $8.2 trillion to a total of $24.1 trillion in value. That's just a hair more than a 50 percent increase in one decade.[7]

The number of households that owned homes reached a peak in 2004, at 69.2 percent. That began to decrease as millions of homeowners found themselves in foreclosure during the Great Recession financial crisis. The Census Bureau reported the percentage of households owning homes has recovered some but remains around 65.5 percent (as of Q4 2021).[8]

Selling You Out of Housing

As noted earlier in our brief discussion of the Great Recession, while both individuals and financial institutions took on too much risk vis-à-vis housing, their outcomes were starkly different. Individuals lost their homes while financial institutions received a bailout.

There could have been a deal cut across the board that benefited everybody, but everybody isn't in the inner circle. Everyone isn't useful in a new financial world order, and if everyone has wealth, that limits the ability of the elite to cement more power.

The wealthy and well-connected benefited during the crisis in multiple ways. Some received direct bailouts. Many were given access to cheap capital. The financial institutions were able to foreclose on homes—taking away the wealth of the individual. These homes were flipped to capital-rich buyers who bought up these assets at bargain prices.

The *New York Times Magazine* reported that "[f]rom 2007 to 2011, 4.7 million households lost homes to foreclosure, and a million more to short sale. Private-equity firms developed new ways to secure credit, enabling them to leverage their equity and acquire an astonishing number of homes."[9]

It was an epic transfer of wealth.

Moreover, it consolidated power with big institutions and has impaired the ability of many Americans to gain wealth via home ownership.

The government bailing out the big financial institutions but not helping individuals keep their homes had another tertiary effect. It put a glut of foreclosed homes into the market, upsetting the balance between supply and demand. The overbuilding during the pre-recession times and the foreclosures created an oversupply of available homes, while the recession put pressure on housing demand.

The US housing market is still feeling the impact. Based on data from Statista, the decade from 2000 to 2009 saw an overbuilding of homes of about two million units above the trend from the previous three decades.[10] The Census Bureau's "New Privately Owned Housing Units Completed" data, looking at solely one-unit structures, shows an additional 1.88 million new structures for that decade over the 1990s.[11]

However, the following decade, 2010–19, saw substantial underbuilding. There were approximately 5.6 million fewer homes built in that decade than in the 1990s, per Statista, and 4.2 million fewer per Census Bureau data.[12]

This cycle of underbuilding has now left the US housing market with too few homes. Various economists have estimated the extent of underbuilding is four to five-plus million homes, consistent with the variability in data cited above.[13] This is just one factor causing prices to skyrocket and keeping many Americans, including young potential homebuyers, out of the market. The market manipulation done by policy ultimately hampered many individuals' ability to create wealth. Instead these individuals are increasing somebody else's wealth via rental payments.

Another enabler of the current housing debacle is the Fed's historic interference in various asset markets via its policy, which has ebbed and flowed somewhat over the last fifteen years but has always favored the wealthy and well-connected.

Their decade-and-a-half policy of artificially suppressed interest rates took from savers and retirees any interest income they would have had on their savings. It transferred the benefits to corporations in the form of plentiful debt with ridiculously low interest costs (and, given the inflationary environment, sometimes negative "real" interest rates, meaning the nominal amount they are paying in financing costs is less than the rate of inflation).

The wealthy received inflated asset values, and the everyday American received historic inflation.

The Fed's policy also gave corporations the motivation to seek yield from wherever they could and the capital to do so. This led institutional investors to compete aggressively with individuals for single-family homes—sometimes entire complexes of them—as I will discuss below.

The Vulturing of Booms and Busts

Does everything economy-related seem to have particularly gone haywire in the last thirty-plus years? That is not a coincidence. The power nexus that includes the Federal Reserve, the Treasury and government, and business interests, from the time of Alan Greenspan's tenure at the Fed, has created a blueprint for wealth transfer.

The "Greenspan put"—the idea that under Fed Chair Greenspan, the Federal Reserve wouldn't let the market fall too much without intervening—led to more risk-taking and more intense boom-and-bust cycles.

What may not be obvious is that booms and busts are extremely profitable for those who are well capitalized—that is, the already wealthy and well-connected. And they are terrible for the little guys.

There is a baseline disadvantage in being small. You don't have access to as many opportunities and you don't have the staying power when things go awry. When the financial boom-and-bust cycle gets further distorted by Fed, Treasury, and other government action, it's even worse.

Those who are wealthy, well capitalized, and have a long-term view will often take on excessive risk to do well in periods of prosperity. When that risk-taking enables a bust, who gets washed out? The little guys, of course! The big investors may suffer temporary setbacks, but they are looking to the future. When the timing is right, they swoop in, buy assets at bargain prices, and wait for the next cycle to begin.

There's a "vulture capital" aspect to these extreme booms and busts. In recent decades, it has come for housing.

One reason housing has become such a long-term wealth generator is that people often unintentionally take a long-term view on housing. They move somewhere to be near a job or to raise a family, so they ignore the boom-and-bust cycles that interfere with wealth. Many people haven't been washed out of their housing opportunities during a bust because they were focused on other things instead of the fluctuating market value of housing. Duration is a critical component of not only generating wealth but also preserving wealth and not being vulnerable to cycles.

Those who don't think long-term and about keeping wealth in the family are often giving up massive gains. I know several people who had divorces and other short-term needs and sold family homes that were bought for five figures. Those homes are now worth seven to eight figures. That is real wealth loss for their respective families.

Of course, profiteers are always seeking to find ways to try to limit your investment duration for their benefit. Home equity loans, reverse mortgages, and other financial products are ways to get you to take short-term gains that can often become long-term losses for your wealth.

In some cases, as happened with the Great Recession bailouts, if you overextend yourself with your home or use your home equity to buy another property, you will find that those who profited in assisting you to overextend are made whole while you lose any wealth you have generated.

The boom-and-bust cycles created by the Fed, Treasury and government, and business interests have driven general economic insecurity and dramatic episodes in the financial and housing markets.

Whether it is the supply-and-demand imbalances in housing, dramatic price inflation of goods and services, or abundant cheap capital for institutional investors, they all set up wealth transfers. They all put you on the path to owning nothing.

Investors, helped by the Fed and the Treasury and government, continue to financialize whatever they can. In housing, this led first to the scope of the Great Recession financial crisis and now to institutional investors competing with you for a home.

Homebuyers, Incorporated

As the cycle of cheap and available debt capital continued after the Great Recession financial crisis into the next decade, it was harder for investors to find "yield" (in layman's terms, assets that would be able to deliver returns on their investments). But investors could not let all of this cheap capital go to waste. As the valuation of stocks increased, professional investors scrambled for other assets to invest in, ultimately driving up prices across markets.

One major asset class that, as a result, saw a substantial increase in corporate investment interest was housing, particularly single-family housing. Houses that individuals and families have bought for decades as a means of creating generational wealth were now also being sought by big corporations.

This was entirely brought about by the Federal Reserve. Meaningful institutional money in single-family rentals didn't exist just over a decade ago!

The *New York Times Magazine* reported in 2020, "Before 2010, institutional landlords didn't exist in the single-family-rental market; now there are 25 to 30 of them, according to Amherst Capital, a real estate investment firm."[14]

I want to say this one more time for emphasis: competing with a large, well-funded corporation to buy a house is a phenomenon that was just created over the last dozen or so years and enabled by Fed and government policy.

Some of these corporations buying up America's single-family houses and turning them into rental properties aren't even based in the United States!

In March 2022, *60 Minutes* did a piece on the subject. Lesley Stahl interviewed Gary Berman, the CEO of Tricon Residential, a publicly traded company based in Toronto, Canada.[15]

At the time, and backed up by recent SEC filings, Tricon Residential owned about 29,000 homes in the US (their website showed an infographic listing 35,262 single-family rental homes, as well as 7,789 stabilized multifamily rental apartments as of September 30, 2022). After they purchase single-family homes, Tricon turns them into rental properties. They are also building new single-family homes with the express intention of renting them, not selling them.[16]

Tricon's 2021 annual report also called out their targeting of the "middle-market" demographic: "Tricon's U.S. single-family rental strategy targets the 'middle-market' resident demographic which consists of over seven million U.S. renter households (source: U.S. Census Bureau). The Company defines the middle-market cohort as those households earning between $70,000 and $110,000 per year and with monthly rental payments of $1,300 to $2,100. These rent levels typically represent approximately 20–25% of household income, which provides each household with meaningful cushion to continue paying rent in times of economic hardship."[17]

Tricon highlights that the middle-class demographic has stable cash flow and the potential to be long-term renters. Tricon's success hinges upon these middle-class individuals renting the American Dream.

Tricon couches the benefits as such: "Tricon offers its residents economic mobility and the convenience of renting a high-quality, renovated home without costly overhead expenses such as maintenance and property taxes, and with a focus on superior customer service."[18] That's quite the spin on not building equity and wealth.

60 Minutes also mentioned the scope of several other companies, noting, "Invitation Homes owns more than 80,000 rental houses, American Homes 4 Rent close to 60,000."[19]

In the fourth quarter of 2021 alone, corporations bought 80,000 homes, which was about 18 percent of all single-family homes sold during that quarter. While not all of those corporate buyers were large corporations (some were small landlords with corporate entities), it is a staggering number and more than 24,000 units higher than the same quarter in the prior year.[20]

It's not just these corporate entities on a stand-alone basis. Working with companies like Tricon and their competitors, some of the biggest names in finance have poured hundreds of millions of dollars into backing the purchase of single-family homes. The names include, through their various entities and whether as investor or lender, BlackRock, the largest asset manager in the world and purveyor of ESG ideals, Blackstone, JPMorgan Chase, Goldman Sachs, and Capital One, among others.[21]

Adding well-capitalized corporate demand affects the single-family housing market and creates pricing pressure in any environment. Adding that to an environment with major supply constraints means that either individuals have to pay more for homes or they are priced out altogether. This is hurting potential homebuyers, including the very large cohort of millennials who are now in the prime age range for home ownership but are finding they can't afford one.

So, with an undersupplied market, corporate buyers—who are flush with Fed-enabled cheap capital and who can waive a whole host of purchasing requirements, including inspections or even viewing a home—make formidable competitors to the average new homebuyer.

Ultimately this puts home ownership outside the reach of millions upon millions of Americans. As Tricon's Berman said to *60 Minutes*, instead "[y]ou can rent the American dream."

That sounds an awful lot like "you will own nothing and be happy."

The way these corporations explain their investment opportunity is insightful.

The Tricon annual report says that "what may be a 'golden decade' for residential assets" has been ushered in and accelerated by Covid policies and resulting behaviors and outcomes. They note:

> Our core single-family rental (SFR) business has been a massive beneficiary of these drivers—record operating metrics and capital inflows have accelerated the institutionalization of the industry, probably by years. Consider some remarkable facts that offer evidence of these exceptional demand trends: in any given week, Tricon has only 200 to 300 homes available for rent but receives up to 10,000 leasing inquiries; Tricon raised more private capital in 2021 than in its previous 32 years of operations combined; and

in the past fiscal year, Tricon's market capitalization more than doubled to $4.2 billion (C$5.3 billion).

While the average American is dealing with inflation, corporate buyers have benefited from access to tons of capital at cheap costs, exacerbating the imbalance between the individual and corporate buyer. And people are clamoring to rent not only because they can't afford to buy, but because the rental market is incredibly tight, too.

Tricon sees this as a huge opportunity for them—a "golden decade," for Pete's sake! The flip side of their "opportunity" is that it shifts individuals from owning their biggest wealth-creating asset to not owning a home at all.

Tricon calls the single-family rental market a story of "capital finding opportunity that didn't previously exist." They tout the strength of their opportunity, saying, "our story is even more compelling because this opportunity arose in the largest and most fragmented asset class in the world." They plan to increase their portfolio of single-family rental homes to 50,000 in just a few years (by the end of 2024).

The story in housing is also one of consolidation of landlords, taking opportunities from smaller landlords and shifting them to the larger ones. Tricon's annual report says, "Over the past decade, the U.S. SFR industry has matured from a largely mom-and-pop cottage business to a professionally managed, institutional-caliber asset class."

Perhaps most staggering is the way access to housing is portrayed. The report states, "Single-family rentals can help solve housing affordability issues by providing an alternative to homeownership, enabling Americans to live in a quality, well-maintained single-family home that they may otherwise be unable to afford or obtain a mortgage to purchase."

This misses the point altogether. Individuals want to be able to afford to buy a house. This does nothing but make that harder for them.

Tricon says they are "Doing Our Part to Solve America's Housing Shortage."

Today's housing affordability issues and rapid home price appreciation are being fueled by a lack of available inventory. New

> supply continues to be severely restricted by environmental restrictions, not-in-my-backyard (NIMBY) politics, a shortage of qualified trades and most recently supply chain bottlenecks that have lengthened build cycles and increased construction costs. . . . To suggest that institutional landlords are responsible for extreme home price appreciation, as some have insinuated, is not only a form of scapegoating but also irresponsible in that it fails to address America's inverted housing supply-demand fundamentals.

Okay, but adding in well-funded, new buyers with cheap capital certainly exacerbates that problem!

But Tricon has a solution.

> Given the broader housing scarcity and rising demand for single-family rentals, Tricon and other participants in the SFR industry are actively trying to address the housing shortage by building new rental communities rather than only acquiring existing homes to meet demand. These build-to-rent single-family communities (BTR) are designed exclusively for rent with amenity packages that frequently rival those of multi-family properties.

They have already identified the scarcity issues in terms of policy that is impacting building, including scarce labor supply and "qualified trades," as they put it, and other issues. Taking land that could be used for new homes that are available to buy, taking labor that could be used to build homes for sale, and using up limited permitting availability for rentals certainly takes away the opportunity for homes to be built that could be bought by individuals. This again shifts wealth creation to the corporate owners and their shareholders instead of leaving it to be claimed by an individual.

Ultimately, Tricon sees these shifts as a trend and a moneymaker for them. They say, "There is a significant runway for growth in the single-family rental industry as only ~3% of the 16 million rental homes in the United States are institutionally owned (source: Green Street U.S. Single-Family Rental Outlook, January 2022)."

Ironically, Tricon, as well as many of the other financial partners involved in this market, touts their commitment to ESG. They have a separate ESG annual report, and mention that their "newest Board member, Renée Glover, is an expert in building communities and affordable housing, and is passionate about ESG." What puts the *S* in social commitment more than taking away wealth-creation opportunities through converting more of the largest driver of household wealth, the homes, into non-owned rental properties?

Invitation Homes is another corporate buyer. Founded in 2012, they are 2.5 times the size of Tricon, with more than 80,000 homes available for lease in sixteen different geographic markets as of the end of December 2021, according to their 2021 10-K filing.[22]

Invitation Homes is under the impression or at least selling the impression that you don't want to own a home. Their 10-K says that they "are meeting the needs of a growing share of Americans who prefer the ease of leasing over the burden of owning a home."

I think they have missed the point. Based on my research, most people who don't own a single-family home for their primary residence can't afford to do so; it's not because of an easy-breezy lifestyle choice.

Of course, this is for the social good. Their 10-K filing states, "At Invitation Homes, we are committed to creating a better way to live and to being a force for positive change, while at the same time advancing efforts that make our company more innovative and our processes more sustainable. Environmental, social, and governance ('ESG') initiatives are an important part of our strategic business objectives and are critical to our long-term success."

Again, the definition of "social" seems to be fairly expansive.

They try to explain further:

> As one of the nation's leading home leasing companies, we have an opportunity and responsibility to contribute to a more inclusive, equitable, and sustainable world. Our mission, vision, and values define our daily actions in delivering on our pledge to be a responsible corporate citizen. Our mission statement "Together with you, we make a house a home" reflects our commitment to a resident-centric business philosophy. . . . We believe that integrating environmental, social, and governance initiatives into our strategic business objectives is critical to our long-term success. In

2021, we completed a formal ESG materiality assessment to identify opportunities for us to make the biggest impact in the areas that our stakeholders prioritize.

Apparently their vision for an inclusive and equitable world does not include home ownership. I guess if nobody owns a home and everyone is a renter, then everyone is on equal and just footing!

Like Tricon, Invitation Homes has growth plans for the future: "We have amassed significant scale within our 16 markets. In these markets, our acquisition strategy has been, and will continue to be, focused on buying, renovating, and operating high quality single-family homes for lease that we believe will appeal to and attract a high quality resident base, that will experience robust long-term demand, and that will benefit from capital appreciation."

The capital appreciation they are looking for is the value appreciation that would normally go to the homeowner, shifted now to the corporate owner.

So, how does Invitation Homes secure these prime properties with capital appreciation opportunities in great neighborhoods? They "collaborate with local market real estate brokers and others, and we leverage these relationships to source off-market acquisition opportunities."

This means they are using their leverage as a repeat buyer, paying in cash without many of the same contingencies that individual buyers would have, to secure preferential access to properties before they hit the market.

American Homes 4 Rent is another major corporate owner of single-family homes that they rent out. According to their 2021 annual report, they had 57,024 single-family residential properties across twenty-two states as of December 31, 2021.[23]

They note that they also sometimes engage in bulk purchases of homes, and that "[i]n addition to our traditional MLS acquisition channel, we continue to acquire newly constructed homes from third-party developers through our National Builder Program."

Like others in the market, they are also focused on building new units for rental.

And they are well capitalized.

In addition to facing corporate competition, they view the traditional homebuyer buying a home instead of renting as their competition. Their annual report says, "We face competition for tenants from other lessors of single-family properties, apartment buildings and condominium units, and the continuing development of single-family properties, apartment buildings and condominium units in many of our markets increases the supply of housing and exacerbates competition for tenants. . . . Additionally, some competing housing options, like home ownerships, may qualify for government subsidies or other incentives that may make such options more affordable and therefore more attractive than renting our properties. These competitive factors will impact our occupancy and the rents we can charge."

It couldn't be any clearer: more options for you to buy or lease hurts their business. *You* will own nothing, but *they* will be happy.

And what happens when corporate owners want to sell some of their portfolios of single-family rental properties? Well, many of them sell them to other corporate buyers, who can soak up the portfolios in their entirety. After a report in June 2022 came out that Starwood Capital Group was exploring selling about three thousand single-family rental properties in two portfolios, a well-known economic commentator who goes by the cheeky pen name "Rudy Havenstein" said in a newsletter, "Since we've now financialized everything on Earth (thanks Ben!), these homes will be sold to a couple of institutional landlords, not 3,000 young families." (Note: the Ben he is referring to is Ben Bernanke, the former Fed chair who expanded this era of easy money policy during the Great Recession.)

This is a critical point that must be underscored. The Federal Reserve, along with the government, has created this unequal and untenable financial situation for Americans. In addition to accelerating a new financial world order globally, at home, they have enabled corporate wealth creation at the expense of the individual. Corporations are now fierce, well-funded competitors to the American Dream, the primary individual wealth creator.

David vs. Goliath

Adding to the challenges of the housing market, smaller landlords have been hindered by government-affiliated mandates that overstepped their legal boundaries. *Time* magazine ran a piece featuring eighty-one-year-old Greta Arceneaux, a landlord for a small number of rental units impacted by government Covid-related eviction moratoriums. *Time* frames these mandates as part of the good-idea-to-bad-outcome model, saying, "While such policies were issued in good faith—they were designed to protect renters who have lost their incomes from losing the roofs over their heads, too—they have leveled a crushing blow to small, independent landlords, like Arceneaux, who rely on a handful of rental units for their livelihoods."[24]

Government interference in the market poisons market mechanisms. Government also always finds a way to favor the wealthy and well-connected and transfer wealth in that direction, regardless of how it may be packaged and promoted to "help the little guy."

The piece, pulling from a 2015 Census report, approximated the number of small or "mom-and-pop" landlords at around 47 percent of the rental market at that time. *Forbes* estimated mom-and-pops accounted for about 77 percent of the small building units, with just more than a third of those landlords being retired and having the rentals as their only source of income.[25] *Time* noted that while big real estate firms would benefit from more than $100 billion worth of CARES Act-related tax breaks, "mom-and-pop landlords, for the most part get nothing. (The CARES Act tax provisions remove caps on individuals' and businesses' ability to write off significant net operating losses, so the benefits go almost entirely to millionaires and billionaires who tend to have the largest balance sheets.)"[26]

Time further quoted Arceneaux, sharing her concerns: "'I don't understand how they can come up with all of this financial aid for the homeless, for renters, for agriculture, for big business, for airplanes,' says Arceneaux, who is a black member of the Coalition of Small Rental Property Owners, a California-based advocacy group that mostly represents black and Latinx landlords. 'And they're forgetting about the small mom-and-pop people that have two units or four units and serve such a great need in the community.'"[27]

The CDC, which was making the federal eviction moratorium mandates outside of its right to do so, was initially given a pass by the Supreme Court, as when the case was raised, the moratoriums had an upcoming expiration date. But in late August 2021, when the CDC sought to extend the federal eviction moratorium, it was rejected by the Supreme Court, which said it was up to Congress to be able to make such an authorization.[28]

That was too late for many small landlords who found themselves in a place all too familiar to the "little guy"; everyone else was bailed out or made whole, while they had to fend for themselves. One of my Twitter followers, @HeyBooBoo16, noted that she "was forced to sell a rental I had due to the government mandated people live in it for free for over a year & still demanded I pay my property taxes etc. . . . lost over $40,000 in rent. . . ."[29]

In addition to taking away wealth-creation opportunities from individuals, the corporate buyer trend is a loss for neighborhoods. Home ownership is a net positive for neighborhoods. People who own the residence where they live are more likely to treat the property with care and make further investments in the property and neighborhood. The neighborhoods become safer as people are more protective of and invested in (quite literally) their own property.

Owning a home gives people a sense of purpose, hope, and pride, along with the opportunity to create generational wealth. It gives neighborhoods more stability as well.

Filmmaker Adam Mariner of Anchor Productions followed a gentleman in Memphis, Tennessee, who was trying to make a difference in the community by helping his renters buy the properties. The renters talked about how doing so gave them "an opportunity to empower themselves." One said, "Knowing that you are paying to own something, versus renting from month to month, I am sure it's going to do something for the mental stability. I got a brother that's disabled and I've got a mother that's disabled, I don't want them to have a thought on not knowing where they're going to live two years from now."[30]

Home ownership is a path to changing people's lives for the better. Yet there's a threat of fewer people owning homes—you will own nothing.

Building Barriers, Not Homes

If helping people gain wealth via home ownership was a priority, it would be much easier and less costly to build homes. But the government, at all levels, keeps doing the very things that keep the American Dream a fantasy.

The National Association of Home Builders regularly studies the costs of regulations on the cost of new housing and its impact on affordable housing in the country. These costs go hand in hand with regulations that make it harder to build, take longer to build, and more costly to build new housing.

The 2021 NAHB study found that regulatory costs across all levels of government were almost $94,000. That accounts for almost a quarter of the total average sales price of a new single-family home at the time the survey was conducted. This amount rose from $65,224 just a decade earlier.[31]

While certainly not all regulation is bad, and some costs are necessary to ensure safety, both the nominal amount and the increase in costs over the past decade point to the excessive level of regulation today.

Other local government policies that restrict building and put up barriers to housing add to the challenge of home ownership for the average American.

Increasing levels of property taxes at the state and local levels also impact home ownership. I personally know several two-income families who had to sell their homes and move to new cities because their yearly property tax burdens doubled or tripled in very short spans of time.

Take Samantha and Payton. A dual-income, middle-class family, Samantha worked in the personal care industry, and Payton worked for a city of Chicago agency. The two worked, saved, and started a family with two beautiful boys. When their oldest was ready for kindergarten, they knew a good education was a priority. So, in 2004, they bought a home for just over $400,000 in the northwest suburbs of Chicago. The home, around three thousand square feet, was perfect for the four-person and two-dog family.[32]

At the time of purchase, the home's assessed property taxes were substantial: around $5,000 per year. But the family decided to stretch to make sure they could keep stability in their home for the boys.

The property taxes kept increasing. Samantha picked up a second job as a babysitter, and Payton picked up another job as well, working for a major transportation company.

Despite them both now working two jobs, the tax burden loomed large. Property taxes that started at $5,000 continued going up. Just fifteen years later, in 2019, their property taxes reached almost $16,000 per year. Samantha and Payton could no longer afford to pay the ongoing cost of living in their home.

Adding insult to injury, the skyrocketing costs of taxes put a damper on the value of homes in the area. Prospective buyers didn't want that burden, either. The family couldn't find a buyer for the house.

Samantha and Payton ended up making an additional $100,000 in improvements to the home to finally find a buyer at just about the same price they had paid back in 2004.

The local government had eaten into their wealth. Huge yearly tax payments chipped away at their savings and any potential equity they would have otherwise had in the house.

To find a place that they could afford with taxes, they moved to the next county. There they were able to afford only a 1,100-square-foot home, which still carried property taxes of $6,500 a year. They continually worry about when those taxes might increase and price them out of their home again, a scenario that has happened not just to them, but also to several of their friends. Some of those friends have moved into town houses, and others are now renting.

The Rent-to-Own Pipeline

Renting isn't a dream, either. A Census Bureau survey from June 1 to June 13, 2022, found that around 15 percent of renters (around 8.4 million renters) were behind on their rent payments. Bloomberg surmised that would likely increase, as many leases come due during summer months, and with the increasing housing market costs, landlords would likely boost rents to be more in line with the higher market rates.[33]

These numbers were higher for certain minority groups (black Americans were almost 25 percent behind) as well as prime earning age groups, such as people ages forty to fifty-four. The survey also said that 3.5 million households reported they were very or somewhat likely to be evicted from their home within two months.[34]

If you can't pay your rent, you are definitely not investing in anything, let alone getting ready to purchase a house.

Airbnb-ing the Neighborhood

In addition to corporations buying up homes to rent, technology has also incentivized investors to purchase homes to rent out by the day, week, and month. Tech platforms like Airbnb and Vrbo have created a massive market for the renting of apartments and single-family homes as temporary or vacation locations.

In some cases, properties up for rent via platforms like Airbnb have taken over entire buildings and even entire neighborhoods. In locales like Galveston, Texas, rental homes are now overtaking meaningful chunks of the town.

In a Slate article, one interviewee talked about the lack of neighbors in their Austin, Texas, neighborhood, saying, "There are neighborhood streets where people used to hang out on their porches and talk. And now you see them replaced with these McMansions that people come into on the weekends and use to throw large parties and then take off." The piece continues, "The McMansions and large parties are possible because houses that used to be rented for a year by people who live in Austin are now rented for a weekend by people who just visit Austin."[35]

In Galveston, Slate estimated that since 2019, around one thousand short-term rentals have been added each year. At that rate, "about a third of the island's housing stock would be short-term rentals within the next five or six years."[36]

Not surprisingly, having a substantial number of homes that are functioning as short-term rentals has an impact on the housing market.

Zaiyan Wei, Wei Chen, and Karen Xie researched the impact of home "sharing"—like short-term and vacation rentals via Airbnb—on home and long-term rental prices. Wei said, "Airbnb is indeed making the real estate market more expensive." The study says, "By enriching its hosts while making housing less affordable for others, Airbnb and other home-sharing platforms may be compromising public affordability for private wealth." Wei added, "It's going to increase the gap between the rich and the poor."[37]

Of course, local governments have found ways to benefit from this trend. The Slate piece on Galveston said, "The city gets to take a 9 percent tax right off the top of every short-term rental. Another 6 percent tax goes to the state." The government wins while more housing is removed from the market for purchase. There is little evidence that any local governments are doing substantial work to make up for the supply decrease, whether by changing permitting rules to make it easier to build or otherwise.[38]

I am a capitalist at heart, and I have no problem with people finding new and unusual ways to make money. However, let's be clear: we are not in a free market when it comes to housing. Restrictive local laws and regulations, government costs, and government meddling in the labor supply have created a nonfree, highly distorted market for housing. Amid this, people are losing home-buying opportunities.

The Barbelling of Housing Values

We have established that owning your primary residence is an important part of building wealth for most households and that it is becoming harder to do so. However, as a new financial world order has come about, even if you do own a home, if you are in the middle class you aren't benefiting quite as much as the already wealthy.

A report from the National Association of Realtors found that from 2010, around 71 percent of the increase in wealth in housing came from high-income households and that the share of housing wealth from middle-income households declined from 43.8 percent in 2010 to 37.5 percent in 2020. Low-income housing wealth fell even more, to "19.8% in 2020, from 28.2% in 2010."[39]

The *Wall Street Journal* reported from that study that "[i]n 2010, high-income homeowners held 28% of all U.S. housing wealth. By 2020, that figure rose to 42.6%."[40]

Another *Journal* piece noted that "Americans in the middle-class income levels experienced significant declines in buying power" and that the supply of affordable homes was shrinking.[41]

The National Association of Realtors' affordability study comparing 2021 to 2019 found that "[h]ouseholds earning between $75,000 and $100,000 could afford to buy 51% of the active housing inventory in December [2021]."[42] That is a substantial seven percentage point decrease from 58 percent in December 2019. The decline for households earning between $100,000 and $125,000 was eight percentage points.

Keeping first-time buyers out of the market delays their start date in building wealth. The *Journal* notes that this could not only reduce their future "nest eggs" but also make it more difficult for those buyers to ever enter the market because of the parallel rises in rents.

Despite the trends in lack of affordability in the US housing market, it is better than its neighbor to the north, Canada, which serves as a warning sign for what the trajectory of housing could become. Below is an analysis showing that housing prices have completely decoupled from disposable income in Canada.

Real Home Prices vs. Real Disposable Income; United States vs. Canada; Percent Change; Q1 1975 to Q1 2022

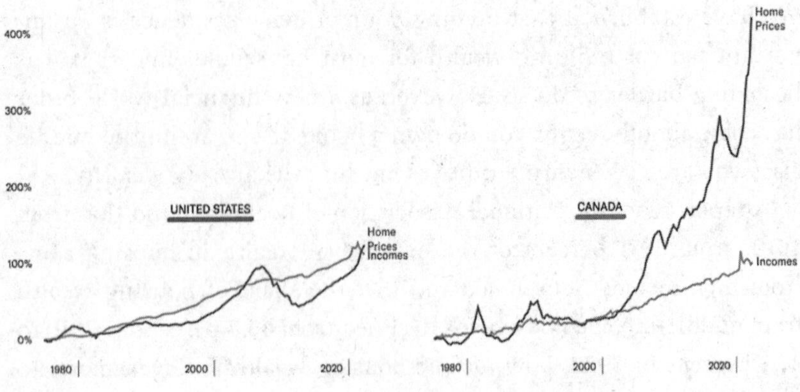

Source: Sam Dogen, Financial Samurai; reprinted with permission. Full source data at https://www.financialsamurai.com/what-if-the-u-s-housing-market-turned-into-the-canadian-housing-market/.

This is resulting from institutional investor purchases and a large number of foreign buyers, including Chinese buyers, as well as building being restricted by provincial and local governments. The housing-cost crisis led Canadian prime minister Justin Trudeau in April 2022 to institute a two-year ban on foreign investors buying homes in Canada.[43]

Foreign buyers have played a material role in the US housing market as well, but they have had nowhere near the impact that we see in Canada. Statista valued the sale of US property to foreign buyers for 2021 at $54.4 billion.[44]

Foreign investment in the US housing market is coming heavily from Canada, Mexico, and China, with the latter playing a smaller role in recent years. Statista has said that such foreign buyers "prefer properties in suburban areas to properties in small towns and central areas of major cities. This is probably why an overwhelming share of sales is detached single-family homes."

Statista also surmises, after speaking with real estate agents, that around 37 percent of these homes end up being rented out by their foreign buyers.

It's not that any one of these factors, like foreign ownership of housing, is a problem in and of itself; it is the sum of all the issues, given the financial backdrop we face going forward.

Buying Land and Water

As we consider the role of reduced access to real estate investments in the future prediction that you will own nothing, I would be remiss not to cover access to the most basic human needs, like food and water.

I know that it is hard to imagine that in a land of abundance like the US, we would one day not have enough food and water to sustain us. But, as the new financial world order comes about, that is a real threat.

I will also mention that, as Thomas Sowell pointed out in *Basic Economics*, in many countries that have faced starvation under centrally planned regimes, it wasn't for an actual lack of food. Rather it was that these entities couldn't get food to the people who needed it, letting the food spoil and the people starve.

If you control a large portion of the food and water supply, you can ultimately control the people.

Land, including farmland and land that has attached water rights, has become a favored investment of the wealthiest individuals, hedge funds, and university endowments that resemble hedge funds. Bill Gates, Jeff Bezos, John Malone, and Harvard University's endowment are just some of the names grabbing up land across the country.

A 2021 CNBC report found that one hundred private landowners owned nearly 2 percent of all the land available in the US, with the majority of that being productive land—ranches, farmland, and forests.[45]

The amount of land that wealthy private landlords hold has been increasing at an alarming clip. According to the *Land Report*, the top one hundred private landowners owned around 27 million acres of land in 2007; that number had increased to 40.2 million acres by 2017. The cutoff to make the top one hundred went from around 76,000 acres in 2008 to 145,000 acres in just about a decade.[46]

John Piotti, CEO of the American Farmland Trust, put it in economic terms. He told CNBC that land is scarce (there is a finite amount of it), and that it is also decreasing in supply in terms of its useful value. He said the US loses two thousand acres of farmland per day (ostensibly due to usage) and that will lead to it becoming even more important—and valuable—over time.[47]

The value of land has also been more stable than other asset classes in times of extreme volatility. Eric O'Keefe, editor of the *Land Report*, told the *Washington Post* that during the Great Recession financial crisis, "productive land correction was less than five percent."[48]

According to the *Post*, "A 2015 paper by the Bureau of Economic Analysis estimated that the total value of land in the Lower 48 states was roughly $23 trillion in 2009, with $1.8 trillion of that value owned by the federal government."[49]

This has brought more institutional investors into the market for farmland. Steve Bruere, president of Peoples Company, a farmland brokerage, management, appraisal, and investment firm, said that "institutional capital is growing and it's becoming a bigger piece of the market. It's about a $3 trillion asset class when you look at the whole US."[50] That's a growing and material part of the overall land market.

These dynamics, among others, have helped push up the value of all kinds of land, including farmland, over the past several decades. According to the American Farm Bureau Federation, using US Department of Agriculture data, the average farm real estate value (which includes land and buildings) by acre was $926 in 1997. In 2022, it was estimated at around $3,800.[51]

Renting Farmers

The US Department of Agriculture estimates that approximately 30 percent of farmland is owned by people who don't actually farm the land themselves.[52] This sets up a scenario where a farmer can earn a living, but not benefit from the rising values of the underlying farmland.

Farmers who do own land today are, as noted by CNBC, often "asset rich but cash poor." They may find themselves in a position where they don't have the financial wherewithal to continue farming. So, they sell the underlying asset, often to a wealthy individual or institutional buyer that is more than happy to snap it up.

This is land that has often been in the family for generations. Farmers make that short-term trade, giving up long-term wealth-creation opportunities.

This leads to the consolidation of ownership of land, food, and water, giving fewer people more control over the food supply.

Holly Rippon-Butler, Land Campaign director at the National Young Farmers Coalition, noted in the CNBC piece that there are not enough young farmers in the industry and that there are fewer farmers with every agricultural census, a disturbing trend in terms of consolidation and anti-diversification, which could impact our food security.[53]

This trend will only be exacerbated as the baby boomers who are currently farmers age out of farming and make legacy decisions regarding their farms. Peoples Company's Steve Bruere estimated that 50 percent of the farmland in the US will turn over in the next twenty-five years.[54]

Unfortunately, given the increasing costs and barriers to getting into farming and the appetite from sophisticated investors, it is likely that more and more farmland will be consolidated.

Per reports, Bill Gates has bought up land in more than eighteen states in less than a decade, using a variety of shell and affiliated companies. The *Land Report* estimated in January 2021 that Gates held around 269,000 acres at that time, and named him America's top farmland owner.[55]

Some of Gates's purchases have sparked outrage in local communities. When it was uncovered that a trust entity associated with Gates bought 2,100 acres of the former Campbell Farms farmland in North Dakota in June 2022, it made the news.

Local community members were unhappy with the purchase for several reasons. One was that Gates had no ties to the community. Another, as reported by the Daily Beast, was that the land "sold for less than what it could have brought within the community," intimating that the seller gave Gates a favorable price for other reasons, perhaps to "rub shoulders" with him.[56] *Agweek* reported that another source of angst stemmed from long-standing legal rules, saying, "North Dakota has an anti-corporate farming law that many people believe keeps large entities from owning farmland and keeps farmland in the control of family farms. This case clearly shows there are workarounds unknown to many people."[57]

North Dakota's attorney general looked into the sale, given the anti-corporate purchasing law. The way the law was written, while corporations and limited liability companies (LLCs) cannot own farmland, individual trusts can, should they intend to lease out the land to farmers. Gates's purchase passed muster given its structure and received state approval.[58]

However, during the time Gates's Red River Trust owns the land, the trust, not the farmer, will benefit from any value appreciation of the land.

Gates's ambitions for useful land are not limited to the US. The *Daily Mail* mocked Gates's interest in creating sustainable farmland in Turkey in November 2021, writing, "Billionaire Bill Gates reportedly shopped for 'hundreds of acres of farmland' in Turkey while vacationing aboard a superyacht that emits an estimated 19 tons of CO_2 a day before heading to the climate change conference in Scotland."[59]

In addition, "green" initiatives are impacting farmland, including the ability to own and farm, as well as pricing. According to Governing.com, the Biden administration is paying "farmers more money not to farm." They say, "The goal is to add 4 million acres of farmland to the Conservation Reserve Program, which takes land out of production to blunt agriculture's environmental impact."[60]

Water Is Life

It's not just land and the food that may be able to be grown on it that has been targeted by investors, but also water. Water rights are complicated, but generally they grant the holder not ownership of water, but the right to take water from a specified source or sources for "beneficial use." In the case of land, the water may be underground on the property, or rights can be given related to other water sources such as rivers, lakes, streams, etc. Of course, "beneficial use" is also subject to interpretation and various shenanigans, as you might imagine.

On the farming side, the interest in water rights has been accelerating the consolidation of farmland, putting it into the hands of fewer individuals, according to the USDA. Their 2018 report, "Three Decades of Consolidation in U.S. Agriculture," discusses the role that seeking water rights has played vis-à-vis farmland. Analyzing the report, writer Eli Francovich said, "Consider, in 1987, more than half of all U.S. cropland was operated by midsize farms that had between 100 and 999 acres of cropland, while 15 percent was operated by large farms with at least 2,000 acres, according to a U.S. Department of Agriculture 2018 report. . . . [O]ver the next 25 years, those numbers shifted dramatically. By 2012, farms with 100–999 acres held 36 percent of cropland, the same share as that held by large farms."[61]

University endowments are also changing the game for land and water. The *Wall Street Journal* reported in 2018 that Harvard had been buying thousands of acres of California vineyards for around six years, which, in December 2018, were estimated to be worth, on a combined basis, more than $300 million and to have increased in value threefold since 2013.[62] Harvard started out in stealth mode under affiliated entities, including one named Brodiaea. The *Journal* wrote that in acquiring these vineyards, Harvard was "acquiring rights to vast sources of water in a region where the earth's warming is making the resource an ever-more-valuable asset."[63]

One rancher who raised cattle and grew grapes was surprised at the prices the entity was willing to pay, saying, "A conventional agricultural business's returns couldn't have justified those prices."[64]

The *Journal* also reported that the day before a local emergency moratorium on "new agricultural wells" was put into effect, "Harvard's Brodiaea filed for permits to drill seven wells deeper than anything else in that part of the county—enough to fill an Olympic-size swimming pool in 90 minutes. One well hit water at 112 feet, but the driller completed the well to 1,200 feet deep, county records show. This would allow it to keep drawing water, even if droughts dropped the groundwater level further."[65]

This rocked the local community, with residents concerned about Harvard having "an outsize influence on the future of groundwater use, leaving smaller rural residents without a voice."[66] Another concern was that the water might be diverted from the area in the long run. One local vineyard owner reportedly wrote to Harvard Management's president, taking issue with the use of LLCs to hide Harvard's activities.

The piece then said, "A Harvard official responded that its investment was 'purely agricultural in nature' and that the vineyards prioritized water conservation."[67]

A 2012 Harvard endowment report stated that natural resources were a targeted asset class "because we believe its physical products are going to be in increasing demand in the global economy over the coming decades."[68]

Harvard's interest in this area remains opaque. In 2020, Wine Industry Insight reported that "[t]wo Harvard-controlled LLCs have deeded over 7,104.74 acres of land in northern San Luis Obispo County for an estimated $120.14 million (based upon $132,159 paid in county real estate transfer taxes). It is unclear whether this was an actual sale or a method for the Harvard LLCs to pull cash out of the assets."[69]

A search of the records of California's secretary of state does show a statement of information filed by Brodiaea Inc. as recently as April 26, 2022.[70]

Water is life, and Americans love life—and water. According to the *Atlantic*, "America consumes more water per capita than just about any other country—more than three times as much as China, and 12 times as much as Denmark." Water isn't used evenly throughout the country. Those in more arid locations tend to use the most. Not including purposes such as power or agriculture, individuals in those drier locations need more water to keep their lawns green as they aren't seeing as much rainfall. Given the warm weather year-round, they also may be filling swimming pools.[71]

The *Atlantic* claims that citizens make "extravagant use" of water "despite scarcity because water is kept artificially cheap." They argue that the amount we pay for water is a tiny fraction of the cost of the infrastructure to deliver it, although I would argue that while it may not be broken out, we pay very handsomely for everything via taxes, including infrastructure. The *Atlantic* breaks out the disparity in water pricing, writing, "Some city users pay $1 for 1,000 gallons.

On farms, water is even cheaper. One thousand gallons of agricultural water in western states can cost as little as a few pennies."[72]

This type of thinking has made water ripe for investors to figure out how they can profit from it. That would be a red flag in normal times. However, it is even more concerning given the confluence of factors and individuals shepherding in a new financial world order. It's staggering to think about water being withheld, in whole or in part, because of social credit or wrongthink.

A *New York Times* piece in 2021 focused on a town in Arizona called Cibola that sits along the Colorado River. They note that a few years back, a subsidiary of MassMutual called Greenstone "quietly bought the rights to most of Cibola's water. Greenstone then moved to sell the water to one of the right places: Queen Creek, a fast-growing suburb of Phoenix 175 miles away, full of tract houses and backyard pools."[73]

The contention was not so much about the transfer, but rather the players. The *Times* wrote, "Transferring water from agricultural communities to cities, though often contentious, is not a new practice. Much of the West, including Los Angeles and Las Vegas, was made by moving water. What is new is for private investors—in this case, an investment fund in Phoenix, with owners on the East Coast—to exert that power."[74]

A county supervisor voiced her concern that the institutional investors would make big money on the backs of the rural counties, which would suffer.[75]

Grady Gammage Jr. of Greenstone was quoted as saying, "The market would say water is far more valuable serving urban populations."[76]

The flip side of this is that it is seen as less valuable in rural communities, including for agricultural use—which is great in theory, but not so great when you need to eat.

That feeds into the concept of more central planning in the new financial world order. Those who think they are "smart" and "know better" will want to direct water resources to their "better uses." But "better" according to whom? We know that this type of thinking has caused all kinds of economic disasters, from stoking historic inflation to a global shortage of fossil fuels. It is incredibly concerning that this thinking is now directly linked to water and, by extension, food.

The possibility to financialize the most important resource for our being, water, has attracted all kinds of large investors to focus on it. The *Times* quoted Matthew Diserio, the president and cofounder of the hedge fund Water Asset Management (WAM), as saying that the US water business is "the biggest emerging market on earth" and "a trillion-dollar market opportunity."[77]

WAM has been investing heavily in water-related investments in and around Colorado, including spending millions of dollars on agricultural land with senior water rights in western Colorado's Grand Valley.[78]

While WAM is leasing its farms to farmers, officials in the community have concerns over its long-term plans. Part of that stems from the company's website, which notes, "Water Property Investor, LP (WPI) will invest primarily in a diversified portfolio of water resources, in the water-stressed Western U.S., purchased at agriculture value. These resources shall then be repackaged and repurposed and sold to higher value municipal, industrial and environmental consumers. . . ."[79]

In addition to private deals to repurpose and repackage water, there is growing support for the creation of a full trading ecosystem around it—a path to the financialization of water.

The *Times* wrote, "Private investors would like to bring in or amplify existing elements of Wall Street for the water industry, such as futures markets and trading that occurs in milliseconds. Most would like to see the price of water, long set in quiet by utilities and governments, rise precipitously. Traders could exploit volatility, whether due to drought, failing infrastructure or government restrictions. Water markets have been called a 'paradise for arbitrage,' an approach in which professionals use trading speed and access to information for profit. The situation has been compared to the energy markets of the late 1990s, in which firms like Enron made money from shortages (some of which, it turned out, traders engineered themselves)."[80]

With names like Enron being thrown about and the recent derivatives market implosion related to housing in 2007–2009, this has serious potential implications.

This entire scenario fits well into the good-idea-gone-bad model. The *Times* said, "The proponents of water markets say they are not in it just for the money." Of course not; they want to see water moved to the "highest and best use," according to them, of course. Why should someone be able to grow crops in the West and make sure their community is sustainable and not have to rely on agriculture elsewhere? It all sounds like a great idea until it impacts you negatively.

Moreover, the benefits gained will likely be reaped by those who already have the wealth, clout, and connections. You will own nothing—or worse, you will have to ration your showers and your drinking water. You may not be able to have access to healthy, real foods. And that's before any social credit is considered. Water is life, and the worst-case scenario is not having enough water to live.

So, water, land, and housing will be at the center of a fight between the political elite, elite businesspeople, activists, other racketeers, and you. What could go wrong?

CHAPTER 9

WORTHLESS PAPER

How the Government's Predatory Education Lending Creates Indentured Servants

Education is what remains after one has forgotten what one has learned in school.

—Albert Einstein

The opposite of creating wealth through the ownership of appreciating assets is the accumulation of liabilities and debts.

Debt can be useful in helping to increase your return on assets, such as when appropriately used to purchase a home or education that delivers a good return on your investment (ROI). In layman's terms, it means you use the debt to make a bigger investment than you could without it, and, over time, if the appreciation on the asset you receive substantially exceeds the cost you had to pay for the debt (including the interest costs and the repayment of the principal amount), the amount you make is enhanced.

However, in certain arenas, debt is being pushed and utilized in a way that is decoupled with achieving ROI. The biggest arena in which this is happening is college debt. In the US, college attendees, whether they had graduated or not, owed $1.6 trillion in college debt principal, aggregately, as of mid-2022.[1]

Now, the nominal amount owed isn't an issue on its own. Individuals have debt related to all kinds of assets and wealth-improving situations. The problem is when loans don't generate an appropriate financial return. College and similar educational loans should be able to be paid back in three to five years to generate an appropriate ROI. If you have to go to graduate school and that lifts your earnings substantially—well into the six figures or more—maybe seven years is okay for payback, but no more than that.

That is not the case for millions of Americans today.

To put it bluntly, college and university degrees have become the biggest legal financial scam in the country, and the US government has morphed into the largest predatory lender in support of it.

Individuals, sometimes even minors with parents cosigning or young individuals who have just turned eighteen, sign up for substantial financial commitments that delay or hinder their ability to create wealth if they can't generate an appropriate investment return. It can even burden their families.

In the age group of thirty-five to forty-nine years of age, 14.5 million Americans still hold more than half a trillion dollars in college loan debt principal (estimated at $630 billion). Over the age of fifty, 8.9 million Americans are still dealing with $393 billion in college debt. None of this includes the interest cost on that debt, which can be substantial, despite the overall low interest rate environment of the last decade and a half.

Amount of Student Debt Owed by Age Group, as of June 30, 2022

Age	Amount Owed ($ in Billions)	Number of Borrowers
24 or younger	$101.7 Billion	6.9 Million
25 to 34	$495.4 Billion	14.9 Million
35 to 49	$629.5 Billion	14.5 Million
50 to 61	$288.9 Billion	6.4 Million
62 and older	$103.9 Billion	2.5 Million

Source: Federal Student Aid; Portfolio by Age and Debt Size, as of June 30, 2022, https://studentaid.gov/data-center/student/portfolio.

The profiteering college education structure is having a major impact on economic freedom and wealth creation for young individuals, as it does not enable a good financial return, or any return on investment in some cases, for too many of those buying educations. Individuals aren't contextualizing their choices about what they want to do and what they may need to do to fulfill their future objectives.

An investment that should be delivering a financial return in a matter of a few years has morphed into a financial burden for millions of people for an extended number of years, with some still burdened with college debt when they are old enough to be eligible for AARP.

This indebted youth-to-college pipeline has ultimately transferred a ton of wealth from young people to colleges and universities at the expense of the young setting out on a path to generate their own wealth.

The power structure of the elites working together has gotten us to a point where university endowments are buying up land and water rights, and college graduates aren't even able to get out of debt, let alone start to make investments.

The Racketeering of Higher Education

The good-idea-to-bad-outcome model has found its ideal victims in those seeking higher education.

First came the wholesale push for education. Now, I believe in education. I think that education is important, learning is a valuable lifelong endeavor, and being well educated is typically an ingredient of success.

However, there are a few truths that need to be addressed.

- Learning is not the same as accreditation.
- Education is not valuable at any price.
- Not all education is equally valuable.
- Paying for the college experience is different than paying for a college degree and must be approached as such.
- The financing of education today is a predatory racket.

People have come to erroneously believe that education has value and, therefore, more education has more value. They believe that education is good and, therefore, higher education will lead to better job opportunities.

This historically has been the case at face value. Those with college degrees, generally and on average, would earn more than those without degrees (again, in general and with exceptions).

This thinking has created an immense number of profiteers, from college preparatory services to the colleges themselves, cheered on by the useful idiots saying that you must go to college, without context.

The profiteers used the cheerleaders to get the message into the zeitgeist that "education is valuable" versus "education is valuable only up to a certain price." While in some respects, being educated (at least in the right things) is "priceless," most young people specifically pursue a college education for the express purpose of increasing the amount of money they make over their careers. While you will hear many on the left call education a "right," it is not—it is an investment.

You can become educated basically for free; many Ivy League and other top-tier schools like MIT have put almost their entire coursework online, accessible at no cost. The democratization of technology and unparalleled access to information means that it has never been easier to educate yourself than it is today.

So, it is not really the education that is being valued; it is the accreditation. What a young person (and sometimes older individuals, too) wants is the piece of paper or the letters after their name that they believe will signify a better chance at improving the amount they can make or getting into a field that they desire that requires such accreditation.

That is an investment. You put out money to get a return on it. Like any other investment, the amount one is willing to pay for it should be based on how much of a return is made from the investment.

Again, I use these terms in their monetary context. It is not to say that lower-paying jobs, like social work, aren't valuable. They have intangible values. But monetarily, social work has a relatively fixed pay scale, and if you pay multiple six figures for an opportunity to do social work, you aren't going to be seeing that same amount of return, or likely any return, and it will impact your ability to create future wealth if you take on debt to finance that. Therefore, the accreditation for that work should cost less than work that has a higher associated pay structure (and in a free market, it would).

The second myth is that more education is directly correlated with the quality of the education. While an Ivy League institution is certainly regarded more highly than a midtier state school, the issue goes deeper. An engineering degree is going to likely land you a higher-paying job than an underwater-basket-weaving degree, and no differentiation is being made for that in the loan process, in the cost of the degrees from the colleges, or by the evaluation of most students and their families.

Duke University recently launched a class called "Building a Global Audience," which is known around the campus as "the TikTok class."[2] While I think it is smart to teach people the ups, downs, and business of social media and how difficult it is to make a living as an influencer (as well as to hopefully tell people you need to be influential before you can be an influencer), you can learn about that online. Duke costs around $80,000 a year for tuition, room, and board, before aid.[3]

At least the TikTok class has some useful value and isn't destructive, which is more than can be said for many classes taught at the university level.

Getting a degree has found many young people struggling to find work commensurate with the value of their degrees. Racking up advanced degrees doesn't necessarily lead to advanced pay, leaving young people heavy in MFAs and PhDs, but not the letters that matter—ROI (return on investment).

With all this in mind, there are a few things we need to look at more deeply.

One is the relative value of college earnings to the earnings of those who don't go to college at all.

Second, the exploding costs of college mean that you are paying substantially more to make more, and the college costs are increasing faster than wage gains.

Third, the immense sticker price of education is leading more young people to take on substantial debt (the average debt load for those with college loans is around $29,000 to $40,000 in the US today, depending on the source).[4] It's estimated that more than 2.5 million borrowers have more than six figures in debt.[5] This means that while an individual may earn a bit more each year, their ability to start generating wealth is hindered.

This entire scenario has become a profiteering racket and a wealth transfer from young people to colleges and universities, the cottage industry around them, and, of course, ancillary financial services companies. And it has been aided and abetted by the government.

What many college graduates end up owning is a piece of paper worth less than they expected, or, sometimes, a worthless piece of paper.

Not surprisingly, not all college degrees and the jobs attained with them are created equal. As shown in a recent study by Georgetown University, the amount that someone makes is highly correlated to their field of study, occupation, and industry, as well as other factors such as location and demographics.[6]

The New York Fed's recent study on the labor market and recent graduates shows an overall median salary mid-career of $72,000 for degree holders. Those with degrees in education and fine arts are well under that amount by mid-career, while degrees related to biochemistry, finance, and engineering are well above it.

See the labor market outcomes chart for the breakdown by major.

On the profiteering front, despite educational careers having the lowest mid-career salaries per the chart, most states require at least a bachelor's degree in order to teach at a taxpayer-funded public school (this isn't always the case for private or charter schools). Of course, the profiteers protect other profiteers.[7]

While candidates may find that a master's degree enhances their prospects of finding a job, particularly in competitive school districts, the pay isn't a lot more.[8] The director of recruiting for the Syracuse City School District told local outlet CNY Central in mid-2022 that their "newly negotiated teacher contract provides new hires who have a master's degree with a $54,400 salary, and those with a bachelor's degree $51,000."

As we look at the value of education, the New York Fed has charted unemployment rates for college graduates versus all workers, and not surprisingly, the college graduate unemployment rate tracks lower than the group as a whole.

Labor Market Outcomes of College Graduates by Major, Updated February 9, 2022

Major	Median Wage Early Career	Median Wage Mid-career	Share with Graduate Degree
Early Childhood Education	$36,000	$43,700	38.8%
Elementary Education	$39,000	$45,400	47.4%
Social Services	$35,000	$50,000	50.5%
Family and Consumer Sciences	$32,000	$51,000	33.5%
Secondary Education	$40,000	$52,000	49.6%
Special Education	$40,000	$52,000	61.8%
Theology and Religion	$36,600	$55,000	43.5%
Health Services	$40,000	$58,000	51.1%
Liberal Arts	$37,400	$60,000	30.4%
Nutrition Sciences	$44,600	$60,000	43.7%
Psychology	$37,000	$60,000	50.4%
Anthropology	$36,000	$60,000	48.8%
Fine Arts	$38,000	$60,000	22.7%
Performing Arts	$34,000	$60,000	38.5%
Sociology	$40,000	$61,000	37.7%
Leisure and Hospitality	$38,000	$63,000	32.8%
Philosophy	$44,000	$65,000	55.7%
Criminal Justice	$40,000	$65,000	22.5%
General Social Sciences	$34,000	$65,000	38.3%
Medical Technicians	$48,000	$65,000	22.4%
History	$40,000	$65,000	50.2%
Agriculture	$44,000	$66,000	21.6%
Public Policy and Law	$50,000	$66,000	43.7%
Foreign Language	$38,000	$67,000	50.9%
Journalism	$40,000	$68,000	26.2%
Mass Media	$41,500	$69,000	18.6%
Environmental Studies	$40,000	$70,000	31.5%
Ethnic Studies	$40,000	$70,000	49.5%
Biology	$40,000	$70,000	63.1%
Commercial Art &and Graphic Design	$40,000	$70,000	12.0%
Business Management	$45,000	$70,000	24.0%
Nursing	$55,000	$71,000	28.3%
Overall	$45,000	$72,000	38.2%

Major	Median Wage Early Career	Median Wage Mid-career	Share with Graduate Degree
Communications	$43,100	$74,000	23.3%
Geography	$46,000	$74,000	34.0%
Chemistry	$45,800	$75,000	64.3%
Earth Sciences	$42,000	$75,000	44.1%
General Business	$45,000	$75,000	24.7%
Accounting	$52,000	$75,000	30.3%
Advertising and Public Relations	$45,000	$78,000	20.4%
Physics	$55,000	$80,000	68.3%
Political Science	$46,000	$80,000	52.2%
Art History	$40,000	$80,000	44.2%
Marketing	$47,000	$80,000	17.6%
Architecture	$50,000	$81,000	41.0%
Information Systems &and Management	$52,000	$81,000	25.0%
International Affairs	$48,000	$82,000	45.0%
Mathematics	$53,000	$85,000	51.7%
Biochemistry	$40,000	$86,000	71.6%
General Engineering	$62,000	$90,000	37.3%
Economics	$60,000	$91,000	41.3%
Industrial Engineering	$69,000	$93,000	39.4%
Construction Services	$60,000	$94,000	9.8%
Business Analytics	$60,000	$95,000	23.5%
Finance	$60,000	$95,000	30.2%
Computer Science	$70,000	$100,000	31.8%
Civil Engineering	$63,000	$100,000	37.0%
Pharmacy	$45,000	$100,000	62.2%
Mechanical Engineering	$68,000	$104,000	40.1%
Electrical Engineering	$70,000	$107,000	47.4%
Aerospace Engineering	$70,000	$110,000	51.8%
Computer Engineering	$74,000	$110,000	41.4%
Chemical Engineering	$70,000	$111,000	49.8%

Source: Federal Reserve Bank of New York, Labor Market for Recent College Graduates, updated February 9, 2022, https://www.newyorkfed.org/research/college-labor-market/index.html#/outcomes-by-major, via US Census Bureau, American Community Survey (IPUMS); US Department of Labor, O*NET.

Unemployment Rates for College Graduates vs. Other Groups, as of July 29, 2022

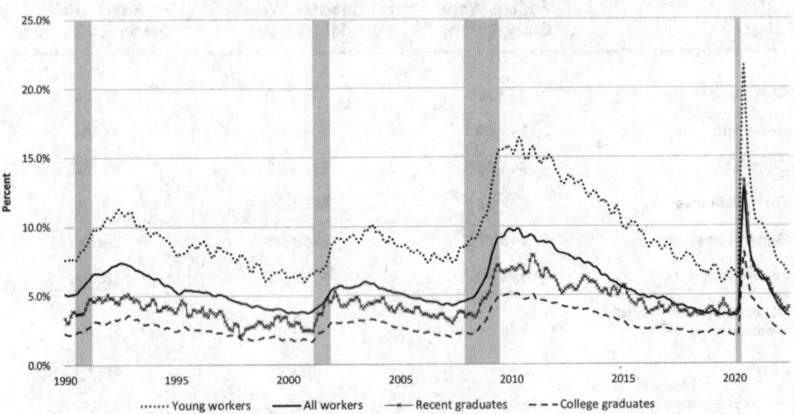

Source: Chart and Table Data for Federal Reserve Bank of New York, Labor Market for Recent College Graduates, Unemployment, as of July 29, 2022, https://www.newyorkfed.org/research/college-labor-market/index.html#/outcomes-by-major.

As we get into looking at wages, the story is more complex.

Distribution of Annual Wages for Recent College Graduates, Updated February 9, 2022

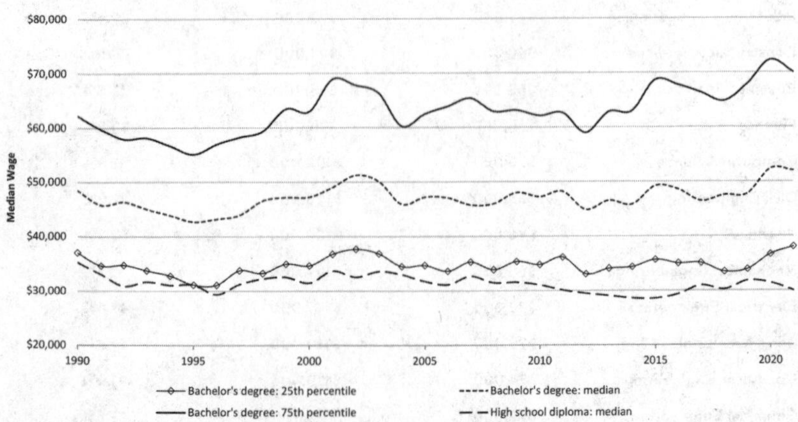

Source: Chart and Table Data for Federal Reserve Bank of New York, Labor Market for Recent College Graduates, Wages, updated February 9, 2022, https://www.newyorkfed.org/research/college-labor-market/index.html#/wages.

The distribution of wages chart shows that the best-performing college graduates are able to secure higher salaries, at the median of the data, than those without degrees. However, this is not the case for everyone. According to Federal Reserve data, roughly 16 percent of high school grads earn more than many workers with a college degree.[9]

It also shows a disparity between college graduates, some of whom may be paying the same cost for their educations.

But this is pure earnings, meaning that these are numbers unadjusted for investment. If you add in the cost of the extra debt and servicing it over time, the benefits would be shown as even less.

Also, continually adding to education doesn't always lead to an exponential boost in earnings. It is estimated that more than one in three workers with a bachelor's degree earns more money than half of workers with a master's degree.[10]

It is important to note again that data is usually presented related to the increased earnings potential from college degrees. But that doesn't equate directly to wealth. The higher earnings, adjusted for taxes, still need to pay down any debt incurred. This is money taken away from the earnings for the life of the loan. Loans also delay the ability to start investing and creating wealth. With the time value of money, this can be a significant disadvantage, especially if the disparity in earnings isn't substantial enough to get the loans paid down quickly.

According to an American Council of Trustees and Alumni report, "High levels of student loan debt have been shown to postpone major life events dramatically, with borrowers reporting delays in saving for retirement (62%), buying a home (55%), marriage (21%), and starting a family (28%)."[11]

Does an education boost your career or keep you owning nothing?

In some cases, like with the millions who are still carrying around that debt well into adulthood, it is a lifelong burden and wealth destroyer.

Economics professor Arindrajit Dube published a chart on Twitter in May 2022 with some further bad news for degree holders. He shared that the college wage premium (the gap in earnings between people with and without college degrees) was falling for the first time since the 1970s. He attributed that to an increase in wages for the lowest earners.[12]

Additionally, there is the widespread misconception that only one type of education fits everyone. As information access has been democratized through the internet, the cost of college should be going down. Becoming well educated is something anyone with discipline and a web connection can do. Also, being educated in a skill is highly valuable and often ignored. Many of the trades, like plumbing, or other skill-based jobs, like being an airline pilot, provide very attractive salaries, and at the time of this writing are experiencing significant labor shortages, as they are being overlooked in favor of attending college.

So, this good intention has gone awry, as rampant profiteering has taken hold. There are all kinds of people who benefit financially from tying up young people with debt and forcing overpriced degrees down their throats. College counselors within high schools and ones that are privately hired, as well as testing and application preparatory coaches, are all pushing their services—which are more valuable the more people there are who want to go to college.

The biggest culprit, though, is the government, which is helping funnel money to schools. They are enriching the administrators at the expense of young Americans.

Tie in the useful idiots—the ones shouting that college is a right and that it's good for society, except that many college grads aren't finding jobs and earning wages that help society any more than if they didn't attend at all—and the school system becomes overpriced at the expense of individual wealth creation.

So, while we can see how earnings potential has been impacted by college, what about college costs?

The Ever-Expanding Cost of College

Where college used to deliver a substantial ROI, the increase in college costs, particularly versus the wage growth that a degree provides, has been thrown completely out of whack. According to *Forbes*, based on Fed data, the price of college had increased at a pace almost eight times faster than wages. They said, "According to figures from the Federal Reserve Bank of St. Louis, the average annual growth in wages was only 0.3% between January 1989 and January 2016. That's right, the cost to attend a university increased nearly eight times faster than wages did. While the cost of a four-year degree exploded to $104,480, real median wages only went from $54,042 to $59,039 between 1989 and 2016."[13]

As a rule, you should never invest six figures to get a five-figure job. The returns will rarely make sense.

One would think that people would understand this and forgo that level of expense for that type of return. However, state-run schooling doesn't seem to teach basic economic and financial concepts. It's almost as if everyone is in this together, wanting you to own nothing without it being obvious.

The increase in college costs without the return is what is driving student loans to be the biggest chunk of nonhousing debt on Americans' personal balance sheets. As of Q2 2022, student loan debt was almost $1.6 trillion, credit card debt was around $900 billion, auto loans were around $1.5 trillion, and other debt was just short of $500 billion.[14]

For the 2020–21 school year, the average tuition and fees for private, nonprofit four-year schools was $37,600 for the academic year, which is more than $150,000 for a four-year degree. This is not just for the Ivy League and elite schools—it is on average! Public schools, which receive substantial state funding, were $9,400 for four-year institutions, which still means an almost $40,000 investment, before housing considerations. These costs keep increasing.[15]

The American Council of Trustees and Alumni (ACTA) put out a report in 2021 called *The Cost of Excess: Why Colleges and Universities Must Control Runaway Spending*, chronicling the out-of-control costs of higher learning. They note that the costs for in-state tuition at public universities, even with record state appropriations, have nearly tripled over the past three decades.

ACTA looked at 1,529 schools, both public and private, and found that increases in spending have correlated very little with increased graduation rates. They have also noted the expansion has been substantially on the noninstructional side: "investment in instructional staff—particularly tenured or tenure-track professors—has been overshadowed by increases in administrative staff, namely well-paid, professional employees."[16]

The mushrooming of administrative and services staff is accounting for a material increase in the cost of higher education, without delivering better outcomes for students in terms of graduation rates or postgraduation opportunities.

To better understand this analysis, note that, definitionally, "academic" is learning-related, "administration" is institutional-related, and "student services," according to the National Center for Education Statistics (NCES), is expenses for "activities whose primary purpose is to contribute to students['] emotional and physical well-being and to their intellectual, cultural, and social development outside the context of the formal instructional program." This may include diversity and inclusion, as well as more standard activities and athletics.

Take a look at the growth in spending of these categories at four-year institutions from 2010 to 2018:

Percentage Growth in Total Spending at Four-Year Public and Private Nonprofit Institutions, 2010 to 2018

	Public	Private Nonprofit
Instruction	16.0%	17.0%
Administration	19.0%	18.0%
Student Services	25.0%	32.0%

Source: American Council of Trustees and Alumni Institute for Effective Governance, "The COST of EXCESS," with Chart Data Sourced via IPEDS, August 2021, https://www.goacta.org/wp-content/uploads/2021/08/The-Cost-of-Excess-FINAL-Full-Report.pdf.

You can see that noninstructional spending growth outpaced that related to learning.

Even on the learning side, ACTA said that "[f]rom 2012 (the earliest year for which comparable staffing data are available) to 2018, colleges and universities prioritized hiring less expensive and often less-credentialed instructional staff and more expensive administrative staff. Spending drove up the price of tuition, which was also correlated with increases in net cost for students."

Their findings noted that on a percentage basis, spending on instruction was two to five-plus times as effective at improving graduation rates (depending on public versus private institution) than spending on administrative endeavors.

Yet these institutions keep spending on administrators and student services.

ACTA cites a New England Center for Investigative Reporting investigation that found that from 1987 to 2012, an average of eighty-seven administrators and professional employees were hired at postsecondary institutions every single workday.

Writer Caroline Simon in *Forbes* looked at a University of California system audit from the state from 2017, examining the snowballing of administrative expenses. She writes, "Between fiscal years 2012–13 and 2015–16, the Office of the President's administrative spending increased by 28%, or $80 million. And ten executives in the office whose salaries were analyzed by the audit made a total of $3.7 million in FY2014—$700,000 more than the combined salaries of their highest-paid state employee counterparts."[17]

Simon notes that for the 1980–81 school year, institutional and student services spending was $13 billion across all institutions (38.5 percent of spending), while instructional spending was $20.7 billion. By the 2014–15 academic year, institutional and student services spending climbed to a whopping $122.3 billion, while instructional climbed to $148 billion, making the former now 45.2 percent of spending. This is not just a blowup in the overall costs but an increase in the percentage of overall spending.[18]

With this explosion in spending, you may be curious as to whether that impacts aid. Surely the reported pricing of tuition and fees (the "sticker price") might be different than what people actually pay? ACTA found that increased sticker prices led to higher amounts paid, "suggesting that tuition discounting has not kept pace with the growth of tuition."

They further noted that even having financial aid didn't keep you from this increased cost burden. ACTA writes, "we found that a $1 increase in in-state public school tuition was associated with an $0.84 increase in net price, while a $1 increase in private school tuition was associated with a $0.42 increase in net price. In other words, increases in sticker price still represent real dollars out of the pockets of students and families."

ACTA did note that trustees at certain schools like Purdue, which has frozen tuition for ten years as of the 2022–23 school year, have tried to stop the price-gouging of students, but that the handful of groups that have stepped up are the exception to the rule.[19]

So, what, or rather who, has enabled colleges to be able to bloat their institutions at the expense of students? The answer lies at the nexus of the power and money grab, as it often does—the government.

The Government Financing Takeover

If you are familiar with my work, you may have heard me share this story before, but I do so here because it is utterly staggering and highly illustrative of the issues we are discussing. In 2019, Congresswoman Maxine Waters, who was chair of the House Financial Services Committee, which oversees the entire financial services sector, was upset about the college loan "crisis." In front of the committee, she grilled the heads of the largest banks in the country about the size and scope of student loans with which individuals all over America had been saddled.

"What are you guys doing to help us with this student loan debt? Who would like to answer first? Mr. Moynihan, big bank," she asked the CEO of Bank of America, Brian Moynihan, who replied, "We stopped making student loans in 2007 or so."

Waters asked the same of the head of Citigroup, who responded that the firm had exited the business in 2009.

Finally, Congresswoman Waters got to Jamie Dimon, the head of JPMorgan Chase, who responded more explicitly, to either end or underscore the embarrassment. He replied, "When the government took over student lending in 2010 or so, we stopped doing all student lending."

Stunningly, the head of the committee that oversees financial services did not know that the government itself had pushed the major banks out of student lending and had taken it over in large part nearly a decade prior.

The government interference with and nationalization of most of the college loan industry has produced dire consequences that have led to the wealth suppression of young people, the opposite of what getting an advanced degree should do.

First, the government's process has provided easy and available financing to young people, who have not been taught in our government-run schools how to evaluate ROI, increasing the demand for college educations. This increased demand with a relatively fixed supply of institutions has been a major driver of cost increases that have greatly outpaced inflation.

Furthermore, the government's student loan endeavors do not use any sort of underwriting standards or process for granting the loans.

There aren't more favorable terms for an A student pursuing an engineering degree with strong job prospects versus a C student pursuing an underwater-basket-weaving degree with fewer prospects.

This process of evaluating risk and pricing it appropriately is done for just about every other type of loan that one takes on, for a reason. Whether it be in impacting the principal balance or the interest rate, the expected risks and outcomes weigh into the loan that someone can take out.

Eliminating any aspects of underwriting has provided more capital to buyers that aren't truly "creditworthy," which has allowed colleges and universities to take advantage of young people, as well as to charge the same or a similar amount for accreditations with wildly different financial prospects for the student "buyer."

Also, built into every other underwriting process is consideration for the chances of full or partial default, which creates a mechanism for the allowance of bankruptcy.

The government has completely upended this process, taking away student loan bankruptcy options in most cases. Without underwriting and bankruptcy, young people are on the hook indefinitely for their debts, with almost no chance of discharge. This, again, has enabled colleges to continually increase their prices without themselves having any skin in the game or having to suffer any consequences or recourse directed back at them.

It has also allowed those firms that provide supplemental student loans to benefit from a government-induced arbitrage opportunity. These firms have little to no bankruptcy risk from the students who hold the loans, yet still charge above-market interest rates as if they do. This has created a scenario where students have been paying very high interest in an otherwise artificially low interest environment, not letting them get ahead in their paydown.

Insider did a series on "hamster wheel" student debt borrowers, those who—despite making regular payments, including some that have exceeded the original principal borrowed—can't get ahead because of interest.

One story included Daniel Tapia, who graduated in approximately 2011, an era of very low interest rates. Despite the overall environment, $60,000 of his loans were taken out privately at a 9 percent interest rate. Insider says that "his student-debt load currently stands at just under $86,000, including $22,000 owned by the government, even after making a decade's worth of monthly payments."[20]

Forty-one years old at the time of the story, Tapia told Insider, "What I don't get is if I took out a certain amount, and I paid that amount already, and I still owe more than I originally owed, it's just nuts. It's mind-boggling to me that this total amount is not going down. It's not going away."

Stories like Daniel's show the wealth transfer that these profiteers are supporting, transferring wealth-creation opportunities from an educated man who can't get ahead of the exorbitant interest on an overpriced education to the financial services provider and college, neither of which bears any meaningful risk.

This all has caused the cost of college to skyrocket, far exceeding inflation or the potential increase in wages one might get for their degree. One 2021 study showed that the cost of college had exceeded the rate of inflation by almost five times over the last fifty years.

American Enterprise Institute's Mark J. Perry, the creator and updater of the price changes chart, which has been referred to as "the chart of the century," looks back on costs over the past two decades. The areas where the government has interfered have risen substantially more quickly than overall inflation. This includes the costs related to higher education.

Perry's commentary on the chart was as follows:

> Based on last week's BLS report on CPI price data through June 2022 I've updated the chart . . . with price changes through the middle of this year. During the most recent 22.5-year period from January 2000 to June 2022, the CPI for All Items increased by 74.4% and the chart displays the relative price increases over that time period for 14 selected consumer goods and services, and for average hourly wages. Seven of those goods and services have increased more than the average inflation rate of 74.4%, led by huge increases in hospital services (+220%), college tuition (+178%), and college textbooks (+162%). . . .[21]

When it comes to profiteering off of secondary education, another issue arises around the scope of the loans. When you take out a loan

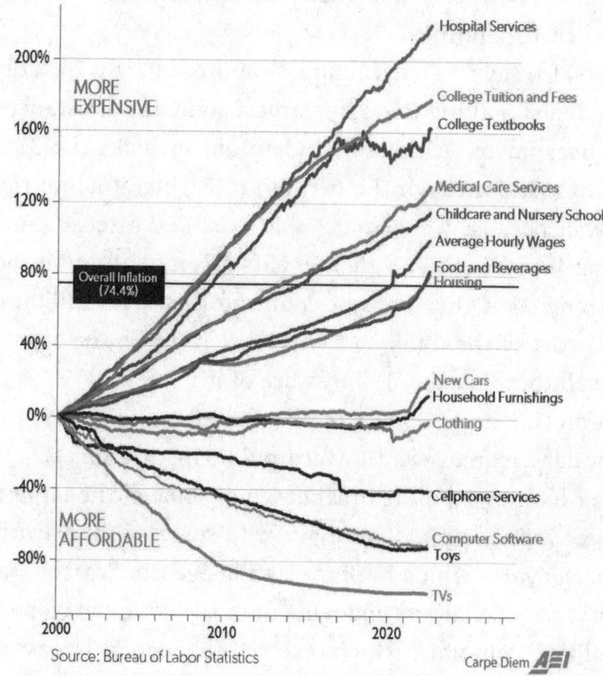

Source: Mark J. Perry, American Enterprise Institute, July 23, 2022. Reprinted with permission.

for other investments, such as a home or a business, you normally can't use that money to get your hair done, per the covenants of the loan that you sign off on. In the case of student loans, some are broad and often not strictly tied to the direct education costs; therefore, expenses like spring break trips (which, I can assure you, are an expense, not an investment) end up being financed from student loans. A survey by LendEDU in 2021 found that almost 57 percent of currently in-school borrowers that were going on spring break planned to use their student loans to help pay for the trip.[22]

A Quarter of a Trillion Dollars in Subsidies per Year

According to the Department of the Treasury's Datalab, for 2018, money from the federal government made up 14 percent of all college revenue. In dollar terms, this was $149 billion for the year, made up of $98 billion in student aid, $41 billion in organizational grants, and $10 billion in contracts.[23] For that year, it was equal to about 3.6 percent of federal spending.[24]

Datalab also says, "Loans comprise approximately 73% of the total aid to students, making them the largest source of assistance from the federal government. Although student aid includes the $11.6 billion investment made through the G.I. Bill of Rights, it is not included in this analysis because we were not able to make a direct connection between that investment and the benefits given to an institution." This sounds to me as if they are not counting this $11.6 billion in GI Bill money as part of the total, so I will leave it out in the aggregate data here as well, but you should be aware of it.[25]

Based on this data, USAFacts says that about 20 percent of federal postsecondary monies went toward public institutions.[26]

Further looking into the breakdown of some of the largest outlays, the biggest federal grants were given to some of the wealthiest universities. Harvard, which I refer to as a hedge fund masquerading as a university, has the largest endowment in the country, valued at north of $41 billion. Columbia, which received the second-largest grant, has an endowment valued at north of $11 billion.

Many individuals who have held high-level positions in government have come from prestigious positions at schools like Harvard. And after their service, many high-ranking officials end up back at Harvard in prestigious positions, including Treasury secretary Larry Summers, who was Harvard's president, and Associate Justice of the Supreme Court Stephen Breyer, who, after retiring from the court, announced he was joining the faculty at Harvard Law. I am sure that this is all purely coincidental.

In terms of federal contracts, again, several well-capitalized universities were among the biggest single contract recipients, including a nearly $1 billion contract to MIT, which has the sixth-largest endowment ($18 billion), and more than a half billion dollars to Stanford in a single contract, which has the fourth-largest endowment (around $29 billion).

On top of federal money (from your taxes), state money (from your taxes) also flows to these universities and colleges. It was reported

Top Five Largest Federal Grant Investments at Colleges/Universities in 2018

University	Grant Investments ($ in Millions)
Harvard University	$179.5
Columbia University	$165.1
Michigan State University	$119.5
Johns Hopkins University	$111.7
Oregon State University	$103.0

Source: "What do universities do with the billions they receive from the government?" USA Facts, https://usafacts.org/articles/what-do-universities-do-with-the-billions-they-receive-from-the-government/; information sourced via Datalab, Explore the Federal Investment in Your Alma Mater, https://datalab.usaspending.gov/colleges-and-universities/, via US Treasury.

Top Five Largest Federal Contract Investments at Colleges/Universities in 2018

University	Contract Investments ($ in Millions)
California Institute of Technology	$2,410.0
University of California–Berkeley	$992.2
Massachusetts Institute of Technology	$939.9
Stanford University	$565.3
Johns Hopkins University	$365.5

Source: "What do universities do with the billions they receive from the government?" USA Facts, https://usafacts.org/articles/what-do-universities-do-with-the-billions-they-receive-from-the-government/; information sourced via Datalab, Explore the Federal Investment in Your Alma Mater, https://datalab.usaspending.gov/colleges-and-universities/.

in 2022 that state financing for postsecondary schools exceeded $100 billion for the first time.

Referencing a report from the State Higher Education Executive Officers Association, Best Colleges said, "This 2022 allocation continues an upward trend in state funding over the past five years, according to the SHEEO report. State support has grown 21.4% since 2017 without counting support provided through the stimulus bills."[27]

Adding together the state and federal money, direct government cash to these universities is about a quarter of a trillion dollars (your dollars!) per year, around 25 percent of their total revenue. This doesn't include any of the cash giveaways to colleges included in the coronavirus CARES Act.

In terms of profiteering and wealth transfers, in addition to getting more wealth to the likes of professionals associated with universities and colleges, such as administrators, the subsidizing of operations has allowed many institutions to continue to grow their endowments. According to the NCES, "At the end of fiscal year 2020, the market value of the endowment funds of colleges and universities was $691 billion, which was 2 percent higher than the beginning of the fiscal year, when the total was $675 billion."[28]

You can see the breakdown of the top twenty, from Harvard to Cornell, in the table that follows.

Again, many of these institutions find themselves receiving large amounts of taxpayer money, despite their financial wherewithal.

Ithaka S+R, a consulting firm with a specialty in education, among other areas, details all the ways that government policy at the federal level enacts a "resource transfer" to colleges and universities, from loans and other direct transfers, like grants, to beneficial tax treatment at multiple levels. They write, "The tax policies that benefit endowments and subsidize higher education, including the charitable deduction for contributions to higher education and the exemption of endowment earnings from income taxation, are blunt policy tools for affecting institutional behavior."[29]

They continue, "Most public and private nonprofit higher education institutions are 501(c)(3) organizations that are exempt from taxes on income generated from their educational missions. Income from endowment assets, donated to both public and private non-profit colleges and universities to further their educational missions, has thus not been taxable. But the recently passed tax law modifies this practice for private institutions with endowments of $500,000 or more per student and at least 500 students." This large-endowment asset tax was passed under the Trump administration.[30]

However, as the taxes apply only to realized capital gains, the actual taxes paid in any given year will be smaller than estimated long-term liabilities listed in endowment reports.[31]

Top 20 Largest Endowment Funds (Degree-Granting Postsecondary Institutions), FY 2020

Rank	Institution	Endowment Market Value End of FY 2020 ($ in Thousands)
1	Harvard University	$41,894,380
2	Yale University	$31,201,686
3	University of Texas System Office	$30,522,120
4	Stanford University	$28,948,111
5	Princeton University	$25,944,283
6	Massachusetts Institute of Technology	$18,381,518
7	University of Pennsylvania	$14,877,363
8	Texas A & M University-College Station	$12,720,530
9	University of Notre Dame	$12,319,422
10	University of Michigan-Ann Arbor	$12,308,473
11	University of California-System Administration Central Office	$12,267,010
12	Columbia University in the City of New York	$11,257,021
13	Emory University	$9,169,028
14	Washington University in St. Louis	$8,489,294
15	Northwestern University	$8,484,706
16	Duke University	$8,474,071
17	University of Chicago	$7,199,521
18	University of Virginia-Main Campus	$7,146,476
19	Vanderbilt University	$6,917,371
20	Cornell University	$6,882,708
--	United States (all institutions)	$691,019,781

Source: National Center for Education Statistics, Endowments, FY 2020, https://nces.ed.gov/fastfacts/display.asp?id=73.

Colleges and universities, particularly at the elite end of the spectrum, are stockpiling cash and generating wealth, while the cost of school is causing young people to forgo wealth creation.

The Millennial-to-Colleges Wealth Transfer

The exploding cost of higher education has created an interesting phenomenon. Millennials are the highest-paid generation (at their age) but have less accumulated wealth. It is not a stretch to connect the dots between their student loan debt burden and this outcome, as well as other Fed and government policies that we have discussed.[32]

Writer and pundit Kevin Drum looked at median household incomes for the boomer, Gen X, and millennial generations at a midpoint of age forty (thirty-five to forty-four).

He says, "Millennials at age ~40 earn quite a bit more than Boomers did at age 40. This is median income adjusted for inflation, so it doesn't include zillionaires and it's real dollars."[33]

Median Household Income by Generation at Age 35–45; Inflation Adjusted

Generation	Median Household Income as Beginning of Generation Turns 40 Years Old
Baby Boomers	$70,000
Gen X	$77,000
Millennials	$85,000

Source: Kevin Drum, "Millennials Are the Highest Paid Generation in American History," September 20, 2021, https://jabberwocking.com/millennials-are-the-highest-paid-generation-in-american-history/, data from US Census Bureau.

Drum also looked at individual income to account for more women in the workforce, which also showed higher earnings for millennials.

However, as we know, in aggregate, despite being a large generation, millennials hold a lower share of wealth (percentage of overall wealth) than previous generations held at the same age. Insider reported, "When boomers were roughly the same age as millennials are now, they owned about 21% of America's wealth, compared to millennials' 5% share today, according to recent Fed data."[34]

The reality of higher debt loads and other factors we have discussed is front and center in the "you will own nothing" prediction.

As discussed, wealth is most highly concentrated in the home. But, with their current balance sheets, millennials don't expect to have that opportunity. CNN reported, "About three-quarters of Boomers and Gen Xers expect to own a home in retirement, while fewer than half of Millennials do."[35]

Looking at overall assets by generation and then real estate wealth by generation, you can see that the early boost in salaries for millennials

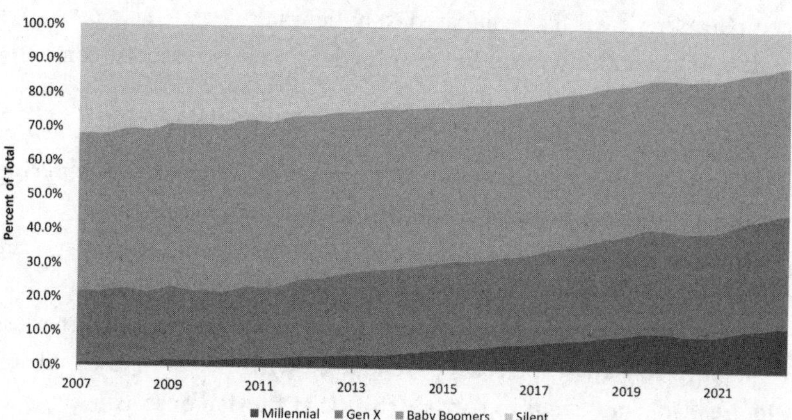

Source: Board of Governors of the Federal Reserve System, Distribution of Household Wealth in the U.S. since 1989, Q1 2007 to Q2 2022, https://www.federalreserve.gov/releases/z1/dataviz/dfa/distribute/chart/#quarter:119;series:Assets;demographic:generation;population:1,3,5,7;units:shares;range:2007.1,2022.2. The Fed notes that distributions by generation are defined by birth year as follows: Silent and Earlier=born before 1946, Baby Boomer=born 1946–1964, Gen X=born 1965–1980, and Millennial=born 1981 or later.

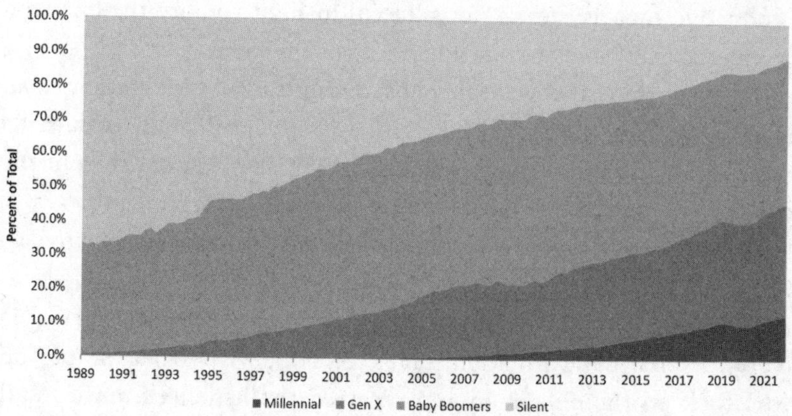

Source: Board of Governors of the Federal Reserve System, Distribution of Household Wealth in the U.S. since 1989, Q3 1989 to Q2 2022, https://www.federalreserve.gov/releases/z1/dataviz/dfa/distribute/chart/#quarter:119;series:Real%20estate;demographic:generation;population:1,3,5,7;units:shares;range;1989.3,2022.2. The Fed notes that distributions by generation are defined by birth year as follows: Silent and Earlier=born before 1946, Baby Boomer=born 1946–1964, Gen X=born 1965–1980, and Millennial=born 1981 or later.

is not translating to more wealth generation. The real estate by generation chart shows how much more quickly Gen X was able to start compounding wealth as compared to millennials.

If you are making more but owning less, that is a bad outcome.

Paying Down Debt and Free College

This transfer of wealth from young people to schools is hampering wealth-creation opportunities for millions of Americans.

That is wrong, and that needs to be fixed. However, the government's—along with the racketeers' and useful idiots'—ideas don't center on a structural change to the issue to make college less expensive and align the costs of schooling with the value they create. No, instead, they want to further shift that burden onto you.

The Biden administration and many members of Congress have been advocating for various levels of student loan forgiveness, including enacting $6 billion in relief for 200,000 students as part of settling a fraud class-action suit related to certain for-profit vocational schools and colleges, and a 2022 student debt relief plan estimated to cost taxpayers between $500 billion and $1 trillion if it survives the court system.[36]

Because the government makes these loans but does not have the productive capacity to create value, ultimately you are the one who grants the loans and the one who forgives the loans.

As discussed, the government's disruption of the student loan market, without underwriting, without any evaluation of returns on investment, and without schools having any risk or "skin in the game," has created this issue.

So, how does the government picking some group of people to have their debts "forgiven" solve anything?

Forgiving these loans unfairly shifts the burden of the costs (via more national debt, inflation, taxes, or otherwise) from the person who took on the obligation and received the benefits from it to all taxpayers. Those who passed up college altogether, those who went to a cheaper school, and those who made sacrifices to pay down their college debts or carry other types of debt burdens would be unfairly penalized by the government picking winners and losers. This ultimately means that working-class people without advanced degrees will be subsidizing the education of those with higher earnings potential.

Postsecondary student loan cancellations are a wealth transfer from the working class to the college-educated class. The debt doesn't go away. It just moves from one place to another.

That is as backward as the day is long.

Student debt jubilees do nothing to help get college costs under control and prevent that same situation from happening in the future. It doesn't put any schools on the hook for selling degrees that aren't worth their costs. It doesn't give them incentives to cut costs. Rather, knowing that the government will intervene, it gives them every incentive to further increase costs without any care for improving outcomes for their students.

As I quoted from Charlie Munger earlier, show me the incentive, and I will show you the outcome.

Selective debt forgiveness gives the government power to pick more winners and losers and ultimately buy more votes.

The colleges win. The wealthy and high earners win or come closer to breaking even. You lose.

Nothing regarding the college cost burden will change until we get the government out of the school lending arena—one that they had no business being in to begin with. Loans should be made through a market-based underwriting process, and with that, the ability of individuals to discharge their student loans through bankruptcy courts should be available to all debt holders.

Students who are taking out loans should be shown, at every step of the process, what their expected return on their investment is, based on their major, school, and other factors, and they should be required to sign off on that as part of the process.

Colleges need to either be part of the underwriting process and hold a piece of the loan or be allowed to be sued if graduates aren't able to use their degrees to better their professional outcomes.

In the meantime, given the cheap debt that has been given to the government and corporations alike for more than a decade, students who do not have the ability today to go through bankruptcy should either be given that option or the rate on their interest paid should be recalculated to an appropriate market rate, and interest paid above that over the past five years should be allowed to be applied to reduce their principal balances.

Or let students sue the schools that price-gouged them.

We are already giving the schools a quarter of a trillion dollars' worth of taxpayer money at the state and local levels each year directly, on top of all other types of benefits and incentives that prop up their profiteering schemes. The least they could do is make the degrees they are selling worthwhile.

Ask yourself, if the government wanted to keep young people from economic prosperity for their lives, would they do anything differently than what they are doing now?

Would this keep them dependent upon the government? Would this make them vote for more government that could "relieve them" of the burdens (those same burdens that were truly created by the government to begin with)?

Profiteering has created a real wealth transfer that benefits the connected and not the average American. Getting more education, in the ultimate ironic twist, may be a predictor of you owning nothing.

CHAPTER 10

THE UPCOMING WEALTH HEIST

The Government's Plan for the Biggest Wealth Transfer in History

We hang the petty thieves and appoint
the great ones to public office.
—Aesop

The transfer of wealth by force is a prominent theme in ensuring you will own nothing, and we have no shortage of those wealth transfers with which to contend. However, there is about to be a historic, free-choice transfer of wealth in the US, assuming that the government doesn't get there first.

Financial consultants Cerulli Associates, who track wealth trends, estimate that within the next twenty-three years there will be a total of $84.4 trillion in wealth transferred.[1] Of that, just more than $11 trillion is set to go to philanthropic endeavors (that's more than the yearly GDP of every country other than the US and China), and a historic $70 trillion is set to be transferred to heirs.[2] I estimate, based on Cerulli Associates' data, that this equates to around 65 percent of the wealth in the hands of individuals in the US set to turn over in the next two and a half decades.

More than a quarter of all wealth in the US (27 percent) is currently estimated to be held by Americans who are, as of the end of Q1 2021, age seventy and older.[3] This, at the time of estimation, was about 157 percent of the US GDP, "more than double the proportion 30 years ago, federal data show," according to the *Wall Street Journal*.

Estimated Wealth Transfers, 2021 to 2045; Dollars in Billions

Year	Estimated Transfer ($ in Billions)
2021–2025	$9,740
2026–2030	$12,411
2031–2035	$16,415
2036–2040	$20,800
2041–2045	$25,056

Source: Cerulli Associates, Cerulli Report, 2021, https://s3.us-east-1.amazonaws.com/cerulli-website-assets/documents/Info-Packs/2021/Cerulli-US-High-Net-Worth-and-Ultra-High-Net-Worth-Markets-2021-Information-Packet.pdf.

This is a ton of wealth that has been earned. Those who have earned it deserve to decide what happens to it. If it ends up in the hands of their designated beneficiaries, it could meaningfully help thwart the efforts to strip ownership and wealth from the average Americans. These beneficiaries will include millennial and Gen X recipients and, to a smaller extent, Gen Z.

Even today, before this epic transfer begins in earnest, inheritances are meaningful for the average American.

A 2019 report by Insider referenced a study that showed the median inheritance size had already moved up by almost 3.7 times over the last three decades, from $15,000 to $55,000. In terms of beneficiaries, Insider said, "They're more middle class than you might imagine. The data show they earn about $69,000 annually—though about 25% earn less than $35,000 a year—have no college degree, and have just $25,000 in retirement savings."[4]

These estimates for inheritances (to date) don't include gifts made prior to someone passing on.

Not only are median inheritances increasing, but averages are as well. The *Wall Street Journal* article reported, "The average inheritance in 2019 was $212,854, up 45% from an inflation-adjusted $146,844 in 1998, according to an analysis of Fed data by economists at a unit of Capital One Financial Corp."[5]

This voluntary, historic financial transfer is an opportunity for the wealth and ownership the older generations have generated to stay with their chosen family members and other beneficiaries. It's an opportunity for you to own something.

It's not just cash, stocks, and bonds at stake but also tangible and intellectual property, including homes, businesses, farms, and land. The Family Owned Business Institute at Grand Valley State University in Michigan estimates that there were approximately 5.5 million family businesses in the US as of 2020.[6] And a 2021 study by PwC found that 67 percent of North American family businesses surveyed "already have next-gen[eration] family members working in the business and anticipate they will become majority shareholders within five years."[7]

This generational wealth transfer can give younger people, who, as we have discussed, are being put on a path to owning nothing, a glimmer of hope for acquiring and building some wealth.

However, the government sees big pools of dollars that represent an opportunity to buy them more power and bail them out of their debt debacle. Using your money to shore up government obligations or make new promises, the coming turnover of wealth will likely turn into a historic cash grab by the government.

You may think it is just the billionaires' dollars that government is after, but billionaires' wealth is a fraction of what's out there (and not nearly enough to make a dent in government spending). Take the top eleven wealthiest individuals in the US as of July 19, 2022 (these eleven were, at that date, among the top seventeen wealthiest people in the world). Their collective estimated wealth at this date, which largely includes their stakes in the value of companies that they have founded and/or grown, was about $1.2 trillion.

While this is undoubtedly a lot of wealth concentrated in a small number of people, it is a fraction of the $84.4 trillion at stake.

Also, even if these assets were confiscated at 100 percent of their value (which couldn't be done without value leakage and is unconstitutional, but play along for the example), it would only be enough to fund the government for less than two and a half months, based on the FY 2022 budget. And then there would be nothing to tax from these folks in the future.[8]

It's not a stretch to conclude that it's the other $83.2 trillion that is set to turn over that would substantially help the government out.

Wealthiest Individuals in the United States; Worldwide Rank by Net Worth; July 19, 2022

Worldwide Rank	Name	Estimated Net Worth	Industry
1	Elon Musk	$223 B	Tech
2	Jeff Bezos	$142 B	Tech
4	Bill Gates	$115 B	Tech
6	Larry Page	$103 B	Tech
7	Sergey Brin	$99 B	Tech
8	Warren Buffett	$99 B	Diversified
9	Steve Ballmer	$92 B	Tech
10	Larry Ellison	$89 B	Tech
15	Charles Koch	$69 B	Industrial
16	Julia Flesher Koch and family	$69 B	Industrial
17	Mark Zuckerberg	$65 B	Tech

Source: Bloomberg Billionaire Index, July 19, 2022, https://www.bloomberg.com/billionaires/?sref=hmG4mtJl.

The Great Underfunding of Liabilities

Under the new financial world order, the government will seek to get its hands on as much of that money as possible. The less wealth you have, the less power you have. The more they take to expand government programs and "promises," the more you are dependent upon the government. You own nothing, and they own you by promising you morsels from the money they took from you. They also use your money to provide for others and, in doing so, "own" them, too.

Layer on top of that the government's current fiscal situation and the need becomes urgent. They need to keep their scheme afloat, which means more money for overall spending, including the giant middlemen transfers of Social Security and Medicare at the federal level and pensions at the state level.

That money has to come from somewhere. The government doesn't produce anything productive, so they must take it directly from you, reduce benefits (which is politically unpopular and often impacts their power grab), or finance it on your behalf (which leads to your existing dollars being worth less and you keeping less of what you earn in the future). It's moving a dollar bill from your left pocket to the right pocket and telling you they gave you a dollar. Or really, the government takes $1.25 from your left pocket, pisses away a dollar (or finds a way to launder it back to their cronies), drops $0.25 in your right pocket, and tries to make you believe that they gave you a quarter.

Uncle Scam

One of the biggest issues at the state and federal levels is unfunded liabilities. Defined benefit plans are a mechanism to transfer wealth with the government as the middleman. Politicians make promises that you will get some payoff in the future based on calculations that are usually aggressive and often complete fantasies. This buys them power today and kicks the can of dealing with the result to some point in the future. It also abets their profiteering cronies in extracting fees.

Social Security, Medicare, and state pensions, as well as some union pensions that the government also helps guarantee, are all set up in this way and, unsurprisingly, have tens of trillions of dollars worth of unfunded liabilities that need to be dealt with (federal government liabilities are estimated at around $129.1 trillion by Truth in Accounting's 2021 Financial State of the Union report).[9]

United States Government Estimated Liabilities Breakdown

Medicare Benefits	$55.1 trillion
Social Security Obligations	$41.2 trillion
Publicly Held Debt	$21.1 trillion
Military and Civilian Retirement Benefits	$9.4 trillion
Other Liabilities	$2.3 trillion

Source: Truth in Accounting, Financial State of the Union, 2021, https://www.truthinaccounting.org/library/doclib/Financial-State-of-the-Union-2020.pdf.

The government needs some way to pay for these promises, and, as noted above, it's just moving Americans' wealth from one place to another.

Now, some people have taken offense at Social Security being labeled a Ponzi scheme, but if it isn't one, it's a first cousin.

The Social Security Trust Fund is "funded" primarily by payroll taxes, paid by both an employee and their employer, or an entrepreneur in full (doubled) if self-employed. It also receives tax revenue from those who pay taxes on benefits received and "interest" on the "reserves" of the trust fund (discussed below) from the US Treasury.

Social Security is a prime example of promised benefits without ownership. In a typical retirement account, you contribute money at your discretion, which is invested in your own account. Your contributions accumulate, and any net gains (interest, dividends, asset appreciation, etc.) grow; you own the full amount in the account when you are ready to redeem the funds.

However, the way the money flows through Social Security and its entire structure is a head-scratcher. While you contribute your earnings, you are not left with a tangible asset that you can pass on to loved ones when you die, should value remain (although, if you are married or have dependents, your survivors may qualify for benefits).

The short explanation of how Social Security works is that you and your employer contribute into a "fund," and you expect to receive some fixed monthly benefit, set by the government, when you retire in the future or should you become disabled. According to the Social Security Administration, for 2021, around 65 million Americans received more than $1 trillion in Social Security benefits. Disabled workers and their dependents account for 13.1 percent of total benefits paid, retired workers and their dependents account for 75.2 percent of total benefits paid, and survivors of the deceased about 11.7 percent of total benefits.[10]

The longer explanation is that, as a worker, you pay money that goes into the "trust fund," but only on "paper" via a bookkeeping entry (alongside the other "revenue," aka funding, described above). That money paid in is immediately used by the US Treasury to pay out any benefits owed to current Social Security beneficiaries. When the amount of money taken in exceeded the amount paid out, as it had in the past, that difference would be "invested" into special-issue US Treasury securities. As explained by David John, formerly of the Heritage Foundation, these special types of Treasury bonds can only be issued to and redeemed by Social Security (that means they are not the type of securities that can be traded in the market).[11]

As also noted in that piece, the Office of Management and Budget under the Clinton administration in 1999 explained the fund flows as, "These [trust fund] balances are available to finance future benefit payments and other trust fund expenditures—but only in a bookkeeping sense. These funds are not set up to be pension funds, like the funds of private pension plans. They do not consist of real economic assets that can be drawn down in the future to fund benefits. Instead, they are claims on the Treasury that, when redeemed, will have to be financed by raising taxes, borrowing from the public, or reducing benefits or other expenditures."

In plain language, the Treasury issues these special securities (which are basically an IOU), puts them into the trust fund via an accounting entry, and the money is used to finance the overall government expenditures.[12]

This is where the gaslighting often occurs, as many news sources will tell you the money is a safe investment in these bonds. However, these bonds aren't like investing in a company. The money isn't being used as an investment to produce a return; the government is spending it. So, it is not like lending money to a company or some other investment where you own a piece of something productive, as these special bonds are only backed by the word of the government. Plus, the interest the Treasury pays isn't derived from a projected return on the bond from an investment; it's made up, too, and it has to be financed by either the money taken in from workers, other taxes, or debt.

All of these mechanisms keep you from the benefits of ownership and keep the government large and powerful.

John C. Goodman, president of the Goodman Institute for Public Policy Research, said in *Forbes* that one cannot "deny, ignore or try to minimize the fact that we have promised future retirees far more than any revenues we expect to collect."

Here's a simpler way to understand this. If everyone decided not to work for one year (which seemed impossible before Covid mandates, but here we are), you wouldn't have all the assets of previous investors sitting in the trust fund to use to pay out, nor would you have bonds or other investments attached to a company that could be liquidated for value or anything else. The lack of money coming in would leave the government without money for the year to pay out. The government would need to either raise taxes or issue more debt to third parties to pay benefits that year. This is why Social Security is considered a shell game or Ponzi-ish scheme.

Hopefully, we won't reach a point where nobody is working (such as in a complete government lockdown scenario). But, as you typically see in pay-in versus pay-out scenarios, with demographic changes bringing on baby boomer recipients more rapidly, Social Security will have more benefits due than the money paid in can cover, which means that the "trust" has a shortfall—an ironic name for sure. This shortfall was projected by Social Security in June 2022 to begin that same year (in 2022). As the system is designed to expect the pay-in to cover the money going out, that means eventually either benefits would need to be cut (which is not politically popular), taxes would need to be raised, and/or debt would need to be issued (which means more interest payments in the government budget, more taxes, and/or more total debt burden, as well as likely printing more money and devaluing the real value of what is paid out).[13]

You may not be bothered by that fix but think of it this way—it is the opposite of the wealth transfer we discussed at the beginning of the chapter. More taxes or debt to finance this flawed system leads to burdening the younger generations to pay for the older generations. It sucks up wealth in an opaque manner. Given the current generational wealth distribution, nobody should be looking to create additional wealth transfers from the younger generations to the older ones.[14]

On top of all of the other arguments that we have discussed, the fact that the government designed the Social Security program to this end and has never fixed it should be illustration enough of why you do not want the government involved in any new or expanded programs of any sort. You don't own your Social Security funds, and the government wants to take more of your wealth to increase their flawed system as the middleman.

According to the Congressional Research Service, over its eighty-seven-year history, Social Security has collected $25.2 trillion and paid out $22.3 trillion, leaving trust fund asset reserves of around $2.9 trillion at the end of 2021.[15]

Trustee projections, according to the Congressional Research Service, show that Social Security will be unable to pay scheduled benefits "in full and on time" starting in 2035.[16]

What Ails Medicare

Medicare, as it stands today, is also at risk regarding its "trust fund status." This table from the Treasury's 2021 Financial Report of the United States Government shows that within a few years Medicare will start having shortfalls that worsen over the next couple of decades.[17]

Trust Fund Status

Fund	Projected Depletion	Projected Post-Depletion Trend
Medicare Hospital Insurance	2026	Trust fund income is projected to cover 91% of benefits in 2026, 78% in 2045, and 91% by 2095
Combined Old-Age Survivors and Disability Insurance	2034	Trust fund income is projected to cover 78% of benefits in 2034 and 74% by 2095

Source: Financial Report of the United States Government, Fiscal Year 2021, Table 1, https://fiscal.treasury.gov/reports-statements/financial-report/current-report.html.

With all of their obligations, as well as their desire to keep expanding government, the 2021 Financial Report of the United States Government shows how completely unsustainable the current government financial trajectory is without some additional changes. Their commentary regarding the debt projections chart, related not to total debt (which would include intragovernmental debt) but solely the debt held by the public, says, "The debt-to-GDP ratio was about 100 percent at the end of FY 2021. Under current policy and based on this report's assumptions, it is projected to reach 701 percent by 2096. The projected continuous rise of the debt-to-GDP ratio indicates that current policy is unsustainable."[18]

You think?

Additionally, the cost of delaying fiscal reform table shows that not addressing this issue will have a meaningful impact on the GDP. These numbers are likely not illustrating a worst-case or even realistic scenario, based on the history of such government projections.

Historical and Current Policy Projections for Debt Held by the Public, 1980 to 2096

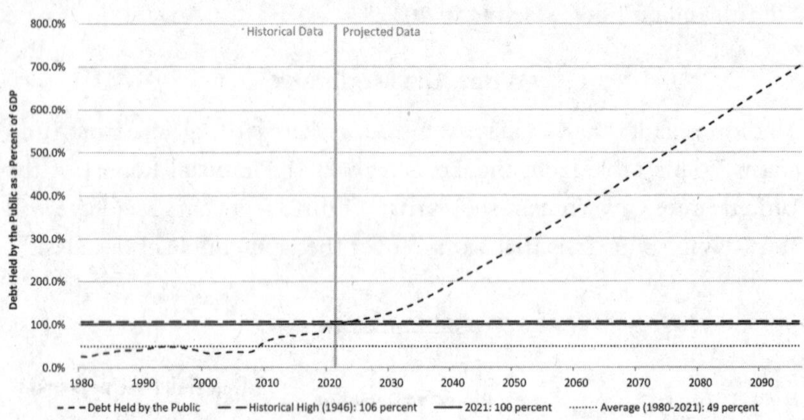

Source: Executive Summary to the Fiscal Year 2021 Financial Report of U.S. Government, Chart 7, https://www.fiscal.treasury.gov/reports-statements/financial-report/unsustainable-fiscal-path.html#chartdiv7es.

Cost of Delaying Fiscal Reform

Period of Delay	Change in Average Primary Surplus
Reform in 2022 (No Delay)	6.2% of GDP between 2022 and 2096
Reform in 2032 (Ten-Year Delay)	7.3% of GDP between 2032 and 2096
Reform in 2042 (Twenty-Year Delay)	9.0% of GDP between 2042 and 2096

Source: Financial Report of the United States Government, Fiscal Year 2021, Page 11, Table 2, https://fiscal.treasury.gov/files/reports-statements/financial-report/2021/fr-02-17-2022-(final).pdf.

They note, "The longer policy action to close the fiscal gap is delayed, the larger the post-reform primary surpluses must be to achieve the target debt-to-GDP ratio at the end of the 75-year period. Future generations are harmed by a policy delay because the higher the primary surpluses are during their lifetimes, the greater is the difference between the taxes they pay and the programmatic spending from which they benefit."[19]

The Pension Mess

On top of federal government obligations, state pension funds are also substantially underfunded. The number is very difficult to nail down, but the American Legislative Exchange Council's (ALEC) 2021 study pegged that liability at more than $8.2 trillion.[20]

Weakness in the markets after being artificially propped up by the Fed added to their woes. As CNN reported in July 2022, "The 100 largest public pension funds in the United States had been funded at just 78.6% of their total obligations at the close of the second quarter, down from 85.5% at the end of 2021 according to analysis by Milliman, an actuarial and consulting firm."[21]

CNN also noted, "Public pensions are borrowing increasing sums to meet their payout obligations," which seems like a really bad idea and the foundation for a future bailout (and is borderline gambling). This included some of the largest pension funds in the nation, including the California Public Employees' Retirement System (CalPERS), as well as the Teacher Retirement System of Texas, the country's fifth-largest public pension fund according to CNN, which they report have been using leverage funds since 2019.

Gambling and taking additional risks are among the only things keeping pensions from imploding, an unwise and unsustainable strategy. This was illustrated across the pond in October 2022 with a UK pension fund crisis, where pensions faced margin calls from the declining value of what they thought were "safe" assets to leverage—government bonds.[22]

The other thing helping some pension funds was President Biden. That is—union pension funds. Some unions, which are supposed to provide better outcomes for the individuals they represent, apparently are about as good as the government when it comes to making promises they can't fulfill. As a result, certain unions are costing you twice: union labor adds costs for the goods and services you buy, and then you also have to bail out their pensions.

As part of the American Rescue Plan passed in March 2021, and with further changes made into and during 2022, President Biden signed into law the Butch Lewis Emergency Pension Plan Relief Act, which helped to bail out what is called "multiemployer pensions." The Pension Benefit Guaranty Corporation (PBGC), a government agency tasked with backstopping pensions, says, "A multiemployer plan is a collectively bargained plan maintained by more than one employer, usually within the same or related industries, and a labor union."

Many union pension plans across the nation are also massively underfunded by billions of dollars. With this bailout, the PBGC had provided "$6.7 billion in Special Financial Assistance" by mid-July 2022 and, at that time, was reviewing applications for another $36.9 billion.[23] The full amount of this taxpayer-funded union pension bailout is estimated to be $74 billion to $91 billion.[24] Worse, no material structural overhauls were made as part of this taxpayer-funded bailout, which means there is a likelihood of more funds being asked for in the future.

Adding insult to injury, this was ongoing, all while the markets were having a historically bad first half of the year. For the first half of 2022, $8.5 trillion in value was wiped from the S&P 500, and an estimated $3.4 trillion in value was lost in retirement funds.[25] Average Americans found their retirement funds down, yet still had to bail out the union funds—another government-enabled wealth transfer.

Almost everything that the government and its cronies touch is underfunded and a future liability. They know this, and it is driving much of the new financial world order behaviors.

These liabilities give the government a big incentive to ensure that you own nothing by getting in between you and your wealth and future inheritances.

The Epic Cash Grab

Given that there is all this cash that the government is salivating over for its needs and wants, what's the plan to shift it from a voluntary wealth transfer (from those who earned it to their families and other beneficiaries) to a forced wealth transfer (to the government)?

The mechanisms rely on wealth taxes and inheritance taxes.

A wealth tax is a ridiculously bad idea. It's an idea so bad that nine European countries have abandoned it. You may want to import cheese, wine, or fashion from Europe, but economic ideas aren't something you want to import from there, particularly economic ideas too progressive for those economically socialist-leaning countries.[26]

Given that these types of taxes are such a bad idea, naturally the Biden administration has been pushing them hard.

Biden's secretary of the Treasury, Janet Yellen (yes, the same Janet Yellen who bungled raising interest rates as Fed chair and couldn't see inflation coming when it was right in front of her), has spent a lot of time trying to sell the "wealth tax that's not really a wealth tax, except that it is" proposal.

In late October 2021, Yellen went on CNN's *State of the Union* program to talk about a proposal that would be a tax on unrealized capital gains of "liquid assets held by extremely wealthy individuals—billionaires . . . I wouldn't call that a wealth tax," Yellen said, but rather a means to "get at capital gains that are an extraordinarily large part of the incomes of the wealthiest individuals and often escape taxation until they are realized and often they're unrealized. . . ."[27]

This complete word salad might be dismissed as the rantings of a crazy person, and the latter notwithstanding, it contains some very dangerous conflations and ideas.

Let's first be clear that "unrealized capital gains" is a theory, not a reality, and it is definitely not income. It is not something to be normalized because it's meaningless in the real world, particularly in that which relates to taxes. We should call it for what they are proposing by it: the unlawful seizure of personal property.

Income taxes are paid on income. You have to actually have income to be taxed on it by the federal government. While it's a deeply flawed system, it is less flawed than trying to tie taxation to wealth.

Unrealized capital gains is the theoretical positive difference at any point in time between what you paid for something (or the cost basis given to it) and what it is estimated to be valued at in the market at that time. I note the positive difference because when you take a risk, the value of an asset can also go down, which would be a theoretical loss up until the time you sell it. But, of course, they never talk about giving you benefits on theoretical losses, only taking theoretical gains.

Because you do not lock in a gain (or loss) until an asset is disposed of, you do not have any income on a given investment until that time. The price could go up and down over time, and you may not be able to find a buyer at a suitable price.

Also, if people who owned large parts of companies, such as company founders, were forced to sell some of their stakes, it would put downward pressure on the stock's overall market price (including from more supply of stock in the market). They would unlikely realize the "estimated" price from such a sale. Plus, the value of all the other shareholders' stock would also decrease.

This would also jeopardize the founder's ownership stake in the business and how the company is ultimately run.

Yellen's intentional conflation of wealth and income is meant to get people to abandon the principle of property rights. Once you cede the principle and believe that the billionaires don't have full property rights, you are saying that the guy with $30,000 doesn't, either.

It's incredibly naïve to think that "they are only going after the billionaire/wealthy" crowd. The government consistently enables wealth transfers to the wealthy and you think that's going to change? Who has the money and connections to support lobbying and their reelection?

Do you think *that's* who they are going after?

"We are going after billionaires" is a trick they use to get you to give up your principles so they can come after you.

The Biden administration isn't seeking to hire eighty-seven thousand new IRS staffers because of "billionaires." They aren't going after the wealthy; they are creating barriers for you.

As we know, even if they took the billionaires' wealth, it wouldn't put a dent in their needs.

Plus, if they did go after the wealthiest individuals, we would have a mass exodus from the country, which would be a substantial hit to tax revenue overall, given that the top 1 percent paid 38.8 percent of 2019 federal income taxes, more than the bottom 90 percent combined, as well as a drag on future productivity and growth.[28] Or the mass selling would force changes in ownership of companies and would upend the stock market, effectively kill ownership opportunities for everyone, and tank the entire financial system.

So, who do you think will end up with loopholes to exploit, and who do you think will end up owning nothing?

It will be sold as going after the wealthy, but what the government truly wants is that $84.4 trillion estimated to turn over, plus the trillions more that are in homes, 401(k)s, IRAs, and other investments. That is the real prize.

Any sort of wealth or capital gains tax has significant implications for individuals. If your stock portfolio is doing well one year, they just may force you to sell your stocks to cover this pretend, theoretical "gain." Or, imagine you bought a house for $300,000. Now, thirty years later, Zillow estimates it is worth $2 million. You could owe taxes on the theoretical $1.7 million difference in value. If you don't have cash available to pay for that—which most likely you won't, because, as we discussed, the largest portion of people's wealth is tied up in their homes—you would have to sell your house to cover that tax bill. Imagine this scenario across every asset class, including family businesses and farms, retirement accounts, or even a painting on your wall.

Think of the farmers we discussed who are "asset rich and cash poor" having to sell their land and rent it back just to operate. Even more of that would happen, leaving only the richest—maybe even eventually the government—as the buyers.

Ultimately, this is why many European nations bid adieu to their attempts at wealth and similar taxes. NPR said of this exit, "it was expensive to administer, it was hard on people with lots of assets but little cash, it distorted saving and investment decisions, it pushed the rich and their money out of the taxing countries—and, perhaps worst of all, it didn't raise much revenue."[29]

Despite that, taxing wealth and property in whatever form remains a temptation for heavily indebted governments and is not likely to go away.

They want to get their hands on this wealth as early as possible, but if that doesn't work, changes to the inheritance tax are another way that government can get their hands on this epic amount of wealth set to be transferred.

The *Wall Street Journal* in 2021 wrote:

> The pending wealth transfers have caught the attention of the Biden administration, which recently proposed reducing a $40 billion annual tax break that has been the cornerstone of estate planning for generations of Americans. Today, people who inherit assets that have risen in value, such as stock held outside retirement accounts, a family home or a three-generation manufacturing company, don't pay capital-gains taxes unless they sell. If they sell, they can exclude gains that occurred during

> the prior owner's lifetime. Under the Biden proposal, the owner's unrealized gains would become taxable in the year of his or her death, although each person would receive a $1 million exemption, plus $250,000 more for residences. The proposal would also raise the top long-term capital gains tax rate from 23.8% to 43.4%.[30]

The *Journal* also noted the impact on family-owned businesses as a sticking point, saying, "Some lawmakers say the changes could force families to sell farms and other businesses to pay the tax bill."[31]

There is wealth to be had, there are government liabilities that need to be addressed, and your ownership opportunities are standing in the way of the latter. It's a make-or-break situation that needs to be monitored and then acted upon very carefully.

It makes you wonder how long the government has been eyeballing boomers' wealth as they have spent like drunken sailors.

It is also worth considering how social credit and CBDCs, along with existing tax policy, could be used as a mechanism for this potential wealth heist.

Between the quest for grabbing your money and the continued debasement of the currency, if you are able to pass on or inherit any money at all, you will then have to worry about what it's worth. The financial war is coming for your wealth from every angle.

CHAPTER 11

OWN EVERYTHING

The Battle to Take Back Your Wealth

> You only have power over people so long as you don't take everything away from them. But when you've robbed a man of everything he's no longer in your power—he's free again.
>
> Aleksandr Solzhenitsyn

You may be demoralized at this point in the reading, but I don't want you to be. I want you to be fired up. I want you to own everything possible, fight back against the infringements on property rights, and build wealth that helps keep economic freedom and the American Dream in place.

You will need more intention in your way of living. This includes actions you can take as an individual, as well as actions you can take as part of a community.

I will share some of my and other experts' best tips regarding the areas we have spoken about. Hopefully, armed with the information I have shared thus far, and some of your own ideas, you will take action.

In areas where new ideas and possibly even rules or regulations need to be implemented, we have to balance the benefits of scale in terms of cost, access, innovation, and other factors with the costs of centralization and consolidation power that also come with scale. Thoughtful approaches are imperative, as we have explored how good ideas can often lead to bad outcomes.

Please note that these are general suggestions for you to explore and research. Any financial advice needs to be individually tailored to you and account for your objectives, current portfolio, risk tolerance, and more. Please consider speaking with a financial advisor to craft a long-term plan tailored for you.

Beef Up Your Balance Sheet

I am a big advocate for doing the opposite of what the lunatics and bad actors are telling you to do. I am also an advocate of "following the money"—learning about and replicating what those in charge do (instead of what they say).

None of the people predicting a lack of ownership by 2030 are giving up their property in their lifetimes. We have seen the wealthiest people accumulate more land, for example. That gives you a signal about land as an investment.

You are going to have to be more disciplined around money and finance. Money isn't everything; you need to balance your life with family, health, and other endeavors. However, a favorite saying I've heard is that while money doesn't buy happiness, it is more comfortable to cry in a Mercedes than on a bicycle. It is also more comfortable to cry on a bicycle than in a cardboard box on the streets. So, you need to actively fight back against the popularization of non-ownership.

Of course, the first step is making sure you are free and clear of any nonproductive debt—the debt used for expenses (versus the debt used to boost your investment returns). Do whatever you can to increase your income and cash flow and decrease your expenses so you can eliminate all your debts.

Doing this requires knowing the difference between expenses and investments. Lean away from expenses as much as possible and lean into investments.

Once you have done that, create a well-diversified investment portfolio that includes more tangible assets. Focus particularly on productive assets that can retain or increase their value, and take a long-term view of asset accumulation and appreciation.

In terms of housing and land, I will discuss that in more detail below.

Regarding business ownership, there are a few ways to approach it as a means of accumulating wealth.

One way to own part of productive companies is via the stock market and buying stock in publicly traded businesses.

If your employer offers a 401(k) match, max that out; that is extra income you can get from your employer, and it is tax deferred.

In terms of overall investments, if you aren't going to do the work to evaluate individual stocks or don't understand them well enough to analyze their metrics, typically owning a diversified set of indices, like the S&P 500, can make sense for a portfolio. If you are going to put in the work to look at individual stock ideas, I always recommend companies with strong balance sheets and big "moats" around their businesses (aka strong competitive advantages).

If things go badly, think about the kinds of companies that are critical and that we can't live without. Those businesses will still have value and may be worthy as investments for your portfolio.

The same diversification approach should be taken with regard to any allocation of funds in bonds or other debt instruments.

Also, look to where the wealthy and well-connected people are investing and advocating. If they feel comfortable in certain arenas and are going to manipulate capital allocation and laws to favor certain companies, pay attention to that. If you can't lick 'em right now, join 'em until you can.

Given the broader trends for the future that we have discussed, make sure to talk to your investment advisor about the appropriate equity position for your portfolio. Suggested allocations may be different today than what was recommended for you in the past.

If you meet the criteria of being an "accredited investor" and can forgo some liquidity, you may want to look into private traditional and alternative investments. At the time of writing, the SEC considered individuals accredited investors if they (including a spouse or partner) had a net worth that exceeded $1 million, excluding their primary residence, or income exceeding $200,000 (individually) or $300,000 (with spouse or partner) for the last two years and expected for the current year.[1]

Looking at private investments can be effective in certain areas. For example, currently, private companies aren't being forced to comply with ESG in the same way that public companies are, and you may find some solid opportunities. Just make sure they aren't in imminent danger of being regulated out of existence and that you understand the fee structures and liquidity constraints that come with private investments.

Get Hedged

You may have concerns related to the dollar's reserve currency status and devaluation and the implications for stocks and equity. That is why you should have a well-diversified portfolio that includes hedges.

In layman's terms, the concept of a hedge is one or more investments positioned to offset the other investments in a portfolio. These are investments expected to go up or remain constant, or at least lose less value, when others in the portfolio go down for various reasons.

Some people think of hedges as insurance policies against the growth areas of their portfolios. I like to say they are positioned on the "FOLM" side of your portfolio versus the "FOMO" side; they are meant for those with the "fear of losing money" to provide stability versus the "fear of missing out" on the high-flying, growth-oriented, and/or more speculative assets and investments. Hedging helps you to protect and preserve your wealth.

Given what we have discussed in this book, hedges are important, and gold and other precious metals should be evaluated as a potential part of your diversified portfolio.

Gold has had an enormously long social contract backing its value. Its value has endured, according to researchers, for at least five thousand years. That's a substantial track record through all kinds of financial cycles. While the past never guarantees the future, it's a compelling data point.

Moreover, we know that several central banks have been shedding dollars and replacing them with gold. If there is a financial reset or collapse, it is possible (though, again, not guaranteed) that gold will play a role in a new global monetary system.[2]

Jim Rickards, the previously discussed economist, author, and financial expert, also suggests holding gold to protect your wealth against the debasement of the dollar (and other currencies). Rickards shared that during an interview at Harvard's Kennedy School of Government, where then-European Central Bank chair Mario Draghi (pre–his prime minister of Italy days) was asked about gold as a reserve asset, Draghi said he never sold an ounce. Draghi's comments included, "Well, you're also asking this to the former governor of the Bank of Italy, and the Bank of Italy is the fourth-largest owner of gold reserves in the world, which is out of all proportion to the size of the country. But I never thought it wise to sell it, because for central banks this is a reserve of safety, it's viewed by the country as such. In the case of nondollar countries, it gives you a value-protection against fluctuations against the dollar, so there are several reasons, risk diversification and so on."[3]

Plus, gold is more portable than people believe. Sadie Sayyah, president of Goldline (with whom I have a working relationship), says that at today's values, a million dollars' worth of gold can fit into a shoe box.

The most important thing for gold in the "own everything" scenario is that you purchase physical gold. If you buy "paper" gold on an exchange, that exchange may not own the underlying gold (you may be buying a promise). It adds a layer of risk in turbulent times.

Entrepreneur and metals investor Jeff Thomas wrote, "The trouble with ETF's is that, since the fund may not actually purchase the gold, since they have only issued a promise to purchase the gold if it becomes necessary, the fund only works as long as gold trading remains fairly stable. If, however, there is ever a rush on the part of purchasers to take delivery of their gold, ETF's will be the first to go under."[4]

So, purchase physical gold if you are going to own it for purposes of our "own everything" endeavor. In addition to gold, you should explore other precious metals, alternative assets, and real estate.

Business Equity

Back to business ownership: if you don't own your own business, look for a job where you can get equity in the value you are helping to build. Many employers are willing to grant stock options as part of a compensation package, whether the firm is a public company or a private company that may be sold, pay dividends, or go public one day. If you believe in the company and the work it and you are doing, this is a way to gain an ownership stake in what you are building and participate in future growth.

If you own a business, you will have to do an in-depth risk assessment and figure out, given the government, Big Tech, and all the issues we have discussed, where your vulnerabilities are and shore them up to have value endure. You may also want to explore exit strategies on an ongoing basis. At some point, it may make sense to lock in the value you have created in your business, take that capital, and diversify it into a broader investment portfolio.

If you are considering buying or building a business, have an advisor help you sort through and prepare for these emerging risk factors on top of your typical business risks.

Also, look into assets that have other uses or may have value during distressing times that you can potentially use as currency. We know that in times of strife, guns and ammunition will have value, but everyday staples can also become valuable as a currency.

The bottom-line message here is to invest, and invest in tangible assets that can grow in value on a risk-adjusted basis.

Fighting ESG and Investment Manipulation

As discussed, the bad actors and profiteers are working overtime to make ESG and derivative initiatives, including impact investing, more prevalent. Their actions include directing capital away from critical resources and other industries and companies they are targeting, as well as slapping an ESG-type label on their products and services as a way to extract fees.

We also saw that many states, from Arizona to Florida and West Virginia, have begun pushing back against ESG and similar endeavors. Get your like-minded neighbors and community groups together and write, call, and show up to state officials to express your concerns over ESG. Tell them you believe it violates the company's fiduciary duty to protect your investments. Lean into the antitrust allegations. Go hard on this. People often march and protest for social issues, but rarely do we see action when it impacts the ability to accumulate wealth and secure our financial foundation.

Communicate to the companies you patronize and invest in. Generate writing campaigns about how ESG is diverting resources away from benefiting shareholders and customers.

Pull your money, patronage, and support from companies that repeatedly act against your interests. Consider a lawsuit if you believe a company's directors have acted in a manner inconsistent with their fiduciary obligation.

Contact local media, stage peaceful protests, and lead awareness campaigns.

Companies are economic animals. They are embracing ESG and other manipulated investment endeavors because that's what they believe will be in their economic interests or at least mitigate their risks. The quickest way to shut ESG down and get companies to switch their positions is to make it in their economic interest to move away from ESG and similar initiatives.

At the time of writing, there were some proposals, like the Index Act, to reduce power from mega-financial companies like BlackRock, State Street, and Vanguard, which not only manage a substantial amount of assets, but in many cases allocate money passively (aka through index funds). *Barron's* reported that these three firms "vote about one quarter of all votes cast at annual meetings."[5]

This gives them more power in voting if they vote "on behalf" of the shareholders. There is both an organic and a legislative movement to allow more individuals to vote, but some issues remain. One is that individuals often don't take the opportunity to vote by proxy. Lee Reiners, executive director of the global financial markets center at Duke University School of Law, told *Barron's* that the issue is more complicated: "The people who are allocating funds to BlackRock, Vanguard, and State Street are state pension funds and union funds, and they're the ones who would then have the right to vote the shares and, in a lot of instances, the people who run these pension funds are of like mind when it comes to ESG issues with BlackRock, Vanguard, and State Street."

This means that more work needs to be done to put pressure on larger managers of capital, such as pension funds, to not abuse their voting power and to allow the individuals represented to have more of a say.

Note that in February 2023, Vanguard distanced itself from some ESG endeavors, including withdrawing from the Net Zero Asset Managers initiative.

Legal action must be taken against the Department of Labor's rule allowing pension managers to consider ESG factors.[6]

Remember again that knowledge is power. Spread the word. Most people aren't even aware of these issues because they are intentionally confusing, and the corporate press is not shining a light on them. The more people you can teach about them, the more allies there will be to fight back.

Additionally, the pipeline to ESG (and similar concepts) becoming normalized starts in school, where kids are indoctrinated about climate. This indoctrination sets them on the path to activism and becoming useful idiots, and eventually they will be bringing those beliefs to work in corporate America. Make sure to teach your kids the truth regarding the environment and other subjects, and extol the merits of economic freedom.

Technology

On the tech front, there needs to be a reasonable standard for companies that operate as infrastructure and digital "town squares." Cutoffs could be based on scale (such as the number of users and/or revenue), volume and scale of competitors, or other metrics. However, anything codified should not act as a mechanism to handicap small players, prevent competition, or otherwise give advantages to the largest companies.

For example, it makes sense to protect the principle of free speech for mega town-square sites like YouTube, Facebook, and Twitter, but not on a small hobby forum for car enthusiasts. The definitions need to be fleshed out yet still vague enough to keep pace with technology (just like free speech applies to computer-generated writing as much as it does to that done with a quill and pen).

Town-square platforms should not be allowed to censor speech unless it goes against the basic principles of free speech, which includes not violating others' natural rights. That means you cannot make threats of actual violence, do something illegal, or interfere with another's privacy, for example, but you can be mean, say things that aren't true, or express unpopular opinions (with exceptions being libel and other actions that infringe on another's rights).

Collusion on censorship or other matters should not be tolerated between the government and any such platforms, nor between platforms.

The platforms should lean toward removing content as a remedy rather than suspending accounts, with the exception of people who flout legal standards several times in a short period. There should be a path to redemption for restoring accounts. Should accounts be suspended, users should be able to, at their discretion, post information on how to otherwise be in contact with them and their work (similar to how a post office can provide a forwarding address when you move).

For this, the platforms get to keep their liability exception as a platform instead of a content publisher.

You should not be forced to grant a license to your content to platform owners or third parties for free, outside of the scope of display on their platform. You should retain ownership of whatever you create.

Other infrastructure, such as web-hosting and payment services, again, properly defined, should not be able to refuse service unless you are conducting illegal activity. Having a moral issue isn't relevant to their providing infrastructure any more than the phone company historically providing phone service to people they may have found objectionable.

Again, no collusion or coordination that would infringe on rights should be tolerated between these entities and other technology companies or government entities.

Ownership of your physical and digital identity is paramount, along with privacy, particularly as surveillance, body ID recognition, and similar tech becomes more pervasive.

Clarity here benefits individual rights, as well as the tech companies. If this isn't codified federally, how will companies be able to build tech that complies with the various state and local regulations? A piece in *Forbes* about having an AI Bill of Rights notes that if laws are made locally, it would be "nearly impossible for a technology vendor to address hundreds of permutations of similar-but-different laws."[7]

Platforms should not be able to censor or meddle in elections, absent existing laws related to foreign election interference.

There are likely some other areas to consider, but this would be a welcome start in protecting rights in a way that isn't also anticompetitive or overly burdensome.

I interviewed Ron Coleman, a partner at Dhillon Law Group and advocate for free speech and religious rights, including internet-related and First Amendment advocacy. He is known for his successful representation of Simon Tam and The Slants and the tenet of free speech in *Matal v. Tam*, whereby the Supreme Court ruled that prohibiting the registration of "disparaging" trademarks was unconstitutional.[8]

Coleman has been active in holding tech accountable to a fair and consistent standard of rules. He told me, "What we're doing is trying to get the courts to recognize this distinction that the government is already using tech companies as proxies for what the government themselves cannot do themselves, and that . . . judges and legislature and legislators and regulators need to take a more mature look at what is going on," in terms of the digital sphere.[9]

Coleman and I agree. While we would like to defer to free market capitalism, what we have today is nowhere near the free market. Coleman referred to it as "state capitalism." He further acknowledged that looking to regulation is tricky because it involves trusting the government, but in some sense, the current state of affairs is even more untenable.

He said, "Right now [the government] is certainly not our friend, and they're not going to become any more of our friends in the in the future. . . . Nonetheless . . . there's no accountability whatsoever in the regime that we are operating under now. The technology companies . . . on the one hand, they don't answer to customers because they're too big to answer the customers, and on the other hand . . . they don't in any meaningful sense answer to shareholders" because of their size and power.

He reminds us that while we want to protect individuals, such as shareholders, from liabilities, there still needs to be accountability at the company level. His example was if an iPhone blows up in someone's hand, the holder of a handful of shares in their retirement account shouldn't be personally liable.

Coleman argues that while there will be mistakes in making legislation and where we draw the "bright line" between these companies that are de facto governments and digital infrastructure, we still need to start somewhere and adapt over time. Otherwise, he warns, we are headed to an "illiberal" system of social credit or worse.

As for solutions, Coleman leans toward private companies being able to have any types of rules they want, but says that those rules need to be applied consistently and as written and not shifted based on politics or other factors. Basically, in my own words, a rigid equal standard.

He also believes individuals need recourse for actions like censorship or termination. His suggestions include not only a process of appeal to be heard but also some type of arbitration if you are not satisfied with the outcome.

Own Your Behaviors

In addition to supporting rights protections, technology's impact lies heavily in your awareness and behaviors.

Outside of the legal realm, consider de-technifying aspects of your life and encouraging others to do the same. Go analog instead of inviting invasive technologies into your home. Alexa isn't your friend, nor is Siri or any of the other robots with cute names.

Most importantly, use your dollars and time to support smaller companies and those making an effort to consider you a partner, not a product. Do what you can to not support companies actively working against you. This is hard, and sometimes making changes come with consequences that don't make sense for you, but where you can, use your resources thoughtfully and intentionally.

And don't forget to make investing in tangible assets a habit if ownership and wealth creation are important to you.

Protecting Your Family from the Government

While it seems like there is little hope for restoring government to its intended purpose, we must use the tools available to us, whether the courts, voting, or lobbying our representatives to try to effect change. This means that you need to take action, which is an important theme in this chapter.

I interviewed Larry Salzman, the director of litigation at Pacific Legal Foundation, a national nonprofit organization that defends Americans from government overreach and abuse. Organizations like Pacific Legal Foundation have been doing tremendous work, using the courts to take on the administrative state at the state and national levels.

Salzman's expertise centers on property rights and economic liberty.

According to his biography, his cases have involved "eminent domain, civil forfeiture, regulatory takings and exactions, the Commerce Clause, and challenges to occupational licensing and 'certificate of need' laws that infringe on the constitutional right to earn a living."[10]

Salzman said, "my earnest belief is that we're probably in a better position today than we have been at any time in the last fifty years, to, at least with respect to law, to challenge what I would call the post–New Deal settlement, whereby courts, would sort of step aside from the administrative and executive branches, and let them regulate to the heart's content, particularly if it involves property or economic rights. That is really under reconsideration."[11]

One case Salzman cites is *Knick v. Township of Scott, Pennsylvania, et al.*, related to the rights of a woman and her small farm in Pennsylvania.[12] He says, "in the course of the decision they said things like, the takings clause or the clause protecting property rights in the Constitution is as important as every other provision of the Bill of Rights and should get equal protection. They said that the property rights are not second-class citizens under the Constitution. So, this court is voicing real support for property rights."

While Salzman notes that some foundational work is going on to restrict the rise of the administrative state, individuals should continue to use the courts (and groups like Pacific Legal Foundation). Also, more work needs to be done via exercising your vote and putting more pressure on your representatives by writing, calling, etc.

You may want to consider donating to or volunteering with organizations and individuals who are doing this type of work and fighting government overreach.

Protecting Your Kids

The indoctrination of kids in many schools around the country is becoming a more significant cause for concern. It impacts future generations' ability to have freedoms and agency and to pursue wealth creation.

As in other areas, many experts suggest getting involved at the school board level.

Moms for Liberty shares a variety of resources and links on their website, including the Protection of Pupil Rights Amendment and related resources, how to submit an open records request, and other expert resources.

Tiffany Justice, a cofounder of Moms for Liberty, emphasized that it is important to expose what is happening in schools as quickly as possible to bring about change.[13]

Justice also said that it is essential for parents to opt their children out of school surveys. This is because the data collected via those surveys are being used for various nefarious purposes, many of which are being pushed by organizations seeking to emphasize social and emotional learning over academic excellence, equity over equality, and collectivism over free choice. "It's how they prime the children for indoctrination," Justice said, "and it's how they prepare a next generation of children to own nothing."[14]

Education Costs

As we explored, one of the key methods to ensure you own nothing is saddling you with debts. Regarding education or accreditation, it is crucial that you (or your friends, acquaintances, and loved ones) don't take on more debt than you can pay back.

My rule of thumb is that you shouldn't graduate with more debt than you will be making three to five years out of school. So, if by year three, you expect to be making $80,000, that would be your maximum debt. Whatever you (or someone you know) take on, cut as many expenses as possible and work to pay it back in no more than five years. The exception is, perhaps, seven years if you are getting an advanced degree where you expect to make multiple six figures. But, again, that is the exception.

If you cannot pay it back and don't work to do so, it will become a burden and a wealth destroyer.

That is, if college even makes sense for your profession. There will be ongoing shortages in lucrative areas from airline piloting to plumbing, so evaluate your options early. Also, more companies are considering certificates to be college equivalents.

If you work in a company, advocate for shifting and expanding what criteria are used to evaluate candidates and work to lessen the reliance on college as a be-all, end-all hiring factor.

Spread this information far and wide. Postsecondary schools can only continue to be complicit in creating barriers to wealth creation if students are willing to take on loans and pay the price.

Housing

Get your hands on tangible property that you can afford. Affordability is the key—buying something that ultimately is out of your price range and that you have to walk away from one day is a waste. So, this needs to be done, as with any investing, with careful thought and analysis.

Buy your own home. If you can buy land and water rights, that is great, too. If you can't, perhaps you and a group of like-minded folks can. Maybe you and a group can help farmers retain their land, work it, and keep it away from large corporate interests and bad actors.

Speak to your accountant in this endeavor, as certain types of land may have associated tax advantages. Farms meeting specific requirements have various available tax breaks, including those related to property taxes.[15]

Generally speaking, look to own property in states that are more friendly to ownership in terms of their laws, including those with lower property taxes. Look for better local governance where you can make an impact.

Jim Rickards is also a proponent of buying real estate, particularly land that has a productive use, whether it is income-generating, land that you can farm, or land from which you can derive other resources, such as water.[16]

And please do make an impact. Run for local office. Encourage those you know and trust to do so as well.

Finally, don't forget that you also have to be able to protect that in which you invest. For land and property, have the appropriate protections in place, from physical protection to insurance protection.

When it comes to exiting properties, there are some actions you can take as well.

Some homeowner associations (HOAs) are fighting back against corporate buyers to preserve property-buying opportunities for individuals and ensure property maintenance.

The *Wall Street Journal* reported that "tactics include placing a cap on the number of homes that can be rented in a particular neighborhood, or requiring that rental tenants be approved by the association board. In most cases, associations need at least a two-thirds majority to pass these measures."[17]

I like this measure better than a pure no-renting or no-corporate-buyer rule, as it gives homeowners more flexibility should the market downturn for limited or extended periods. It can also ensure that smaller landlords aren't pushed out of the market.

Of course, some states are going to make it difficult. Not surprisingly, California is one of them. The *Journal* reports, "As part of an effort to encourage homeowners to build small rental properties on their land, California now prohibits associations from imposing some limits on long-term leases."[18]

Personally, consider not selling your home to a corporate or foreign buyer unless you have substantially exhausted your options to sell to another individual. I want you to get as much as possible for your home sale, but remember that in a free market, your choices are important, too.

Larry Salzman of Pacific Legal Foundation has also been working to ensure that your home isn't taken for small infractions, such as not paying a fine. Salzman calls it home equity theft, and he says there are still twelve states where if you get behind on property taxes, for example, they don't just come after that amount: they can foreclose on the entire home and take any equity above and beyond what is owed.[19]

Pacific Legal Foundation is working to end this practice in all states where it exists, having been successful in defending clients in various states. They are not only petitioning the Supreme Court but have also been successful in drafting legislation accepted at the state level.

Salzman also suggests that pushing back on zoning laws is a way to ensure more prosperity, noting that, like our good-idea-to-bad-outcome model, some of the intentions make sense, but they have become onerous and extremely costly over time.

Inheritance Planning

As we reviewed in the previous chapter, inheritances are estimated to be worth $84.4 trillion in the next two and a half decades. You must do everything you can to preserve that wealth for your heirs.

The government is likely counting on the masses not doing robust estate planning; that way, it will be much easier for them to seize that wealth.

That means hiring an estate planner. Andrew Egan, an estate planning expert and fiduciary litigator at Bressler, Amery & Ross, said that while for many middle-class Americans a bulk of assets pass down through beneficiary designations, it still makes sense to put more structured legacy plans in place. This likely includes a will and one or more trusts, which may seem scary and sophisticated, but shouldn't be. He noted that trusts can be tools to help protect passing your assets with less of a tax burden.[20]

Egan emphasized that it is critical to get professional help, as different states have varying rules, regulations, and tax provisions that you need to be aware of on top of any federal laws and taxes.

Planning now is important, as rules often change, but Egan noted that previous actions may be "grandfathered in" when rule changes are made. Acting now can help you possibly avoid future rule changes (although not 100 percent guaranteed).

As a way to avoid future inheritance grabs, gifting assets during your lifetime can also be a hedge against that possibility. Egan says that you can gift money or assets worth up to $16,000 (based on 2022 limits) per person per calendar year and that the amount often is revised upward over time. Gifting, within limits, can be an effective way to transfer wealth over time to loved ones and not have to worry about changes to inheritance taxes and rules.

A quick plug from the author here: consider filling out a legacy planning system, like the one I created (Future File, at FutureFile.com), so that your loved ones know your wishes and information and can access everything they need should something happen to you.

Egan also noted that talking to your estate planner about long-term care planning is critical in terms of maintaining your wealth. As people are living longer, more of their wealth is being eaten up by the skyrocketing costs of care later in life. Planning for that with a professional can also be helpful in terms of preserving wealth for future generations.

As an individual or, again, with community groups, actively speak out against any forms of wealth taxes or enhanced estate taxes for anyone. Once that door is opened, as we have seen, class creep comes in. If you are okay with billionaires' wealth being confiscated, it won't be long until it happens to you.

Be diligent and vehement, including calling your representatives.

Fighting Social Credit

Writer Spencer Lindquist eloquently surmised that "[t]he enforcers of America's emergent social credit system are most empowered when they can cut you off not only from your job, but from your community and all other sources of support. The remedy? Establish genuine, in-person authentic communities built around shared values."[21]

Lindquist further notes the difference between online and offline "friends" and connections, and how they may be valuable should you be accused of wrongthink. As others, including radio and TV host Jesse Kelly, have advocated, building strong communities with like-minded people who will be your allies in pushing back against systematic nonsense is critical. Kelly has suggested moving to states and locales to what he dubs "Balkanize" (aka fortify) them and becoming an activist where you live. His suggestions have included getting onto local school boards and running for city council or state house positions, as well as patronizing businesses and hiring people who are of like mind.[22]

Lindquist reminds us:

> These same social bonds that can protect you from cancellation must be put to use in a proactive, not just defensive, capacity. Voting isn't enough. Get involved in all aspects of public life. Run for office, write for local papers, show up to school board meetings, and be present anywhere voices are heard or decisions are made.
>
> Use these grassroots bonds to build high-trust communities that can propel members to powerful positions. In those capacities, they'll be able to provide air cover for the grassroots by leveraging their institutional support for the benefit of the community.[23]

Action is a recurring and crucial theme in this chapter. You cannot be passive and expect that you will have the same opportunities available. You must be willing to go on the offensive to protect your rights, individually or with others by your side.

Fighting the Fed and the Devaluation of the Dollar

Central banking is a failed experiment. At least for the average person. While it may have served the intentions of those elites it has benefited, it needs to be stopped to preserve any value that remains today in the US dollar.

While many people would tell you to end the Fed, the need is more nuanced than that. What should be ended is their powers. Ending the institution and moving the ability to print dollars from nowhere and increase the money supply on a whim to Congress would be even worse than where it stands today.

The current mess needs to be cleaned up and monetary expansion frozen until productivity can catch up. Then any monetary expansion needs to be tied to productivity, similar to one of the ideas floated by Milton Friedman, the "K-percent Rule," many years ago. Friedman said that the money supply would grow in concert with GDP growth (or another modest growth proxy that was constant each year) to stabilize the economy and remove the Fed's ability to "print" money ad hoc.[24]

Fiat currency also needs to be shifted to something tangible to remove the ability for Congress to spend at its whim and the central bank or any other entity to devalue the dollar at its whim as well.

A CBDC should be opposed at every turn. Even if it is promised not to be retail-facing, as we discussed, once you build the monster, it will only grow in power.

If it does come to fruition, don't voluntarily use it. That doesn't mean that the government won't try to force it upon us, but we must do everything we can to keep it from succeeding.

Bitcoin and Cryptocurrency

Cryptocurrency, including Bitcoin, has emerged partly to counteract the damage done to the dollar and other currencies around the globe by central banks.

As it is nascent, it's unclear whether Bitcoin fills that void long-term. I think Bitcoin, the blockchain, and other cryptocurrencies are worth keeping an eye on and learning more about, but I want to give you some thoughts as you draw your own conclusions.

Everything of value has value because of a social contract. When people agree and trust the value that something conveys, it is considered to have that value. And that value can fluctuate over time based on the number of people who agree and trust in that value, as well as the scarcity of and demand for the underlying item of value.

While many assets have longer track records, cryptocurrencies have a decade-and-a-half track record or less, depending on the crypto. That doesn't mean that one or more cryptocurrencies don't have the opportunity to endure; it just provides less data on how it thrives or survives in different economic and geopolitical situations.

Cryptocurrencies' lack of malleability in the physical world, their limits as a medium of exchange, and their tie to technology should be considered. Also, the industry has been rocked by hacking, fraud, and other woes, so understanding where there are issues and vulnerabilities is imperative.

My father left me with a handful of foundational financial principles. One of the key ones was never invest in something you don't understand. I am sure you could explain what a gold chain or a restaurant chain is, but do you know what a blockchain is? Cryptocurrencies—even the most established—have a learning curve. Do your research before you allocate any substantial investment.

Anything decentralized and outside of government financial systems is subject to legal threats. In the US, gold was recalled by the government under President Franklin D. Roosevelt during the Great Depression, and individuals did receive some compensation in exchange. Today the US government and other developed countries' governments seem more concerned with cryptocurrencies, and are actively considering different legislations and competitive digital centralized currencies.

Investor and *The Big Short* subject Michael Burry tweeted, I don't hate BTC [Bitcoin] . . . the long term future is tenuous for decentralized crypto in a world of legally violent, heartless centralized governments with lifeblood interests in monopolies on currencies.[25]

I think that's a tremendous risk. As discussed in Chapter 5, nations are seeking digital currencies to increase centralization. Control over money is a power that they don't want to give up, and they are likely to legislate, tax, and even be prepared to fight for that sovereign power.

While struggling countries are turning to Bitcoin, more established ones have been adding to their gold reserves. According to the World Gold Council, in 2021, central banks around the world added almost 456 tonnes of gold to their reserves, some of that to replace fiat-currency-based reserves, as well as 1,136 tonnes through the end of 2022, the highest amount on record.[26]

While behaviors shift as the economy shifts, I like to look at what the wealthy and powerful are doing as a data point.

The big question is long-term adoption.

As more time passes, this information is bound to change, so, like other investments, you should revisit it periodically. Remember, nobody can predict the future, and a slew of variables can change the course of history.

Economist Nouriel Roubini had been vocal against cryptocurrencies. He told Yahoo Finance in regards to Bitcoin, "It's not scaleable, it's not secure, it's not decentralized, it's not a currency."[27] But Roubini hasn't written off crypto entirely. He has recently been exploring ways to combine blockchain technology with real-world assets to hedge against the issues with fiat money. In combination with a team from Dubai, he is looking at creating a hybrid digital coin. Bloomberg reports, "Unlike many cryptocurrencies, Roubini stresses that the coin would be backed by real assets—a mix of short-term U.S. Treasuries, gold and U.S. property (in the form of real estate investment trusts, or REITs). . . ."[28]

So, his digital alternative is still backed by tangible, hard assets like real estate and gold, as we have been discussing. This is another endorsement for falling back on owning hard assets.

Other pro-asset individuals have included Berkshire Hathaway superinvestors Warren Buffett and Charlie Munger.

Munger has referred to cryptocurrency as a "turd" and "an investment in nothing."[29]

At Berkshire Hathaway's 2022 shareholder meeting, Buffett said he would take a 1 percent stake in all the real estate in the United States or all the farmland in the United States for $25 billion but wouldn't buy the world's supply of bitcoin for $25, saying, "I'll have to sell it back to you one way or another. It isn't going to do anything."[30]

Note again the advocacy from these investment pros for hard assets.

Despite their track records, Munger and Buffett could be wrong. They aren't as focused on disruptive technologies, and times have shifted. However, their focus on what produces value and is a productive asset is important vis-à-vis our broader discussion.

Also, it is worth noting that Berkshire made an investment in 2022 in a digital bank in Latin America that is considered "crypto-friendly," called Nubank. So, despite their protests, there is still some dabbling in at least related areas.[31]

Ultimately, cryptocurrencies have a valid and vital mandate to try to keep money from being manipulated and destroyed in value. Whether they can accomplish that in the long run is still a guess and heavily dependent upon any potential future attempts by governments and central banks to thwart them. Their risk should be evaluated in terms of risk-adjusted return and your desired risk tolerance.

Pursue Happiness—and Assets

Ron Coleman made a plea for courage and stepping up to take back your freedom. He said that you need to lessen your dependence on big organizations and make your income as "unfragile as possible."[32]

Coleman said, "[E]veryone who works for a major corporation or . . . that serves major corporations or anything like it, these people need to understand that either they're going to agree to . . . lose their independence and to become zombies, or they're going to be flushed out. And if they're going to be flushed out they may as well be flushed out now, so they can begin the process of building an independent way to do what they want to do, and to do what they believe is right so that they can live less of their life in fear and more of their life in being true to themselves once they do that."

Coleman says that speaking up without anonymity can help change the tide of what is considered popular opinion and make some bad actors back off.

He added, "We haven't lost everything yet. There are certain battlefields that we're not going to be able to return to for a very, very long time. These include major cities . . . [and] academia . . . but there are fights that we can win a lot faster. And I would say we should be focusing on those and you know getting the relatively lower line fruit, and also preventing more institutions and more sectors of system from being irredeemable."

He noted that you need to be free in your conscience if you want to be free in all realms. That includes the ability to pursue wealth creation and enjoy other freedoms.

You Are the Counter-revolution

With this financial war and new financial world order upon us, and with the confluence of events and individuals trying to take away your rights, including your property rights and your opportunities to create wealth, the battles are still playing out.

You can win.

Be intentional about creating a well-diversified portfolio for yourself, speaking up and educating others on issues, and taking action individually and with like-minded community members.

The elites are gunning to come out on top and using their propaganda machines to gaslight you. Don't let them.

You will not be happy if you own nothing. The pursuit of happiness runs directly through the town of ownership.

You can stop this from happening. You can fight back.

Gather your friends, family, and community together, make plans, and protect your property rights.

Own everything you can.

ACKNOWLEDGMENTS

This is both my favorite and least favorite part of writing a book: my favorite because I have so much gratitude, and my least favorite because there are so many people I want to thank and to whom I have gratitude and know that I will inevitably miss some.

To that end, I am again keeping this short and sweet, with an extra thank-you to the following people directly connected to this work:

First, to my best friend and love, Kurt. You are so special to me and an incredible partner in life and work. You were integral in all aspects of this book, from helping to shape and elevate the content to doing research, sometimes unintentionally, to reading drafts and more.

To Tracey, my sister and right hand, who makes all of my work better, and to Mike, for being part of our inner circle and keeping us filled with laughter to help balance these serious subjects.

To my editor, Eric Nelson, who always pushes for big ideas and tries to make them even better and more relevant. And to my assistant editor, James Neidhardt, who also had to do some extra heavy lifting here. I appreciate both of your efforts and am proud of the work we did and of our collaboration.

To Henry Bernard, who came in at the eleventh hour to help solve an unexpected issue. I am beyond appreciative of you.

To Glenn Beck, for your support and mentorship. I have learned much from you and you helped, from day one, to shape the foundation for this material—many thanks and much gratitude to you. Thank you as well for lending your voice to the endorsement of the book.

To Dana Loesch, Charles Payne, and Michael Shellenberger, thank you for your enthusiastic endorsements of the book and your powerful words.

To Bridget Phetasy, for being a "mensch," always having my back, elevating my work, and your overall support and friendship.

To Emily Barsh, for your thoughtful insights in the early days of shaping the material.

To Rikki Ratliff-Fellman, for your incredible help in finding, shaping, and communicating material, including material relevant to this book. I appreciate your incredible talents and our work together.

To Sarah Kolk, for your endless list of talents and your willingness to be helpful in just about every way.

To Pete Garceau, thank you for an absolutely perfect cover design. You knocked it out of the park.

To Jim Rickards, Ron Coleman, Tiffany Justice, Andrew Egan, and Larry Salzman for taking the time to lend your expertise to the book. And to those who were interviewed and wanted to remain anonymous or were not used, I appreciate you as well.

To the rest of the staff at Broadside and HarperCollins, including Theresa Dooley in publicity and Tom Hopke in marketing, thank you for all your efforts. I also want to thank the copyediting and production staff as well.

To Alan Roby, who has guided my professional journey and kept me sane along the way.

To Alex Epstein, for generously sharing your advice and insights on marketing.

To all of my collaborators and colleagues, I appreciate you.

To my extended family, you know who you all are, thank you for your love. I am proud to be part of such a special and loving group.

To all the many thinkers and economists, past and present, who have shaped the discourse around capitalism, free markets, and individual rights, I am again humbled by the opportunity to build upon your work.

To everyone who has worked hard and participated in creating their own American Dream, I am proud to pursue that dream alongside you.

To my parents, who are no longer with us, thank you for the foundation of self-confidence, work ethic, straightforwardness, and gratitude. I love you and miss you every day.

Finally, I would like to acknowledge the typos, formatting errors, data errors, inconsistencies, and other issues that made it into this book. Congratulations, you managed to slip by several different people and at least one hundred readings of the manuscript. Well done.

NOTES

Introduction: The Coming War

1. Credit Suisse Research Institute, "Global Wealth Report 2022," Credit Suisse, September 2022, https://www.credit-suisse.com/about-us/en/reports-research/global-wealth-report.html.

Chapter 1: Socially Unacceptable

1. "How Communities Are Thanking Health Care Workers During COVID-19," Eisenhower Health, May 5, 2020, https://careers.eisenhowerhealth.org/for-fun/how-communities-are-thanking-health-care-workers-during-covid-19/.

2. "Nurse Shares Story on Losing Job over Vaccine Mandates | Interview," TrialSite News YouTube channel, October 20, 2021, https://www.youtube.com/watch?v=CcznN1Zrzaw. Only first name shared for privacy.

3. Ibid.

4. Ibid.

5. "Executive Order on Requiring Coronavirus Disease 2019 Vaccination for Federal Employees," The White House, September 9, 2021, https://www.whitehouse.gov/briefing-room/presidential-actions/2021/09/09/executive-order-on-requiring-coronavirus-disease-2019-vaccination-for-federal-employees/.

6. Michael Doudna, "VERIFY: Yes, if you are fired from your job for refusing a vaccine mandate, you could lose unemployment benefits," NBC12 News, September 22, 2021, https://www.12news.com/article/news/verify/verify-yes-if-you-are-fired-from-your-job-for-refusing-a-vaccine-mandate-you-could-lose-unemployment-benefits/75-668ce849-d5a0-42f5-ac92-70542233788f.

7. Ibid.

8. Emma Colton, "Weeks after Minnesota nurses warn of staffing crisis, Mayo Clinic fires 700 unvaccinated workers," Fox News, January 5, 2022, https://www.foxnews.com/us/mayo-clinic-unvaccinated-700-employees-fired-staffing-crisis-minnesota.

9. Suzie Ziegler, "1,430 unvaccinated NYC employees fired, including 36 NYPD cops," Police1, February 16, 2022, https://www.police1.com/coronavirus-covid-19/articles/1430-unvaccinated-nyc-employees-fired-including-36-nypd-cops-NUqxKJtXDu9yhocy/.

10. Dave Muoio, "How many employees have hospitals lost to vaccine mandates? Here are the numbers so far," Fierce Healthcare, February 22, 2022, https://www.fiercehealthcare.com/hospitals/how-many-employees-have-hospitals-lost-to-vaccine-mandates-numbers-so-far.

11. Meghann Myers and Leo Shane III, "The vast majority of troops kicked out for COVID vaccine refusal received general discharges," *Military Times*, April 27, 2022, https://www.militarytimes.com/news/pentagon-congress/2022/04/27/the-vast-majority-of-troops-kicked-out-for-covid-vaccine-refusal-received-general-discharges/.

12. Steve Beynon, "Army Cuts Off More Than 60K Unvaccinated Guard and Reserve Soldiers from Pay and Benefits," Military.com, July 6, 2022, https://www.military.com/daily-news/2022/07/06/army-cuts-off-more-60k-unvaccinated-guard-and-reserve-soldiers-pay-and-benefits.html.

13. Tom Hals, "U.S. judge blocks last remaining Biden admin COVID-19 vaccine rule," Reuters via Yahoo News, December 7, 2021, https://news.yahoo.com/u-judge-blocks-covid-vaccine-173254136.html.

14. Mario Perez, "Spotify Employees Reportedly Want to Cancel Joe Rogan's Show," Blast, July 7, 2021, https://theblast.com/75295/spotify-employees-want-to-cancel-joe-rogans-show/; Katherine Rosman, Ben Sisario, Mike Isaac, and Adam Satariano, "Spotify Bet Big on Joe Rogan. It Got More Than It Counted On," *New York Times*, February 17, 2022, https://www.nytimes.com/2022/02/17/arts/music/spotify-joe-rogan-misinformation.html.

15. Matt Pearce and Wendy Lee, "Spotify Ceo Tells Employees Why the Company Doesn't Edit Joe Rogan: It's a Platform," *Los Angeles Times*, February 2, 2022, https://www.latimes.com/entertainment-arts/story/2022-02-02/la-ent-spotify-rogan-platform.

16. Chris Willman, "In Removing Neil Young's Music, Spotify Didn't Need to Listen to the Artist,

but Did Have to Heed His Label," *Variety*, January 27, 2022, https://variety.com/2022/music/news/neil-young-spotify-takedown-request-warner-records-remove-1235165611/.

17. Pearce and Lee, "Spotify Ceo Tells Employees Why the Company Doesn't Edit Joe Rogan: It's a Platform."

18. Lee Brown, "Joe Rogan calls attempt to cancel him over podcast a 'hit job,'" *New York Post*, February 9, 2022, https://nypost.com/2022/02/09/joe-rogan-slams-attempt-to-cancel-him-over-spotify-podcast/.

19. Ben Cost, "Joe Rogan on cancel culture attempt: 'I gained 2 million subscribers,'" *New York Post*, April 25, 2022, https://nypost.com/2022/04/25/joe-rogan-on-cancel-culture-attempt-i-gained-2m-subscribers/.

20. Zoe Christen Jones, "Netflix employees stage walkout over Dave Chappelle special," CBS News, October 25, 2021, https://www.cbsnews.com/news/dave-chappelle-netflix-employees-walkout/.

21. Téa Kvetenadze, "Netflix Suspends Employees for Crashing Meeting Amid Chappelle Transphobia Controversy," *Forbes*, October 11, 2021, https://www.forbes.com/sites/teakvetenadze/2021/10/11/netflix-suspends-employees-for-crashing-meeting-amid-chappelle-transphobia-controversy/?sh=29278e5317f0.

22. Todd Spangler, "Netflix Updates Corporate Culture Memo, Adding Anti-Censorship Section and a Vow to 'Spend Our Members' Money Wisely,'" *Variety*, May 12, 2022, https://variety.com/2022/digital/news/netflix-culture-memo-update-censorship-spending-1235264904/.

23. Charles Creitz, Fox News, "Nicholas Sandmann Reaches Settlement with Nbc in Covington Catholic High School Controversy," *New York Post*, December 18, 2021, https://nypost.com/2021/12/18/covington-catholic-graduate-nicholas-sandmann-settlement-with-nbc/.

24. Katja Drinhausen and Vincent Brussee, "China's Social Credit System in 2021: from Fragmentation towards Integration," MERICS, March 3, 2021 updated May 9, 2022, https://merics.org/en/report/chinas-social-credit-system-2021-fragmentation-towards-integration.

25. Drew Donnelly, PhD, "China Social Credit System Explained—What Is It & How Does It Work?" Horizons, July 22, 2022, https://nhglobalpartners.com/china-social-credit-system-explained/.

26. Drinhausen and Brussee, "China's Social Credit System in 2021."

27. Katie Jones, "The Game of Life: Visualizing China's Social Credit System," Visual Capitalist, September 18, 2019, https://www.visualcapitalist.com/the-game-of-life-visualizing-chinas-social-credit-system/.

28. Donnelly, "China Social Credit System Explained."

29. Jessica Reilly, Muyao Lyu, and Megan Robertson, "China's Social Credit System: Speculation vs. Reality," *Diplomat*, March 30, 2021, https://thediplomat.com/2021/03/chinas-social-credit-system-speculation-vs-reality/.

30. Drinhausen and Brussee, "China's Social Credit System in 2021."

31. Reilly et al, "China's Social Credit System: Speculation vs. Reality."

32. Sam Peach, "Why Did Alibaba's Jack Ma Disappear for Three Months?" BBC News, March 20, 2021, https://www.bbc.com/news/technology-56448688.

33. Eva Dou and Lyric Li, "Alibaba's Jack Ma Reemerges from Three-Month Absence after Clash with Beijing," *Washington Post*, January 20, 2021, https://www.washingtonpost.com/world/asia_pacific/jack-ma-alibaba-ant-china/2021/01/20/eb6b5d32-5adb-11eb-a849-6f9423a75ffd_story.html; Yong Xiong and Laura He, "Jack Ma to Relinquish Control of Ant Group," CNN, January 7, 2023, https://www.cnn.com/2023/01/07/intl_business/jack-ma-ant-group-restructuring-intl-hnk/index.html.

34. Drinhausen and Brussee, "China's Social Credit System in 2021."

35. Jones, "The Game of Life,"; Zhou Jiaquan, "Drones, Facial Recognition and a Social Credit System: 10 Ways China Watches Its Citizens," *South China Morning Post*, August 4, 2018, https://www.scmp.com/news/china/society/article/2157883/drones-facial-recognition-and-social-credit-system-10-ways-china.

36. Donnelly, "China Social Credit System Explained."

37. Rishi Iyengar, "Shanghai Citizens May Soon Have Their Credit Scores Lowered for Not Visiting Their Parents," *Time*, April 12, 2016, https://time.com/4290234/china-shanghai-parents-visit-credit-score-lower/.

38. "China's Social Credit System," Bertelsmann Stiftung, https://i.gzn.jp/img/2020/01/08/china-social-credit-system/01.png.

39. "China's Social Credit System"; Jones, "The Game of Life."

40. Alisa Chang (Host), "What It's Like to Be on the Blacklist in China's New Social Credit System," NPR, October 31, 2018, https://www.npr.org/2018/10/31/662696776/what-its-like-to-be-on-the-blacklist-in-chinas-new-social-credit-system.

41. Ibid.

42. Wenxin Fan, "In One Chinese City, Protesters Find Themselves Thwarted by a Red Health Code," *Wall Street Journal*, June 16, 2022, https://www.wsj.com/articles/in-one-chinese-city-protesters-find-themselves-thwarted-by-a-red-health-code-11655437726.

43. Davos Agenda 2021, "This New Approach to Credit Scoring Is Accelerating Financial Inclusion in Emerging Economies," World Economic Forum, January 20, 2021, https://www.weforum.org/agenda/2021/01/this-new-approach-to-credit-scoring-is-accelerating-financial-inclusion/.

44. Ibid.

45. Ibid.

46. Ibid.

47. Ibid.

48. Rose Eveleth, "What If Your Social Media Activity Affected Your Credit Score?" Slate, April 8, 2019, https://slate.com/technology/2019/04/forms-from-future-social-media-credit-score.html.

49. Roger Koppl and Abigail Devereaux, "Biden Establishes a Ministry of Truth," *Wall Street Journal*, May 1, 2022, https://www.wsj.com/articles/biden-establishes-a-ministry-of-truth-disinformation-governance-board-partisan-11651432312.

50. Daniel Dale, "Fact Check: White House Tweet Falsely Claims 'There Was No Vaccine Available' When Biden Took Office," CNN, May 13, 2022, https://www.cnn.com/2022/05/13/politics/fact-check-white-house-no-vaccine-available-tweet/index.html.

51. Betsy Woodruff Swan and Daniel Lippman, "Small Group, Big Headache: Inside DHS' Messy Disinformation Governance Board Launch," *Politico*, May 5, 2022, https://www.politico.com/news/2022/05/05/dhs-disinformation-board-mayorkas-00030123.

52. Benjamin Hart, "Poorly Conceived Biden Disinformation Board Put on Pause," *New York*, May 18, 2022, https://nymag.com/intelligencer/2022/05/poorly-conceived-biden-disinformation-board-put-on-pause.html.

53. Ibid.

54. Steven Nelson, "White House 'Flagging' Posts for Facebook to Censor over COVID 'Misinformation,'" *New York Post*, July 15, 2021, https://nypost.com/2021/07/15/white-house-flagging-posts-for-facebook-to-censor-due-to-covid-19-misinformation/.

55. Tom Bartlett, "The Vaccine Scientist Spreading Vaccine Misinformation," *Atlantic*, August 12, 2021, https://www.theatlantic.com/science/archive/2021/08/robert-malone-vaccine-inventor-vaccine-skeptic/619734/; @pbhushan1, Twitter, December 29, 2021, https://twitter.com/pbhushan1/status/1476399667084546050?s=20&t=9Z_V0JccJnFCWariSOY2-Q.

56. Kara Frederick, "Sleepwalking into a China-Style Social Credit System," Heritage Foundation, March 4, 2022 https://www.heritage.org/technology/commentary/sleepwalking-china-style-social-credit-system.

57. Ibid.

58. Lora Ries and James Jay Carafano, "Homeland Security's Rebooted Disinformation Plan Is No Better Than the First," Heritage Foundation, May 25th, 2022, https://www.heritage.org/civil-rights/commentary/homeland-securitys-rebooted-disinformation-plan-no-better-the-first.

59. Kery Murakami, "$750M Headed to States for New Gun Control Initiatives," Route Fifty, June 24, 2022, https://www.route-fifty.com/public-safety/2022/06/congress-sends-gun-safety-bill-biden-signature/368588/.

60. Tucker Carlson, "Red Flag Laws Will Not End Mass Shootings but Will End Due Process," Fox News, June 13, 2022, https://www.foxnews.com/opinion/tucker-carlson-red-flag-laws-mass-shootings-due-process.

61. Ibid.

62. Zach Williams, "NY Senate OKs Bill Barring Guns in Times Square, Requiring Social Media Info for Permit," *New York Post*, July 1, 2022, https://nypost.com/2022/07/01/new-york-bill-would-require-social-media-info-for-gun-carry-permit/; Jackie Napier, "State Supreme Court Judge in Rochester Rules NYS Red Flag Law Unconstitutional," ABC 13 WHAM, December 30, 2022, https://13wham.com/news/local/state-supreme-court-judge-in-rochester-rules-nys-red-flag-law-unconstitutional-thomas-moran-dan-strollo-erpo-payton-gendron-buffalo-tops-shooting.

63. "Excelsior Pass Plus: Frequently Asked Questions," New York State, https://covid19vaccine.health.ny.gov/excelsior-pass-plus-frequently-asked-questions.

64. Ibid.

65. ID2020 website, https://id2020.org/.

66. Ibid.

67. Ibid.; IDEO.org, https://www.ideo.org/.

68. Paul Vieira, "What Is the Freedom Convoy? Trucker Protests in Canada Explained," *Wall Street Journal*, February 24, 2022, https://www.wsj.com/articles/freedom-convoy-canada-trucker-protest-what-11644441237.

69. Ibid.

70. Ibid.

71. Ibid.

72. Ibid.

73. GoFundMe, "UPDATE: GoFundMe to Refund All Freedom Convoy 2022 Donations (2/5/2022)," Medium, February 4, 2022, updated February 5, 2022, https://medium.com/gofundme-stories/update-gofundme-statement-on-the-freedom-convoy-2022-fundraiser-4ca7e9714e82.

74. Micah Lee, "Oath Keepers, Anti-Democracy Activists, and Others on the Far Right Are Funding Canada's 'Freedom Convoy,'" Intercept, February 17, 2022, https://theintercept.com/2022/02/17/freedom-convoy-givesendgo-canada-oath-keepers-funding/.

75. Grant LaFleche and Alex McKeen, "Who's Funding the 'Freedom Convoy'? What Leaked Data Suggests about GiveSendGo Donors," *Toronto Star*, February 14, 2022 https://www.thestar.com/news/canada/2022/02/14/whos-funding-the-freedom-convoy-what-leaked-data-suggests-about-givesendgo-fundraising.html; Bryan Passifiume, "American billionaire, Canadian civil servants among donors leaked in GiveSendGo hack," *National Post*, February 14, 2022, updated February 15, 2022, https://nationalpost.com/news/civil-servants-nasa-employees-and-an-american-billionaire-among-donors-leaked-in-givesendgo-hack.

76. Klaus Schwab, speech at John F. Kennedy School of Government, Harvard University, September 20, 2017, https://www.youtube.com/watch?v=SjxJ1wPnkk4.

77. "Chrystia Freeland," Columbia University World Leaders Forum, https://worldleaders.columbia.edu/directory/chrystia-freeland.

78. Sarah Turnbull, "Freeland Says Some Protesters' Accounts Have Been Frozen, More to Come," CTV News, February 17, 2022, https://www.ctvnews.ca/politics/freeland-says-some-protesters-accounts-have-been-frozen-more-to-come-1.5785343.

79. Editors of *Encyclopaedia Britannica*, "Hitler Youth," *Britannica*, https://www.britannica.com/topic/Hitler-Youth.

80. "Your Child's Rights and What to Do about Them," Southeastern Legal Foundation, https://www.slfliberty.org/wp-content/uploads/sites/12/2022/05/SLFParentGuidebook.pdf.

81. "Department of Justice Is Using the PATRIOT Act to Investigate Parents," Moms for Liberty, May 12, 2022, https://www.momsforliberty.org/news/doj-to-investigate-parents/.

82. Adam Sullivan, "NH parental bill of rights falls short," WCAX 3, May 24, 2022, https://www.wcax.com/2022/05/24/nh-parental-bill-rights-falls-short/; "HB1431-FN-L," General Court of New Hampshire, https://www.gencourt.state.nh.us/bill_status/billinfo.aspx?id=1378&inflect=2.

83. "Cameras in the Classroom," *Education Next*, February 9, 2022, https://www.educationnext.org/cameras-in-the-classroom-iowa-florida-lawmakers-introduce-bills/.

84. Tiffany Justice, video interview, August 22, 2022.

85. "FBI Child ID App," FBI, https://www.fbi.gov/news/apps/child-id-app.

Chapter 2: A New Financial World Order, Part I

1. Eleanor Watson, "100 Days of War in Ukraine: A Timeline," CBS News, June 3, 2022, https://www.cbsnews.com/news/ukraine-russia-war-timeline-100-days/.

2. Ellen Nakashima and Felicia Sonmez, "U.S. Targets Major Russian Banks and Tech Sector with Sweeping Sanctions and Export Controls following Ukraine Invasion," *Washington Post*, February 24, 2022, https://www.washingtonpost.com/politics/2022/02/24/russia-sanctions-ukraine-biden/.

3. Alan Rappeport, "U.S. Escalates Sanctions with a Freeze on Russian Central Bank Assets," *New York Times*, February 28, 2022, https://www.nytimes.com/2022/02/28/us/politics/us-sanctions-russia-central-bank.html; Nicholas Gordon, "Banks are stopping Putin from tapping a $630 billion war chest Russia stockpiled before invading Ukraine," *Fortune*, March 3, 2022, https://fortune.com/2022/03/03/russia-sanctions-central-bank-ruble-us-eu-foreign-reserves/.

4. Ben Aris, "Russia Has Become an Agricultural Powerhouse, but Remains a Net Importer of

Food," Newsbase, April 20, 2020, https://www.intellinews.com/russia-has-become-an-agricultural-powerhouse-but-remains-a-net-importer-of-food-181359/.

5. Eddie Spence, "The $140 Billion Question: Can Russia Sell Its Huge Gold Pile?" Bloomberg, March 16, 2022, https://www.bloomberg.com/news/articles/2022-03-16/the-140-billion-question-can-russia-sell-its-huge-gold-pile?sref=hmG4mtJl.

6. Irina Ivanova, "Russia's Ruble Is the Strongest Currency in the World This Year," CBS News, June 28, 2022, https://www.cbsnews.com/news/russia-ruble-currency-2022/; Elliot Smith, "As Inflation Slows and the Ruble Rallies, Russia Is Hoping to Avoid a Financial Crisis," CNBC, May 18 2022, https://www.cnbc.com/2022/05/18/as-inflation-slows-and-ruble-rallies-russia-is-hoping-to-avoid-a-crisis.html.

7. Lauri Myllyvirta, Hubert Thieriot, Andrei Ilas, and Oleksii Mykhailenko, "Financing Putin's War: Fossil Fuel Imports from Russia in the First 100 Days of the Invasion," Centre for Research on Energy and Clean Air, June 12, 2022, https://energyandcleanair.org/publication/russian-fossil-exports-first-100-days.

8. Franklin Monsour and Kristina Arianina, "How Does the U.S. Take Ownership of Russian Oligarchs' Assets?" Bloomberg Law, March 18, 2022, https://news.bloomberglaw.com/us-law-week/how-does-the-u-s-take-ownership-of-russian-oligarchs-assets.

9. Editors of *Encyclopaedia Britannica*, "Eighty Years' War," *Britannica*, https://www.britannica.com/event/Eighty-Years-War.

10. Ray Dalio, "Changing World Order: Chapter 4: The Big Cycles of the Dutch and British Empires and Their Currencies," LinkedIn, May 21, 2020, https://www.linkedin.com/pulse/big-cycles-over-last-500-years-ray-dalio/.

11. Ibid.

12. Irina Damascan, "The Dutch Invented the Stock Market and Here's Why That's Important during the Coronavirus Outbreak," Medium, March 19, 2020, https://medium.com/dataseries/the-dutch-invented-the-stock-market-and-heres-why-that-s-important-during-the-coronavirus-outbreak-4482b100daee.

13. Andrew Beattie, "What Was the First Company to Issue Stock?" Investopedia, Updated June 30, 2022, https://www.investopedia.com/ask/answers/08/first-company-issue-stock-dutch-east-india.asp.

14. Ray Dalio, "Changing World Order: Chapter 4."

15. Ibid.

16. Editors of *Encyclopaedia Britannica*, "Congress of Vienna," *Britannica*, https://www.britannica.com/event/Congress-of-Vienna.

17. Ibid.; Ray Dalio, "Changing World Order: Chapter 4."

18. Deborah D'Souza, "How London Became the World's Financial Hub," Investopedia, June 25, 2019, https://www.investopedia.com/how-london-became-the-world-s-financial-hub-4589324.

19. Ray Dalio, "Changing World Order: Chapter 4."

20. Matthew Johnston, "How New York Became the Center of American Finance," Investopedia, March 31, 2022, https://www.investopedia.com/articles/investing/022516/how-new-york-became-center-american-finance.asp.

21. "Creation of the Bretton Woods System," Federal Reserve History, November 22, 2013, https://www.federalreservehistory.org/essays/bretton-woods-created.

22. Yi Wen and Brian Reinbold, "The Changing Relationship between Trade and America's Gold Reserves," Federal Reserve Bank of St. Louis, May 4, 2020, https://www.stlouisfed.org/publications/regional-economist/first-quarter-2020/changing-relationship-trade-americas-gold-reserves.

23. "Creation of the Bretton Woods System."

24. Ibid.

25. Ibid.

26. Ibid.

27. Ibid.

28. Jim Rickards, video interview, August 24, 2022; Arnold Beichman, "Guilty as Charged," Hoover Institution, April 30, 1999, https://www.hoover.org/research/guilty-charged.

29. Ashok Rao, "This Soviet spy created the US-led global economic system," Vox, August 24, 2014, https://www.vox.com/2014/8/24/6057119/harry-dexter-white-ben-steil.

30. "Gold Reserve Act of 1934," Federal Reserve History, November 22, 2013, https://www.federalreservehistory.org/essays/gold-reserve-act.

31. James Eagle, "Here's How Reserve Currencies Have Evolved Over 120 Years," Visual Capitalist, December 8, 2021, https://www.visualcapitalist.com/cp/how-reserve-currencies-evolved-over-120-years/.

32. Michael Bordo, "The Operation and Demise of the Bretton Woods System: 1958 to 1971," VoxEU, April 23, 2017, https://voxeu.org/article/operation-and-demise-bretton-woods-system.

33. Sarah Pruitt, "The Post World War II Boom: How America Got into Gear," History, May 14, 2020, https://www.history.com/news/post-world-war-ii-boom-economy.

34. "Luke Gromen," *The Grant Williams Podcast*, March 11, 2022, https://www.grant-williams.com/podcast/0028-luke-gromen.

35. "Nixon Ends Convertibility of U.S. Dollars to Gold and Announces Wage/Price Controls," Federal Reserve History, November 22, 2013, https://www.federalreservehistory.org/essays/gold-convertibility-ends.

36. Ibid.

37. John Paul Koning, "The Losing Battle to Fix Gold at $35, Part II," Mises Institute, March 31, 2009, https://mises.org/library/losing-battle-fix-gold-35-part-ii.

38. *Fresh Air*, "Underground Cities and 'Ghost' Miners': What Some People Do for Gold," WBEZ/NPR, December 3, 2013, https://www.npr.org/2013/12/03/248245685/underground-cities-and-ghost-miners-what-some-people-do-for-gold.

39. Richard Nixon, "Address to the Nation Outlining a New Economic Policy: 'The Challenge of Peace,'" American Presidency Project, August 15, 1971, https://www.presidency.ucsb.edu/documents/address-the-nation-outlining-new-economic-policy-the-challenge-peace.

40. Michael J. Graetz, "A 'Barbarous Relic': The French, Gold, and the Demise of Bretton Woods," Columbia Law School Scholarship Archive, 2016, https://scholarship.law.columbia.edu/cgi/viewcontent.cgi?article=3545&context=faculty_scholarship.

41. Will Kenton, "Nixon Shock," Investopedia, July 1, 2021, https://www.investopedia.com/terms/n/nixon-shock.asp.

42. Editors of *Encyclopaedia Britannica*, "Arab Oil Embargo," *Britannica*, https://www.britannica.com/event/Arab-oil-embargo.

43. Zaw Thiha Tun, "How Petrodollars Affect the U.S. Dollar," Investopedia, March 30, 2022, https://www.investopedia.com/articles/forex/072915/how-petrodollars-affect-us-dollar.asp.

44. "Oil Shock of 1973–74," Federal Reserve History, November 22, 2013, https://www.federalreservehistory.org/essays/oil-shock-of-1973-74.

45. Bernard Gwertzman, "'Milestone' Pact Is Signed by U.S. and Saudi Arabia," *New York Times*, June 9, 1974, https://www.nytimes.com/1974/06/09/archives/milestone-pact-is-signed-by-us-and-saudi-arabia-acclaimed-by.html.

46. Andrea Wong, "The Untold Story Behind Saudi Arabia's 41-Year U.S. Debt Secret," Bloomberg, May 30, 2016, https://www.bloomberg.com/news/features/2016-05-30/the-untold-story-behind-saudi-arabia-s-41-year-u-s-debt-secret#xj4y7vzkg?sref=hmG4mtJl.

47. Ibid.

48. Ibid.

49. "Luke Gromen," *The Grant Williams Podcast*; phrase credited to iTulip founder Eric Janszen.

50. Jeanna Smialek, "Powell Admires Paul Volcker. He May Have to Act Like Him," *New York Times*, March 14, 2022, https://www.nytimes.com/2022/03/14/business/economy/powell-fed-inflation-volcker.html.

51. "Recent Developments in Oil Prices," ECB Monthly Bulletin, May 2005, https://www.ecb.europa.eu/pub/pdf/other/mb200505_focus01.en.pdf.

52. "Timeline: Half a Century of Oil Price Volatility," Reuters, November 20, 2008, https://www.reuters.com/article/us-oil-prices/timeline-half-a-century-of-oil-price-volatility-idUKTRE4AJ3ZR20081120.

53. "Crude Oil Prices—70 Year Historical Chart," Macrotrends, https://www.macrotrends.net/1369/crude-oil-price-history-chart.

54. "Major Foreign Holders of Treasury Securities," US Treasury, https://ticdata.treasury.gov/Publish/mfh.txt.

55. Zhou Xiaochuan, "Reform the international monetary system," Bank for International Settlements, March 23, 2009, https://www.bis.org/review/r090402c.pdf.

56. Robert Fisk, "The Demise of the Dollar," *Independent*, October 6, 2009, https://www.independent.co.uk/news/business/news/the-demise-of-the-dollar-1798175.html.

57. Luke Gromen, *The Mr. X Interviews*, vol. 1 (Lake Placid, NY: Aviva Publishing, 2018).

58. Ibid.

59. Ibid.

60. Ibid.

61. Ben S. Bernanke, "The Dollar's International Role: An 'Exorbitant Privilege'?" Brookings Institution, January 7, 2016, https://www.brookings.edu/blog/ben-bernanke/2016/01/07/the-dollars-international-role-an-exorbitant-privilege-2/.

62. Gwynn Guilford and Corinne Purtill, "The US Can Eliminate Its Trade Deficit or Run the World's Dominant Currency—but Not Both," Quartz, May 2, 2018, updated July 20, 2022, https://qz.com/1266044/why-does-the-us-run-a-trade-deficit-to-maintain-the-dollars-privileged-position/.

63. Ibid.

64. Ray Dalio, *Principles for Dealing with the Changing World Order* (New York: Avid Reader Press, 2021), 13.

65. Marc Faber, "Once Asset Prices Drive the Real Economy, Standards of Living Become Vulnerable to Declines in Asset Prices," Gloom Boom Doom, Monthly Market Commentary: May 1, 2022, https://www.gloomboomdoom.com/.

66. Jared Bernstein, "Dethrone 'King Dollar,'" *New York Times*, August 27, 2014, https://www.nytimes.com/2014/08/28/opinion/dethrone-king-dollar.html.

67. Susan Lund et al., "Risk, Resilience, and Rebalancing in Global Value Chains," McKinsey & Company, August 6, 2020, https://www.mckinsey.com/business-functions/operations/our-insights/risk-resilience-and-rebalancing-in-global-value-chains.

Chapter 3: A New Financial World Order, Part II

1. Tom Bethell, "Property Rights, Prosperity and 1,000 Years of Lessons," *Wall Street Journal*, December 27, 1999, https://www.wsj.com/articles/SB945995080635655672.

2. Milton Friedman, *Commanding Heights* Interview, Part 1, PBS, https://www-tc.pbs.org/wgbh/commandingheights/press_site/people/pdf/friedman_intv.pdf.

3. Milton Friedman, *Commanding Heights* interview, PBS, n.d., http://www.pbs.org/wgbh/commandingheights/press_site/people/friedman_intv.html.

4. Ayn Rand, "POV: Man's Rights; The Nature of Government," in *The Virtue of Selfishness* (Ayn Rand Institute, 1963), https://ari.aynrand.org/issues/government-and-business/individual-rights/.

5. Rose and Milton Friedman, *Two Lucky People: Memoirs*, quoted in Ken Blackwell, "Milton Friedman's Property Rights Legacy," *Forbes*, July 31, 2014, https://www.forbes.com/sites/realspin/2014/07/31/milton-friedmans-property-rights-legacy/?sh=3140037a6635.

6. Blackwell, "Milton Friedman's Property Rights Legacy."

7. Bethell, "Property Rights, Prosperity and 1,000 Years of Lessons."

8. "Regulatory Costs Add a Whopping $93,870 to New Home Prices," National Association of Home Builders, May 6, 2021, https://www.nahb.org/blog/2021/05/regulatory-costs-add-a-whopping-93870-to-new-home-prices/.

9. "To Serve Man (*The Twilight Zone*)," Wikipedia, https://en.wikipedia.org/wiki/To_Serve_Man_(The_Twilight_Zone).

10. Mark J. Perry, "50 Years of Failed Doomsday, Eco-pocalyptic Predictions; the So-called 'Experts' Are 0-50," Carpe Diem/AEI, September 23, 2019, https://www.aei.org/carpe-diem/50-years-of-failed-doomsday-eco-pocalyptic-predictions-the-so-called-experts-are-0-50/.

11. "George Carlin: Jamming in New York (1992)—Transcript," Scraps from the Loft, April 6, 2017, https://scrapsfromtheloft.com/comedy/george-carlin-jamming-new-york-1992-full-transcript/.

12. Keith Reed, "BLM Co-Founder Says She Put $6 Million Home to Personal Use," The Root, May 10, 2022, https://www.theroot.com/blm-co-founder-says-she-put-6-million-home-to-personal-1848904788; Paul Meara, "Black Lives Matter Leaders Sue Former Executive Accused of Siphoning $10 Million for Personal Use," BET, September 6, 2022, https://www.bet.com/article/w0hjnf/black-lives-matter-leaders-sue-former-executive-10-million-personal; Erika D. Smith, "In this Black Lives Matter family feud, we'll get transparency. But at what cost?" *Los Angeles Times*, September 4, 2022, https://www.latimes.com/california/story/2022-09-04/black-lives-matter-blm-lawsuit-stealing-donations-cost-movement.

13. "Klaus Schwab," Wikipedia, https://en.wikipedia.org/wiki/Klaus_Schwab.

14. "A Partner in Shaping History: The First 40 Years," World Economic Forum, 2010, https://

www3.weforum.org/docs/WEF_First40Years_Book_2010.pdf; Ceri Parker, "The World Economic Forum at 50: a Timeline of Highlights from Davos and Beyond," World Economic Forum, December 20, 2019, https://www.weforum.org/agenda/2019/12/world-economic-forum-davos-at-50-history-a-timeline-of-highlights/.

15. "Professor Dr.-Ing. Klaus Schwab," Amazon, https://www.amazon.com/Professor-Dr-Ing-Klaus-Schwab/e/B00IZOATS6?ref=sr_ntt_srch_lnk_7&qid=1654705430&sr=1-7.

16. Haig Simonian, "Interview: Klaus Schwab," FT.com via Wayback Machine, January 22, 2008, https://web.archive.org/web/20090604034329/http:/www.ft.com/cms/s/0/0304411c-c5e8-11dc-8378-0000779fd2ac%2Cdwp_uuid%3D01b19234-b4b2-11dc-990a-0000779fd2ac.html?nclick_check=1.

17. Parker, "The World Economic Forum at 50."

18. "Heidrick & Struggles Helps Identify Young Global Leaders for World Economic Forum," press release, March 16, 2009, https://heidrick.gcs-web.com/news-releases/news-release-details/heidrick-struggles-helps-identify-young-global-leaders-world.

19. @JamesMelville, Twitter, February 1, 2022, https://twitter.com/JamesMelville/status/1488472558425063430?s=20&t=FzhBQJQrB5VUXbOytLg39Q; Adham Hamed, "Did Klaus Schwab Reveal How the World Economic Forum Infiltrates Governments?" *Al-Estiklal*, August 29, 2022, https://www.alestiklal.net/en/view/12516/did-klaus-schwab-just-reveal-how-the-world-economic-forum-infiltrates-governments.

20. "Can You Rent Everything You Need in Life," World Economic Forum, YouTube, January 31, 2017, https://www.youtube.com/watch?v=Kpz6K1sSIPY.

21. "World Economic Forum's '8 Predictions for the World in 2030,'" Flow State, YouTube, January 2, 2021, https://www.youtube.com/watch?v=MKwENH-m4oU; @WEF, Twitter, April 9, 2018, https://twitter.com/wef/status/983378870819794945?s=20&t=O1782NwYJgDEinsrSAQx-w; Ceri Parker, "8 predictions for the world in 2030," World Economic Forum, November 12, 2016, https://www.weforum.org/agenda/2016/11/8-predictions-for-the-world-in-2030/.

22. Sarah Todd, "Psychologists Say a Good Life Doesn't Have to Be Happy, or Even Meaningful," World Economic Forum, August 24, 2021, https://www.weforum.org/agenda/2021/08/research-good-life-happy-meaningful.

23. Eugene Garla, "Cyber Polygon Furthers Great Reset Agenda of Centralized Power & Surveillance," Sociable, July 13, 2021, https://sociable.co/government-and-policy/cyber-polygon-great-reset-centralized-power-surveillance/.

24. Oliver Cann, "Who Pays for Davos?" World Economic Forum, January 16, 2017, https://www.weforum.org/agenda/2017/01/who-pays-for-davos/.

25. Ryan Heath, "Davos Is Dead," *Politico*, December 20, 2021, https://www.politico.com/news/2021/12/20/davos-is-dead-525732#:~:text=In%202020%2C%20WEF's%20Davos%20conference,to%20access%20this%20guest%20list.

26. "Annual Report: 2020–2021," World Economic Forum, https://www3.weforum.org/docs/WEF_Annual_Report_2020_21.pdf, 98.

27. Adam Andrzejewski, "$60 Million from U.S. Taxpayers So WEF Can Fund 'Playground' for World's Billionaires?" Defender, May 20, 2022, https://childrenshealthdefense.org/defender/wef-u-s-taxpayers-funding/.

28. "Knurrende Zustimmung vom Ständerat zu WEF-Geldern," SRF, June 11, 2021, https://www.srf.ch/news/schweiz/geld-fuer-sicherheit-am-wef-knurrende-zustimmung-vom-staenderat-zu-wef-geldern.

29. "The U.S. Government and the World Health Organization," KFF, May 19, 2022, https://www.kff.org/coronavirus-covid-19/fact-sheet/the-u-s-government-and-the-world-health-organization/.

30. "What we do," World Health Organization, https://www.who.int/about.

31. @CriticalSway, Twitter, May 17, 2022, https://twitter.com/CriticalSway/status/1526464507438157827?s=20&t=1wbtO_AgZMbvNldh4zUG7Q.

32. "WHO Battles Opposition to Push for Pandemic Treaty," *Taipei Times*, June 9, 2022, https://www.taipeitimes.com/News/world/archives/2022/06/09/2003779620.

33. "The U.S. Government and the World Health Organization," KFF.

34. Richard Roth and Maegan Vazquez, "US Officially Rejoins Controversial UN Human Rights Council," CNN, October 14, 2021, https://www.cnn.com/2021/10/14/politics/us-united-nations-human-rights-council.

35. World Bank, "United Nations and Its Relationship to the World Bank Group," World Bank Group eLibrary, October 2015, https://elibrary.worldbank.org/doi/10.1596/978-1-4648-0484-7_united_nations_and; https://ebrary.net/14983/economics/united_nations_relationship_world_bank_group.

36. Joe Sommerlad, "What Is the Bilderberg Group and Are Its Members Really Plotting the New World Order?" *Independent*, May, 28, 2019, https://www.independent.co.uk/news/world/europe/bilderberg-group-conspiracy-theories-secret-societies-new-world-order-alex-jones-a8377171.html.

37. Ruslana Lishchuk, "Streaming Services and Tech Giants Compared to Countries," Mackeeper, August 13, 2021, https://mackeeper.com/blog/tech-giants-as-countries/; "Facebook Statistics and Trends," Datareportal, https://datareportal.com/essential-facebook-stats.

38. "Remarks by President Biden Before Business Roundtable's CEO Quarterly Meeting," The White House, March 21, 2022, https://www.whitehouse.gov/briefing-room/speeches-remarks/2022/03/21/remarks-by-president-biden-before-business-roundtables-ceo-quarterly-meeting/.

Chapter 4: The Incredible Shrinking Dollar

1. Frédéric Bastiat, "Economic Sophisms," *Physiology of Plunder*, 1848 (Second Series), ch. 1.

2. Jack Weatherford, *In Money We Trust*, PBS, https://www.pbs.org/video/in-money-we-trust-ox6o7a/.

3. Bruce Bartlett, "How Excessive Government Killed Ancient Rome," *Cato Journal* 14, no. 2 (Fall 1994), https://www.cato.org/sites/cato.org/files/serials/files/cato-journal/1994/11/cj14n2-7.pdf; Joseph R. Peden, "Inflation and the Fall of the Roman Empire," Mises Institute, October 19, 2017, https://mises.org/library/inflation-and-fall-roman-empire.

4. Weatherford, *In Money We Trust*; "History of Hard Money: The Roman Empire," Vaulted, March 23, 2022, https://vaulted.com/history-of-hard-money-the-roman-empire/; Marc Faber, "Economy and Empire," *Forbes*, June 10, 2002, https://www.forbes.com/global/2002/0610/064.html?sh=5ecd55186381.

5. Peden, "Inflation and the Fall of the Roman Empire"; "History of Hard Money: The Roman Empire"

6. Steve Forbes, "In Money We Trust."

7. "A Message from the President of the United States," Internet Archive, *Saturday Night Live*, Season 4, Episode 4, November 4, 1978, https://archive.org/details/saturday-night-live-s-04-e-04-steve-martin-van-morrison-11-04-1978.

8. Ibid.

9. "Cost-of-Living Adjustment (COLA) Information for 2022," Social Security Administration, https://www.ssa.gov/cola/.

10. Ajay S. Mookerjee, "What If Central Banks Issued Digital Currency?" *Harvard Business Review*, October 15, 2021, https://hbr.org/2021/10/what-if-central-banks-issued-digital-currency.

11. U.S. Inflation Calculator, https://www.usinflationcalculator.com/.

12. Federal Reserve Bank of St. Louis, "Functions of Money," *The Economic Lowdown* (podcast), https://www.stlouisfed.org/education/economic-lowdown-podcast-series/episode-9-functions-of-money.

13. "Open Market Operations," Board of Governors of the Federal Reserve System, https://www.federalreserve.gov/monetarypolicy/openmarket.htm.

14. J. Paul Getty quotes, Goodreads, https://www.goodreads.com/quotes/214064-if-you-owe-the-bank-100-that-s-your-problem-if.

15. "Robert E. Rubin (1995–1999)," US Department of the Treasury, https://home.treasury.gov/about/history/prior-secretaries/robert-e-rubin-1995-1999; "Robert Rubin," Wikipedia, https://en.wikipedia.org/wiki/Robert_Rubin.

16. "Current Member Biography: Lawrence H. Summers," Group of Thirty, https://group30.org/members/bio_current/summers.

17. "Timothy Geithner Fast Facts," CNN, updated August 2, 2022, https://www.cnn.com/2013/02/25/us/timothy-geithner-fast-facts/index.html.

18. "Ben Bernanke Fast Facts," CNN, November 25, 2021, https://www.cnn.com/2013/02/20/us/ben-bernanke-fast-facts/index.html.

19. Alex Thompson and Theodoric Meyer, "Janet Yellen Made Millions in Wall Street, Corporate Speeches," *Politico*, January 1, 2021, https://www.politico.com/news/2021/01/01/yellen-made-millions-in-wall-street-speeches-453223.

20. Heather Perlberg and Sonali Basak, "Trump Treasury Secretary Mnuchin Raises $2.5 Billion Fund," Bloomberg, September 20, 2021, https://www.bloomberg.com/news/articles/2021-09-20/trump-treasury-secretary-steven-mnuchin-raises-2-5-billion-fund?sref=hmG4mtJl.

21. Eric Dash and Louise Story, "Rubin Leaving Citigroup; Smith Barney for Sale," *New York Times*, January 9, 2009, https://www.nytimes.com/2009/01/10/business/10rubin.html?_r=1&hp.

22. James Doubek, "Former Treasury Secretary Paul O'Neill Dies at 84," NPR, April 18, 2020, https://www.npr.org/2020/04/18/837917748/former-treasury-secretary-paul-oneill-dies-at-84; Will Dunham, "Former U.S. Treasury Secretary and Iraq War Critic Paul O'Neill dies at 84: WSJ," Reuters, April 18, 2020, https://www.reuters.com/article/us-people-paul-o-neill/former-u-s-treasury-secretary-and-iraq-war-critic-paul-oneill-dies-at-84-wsj-idUSKBN2200MW.

23. Joseph Kahn, "Former Treasury Secretary Joins Leadership Triangle at Citigroup," *New York Times*, October 27, 1999, https://www.nytimes.com/1999/10/27/business/former-treasury-secretary-joins-leadership-triangle-at-citigroup.html; Jeff Cox, "Bernanke, Paulson and Geithner Say They Bailed Out Wall Street to Help Main Street," CNBC, September 12, 2018, https://www.cnbc.com/2018/09/12/bernanke-paulson-and-geithner-say-they-bailed-out-wall-street-to-help-main-street.html; Jeanna Smialek, "Top U.S. Officials Consulted with BlackRock as Markets Melted Down," *New York Times*, June 24, 2021, https://www.nytimes.com/2021/06/24/business/economy/fed-blackrock-pandemic-crisis.html; Pete Schroeder and Michelle Price, "U.S. Fed hires BlackRock to help execute mortgage-backed securities purchases," Reuters, March 24, 2020, https://www.reuters.com/article/us-health-coronavirus-fed-banks/u-s-fed-hires-blackrock-to-help-execute-mortgage-backed-securities-purchases-idUSKBN21B3E0.

24. "The Budget and Economic Outlook: 2022 to 2032," Congressional Budget Office, May 2022, https://www.cbo.gov/publication/58147.

25. "Interest Costs on the National Debt Projected to Nearly Triple over the Next Decade," Peter G. Peterson Foundation, July 22, 2021, https://www.pgpf.org/blog/2021/07/interest-costs-on-the-national-debt-projected-to-nearly-triple-over-the-next-decade.

26. Jordan Major, "Major Central Banks Have Printed $25 Trillion since 2008, Data Shows," Finbold, November 12, 2021, https://finbold.com/major-central-banks-have-printed-25-trillion-since-2008-data-shows/.

27. Jeff Cox, "Inflation Climbs Higher than Expected in June as Price Index Rises 5.4%," CNBC, July 13, 2021, https://www.cnbc.com/2021/07/13/consumer-price-index-increases-5point4percent-in-june-vs-5percent-estimate.html.

28. Saleha Mohsin, "Yellen Sees Recent Inflation as Transitory Rather Than Permanent," Bloomberg, June 5, 2021, https://www.bloomberg.com/news/articles/2021-06-05/yellen-sees-recent-inflation-as-transitory-rather-than-permanent?sref=hmG4mtJl.

29. Christopher Condon, "Yellen Sticks with 'Transitory' View of U.S. Inflation," Bloomberg, October 12, 2021, https://www.bloomberg.com/news/articles/2021-10-12/yellen-sticks-with-transitory-view-of-higher-u-s-inflation?sref=hmG4mtJl.

30. Jeff Cox, "Inflation Rose 9.1% in June, Even More than Expected, as Consumer Pressures Intensify," CNBC, July 13, 2022, https://www.cnbc.com/2022/07/13/inflation-rose-9point1percent-in-june-even-more-than-expected-as-price-pressures-intensify.html; Jeff Cox, "Wholesale prices shoot up near-record 11.3% in June on surge in energy costs," CNBC, July 14, 2022, https://www.cnbc.com/2022/07/14/producer-price-index-june-2022-gain-11point3percent-on-surge-in-energy-costs.html.

31. "M2," Investopedia, updated January 10, 2022, https://www.investopedia.com/terms/m/m2.asp.

32. Morgan Housel, "The Fed Isn't Printing as Much Money as You Think," March 8, 2021, Collaborative Fund, https://www.collaborativefund.com/blog/the-fed-isnt-printing-as-much-money-as-you-think/.

33. Saqib Iqbal Ahmed, "S&P 500 Ends Brutal First Half '22 with Largest Percentage Loss since 1970," Reuters, June 30, 2022, https://www.reuters.com/markets/europe/brutal-first-half-22-track-shave-8-trillion-off-sp-500-2022-06-30/; Kerry Hannon, "Retirement Savers Lose over $3 Trillion in Stock Market Retreat," Yahoo News, June 23, 2022, https://news.yahoo.com/retirement-savers-lose-stock-market-201508667.html.

34. "Personal Saving Rate," FRED, https://fred.stlouisfed.org/series/PSAVERT.

35. "Personal Saving Rate," Bureau of Economic Analysis, December 23, 2022, https://www.bea.gov/data/income-saving/personal-saving-rate.

36. "Household Debt and Credit, 2022: Q2," Federal Reserve Bank of New York, August 2022, https://www.newyorkfed.org/medialibrary/interactives/householdcredit/data/pdf/HHDC_2022Q2.

37. @LetEvery1Invest, Twitter, April 27, 2022, https://twitter.com/LetEvery1Invest/status/1519503228882370561?s=20&t=f2jypC4rQF_dZr5fzbnvaQ.

38. James V. Grimaldi, Coulter Jones and Joe Palazzolo, "131 Federal Judges Broke the Law by

Hearing Cases Where They Had a Financial Interest," *Wall Street Journal,* September 28, 2021, https://www.wsj.com/articles/131-federal-judges-broke-the-law-by-hearing-cases-where-they-had-a-financial-interest-11632834421.

39. Paul Lamonica, "More than $7 Trillion Has Been Wiped Out from the Stock Market This Year," CNN, May 12, 2022, https://www.cnn.com/2022/05/12/investing/stocks-bear-market/index.html.

Chapter 5: Digital Dollar Destitution

1. Adeel Hassan and Andrea Kannapell, "These Are the U.S. States Trying Lotteries to Increase Covid Vaccinations," *New York Times,* July 3, 2021, https://www.nytimes.com/2021/07/03/world/covid-vaccine-lottery.html.

2. "What Is Lawful Money? How Is It Different from Legal Tender?" Board of Governors of the Federal Reserve System, https://www.federalreserve.gov/faqs/money_15197.htm.

3. Shobhit Seth, "What Is a Central Bank Digital Currency (CBDC)," Investopedia, March 19, 2022, https://www.investopedia.com/terms/c/central-bank-digital-currency-cbdc.asp.

4. Ibid.

5. Ibid.

6. Kevin Voigt and Andy Rosen, "Cryptocurrency: What It Is and How It Works," Nerdwallet, June 13, 2022, https://www.nerdwallet.com/article/investing/cryptocurrency; Carmen Reinicke, "Bitcoin Has Lost More than 50% of Its Value This Year. Here's What You Need to Know," CNBC, June 15, 2022, https://www.cnbc.com/2022/06/15/bitcoin-has-lost-more-than-50percent-of-its-value-this-year-what-to-know.html.

7. Adam Hayes, "10 Important Cryptocurrencies Other Than Bitcoin," Investopedia, July 8, 2022, https://www.investopedia.com/tech/most-important-cryptocurrencies-other-than-bitcoin/.

8. Ibid.

9. Ibid.

10. "Executive Order on Ensuring Responsible Development of Digital Assets," The White House, March 9, 2022, https://www.whitehouse.gov/briefing-room/presidential-actions/2022/03/09/executive-order-on-ensuring-responsible-development-of-digital-assets/.

11. Gregory A. Keoleian and Martin C. Heller, "Implications of Future US Diet Scenarios on Greenhouse Gas Emissions," Center for Sustainable Systems, University of Michigan, January 13, 2020, https://css.umich.edu/publications/research-publications/implications-future-us-diet-scenarios-greenhouse-gas-emissions.

12. "Digital Currency: Yuan Comes with an Expiry Date: Spend or It Will Vanish," ETBFSI, April 14, 2021, https://bfsi.economictimes.indiatimes.com/news/policy/digital-currency-yuan-comes-with-an-expiry-date-spend-or-it-will-vanish/82059471.

13. Russ Wiles, "Biden Plan Would Give IRS More Power to Track $600 Bank Accounts: What You Need to Know," AZ Central, October 9, 2021, https://www.azcentral.com/story/money/business/2021/10/09/what-you-need-know-biden-plan-track-600-bank-accounts/6052734001/.

14. @CBSEveningNews, Twitter, October 12, 2021, https://twitter.com/CBSEveningNews/status/1448018574115737602?s=20&t=irLtSxPeRchxq9VSuOzU2Q.

15. Greg Baer and Paige Pidano Paridon, "The Waning Case for a Dollar CBDC," Bank Policy Institute, February 18, 2022, https://bpi.com/the-waning-case-for-a-dollar-cbdc/.

16. Ibid.

17. Ibid.

18. Ajay S. Mookerjee, "What If Central Banks Issued Digital Currency?" *Harvard Business Review,* October 15, 2021, https://hbr.org/2021/10/what-if-central-banks-issued-digital-currency.

19. "119 Impressive Cybersecurity Statistics: 2023 Data & Market Analysis," Finances Online, https://financesonline.com/cybersecurity-statistics/; Rob Sobers, "166 Cybersecurity Statistics and Trends," Updated July 8, 2022, https://www.varonis.com/blog/cybersecurity-statistics.

20. Patrick Howell O'Neill, "A $620 Million Hack? Just Another Day in Crypto," *MIT Technology Review,* April 15, 2022, https://www.technologyreview.com/2022/04/15/1050259/a-620-million-hack-just-another-day-in-crypto/.

21. Mookerjee, "What If Central Banks Issued Digital Currency?"

22. Amnon Samid, "What I Learned from My Role in Digitizing the Yuan," Forkast, February 4, 2022, https://forkast.news/digital-yuan-cbdc-china-central-bank-currency/; Sebastian Banescu et al., "4 key cybersecurity threats to new central bank digital currencies," World Economic Forum, November 20, 2021, https://www.weforum.org/agenda/2021/11/4-key-threats-central-bank-digital-currencies/.

23. William Turton and Kartikay Mehrotra, "Hackers Breached Colonial Pipeline Using Compromised Password," Bloomberg, June 4, 2021, https://www.bloomberg.com/news/articles/2021-06-04/hackers-breached-colonial-pipeline-using-compromised-password; Kevin Collier, "Meat Supplier JBS Paid Ransomware Hackers $11 Million," CNBC, June 9, 2021, https://www.cnbc.com/2021/06/09/jbs-paid-11-million-in-response-to-ransomware-attack-.html.

24. Kristalina Georgieva, "The Future of Money: Gearing Up for Central Bank Digital Currency," International Monetary Fund, February 9, 2022, https://www.imf.org/en/News/Articles/2022/02/09/sp020922-the-future-of-money-gearing-up-for-central-bank-digital-currency; "Central Bank Digital Currency Tracker," Atlantic Council, https://www.atlanticcouncil.org/cbdctracker/.

25. Andrea Shalal and David Lawder, "G7 Finance Officials Endorse Principles for Central Bank Digital Currencies," Reuters, October 13, 2021, https://www.reuters.com/business/g7-finance-officials-endorse-principles-central-bank-digital-currencies-2021-10-14/.

26. Jeffrey A. Brill et al., "Central Banks Consider Digital Currency Pros and Cons in US and Europe," Skadden, Arps, Slate, Meagher & Flom LLP and Affiliates, January 19, 2022, https://www.skadden.com/insights/publications/2022/01/2022-insights/regulation-enforcement-and-investigations/central-banks-consider-digital-currency-pros-and-cons.

27. Colin Brightfield, "Central Bank Digital Currencies (CBDCs) Are Coming Soon," How-To Geek, April 27, 2022, https://www.howtogeek.com/798159/central-bank-digital-currencies-cbdcs-are-coming-soon/.

28. "Digital Currency Governance Consortium," World Economic Forum, https://www.weforum.org/communities/digital-currency-governance-consortium; Daniel Israel, "A Summary: Why Are the World Economic Forum (WEF) & Rockefeller Foundation So Intent on Implementing a Digital ID, Digital Currency & Social Credit Score System?" Medium, February 10, 2022, https://medium.com/@daniel_israel/a-summary-why-are-the-world-economic-forum-wef-rockefeller-foundation-so-intent-on-f646c3a278aa.

29. Philipp Hildebrand, "Davos Brief: a Fundamental Rethink," BlackRock Investment Institute, January 25, 2021, https://www.blackrock.com/us/individual/insights/blackrock-investment-institute/davos-brief.

30. Joe Silverstein, "Billionaire Investor Ray Dalio Says China Is a Rising Power, Warns That Inflation and Debt Will Destroy US," Fox News, May 3, 2022, https://www.foxnews.com/media/billionaire-investor-ray-dalio-china-rising-power-warns-inflation-debt-destroy-us.

31. Theodore Benzmiller, "China's Progress Towards a Central Bank Digital Currency," Center for Strategic & International Studies, April 19, 2022, https://www.csis.org/blogs/new-perspectives-asia/chinas-progress-towards-central-bank-digital-currency.

32. Lorand Laskai, "Let's Start with What China's Digital Currency Is Not," Digichina, Stanford University, March 8, 2022, https://digichina.stanford.edu/work/lets-start-with-what-chinas-digital-currency-is-not/.

33. Benzmiller, "China's Progress Towards a Central Bank Digital Currency."

34. Christina Majaski, "Yuan vs. Renminbi: What's the Difference?" Investopedia, July 5, 2022, https://www.investopedia.com/articles/forex/061115/yuan-vs-rmb-understanding-difference.asp.

35. Benzmiller, "China's Progress Towards a Central Bank Digital Currency."

36. Allen K. Wan, Amanda Wang, Yujing Liu, and Zheping Huang, "China's Much-Hyped Digital Yuan Fails to Impress Early Users," Bloomberg, May 9, 2021, https://www.bloomberg.com/news/articles/2021-05-09/china-s-much-hyped-digital-yuan-fails-to-impress-early-users?sref=VZPf2pAM.

37. Ananya Kumar, "A Report Card on China's Central Bank Digital Currency: The e-CNY," Atlantic Council, March 1, 2022, https://www.atlanticcouncil.org/blogs/econographics/a-report-card-on-chinas-central-bank-digital-currency-the-e-cny/.

38. Ibid.

39. Ibid.

40. Ibid.

41. Ibid.

42. Jing Yang and AnnaMaria Andriotis, "At the Winter Olympics, Beijing's Digital Yuan Push Puts Visa in a Bind," *Wall Street Journal*, February 9, 2022, https://www.wsj.com/articles/beijings-digital-currency-push-at-winter-olympics-puts-visa-in-a-bind-11644402602; Benzmiller, "China's Progress Towards a Central Bank Digital Currency."

43. Frank Tang, "China's Digital Currency Racks up 'a Couple of Million' Yuan of Payments per

Day at the Beijing Winter Olympics," *South China Morning Post*, February 16, 2022, https://www.scmp.com/economy/china-economy/article/3167271/chinas-digital-currency-racks-couple-million-yuan-payments.

44. Baer and Paridon, "The Waning Case for a Dollar CBDC."

45. Dante Disparte, "A Central Bank Digital Currency Would Be Bad for the US," Coindesk, May 17, 2021, https://www.coindesk.com/policy/2021/05/17/a-central-bank-digital-currency-would-be-bad-for-the-us/.

46. Ibid.

47. Derek Andersen, "Ex-Fed Vice-Chair Quarles Has Lost None of His Fervor in Opposing US CBDC," Cointelegraph, May 3, 2022, https://cointelegraph.com/news/ex-fed-vice-chair-quarles-has-lost-none-of-his-fervor-in-opposing-us-cbdc.

48. Ibid.

49. Baer and Paridon, "The Waning Case for a Dollar CBDC."

50. Ibid.

51. Christopher J. Waller, "Christopher J Waller: CBDC—A Solution in Search of a Problem?" Bank for International Settlements, August 5, 2021, https://www.bis.org/review/r210806a.htm.

52. "Central Bank Digital Currency (CBDC) Feedback Form," Board of Governors of the Federal Reserve System, May 21, 2022, https://www.federalreserve.gov/apps/forms/cbdc.

53. Matthew Malloy, Francis Martinez, Mary-Frances Styczynski, and Alex Thorp, "Retail CBDC and U.S. Monetary Policy Implementation: A Stylized Balance Sheet Analysis," Federal Reserve Board, April 2022, https://www.federalreserve.gov/econres/feds/files/2022032pap.pdf.

54. Brill et al., "Central Banks Consider Digital Currency Pros and Cons in US and Europe."

55. Andrea Shalal and David Lawder, "G7 Finance Officials Endorse Principles for Central Bank Digital Currencies," Reuters, October 13, 2022, https://www.reuters.com/business/g7-finance-officials-endorse-principles-central-bank-digital-currencies-2021-10-14/.

Chapter 6: The Technocracy and Digital Rights

1. Nico DeMattia, "BMW Makes Heated Seats an $18/Month Subscription Service—Again," The Drive, July 11, 2022, https://www.thedrive.com/news/bmw-is-charging-a-subscription-fee-for-heated-seats-again; James Vincent, "BMW starts selling heated seat subscriptions for $18 a month," The Verge, July 12, 2022,https://www.theverge.com/2022/7/12/23204950/bmw-subscriptions-microtransactions-heated-seats-feature.

2. Will Kenton, "Technocracy Definition," Investopedia, September 26, 2021, https://www.investopedia.com/terms/t/technocracy.asp.

3. @CarolJSRoth, Twitter, July 12, 2022, https://twitter.com/caroljsroth/status/1547046712115617794/photo/2.

4. @CarolJSRoth, Twitter, July 18, 2022, https://twitter.com/caroljsroth/status/1549154618021650443?s=20&t=j56AMs3nlpDTsyzqwoxlyA.

5. James Gordon, "'The Lil Bird and I Are Now the Best of Friends': Journalist Alex Berenson Returns to Twitter as Social Media Giant Admits He Shouldn't Have Been Banned for Questioning COVID Vaccines," *Daily Mail*, July 8, 2022, updated July 9, 2022, https://www.dailymail.co.uk/news/article-10996987/Journalist-Alex-Berenson-reinstated-Twitter-suing-violation-Amendment.html; Alex Berenson, "@alexberenson," Substack, July 6, 2022, https://alexberenson.substack.com/p/alexberenson/.

6. "Mobile Operating System Market Share Worldwide," Statcounter, https://gs.statcounter.com/os-market-share/mobile/worldwide.

7. Ruslana Lishchuk, "How Large Would Tech Companies Be If They Were Countries?" Mackeeper, August 13, 2021, https://mackeeper.com/blog/tech-giants-as-countries/; "Facebook Statistics and Trends," Datareportal https://datareportal.com/essential-facebook-stats.

8. "Digital Revolution," December 12, 2017, Techopedia, https://www.techopedia.com/definition/23371/digital-revolution.

9. Fakhri Ahmadov, "How the Last 10 Years of Business Changed Everything," World Economic Forum, May 8, 2017, https://www.weforum.org/agenda/2017/05/how-tech-giants-changed-the-business-world/.

10. "Our Partners," World Economic Forum, https://www.weforum.org/partners/.

11. Raymond Zhong, "China Fines Alibaba $2.8 Billion in Landmark Antitrust Case," *New York Times*, April 9, 2021, https://www.nytimes.com/2021/04/09/technology/china-alibaba-monopoly-fine.html; Paul Mozur, Cecilia Kang, Adam Satariano, and David McCabe, "A Global Tipping Point

for Reining In Tech Has Arrived," *New York Times*, April 20, 2021, updated April 30, 2021, https://www.nytimes.com/2021/04/20/technology/global-tipping-point-tech.html.

12. @TrungTPhan, Twitter, July 25, 2022, https://twitter.com/TrungTPhan/status/1551772934493986816?s=20&t=w0VofhEMFWmYdYLuhFOpQw.

13. Terry Gross, "How 5 Tech Giants Have Become More Like Governments Than Companies," NPR, October 26, 2017, https://www.npr.org/2017/10/26/560136311/how-5-tech-giants-have-become-more-like-governments-than-companies.

14. Daniel Broudy and Makoto Arakaki, "Who Wants to Be a Slave? The Technocratic Convergence of Humans and Data," *Frontiers in Communication*, June 12, 2020, https://www.frontiersin.org/articles/10.3389/fcomm.2020.00037/full.

15. Sunil Johal, "Technology Will Make Today's Government Obsolete and That's Good," The Conversation, November 29, 2017, https://theconversation.com/technology-will-make-todays-government-obsolete-and-thats-good-86430.

16. Rodrigo Fernandez, Tobias J. Klinge, Reijer Hendrikse, and Ilke Adriaans, "How Big Tech Is Becoming the Government," *Tribune*, May 2, 2021, https://tribunemag.co.uk/2021/02/how-big-tech-became-the-government.

17. Giovanni De Gregorio, "How Big Tech Is Changing Who's in Charge of Our Rights and Freedoms," The Conversation, November 16, 2021, https://theconversation.com/how-big-tech-is-changing-whos-in-charge-of-our-rights-and-freedoms-171157.

18. Ibid.

19. Tristan Greene, "Majority of Europeans Would Replace Government with AI—Oof, They're so Wrong," TNW, May 27, 2021, https://thenextweb.com/news/majority-europeans-replace-government-ai-why-wrong.

20. Mozur et al., "A Global Tipping Point for Reining In Tech Has Arrived."

21. Ibid.

22. Ibid.

23. Marietje Schaake, "How Democracies Can Claim Back Power in the Digital World," *MIT Technology Review*, September 29, 2020, https://www.technologyreview.com/2020/09/29/1009088/democracies-power-digital-social-media-governance-tech-companies-opinion/.

24. Ibid.

25. Sui-Lee Wee, "China Reassures Homeowners Worried About Land Rights," *New York Times*, December 26, 2016, https://www.nytimes.com/2016/12/26/business/china-wenzhou-land-lease.html.

26. Schaake, "How Democracies Can Claim Back Power in the Digital World."

27. Emily Baker-White, "Leaked Audio from 80 Internal TikTok Meetings Shows That US User Data Has Been Repeatedly Accessed from China," BuzzFeed News, June 17, 2022, https://www.buzzfeednews.com/article/emilybakerwhite/tiktok-tapes-us-user-data-china-bytedance-access.

28. Libby Emmons, "PayPal Permanently Bans Journalist Ian Miles Cheong's Account," Post Millennial, January 5, 2022, https://thepostmillennial.com/paypal-permanently-bans-journalist-ian-miles-cheongs-account.

29. @DavidSacks, Twitter, January 5, 2022, https://twitter.com/davidsacks/status/1478831627992121344.

30. Amanda Pérez Pintado, "PayPal Controversy: App Backtracks on New Policy to Fine $2500 for Misinformation," *USA Today*, October 13, 2022, https://www.usatoday.com/story/money/2022/10/13/paypal-misinformation-policy-sparks-backlash-many-users-delete-app/10486413002/.

31. Sara Morrison, "Why Attorney General Bill Barr Is Mad at Apple," Vox, May 18, 2020, https://www.vox.com/recode/2020/5/18/21262731/fbi-apple-unlock-iphone-encryption-bill-barr-alshamrani.

32. Nick Summers, "Amazon One Uses Your Palm to Approve Store Purchases," Engadget, September 29, 2020, https://www.engadget.com/amazon-one-palm-recognition-go-stores-seattle-100718649.html; Jon Fingas, "Mastercard's pay-with-a-smile test is bound to rile privacy advocates (updated)," Engadget, May 17, 2022, https://www.engadget.com/mastrercard-biometric-checkout-pay-by-smiling-153808508.html?src=rss.

33. Sherry Lichtenberg, PhD, "Telecommunications Carrier of Last Resort: Necessity or Anachronism?" National Regulatory Research Institute, February 13, 2016, https://pubs.naruc.org/pub.cfm?id=81D3624D-BA04-F949-4859-E071E9D211F3; "Phone service for all, no matter what kind," Reuters, March 28, 2012, https://www.reuters.com/article/idUS179030969720120328.

34. "Terms of Service," Twitter, July 10, 2022, https://twitter.com/en/tos.

35. Ibid.

36. Jonathan L. Fischer, "The Evil List," Slate, January, 15, 2020 https://slate.com/technology/2020/01/evil-list-tech-companies-dangerous-amazon-facebook-google-palantir.html.

37. Ibid.

38. @BBGNewEconomy, Twitter, May 19, 2022, https://twitter.com/BBGNewEconomy/status/1527389224282075137.

39. Simon Parkin, "Has Dopamine Got Us Hooked on Tech?" *Guardian*, March 4, 2018, https://www.theguardian.com/technology/2018/mar/04/has-dopamine-got-us-hooked-on-tech-facebook-apps-addiction; Olivia Solon, "Ex-Facebook President Sean Parker: Site Made to Exploit Human 'Vulnerability,'" *Guardian*, November 9, 2017, https://www.theguardian.com/technology/2017/nov/09/facebook-sean-parker-vulnerability-brain-psychology.

40. Vann Vicente, "What Are Online 'Whales'?" How-to Geek, January 25, 2022, https://www.howtogeek.com/725959/what-are-online-whales/.

41. Nicole Casperson, "Robinhood Drops the Confetti, but Advisers Aren't Convinced," Investment News, April 6, 2021, https://www.investmentnews.com/robinhood-drops-the-confetti-but-advisers-arent-convinced-204828.

42. Keith Zhai, "China Limits Online Videogames to Three Hours a Week for Young People," *Wall Street Journal*, August 31, 2021, https://www.wsj.com/articles/china-sets-new-rules-for-youth-no-more-videogames-during-the-school-week-11630325781.

43. Albert Khoury, "Delete TikTok—Here's What the Chinese Company Collects about You," Komando.com, July 1, 2022, https://www.komando.com/security-privacy/tiktok-chinese-spy-tool/844334/; Arol Wright, "FCC Commissioner Calls TikTok Chinese Spyware and Wants It Pulled from Mobile App Stores," Android Police, June 29, 2022, https://www.androidpolice.com/fcc-commissioner-labels-tiktok-spyware-app-store-removal/.

44. "Big Tech's Supersized Ambitions," *Economist*, January 22, 2022, https://www.economist.com/leaders/2022/01/22/big-techs-supersized-ambitions.

45. Ibid.

46. "In-Game Purchase," ironSource, https://www.is.com/glossary/in-game-purchase/.

47. Noah Manskar, "Jack Dorsey Says Blocking Post's Hunter Biden Story Was 'Total Mistake'—but Won't Say Who Made It," *New York Post*, March 25, 2021, https://nypost.com/2021/03/25/dorsey-says-blocking-posts-hunter-biden-story-was-total-mistake/.

48. Julia Carrie Wong, "The Cambridge Analytica Scandal Changed the World—but It Didn't Change Facebook," *Guardian*, March 18, 2019, https://www.theguardian.com/technology/2019/mar/17/the-cambridge-analytica-scandal-changed-the-world-but-it-didnt-change-facebook.

49. Sam Meredith, "Facebook–Cambridge Analytica: A Timeline of the Data Hijacking Scandal," CNBC, April 10, 2018, https://www.cnbc.com/2018/04/10/facebook-cambridge-analytica-a-timeline-of-the-data-hijacking-scandal.html.

50. Joseph Menn, "Spy Agency Ducks Questions about 'Back Doors' in Tech Products," Reuters, October 28, 2020, https://www.reuters.com/article/us-usa-security-congress-insight/spy-agency-ducks-questions-about-back-doors-in-tech-products-idUSKBN27D1CS.

51. Broudy and Arakaki, "Who Wants to Be a Slave?"

52. Ibid.

Chapter 7: Socially Unacceptable, the Business Edition

1. Dan Katz, "Markets Have ESG Tunnel Vision," *Barron's*, May 27, 2022, https://www.barrons.com/articles/markets-have-esg-tunnel-vision-51653683236.

2. Paul Clarke, "Bank of America CEO Brian Moynihan: ESG transition is a 'big business opportunity,'" *Financial News*, May 24, 2022, https://www.fnlondon.com/articles/bank-of-america-ceo-brian-moynihan-esg-transition-is-a-big-business-opportunity-20220524.

3. Christine Williamson, "BlackRock AUM recedes from $10 trillion high," Pensions&Investments, April 13, 2022, https://www.pionline.com/money-management/blackrock-aum-recedes-10-trillion-high.

4. Andrew Ross Sorkin, "BlackRock C.E.O. Larry Fink: Climate Crisis Will Reshape Finance," *New York Times*, January 14, 2020, updated February 24, 2020, https://www.nytimes.com/2020/01/14/business/dealbook/larry-fink-blackrock-climate-change.html.

5. Laurence D. Fink, "Sustainability as BlackRock's New Standard for Investing," BlackRock's 2020 letter to clients, https://www.blackrock.com/corporate/investor-relations/2020-blackrock-client-letter.

6. Laurence D. Fink, "A Fundamental Reshaping of Finance," Larry Fink's 2020 letter to CEOs, https://www.blackrock.com/corporate/investor-relations/2020-larry-fink-ceo-letter.

7. Ibid.

8. Cam Simpson and Saijel Kishan, "How BlackRock Made ESG the Hottest Ticket on Wall Street," Bloomberg, December 31, 2021, https://www.bloomberg.com/news/articles/2021-12-31/how-blackrock-s-invisible-hand-helped-make-esg-a-hot-ticket?sref=hmG4mtJl.

9. Ibid.

10. William Power, "Does Sustainable Investing Really Help the Environment?" *Wall Street Journal*, November 7, 2021, https://www.wsj.com/articles/sustainable-investing-good-for-environment-11636056370.

11. Lewis Braham, "Why This ESG Fund Isn't Afraid of Energy Stocks," *Barron's*, April 28, 2022, https://www.barrons.com/articles/esg-fund-apple-amazon-energy-stocks-51651096987.

12. Frances Schwartzkopff and Saijel Kishan, "ESG Funds Managing $1 Trillion Are Stripped of Sustainable Tag by Morningstar," Bloomberg, February 10, 2022, https://www.bloomberg.com/news/articles/2022-02-10/funds-managing-1-trillion-stripped-of-esg-tag-by-morningstar?sref=hmG4mtJl.

13. Matt Cook, "The Rise of ESG and Its Impact on the Energy Industry," Lewis Davey, April 7, 2022, https://www.lewisdavey.com/blog/the-rise-of-esg-and-its-impact-on-the-oil-and-gas-industry.

14. Jude Clemente, "ESG and the Dangerous Structural Increase in the Price of Oil," *Forbes*, February 13, 2022, https://www.forbes.com/sites/judeclemente/2022/02/13/esg-and-the-dangerous-structural-increase-in-the-price-of-oil/?sh=24b9c9757b04.

15. Dan Eberhart, "Time for Investors to Loosen the Reins on Shale Producers," *Forbes*, January 25, 2022, https://www.forbes.com/sites/daneberhart/2022/01/25/time-for-investors-to-loosen-the-reins-on-shale-producers/?sh=795264a54861.

16. Clemente, "ESG and the Dangerous Structural Increase in the Price of Oil."

17. Chris Isidore, "Average US Gas Price Dips below $5 a Gallon," CNN, June 19, 2022, https://www.cnn.com/2022/06/19/energy/gas-prices-fall-below-5-dollars/index.html.

18. Tyler Olson, "As Biden Asks Saudis for Oil Help, US Energy Reps Say They're Tired of 'Vilification,'" Fox Business, July 14, 2022, https://www.foxbusiness.com/politics/biden-asks-saudis-oil-help-us-energy-reps-theyre-tired-vilification.

19. Ahmad Ghaddar, Alex Lawler, and Rowena Edwards, "OPEC+ Agrees Deep Oil Production Cuts, Biden Calls It Shortsighted," Reuters, October 5, 2022, https://www.reuters.com/business/energy/opec-heads-deep-supply-cuts-clash-with-us-2022-10-04/.

20. Priscila Azevedo Rocha, Anna Shiryaevskaya, and Todd Gillespie, "European Energy Prices Soar as Russian Curbs Risk Economic Pain," Bloomberg, July 26, 2022, https://www.bloomberg.com/news/articles/2022-07-26/french-electricity-price-hits-record-high-as-gas-costs-soar?sref=hmG4mtJl; Melissa Eddy, "German Inflation Hits 8.5 Percent, Again Driven by High Energy Prices," *New York Times*, July 28, 2022, https://www.nytimes.com/2022/07/28/business/germany-inflation.html.

21. Sam Meredith, "Russia Is Set to Switch off the Gas for Work on a Key Pipeline—and Germany Fears the Worst," CNBC, July 5, 2022, https://www.cnbc.com/2022/07/05/germany-fears-russian-gas-flows-could-be-about-to-stop-for-good.html.

22. Abby Wallace, "Germany Starts Rationing Hot Water and Turning down the Heating in Case Russia Cuts off Its Natural Gas Supplies," Insider, July 8, 2022, https://www.businessinsider.com/germany-gas-crisis-landlords-lowering-the-heating-shortages-russia-ukraine-2022-7.

23. Chris Flood, "Energy Crisis Prompts ESG Rethink on Oil and Gas," *Financial Times*, July 17, 2022, https://www.ft.com/content/c45692c7-8695-438d-9414-33137be91e79.

24. Ibid.

25. Kate Abnett, "EU Parliament Backs Labelling Gas and Nuclear Investments as Green," Reuters, July 6, 2022, https://www.reuters.com/business/sustainable-business/eu-parliament-vote-green-gas-nuclear-rules-2022-07-06/; America Hernandez, "Parliament Votes to Give Green Labels to Nuclear and Gas," *Politico*, July 6, 2022, https://www.politico.eu/article/parliament-votes-to-give-green-labels-to-nuclear-and-gas/.

26. "History of ESG," Preqin, https://www.preqin.com/preqin-academy/lesson-5-esg/history-of-esg.

27. "Secretary-General Proposes Global Compact on Human Rights, Labour, Environment, in Address toWorld Economic Forum in Davos," press release, United Nations, February 1, 1999, https://press.un.org/en/1999/19990201.sgsm6881.html.

28. Ibid.

29. "History of ESG," Preqin.

30. "Evolution of ESG," Breckinridge Capital Advisors, August 12, 2021, https://breckinridge-fs.s3.amazonaws.com/files/uploads/evolution-of-esg-timeline.pdf.

31. "Secretary-General Launches 'Principles for Responsible Investment' Backed by World's Largest Investors," press release, United Nations, April 27, 2006, https://press.un.org/en/2006/sg2111.doc.htm.

32. "History of ESG," Preqin; "About the PRI," Principles for Responsible Investing, United Nations, https://www.unpri.org/about-us/about-the-pri; "Signatory Directory," Principles for Responsible Investing, United Nations, https://www.unpri.org/signatories/signatory-resources/signatory-directory.

33. "About the PRI," UN.

34. Ibid.

35. "History of ESG," Preqin; Kayla Barnes, "A History of How Modern ESG Came to Be," sgENGAGE, May 6, 2021, https://npengage.com/companies/esg-history/.

36. "Sustainable Development Impact Summit 2017 Report," World Economic Forum, September 18–19, 2017, https://www3.weforum.org/docs/WEF_SDIS17_report.pdf; "2019 Investment Stewardship Annual Report," BlackRock, August 2019, https://www.blackrock.com/corporate/literature/publication/blk-annual-stewardship-report-2019.pdf.

37. "Embracing the New Age of Materiality Harnessing the Pace of Change in ESG," World Economic Forum, March 2020, https://www3.weforum.org/docs/WEF_Embracing_the_New_Age_of_Materiality_2020.pdf.

38. "The Future of Sustainable and Impact Investing," World Economic Forum via Wayback Machine, http://web.archive.org/web/20200624155720/https://www.weforum.org/projects/mainstreaming-sustainable-and-impact-investing.

39. "Embracing the New Age of Materiality Harnessing the Pace of Change in ESG," WEF.

40. Ibid.

41. Ibid.

42. Glenn Beck, *The Great Reset* (New York: Forefront Books, 2022), 173; "Toward Common Metrics and Consistent Reporting of Sustainable Value Creation," World Economic Forum, January 2020, https://www3.weforum.org/docs/WEF_IBC_ESG_Metrics_Discussion_Paper.pdf.

43. Andrew Holt, "Shift from shareholder value to stakeholder-focused model for top US firms," *IR Magazine*, August 23, 2019, https://www.irmagazine.com/esg/shift-shareholder-value-stakeholder-focused-model-top-us-firms; "About Us," Business Roundtable, https:/www.businessroundtable.org/about-us.

44. Nir Kossovsky, "Fulfilling the Promise of The Business Roundtable's Statement on Corporate Purpose," *IR Magazine*, August 25, 2021, https://www.irmagazine.com/esg/fulfilling-promise-business-roundtables-statement-corporate-purpose.

45. CFR.org Editors, "Funding the United Nations: How Much Does the U.S. Pay?" Council on Foreign Relations, April 4, 2022, https://www.cfr.org/article/funding-united-nations-what-impact-do-us-contributions-have-un-agencies-and-programs.

46. "World Economic Forum and UN Sign Strategic Partnership Framework," press release, World Economic Forum, June 13, 2019, https://www.weforum.org/press/2019/06/world-economic-forum-and-un-sign-strategic-partnership-framework/.

47. "BlackRock," https://www.weforum.org/organizations/blackrock-inc.

48. "Sri Lanka GDP 1960–2022," Macrotrends via World Bank, https://www.macrotrends.net/countries/LKA/sri-lanka/gdp-gross-domestic-product; Ziaul Hoque, "How Sri Lanka's Booming Economy Ended in the Worst Crisis in Its History," *Daily Star*, April 2, 2022, https://www.thedailystar.net/weekend-read/news/missteps-and-misfortunes-2996116.

49. "World's Largest Fund Manager Blackrock Speaks up for Sri Lanka," Daily FT, June 6, 2014, https://www.ft.lk/Special-Report/worlds-largest-fund-manager-blackrock-speaks-up-for-sri-lanka/22-303026.

50. Ranil Wickremesinghe, "Davos 2016: the Future of Sri Lanka's Economy," World Economic Forum, January 19, 2016, https://www.weforum.org/agenda/2016/01/the-future-of-sri-lanka-s-economy/.

51. Ranil Wickremesinghe, "Sri Lanka PM: This is how I will make my country rich by 2025," World Economic Forum, August 29, 2018, https://www.weforum.org/agenda/2018/08/this-is-how-we-will-make-sri-lanka-rich-by-2025/.

52. "Vision 2025: Sri Lanka's Path to Prosperity," World Bank, October 17, 2017, https://www.worldbank.org/en/news/feature/2017/10/17/vision-2025-sri-lankas-path-to-prosperity; Michel Chossudovsky, "World Bank," *Britannica*, https://www.britannica.com/topic/World-Bank.

53. Ted Nordhaus and Saloni Shah, "In Sri Lanka, Organic Farming Went Catastrophically Wrong," FP, March 5, 2022, https://foreignpolicy.com/2022/03/05/sri-lanka-organic-farming-crisis/.

54. "Sri Lanka's Environmental Factors," World Economics Research, https://worldeconomics.com/ESG/Environment/Sri%20Lanka.aspx.

55. Ibid.

56. Hannah Ellis-Petersen, "'It Will Be Hard to Find a Farmer Left': Sri Lanka Reels from Rash Fertiliser Ban," *Guardian*, April 20, 2022, https://www.theguardian.com/world/2022/apr/20/sri-lanka-fertiliser-ban-president-rajapaksa-farmers-harvests-collapse.

57. Uditha Jayasinghe and Devjyot Ghoshal, "Fertiliser Ban Decimates Sri Lankan Crops as Government Popularity Ebbs," Reuters, March 3, 2022, https://www.reuters.com/markets/commodities/fertiliser-ban-decimates-sri-lankan-crops-government-popularity-ebbs-2022-03-03/.

58. Jessie Yeung, "Sri Lanka Is Facing an Economic and Political Crisis. Here's What You Need to Know," CNN, April 6, 2022, https://www.cnn.com/2022/04/05/asia/sri-lanka-economic-crisis-explainer-intl-hnk/index.html.

59. Ibid.; Reuters, "Sri Lanka President Declares Public Emergency after Protests against Economic Crisis," *Guardian*, April 2, 2022, https://www.theguardian.com/world/2022/apr/02/sri-lanka-president-declares-public-emergency-after-protests-against-economic-crisis.

60. Reuters, "Sri Lanka President Declares Public Emergency."

61. Ellis-Petersen, "'It Will Be Hard to Find a Farmer Left': Sri Lanka Reels from Rash Fertiliser Ban."

62. Ibid.

63. Nordhaus and Shah, "In Sri Lanka, Organic Farming Went Catastrophically Wrong."

64. Rhea Mogul and Iqbal Athas, "Sri Lanka's Economy Has 'Completely Collapsed,' Prime Minister says," CNN, June 23, 2022, https://www.cnn.com/2022/06/23/asia/sri-lanka-economy-collapse-prime-minister-intl-hnk/index.html.

65. "Sri Lankan President Resigns after Fleeing Country amid Economic Crisis," Ireland Live, July 15, 2022, https://www.ireland-live.ie/news/world/861200/sri-lankan-president-resigns-after-fleeing-country-amid-economic-crisis.html.

66. Yeung, "Sri Lanka Is Facing an Economic and Political Crisis. Here's What You Need to Know."

67. Ibid.

68. "Ghana's Environmental Factors," World Economics Research, https://worldeconomics.com/ESG/Environment/Ghana.aspx; "'Total System Shutdown' as Ghana Hit by Countrywide Power Blackout," Fin24, March 8, 2021, https://www.news24.com/fin24/Economy/Africa/total-system-shutdown-as-ghana-hit-by-countrywide-power-blackout-20210308.

69. Mike Corder, "Explainer: Why Are Dutch Farmers Protesting over Emissions?" The Journal, July 8, 2022, https://www.nujournal.com/news/agribusiness/2022/07/08/explainer-why-are-dutch-farmers-protesting-over-emissions/.

70. Chris Lyddon, "Focus on the Netherlands," World-Grain.com, May 27, 2021, https://www.world-grain.com/articles/15349-focus-on-the-netherlands; Corder, "Explainer: Why Are Dutch Farmers Protesting over Emissions?"

71. "Mark Rutte," World Economic Forum, https://www.weforum.org/agenda/authors/mark-rutte.

72. "Food Action Alliance," World Economic Forum, September 2021, https://weforum.ent.box.com/s/wenkz4o4x5s1eegt20wpz8s2l4hknye2.

73. "Global Leaders Unite Under the Food Action Alliance to Deliver a Better Future for the People and the Planet," press release, World Economic Forum, January 22, 2020, https://www.weforum.org/press/2020/01/global-leaders-unite-under-the-food-action-alliance-to-deliver-a-better-future-for-the-people-and-the-planet/.

74. Ibid.

75. "Food Innovation Hubs Put Farmers at Head of the Table for Systems Change," press release, World Economic Forum, January 27, 2021, https://www.weforum.org/press/2021/01/food-innovation-hubs-put-farmers-at-head-of-the-table-for-systems-change/.

76. Ibid.

77. Al Root, "Tesla Got Kicked Out of the S&P 500 ESG Index. Elon Musk Calls ESG a 'Scam,'" *Barron's*, May 18, 2022, https://www.barrons.com/articles/tesla-s-p-500-esg-index-51652886703.

78. @elonmusk, Twitter, May 18, 2022, https://twitter.com/elonmusk/status/1526958110023245829?s=20&t=BTIibHg6Ttz5PaY-SEd16Q; @elonmusk, Twitter, May 18, 2022, https://twitter.com/elonmusk/status/1526960512231153664?s=20&t=BTIibHg6Ttz5PaY-SEd16Q'; @elonmusk, Twitter, May 18, 2022, https://twitter.com/elonmusk/status/1526961470562508802?s=20&t=BTIibHg6Ttz5PaY-SEd16Q.

79. "About GRI," Global Reporting Initiative, https://www.globalreporting.org/about-gri/.

80. "Bernie Marcus," New Georgia Encyclopedia, https://www.georgiaencyclopedia.org/articles/business-economy/bernie-marcus-b-1929/.

81. Samuel Etienne and Ewa Krukowska, "Private Jets, Amazon Orders Set to Escape Higher EU Energy Taxes," Bloomberg, July 9, 2021, https://www.bloomberg.com/news/articles/2021-07-09/private-jets-amazon-orders-set-to-escape-higher-eu-energy-taxes?sref=hmG4mtJl.

82. John Ainger and Steven Arons, "Weapons Group Points to Ukraine in Bid to Shape ESG Rulebook," Bloomberg, February 28, 2022, https://www.bloomberg.com/news/articles/2022-02-28/weapons-group-points-to-ukraine-in-bid-to-shape-eu-s-esg-rules?sref=hmG4mtJl.

83. "Proposed Rule—Prudence and Loyalty in Selecting Plan Investments and Exercising Shareholder Rights," Federal Register, October 14, 2021, https://www.federalregister.gov/documents/2021/10/14/2021-22263/prudence-and-loyalty-in-selecting-plan-investments-and-exercising-shareholder-rights; "Prudence and Loyalty in Selecting Plan Investments and Exercising Shareholder Rights," Federal Register, December 1, 2022, https://www.federalregister.gov/documents/2022/12/01/2022-25783/prudence-and-loyalty-in-selecting-plan-investments-and-exercising-shareholder-rights.

84. Vivek Ramaswamy and Alex Acosta, "Biden's ESG Tax on Your Retirement Fund," *Wall Street Journal,* July 19, 2022, https://www.wsj.com/articles/bidens-esg-tax-on-your-retirement-fund-pension-planning-regulation-climate-change-investment-returns-portfolios-11658245467.

85. "29 CFR Part 2550: Prudence and Loyalty in Selecting Plan Investments and Exercising Shareholder Rights," Department of Labor, Employee Benefits Security Administration, https://www.dol.gov/sites/dolgov/files/ebsa/temporary-postings/prudence-and-loyalty-in-selecting-plan-investments-and-exercising-shareholder-rights-final-rule.pdf.

86. Beck, *The Great Reset*, 177.

87. "Kevin Stiroh to Step Down as Head of New York Fed Supervision to Assume New System Leadership Role at Board of Governors on Climate," Federal Reserve Bank of New York, January 25, 2021, https://www.newyorkfed.org/newsevents/news/aboutthefed/2021/20210125.

88. Governor Lael Brainard, "Financial Stability Implications of Climate Change," Board of Governors of the Federal Reserve System, March 23, 2021, https://www.federalreserve.gov/newsevents/speech/brainard20210323a.htm.

89. Daniel F. C. Crowley et al., "Biden Administration ESG Activity Accelerates," *National Law Review*, June 7, 2021, https://www.natlawreview.com/article/biden-administration-esg-activity-accelerates.

90. "SEC Proposes to Enhance Disclosures by Certain Investment Advisers and Investment Companies About ESG Investment Practices," press release, US Securities and Exchange Commission, May 25, 2022, https://www.sec.gov/news/press-release/2022-92.

91. Michelle A. Williams and Patricia Geli, "ESG Is Not Enough. It's Time to Add an H," Yahoo Finance, March 14, 2022, https://finance.yahoo.com/news/esg-not-enough-time-add-122500968.html.

92. Megan Gosch, "Industry Insight: A Shift for the Ages," NOLN, January 1, 2021, https://www.noln.net/articles/4911-industry-insight-a-shift-for-the-ages.

93. Winnie Yeh, "3 Circular Economy Approaches to Reduce Demand for Critical Metals," World Economic Forum, July 18, 2022, https://www.weforum.org/agenda/2022/07/3-circular-approaches-to-reduce-demand-for-critical-minerals/.

94. Thomas Birr and Carsten Stöcker, "Goodbye Car Ownership, Hello Clean Air: Welcome to the Future of Transport," World Economic Forum, December 16, 2016, https://www.weforum.org/agenda/2016/12/goodbye-car-ownership-hello-clean-air-this-is-the-future-of-transport/.

95. Mark Brnovich, "ESG May Be an Antitrust Violation," *Wall Street Journal*, March 6, 2022, https://www.wsj.com/articles/esg-may-be-an-antitrust-violation-climate-activism-energy-prices-401k-retirement-investment-political-agenda-coordinated-influence-11646594807.

96. Ibid.

97. Lydia Nusbaum, "Gov. DeSantis Takes Stand Against 'Woke' Standards That Are 'Politicizing' the Economy, Targeting Disfavored Industries," Florida's Voice, July 27, 2022, https://flvoicenews.com/gov-desantis-takes-stand-against-woke-standards-that-are-politicizing-the-economy-targeting-disfavored-industries/.

98. Ibid.

99. Mary Rooke, "West Virginia Blocks Wall Street Titans Pushing ESG Agenda," Daily Caller, July 28, 2022, https://dailycaller.com/2022/07/28/west-virginia-blocks-banks-esg-coal/.

100. "Restricted Financial Institution List," West Virginia Treasury, July 28, 2022, https://www.wvtreasury.com/portals/wvtreasury/content/legal/memorandum/Restricted-Financial-Institutions-List.pdf.

101. @billmckibben, Twitter, August 1, 2022, https://twitter.com/billmckibben/status/1554139525592616962?s=20&t=R37B_f9MQh4oQRV9zsdtIg.

102. Will Schmitt, "BNY Mellon Fined $1.5m by Sec for Misleading ESG Fund Statements," Citywire, May 23, 2022, https://citywireusa.com/professional-buyer/news/bny-mellon-fined-1-5m-by-sec-for-misleading-esg-fund-statements/a2388180?linkSource=article-body; Margaryta Kirakosian and Philipp Fischer, "German Police Raid Deutsche Fund Arm over Greenwashing Allegations," Citywire, May 31, 2022, https://citywireusa.com/professional-buyer/news/german-police-raid-deutsche-fund-arm-over-greenwashing-allegations/a2388824.

103. Editorial Board, "A Financier Tells Some Climate-Change Truths," *Wall Street Journal*, May 23, 2022, https://www.wsj.com/articles/a-financier-tells-some-climate-truths-stuart-kirk-hsbc-mark-carney-11653340776.

104. Ibid.

105. Ibid.

106. @TheEconomist, Twitter, July 21, 2022, https://twitter.com/TheEconomist/status/1550083579941490688?s=20&t=o3NGVdoRTX98MTMbvoUUnQ.

107. Roy Swan, "Investors Are Embracing ESG but Avoiding Impact. What They're Missing," *Barron's*, July 27, 2022, https://www.barrons.com/articles/investors-embracing-esg-but-avoiding-impact-51658862821.

108. @renexgirard, Twitter, July 28, 2022, https://twitter.com/renexgirard/status/1552548719718895616?s=20&t=YHqPy-DTxggeIbVK8G4BpQ.

Chapter 8: Renting the American Dream

1. Daisuke Wakabayashi, "As China's Economy Stumbles, Homeowners Boycott Mortgage Payments," *New York Times*, August 17, 2022, https://www.nytimes.com/2022/08/17/business/china-economy-real-estate-crisis.html.

2. Neil Bhutta et al., "Changes in U.S. Family Finances from 2016 to 2019: Evidence from the Survey of Consumer Finances," Federal Reserve Bulletin, September 2020, https://www.federalreserve.gov/publications/files/scf20.pdf; Fan-Yu Kuo, "Homeownership Remains Primary Driver of Household Wealth," National Association of Home Builders' Eye on Housing, February 16, 2021, https://eyeonhousing.org/2021/02/homeownership-remains-primary-driver-of-household-wealth/.

3. Jonathan Eggleston, Donald Hays, Robert Munk, and Briana Sullivan, "The Wealth of Households: 2017," Page 2, Table 2, US Census Bureau, August 2020, https://www.census.gov/content/dam/Census/library/publications/2020/demo/p70br-170.pdf.

4. Neil Bhutta et al., "Changes in U.S. Family Finances from 2016 to 2019: Evidence from the Survey of Consumer Finances"; Fan-Yu Kuo, "Homeownership Remains Primary Driver of Household Wealth."

5. Fan-Yu Kuo, "Homeownership Remains Primary Driver of Household Wealth."

6. Ibid.

7. Nicole Friedman, "U.S. Housing Wealth Skewed Even More Toward Affluent Over Past Decade," *Wall Street Journal*, March 9, 2022, https://www.wsj.com/articles/u-s-housing-wealth-skewed-even-more-toward-affluent-over-past-decade-11646838000.

8. Ibid.

9. Francesca Mari, "A $60 Billion Housing Grab by Wall Street," *New York Times Magazine*, March 4, 2020, https://www.nytimes.com/2020/03/04/magazine/wall-street-landlords.html.

10. "Number of Homes Built in the United States between 1900 and 2021," Statista, February 25, 2022, https://www.statista.com/statistics/1041889/construction-year-homes-usa/.

11. Historical Data: "Housing Units Completed," US Census Bureau. https://www.census.gov/construction/nrc/historical_data/index.html.

12. "Number of Homes Built in the United States between 1900 and 2021," Statista; Ibid.

13. "Number of Homes Built in the United States between 1900 and 2021," Statista; George Ratiu, "US Housing Supply Continues to Lag Household Formations," Realtor.com, September 9, 2021, https://www.realtor.com/research/us-housing-supply-continues-to-lag-household-formations/.

14. Mari, "A $60 Billion Housing Grab by Wall Street."

15. Lesley Stahl, "Would-Be Home Buyers May Be Forced to Rent the American Dream, Rather than Buy It," CBS News, *60 Minutes*, March 20, 2022, https://www.cbsnews.com/news/rising-rent-prices-60-minutes-2022-03-20/.

16. "Investing with Tricon Residential," Tricon Residential, https://investors.triconresidential.com/company-profile/default.aspx.

17. "Tricon Residential 2021 Annual Report," 29, https://s29.q4cdn.com/296929481/files/doc_financials/2021/ar/Tricon-2021-Annual-Report_May1622.pdf.

18. Ibid.

19. Stahl, "Would-Be Home Buyers."

20. Dana Anderson and Sheharyar Bokhari, "Real Estate Investors Are Buying a Record Share of U.S. Homes," Redfin, February 16, 2022, updated April 6, 2022, https://www.redfin.com/news/investor-home-purchases-q4-2021/.

21. Elena Botella, "Investment Firms Aren't Buying All the Houses. But They Are Buying the Most Important Ones," Slate, June 19, 2021, https://slate.com/business/2021/06/blackrock-invitation-houses-investment-firms-real-estate.html; Hudson Cashdan, "Modeling an Asset Class: Why Wall Street May Be in the Single-family Rental Market for Keeps," Toptal Finance, https://www.toptal.com/finance/real-estate/wall-street-buying-single-family-homes; "Invitation Homes Announces New $725 Million Sustainability-Linked Seven-Year Term Loan," press release, June 22, 2022, https://www.businesswire.com/news/home/20220622005289/en/Invitation-Homes-Announces-New-725-Million-Sustainability-Linked-Seven-Year-Term-Loan.

22. "Invitation Homes Inc., 10-K," February 22, 2022, https://d18rn0p25nwr6d.cloudfront.net/CIK-0001687229/0d03f6ff-fb4f-443b-add2-aec95b8e441d.html.

23. "American Homes Annual Report," 2021, https://s26.q4cdn.com/445305060/files/doc_financials/2021/ar/AMH-2021-Annual-Report.pdf.

24. Abby Vesoulis, "How Eviction Moratoriums Are Hurting Small Landlords—and Why That's Bad for the Future of Affordable Housing," *Time*, June 11, 2020, https://time.com/5846383/coronavirus-small-landlords/.

25. Natalie Campisi, "What Mom-And-Pop Landlords Can Do to Relieve Eviction Ban Pressure," *Forbes*, February 15, 2021, https://www.forbes.com/advisor/mortgages/what-mom-and-pop-landlords-can-do-to-relieve-eviction-ban-pressure/.

26. Vesoulis, "How Eviction Moratoriums Are Hurting Small Landlords."

27. Ibid.

28. Amy Howe, "Court lifts federal ban on evictions," SCOTUSblog, August 26, 2021, https://www.scotusblog.com/2021/08/court-lifts-federal-ban-on-evictions/.

29. @HeyBooBoo16, Twitter, June 29, 2022, https://twitter.com/HeyBooBoo16/status/1542366315972661248?s=20&t=wKV4mIpE5DHmgL3fKFO9yg.

30. *Over Asking Price*, rough cut, Anchor Productions.

31. "Regulatory Costs Add a Whopping $93,870 to New Home Prices," National Association of Home Builders, May 6, 2021, https://www.nahb.org/blog/2021/05/regulatory-costs-add-a-whopping-93870-to-new-home-prices/.

32. Phone interview, July 14, 2022; names changed to protect privacy.

33. "Week 46 Household Pulse Survey: June 1–June 13," US Census Bureau, June 22, 2022, https://www.census.gov/data/tables/2022/demo/hhp/hhp46.html; Alexandre Tanzi, "More Than 8 Million Americans Are Late on Rent as Prices Increase," Bloomberg, June 24, 2022, https://www.bloomberg.com/news/articles/2022-06-24/over-8-million-americans-are-late-on-rents-as-prices-increase?sref=hmG4mtJl.

34. Ibid.

35. Mary Wilson, "What Happens When Airbnb Swallows Your Neighborhood," Slate, October 12, 2021, https://slate.com/business/2021/10/airbnb-housing-shortage-luxury-vacation-rental-galveston-texas.html.

36. Ibid.

37. Melvin Durai, "What Does Airbnb Do to the Local Housing Market? Make It Less Affordable," Purdue University, August 18, 2021, https://www.krannert.purdue.edu/news/features/home.php?research=7145.

38. Wilson, "What Happens When Airbnb Swallows Your Neighborhood."

39. Friedman, "U.S. Housing Wealth Skewed."

40. Ibid.

41. Nicole Friedman, "In Covid-19 Housing Market, the Middle Class Is Getting Priced Out," *Wall Street Journal*, February 7, 2022, https://www.wsj.com/articles/in-covid-19-housing-market-the-middle-class-is-getting-priced-out-11644246000?mod=article_inline.

42. Ibid.

43. "Canada Bans Foreign Home Buyers for Two Years to Cool Market," Associated Press, April 7, 2022, https://apnews.com/article/business-chrystia-freeland-justin-trudeau-ontario-canada-999eedee72d9fd63e73576efd2bb3535.

44. "U.S. Foreign Property Investment—Statistics & Facts," Statista, June 24, 2022, https://www.statista.com/topics/4455/foreign-property-investment-in-the-us/.

45. Nathaniel Lee, Lindsey Jacobson, and Jason Reginato, "Why Bill Gates Is Buying up U.S. Farmland," CNBC, August 20, 2021, https://www.cnbc.com/video/2021/08/20/why-us-farmland-is-attracting-ultra-wealthy-investors.html.

46. "The Land Report," https://landreport.com/; Christopher Ingraham, "American Land Barons: 100 Wealthy Families Now Own Nearly as Much Land as That of New England," *Washington Post*, December 21, 2017, https://www.washingtonpost.com/news/wonk/wp/2017/12/21/american-land-barons-100-wealthy-families-now-own-nearly-as-much-land-as-that-of-new-england/.

47. Lee, Jacobson, and Reginato, "Why Bill Gates Is Buying up U.S. Farmland."

48. Ingraham, "American Land Barons."

49. Ibid.

50. Lee, Jacobson, and Reginato, "Why Bill Gates Is Buying up U.S. Farmland."

51. "Farm Inputs: U.S. Agricultural Land Values Show Record Increase," American Farm Bureau Federation, August 8, 2022, https://www.fb.org/market-intel/farm-inputs-u.s.-agricultural-land-values-show-record-increase.

52. Rida Morwa, "Bill Gates Buys Farmland, We Buy Income," Seeking Alpha, October 22, 2021, https://seekingalpha.com/article/4461001-bill-gates-buys-farmland-we-buy-income.

53. Lee, Jacobson, and Reginato, "Why Bill Gates Is Buying up U.S. Farmland."

54. Ibid.

55. Eric O'Keefe, "Bill Gates: America's Top Farmland Owner," Land Report, January 11, 2021, https://landreport.com/2021/01/farmer-bill/.

56. Noah Kirsch, "North Dakotans Freak Over Bill Gates Land-Buying Mystery," Daily Beast, June 25, 2022, https://www.thedailybeast.com/north-dakotans-freak-over-bill-gates-land-buying-mystery.

57. Jenny Schlecht, "A Company Associated with Bill Gates Bought Some Land. Why Do We Care?" *Agweek*, June 20, 2022, https://www.agweek.com/opinion/columns/a-company-associated-with-bill-gates-bought-some-land-why-do-we-care.

58. Keith Griffith, "Bill Gates Wins Legal Approval to Buy Huge Swath of North Dakota Farmland Worth $13.5m after Outcry from Residents Who Say They Are Being Exploited by the Ultra-Rich," *Daily Mail*, June 30, 2022, updated July 1, 2022, https://www.dailymail.co.uk/news/article-10971639/Bill-Gates-wins-legal-approval-buy-huge-swath-North-Dakota-farmland-worth-13-5M.html.

59. Adam Manno and Jack Wright, "Bill Gates Shops for 'Hundreds of Acres of Farmland' to Create 'Sustainable Farm in Turkey' from aboard His $2 Million-a-Week Rental Yacht after Celebrating Lavish 66th Birthday Party with Jeff Bezos," *Daily Mail*, November 3, 2021, https://www.dailymail.co.uk/news/article-10162419/Bill-Gates-shops-hundreds-acres-sustainable-farmland-aboard-2M-week-rental-yacht.html.

60. H. Claire Brown, "The Biden Administration Will Pay Farmers More Money Not to Farm," Governing, May 2, 2021, https://www.governing.com/now/the-biden-administration-will-pay-farmers-more-money-not-to-farm.

61. James M. MacDonald, Robert A. Hoppe, and Doris Newton, "Three Decades of Consolidation in U.S. Agriculture," US Department of Agriculture, March 2018, https://www.ers.usda.gov/webdocs/publications/88057/eib-189.pdf; Eli Francovich, "As West Withers Corporations Consolidate Land and Water Rights," Columbia Insight, December 6, 2021, https://columbiainsight.org/as-west-withers-corporations-consolidate-land-and-water-rights/.

62. Russell Gold, "Harvard Quietly Amasses California Vineyards—and the Water Underneath," *Wall Street Journal*, December 10, 2018, https://www.wsj.com/articles/harvard-quietly-amasses-california-vineyardsand-the-water-underneath-1544456396.

63. Ibid.

64. Ibid.

65. Ibid.

66. Ibid.

67. Ibid.

68. Ibid.

69. Lewis Perdue, "Harvard-Controlled LLC in $120+ Million Deal with Anonymous LLC Connected with Canadian Pension Fund," Wine Industry Insight subscriber email, August 16, 2020, https://wineindustryinsight.com/emed_message.php?id=3508.

70. "Statement of Information," State of California Office of the Secretary of State, https://bizfileonline.sos.ca.gov/search/business.

71. Abrahm Lustgarten and ProPublica, "A Free-Market Plan to Save the American West from Drought," *Atlantic*, March 2016, https://www.theatlantic.com/magazine/archive/2016/03/a-plan-to-save-the-american-west-from-drought/426846/.

72. Ibid.

73. Ben Ryder Howe, "Wall Street Eyes Billions in the Colorado's Water," *New York Times*, January 3, 2021, https://www.nytimes.com/2021/01/03/business/colorado-river-water-rights.html.

74. Ibid.

75. Ibid.

76. Ibid.

77. Ibid.

78. Nelson Harvey, "Betting on Water Shortages? A Hedge Fund Buys Water Rights in Grand Valley," Water Education Colorado, August 8, 2018, https://www.watereducationcolorado.org/fresh-water-news/betting-on-water-shortages-a-hedge-fund-buys-water-rights-in-grand-valley/.

79. Ibid.

80. Howe, "Wall Street Eyes Billions in the Colorado's Water."

Chapter 9: Worthless Paper

1. Federal Reserve Bank of New York, "Household Debt: Non Housing Debt Balance Chart," Q2 2022, press release, "Total Household Debt Surpasses $16 Trillion in Q2 2022; Mortgage, Auto Loan, and Credit Card Balances Increase," https://www.newyorkfed.org/microeconomics/hhdc.

2. Claire Ballentine, Misyrlena Egkolfopoulou, and Paulina Cachero, "Colleges Are Launching TikTok Classes for Influencers Making $5,000 a Post," Bloomberg, May 6, 2022, https://www.bloomberg.com/news/articles/2022-05-06/how-to-become-tiktok-influencer-there-s-a-college-class-for-that?sref=hmG4mtJl.

3. "Undergraduate Tuition & Fees," Duke University, Financial Services Bursar, https://finance.duke.edu/bursar/TuitionFees/tuition.

4. Alicia Hahn and Jordan Tarver, "2022 Student Loan Debt Statistics: Average Student Loan Debt," *Forbes*, June 9, 2022, https://www.forbes.com/advisor/student-loans/average-student-loan-statistics/; Daniel Kurt, "Student Loan Debt: 2021 Statistics and Outlook," Investopedia, April 9, 2022, https://www.investopedia.com/student-loan-debt-2019-statistics-and-outlook-4772007.

5. Adam Looney, David Wessel, and Kadija Yilla, "Who Owes All That Student Debt? and Who'd Benefit If It Were Forgiven?" Brookings Institution, January 28, 2020, https://www.brookings.edu/policy2020/votervital/who-owes-all-that-student-debt-and-whod-benefit-if-it-were-forgiven/.

6. Anthony P. Carnevale, Ban Cheah, and Emma Wenzinger, "The College Payoff—More Education Doesn't Always Mean More Earnings," Georgetown University, 2021, https://cew.georgetown.edu/cew-reports/collegepayoff2021/#resources.

7. Kathy Deady, "Yes, You Can Become a Teacher Without a Degree in Education. Here's How," Teachaway, April 4, 2022, https://www.teachaway.com/blog/can-you-become-teacher-without-teaching-degree.

8. Conor Wight, "SCSD Responds to Teacher Shortage as Some School Districts Struggle to Fill Vacancies," CNYCentral, July 13, 2022, https://cnycentral.com/news/local/scsd-responds-to-teacher-shortage-as-some-school-districts-struggle-to-fill-vacancies.

9. Jessica Dickler, "More Education Doesn't Always Get You More Money, Report Finds," CNBC, October 13, 2021, https://www.cnbc.com/2021/10/13/more-education-doesnt-always-get-you-more-money-report-finds.html.

10. Carnevale et al., "The College Payoff."

11. "The Cost of Excess," American Council of Trustees and Alumni Institute for Effective Governance, August 2021, https://www.goacta.org/wp-content/uploads/2021/08/The-Cost-of-Excess-FINAL-Full-Report.pdf.

12. @arindube, Twitter, May 20, 2022, https://twitter.com/arindube/status/1527829083245236224?s=20&t=hFZeZtBRjXannz1jIiJcLw.

13. Camilo Maldonado, "Price of College Increasing Almost 8 Times Faster Than Wages," *Forbes*, July 24, 2018, https://www.forbes.com/sites/camilomaldonado/2018/07/24/price-of-college-increasing-almost-8-times-faster-than-wages/?sh=d02a0cf66c1d.

14. Federal Reserve Bank of New York, "Total Household Debt Surpasses $16 Trillion in Q2 2022."

15. "Tuition Costs of Colleges and Universities," National Center for Education Statistics, https://nces.ed.gov/fastfacts/display.asp?id=76.

16. "The Cost of Excess."

17. Caroline Simon, " Bureaucrats and Buildings: The Case for Why College Is So Expensive," *Forbes*, September 5, 2017, https://www.forbes.com/sites/carolinesimon/2017/09/05/bureaucrats-and-buildings-the-case-for-why-college-is-so-expensive/?sh=5485a882456a.

18. Ibid.

19. "The Cost of Excess."

20. Ayelet Sheffey, "'It's Mind-Boggling to Me That This Total Amount Is Not Going Down. It's Not Going Away': 2 Borrowers Describe the Crushing Interest That Keeps Them from Paying off Their Debt," Insider, August 23, 2022, https://www.businessinsider.com/interest-on-student-loan-debt-is-crushing-borrowers-2021-8.

21. Mark J. Perry, "Chart of the Day. . . . or Century?" American Enterprise Institute, July 23, 2022, https://www.aei.org/carpe-diem/chart-of-the-day-or-century-8/.

22. Mike Brown, "Can You Use Student Loans For Spring Break?" Lendedu, September 3, 2021, https://lendedu.com/blog/student-loans-for-spring-break/.

23. "Explore the Federal Investment in Your Alma Mater," Datalab, https://datalab.usaspending.gov/colleges-and-universities/.

24. "What Do Universities Do with the Billions They Receive from the Government?" USAFacts, November 3, 2021, https://usafacts.org/articles/what-do-universities-do-with-the-billions-they-receive-from-the-government/.

25. "Explore the Federal Investment in Your Alma Mater," Datalab.

26. "What Do Universities Do with the Billions They Receive from the Government?" USAFacts.

27. Matthew Arrojas, "State Funding for Colleges, Universities Hits All-Time High," Best Colleges, February 3, 2022, https://www.bestcolleges.com/news/2022/02/03/state-funding-for-colleges-grapevine-report/.

28. "Endowments," National Center for Education Statistics, FY 2020, https://nces.ed.gov/fastfacts/display.asp?id=73.

29. Sandy Baum, Catharine Bond Hill, and Emily Schwartz, "College and University Endowments in the Public Interest?" Ithaka S+R, May 22, 2018, https://sr.ithaka.org/publications/college-and-university-endowments/.

30. Ibid.

31. Rick Seltzer, "How Much Are Most Colleges Paying in Endowment Tax?" Inside Higher Ed, February 18, 2020, https://www.insidehighered.com/news/2020/02/18/wealthiest-universities-are-paying-big-endowment-tax-bills-how-much-are-others-who.

32. Hillary Hoffower and Andy Kiersz, "Millennials Make More Money than Any Other Generation Did at Their Age, but Are Way Less Wealthy. The Affordability Crisis Is to Blame," Insider, September 22, 2021, https://www.businessinsider.com/millennials-highest-earning-generation-less-wealthy-boomers-2021-9.

33. Kevin Drum, "Millennials Are the Highest Paid Generation in American History," September 20, 2021, https://jabberwocking.com/millennials-are-the-highest-paid-generation-in-american-history/.

34. Hoffower and Kiersz, "Millennials Make More Money than Any Other Generation Did at Their Age, but Are Way Less Wealthy."

35. Nicole Goodkind, "Millennials Are Ahead of Their Parents in Retirement Savings," CNN, April 27, 2022, https://www.cnn.com/2022/04/27/investing/retirement-millennials-boomers-saving-more/index.html.

36. Stacy Cowley, "Government to Cancel $6 Billion in Student Loans for Defrauded Borrowers," *New York Times*, June 23, 2022, https://www.nytimes.com/2022/06/23/business/student-loan-debt-fraud-settlement.html; Gabriel T. Rubin and Amara Omeokwe, "Biden's Student-Debt-Forgiveness Plan May Cost Up to $1 Trillion, Challenging Deficit Goals," *Wall Street Journal*, September 5, 2022, https://www.wsj.com/articles/bidens-student-debt-forgiveness-plan-may-cost-up-to-1-trillion-challenging-deficit-goals-11662370201.

Chapter 10: The Upcoming Wealth Heist

1. "U.S. High-Net-Worth and Ultra-High-Net-Worth Markets 2021," Cerulli Report, 2021, https://s3.us-east-1.amazonaws.com/cerulli-website-assets/documents/Info-Packs/2021/Cerulli-US-High-Net-Worth-and-Ultra-High-Net-Worth-Markets-2021-Information-Packet.pdf.

2. "GDP by Country," Worldometer, https://www.worldometers.info/gdp/gdp-by-country/.

3. Ben Eisen and Anne Tergesen, "Older Americans Stockpiled a Record $35 Trillion. The Time Has Come to Give It Away," *Wall Street Journal*, July 2, 2021, https://www.wsj.com/articles/older-americans-35-trillion-wealth-giving-away-heirs-philanthropy-11625234216.

4. Tanza Loudenback, "The Typical American Heir Is Now a Middle-Class 50-Something Who Puts the Money toward Retirement," Insider, November 21, 2019, https://www.businessinsider.com/personal-finance/older-americans-get-more-inheritances-use-for-retirement-2019-11.

5. Eisen and Tergesen, "Older Americans Stockpiled a Record $35 Trillion."

6. "Family Firm Facts," Grand Valley State University, Family Owned Business Institute, https://www.gvsu.edu/fobi/family-firm-facts-5.htm.

7. Jonathan Flack, "2021 Family Business Survey: US Findings," PwC, https://www.pwc.com/us/en/services/trust-solutions/private-company-services/library/family-business-survey.html.

8. "Historical Tables, 1.1," The White House, https://www.whitehouse.gov/omb/budget/historical-tables/.

9. "Financial State of the Union 2021," Truth in Accounting, April 15, 2021, https://www.truthinaccounting.org/library/doclib/Financial-State-of-the-Union-2020.pdf.

10. "Fact Sheet," US Social Security Administration, https://www.ssa.gov/news/press/factsheets/basicfact-alt.pdf; "Mandatory Spending in 2019: An Infographic," Congressional Budget Office, April 15, 2020, https://www.cbo.gov/publication/56325.

11. David John, "Misleading the Public: How the Social Security Trust Fund Really Works," Heritage Foundation, September 2, 2004, https://www.heritage.org/social-security/report/misleading-the-public-how-the-social-security-trust-fund-really-works.

12. Ibid.

13. "Summary: Actuarial Status of the Social Security Trust Funds," US Social Security Administration, June 2022, https://www.ssa.gov/policy/trust-funds-summary.html; "Social Security Primer," 2, Congressional Research Service, July 6, 2022, https://crsreports.congress.gov/product/pdf/R/R42035.

14. Nicole Lyn Pesce, "This Depressing Chart Shows the Jaw-Dropping Wealth Gap between Millennials and Boomers," MarketWatch, December 28, 2019, https://www.marketwatch.com/story/this-depressing-chart-shows-the-jaw-dropping-wealth-gap-between-millennials-and-boomers-2019-12-04.

15. "Social Security Primer," 2.

16. Ibid.

17. "Financial Report of the United States Government," Bureau of the Fiscal Service, FY 2021, https://fiscal.treasury.gov/reports-statements/financial-report/current-report.html.

18. Ibid.

19. Ibid.; "FY 21 Financial Report of the United States Government," https://fiscal.treasury.gov/files/reports-statements/financial-report/2021/fr-02-17-2022-(final).pdf.

20. Thomas Savidge and Jonathan Williams, "Unaccountable and Unaffordable," American Legislative Exchange Council, 2021, https://alec.org/wp-content/uploads/2022/06/UAUA-6th-Edition-WEB-1.pdf.

21. Nicole Goodkind, "The Market Meltdown Threatening Pensions for Millions of Americans," CNN, July 14, 2022, https://www.cnn.com/2022/07/14/investing/pensions-markets-unfunded/index.html.

22. Nishant Kumar, "Hedge Fund Titan Warns UK Pension Crisis Is Just the Start," Bloomberg, October 17, 2022, https://www.bloomberg.com/news/articles/2022-10-17/hedge-fund-titan-warns-uk-pension-crisis-is-just-the-start?sref=hmG4mtJl.

23. "PBGC Issues Final Rule on Special Financial Assistance," press release, Pension Benefit Guaranty Corporation, July 6, 2022, https://www.pbgc.gov/news/press/releases/pr22-28.

24. "Fact Sheet—Special Financial Assistance for Financially Troubled Multiemployer Plans," Pension Benefit Guaranty Corporation, July 6, 2022, https://www.pbgc.gov/sites/default/files/sfa/factsheet.pdf.

25. Robert Besser, "S&P 500 Lost $8 Trillion in First Half of 2022," India's News.Net, July 3, 2022, https://www.indiasnews.net/news/272608014/sp-500-lost-8-trillion-in-first-half-of-2022; Kerry Hannon, "Retirement savers lose over $3 trillion in stock market retreat," Yahoo Money, June 23, 2022·https://news.yahoo.com/retirement-savers-lose-stock-market-201508667.html.

26. Greg Rosalsky, "If a Wealth Tax Is Such a Good Idea, Why Did Europe Kill Theirs?" *Planet Money* (podcast), NPR, February 26, 2019, https://www.npr.org/sections/money/2019/02/26/698057356/if-a-wealth-tax-is-such-a-good-idea-why-did-europe-kill-theirs.

27. @TheHill, Twitter, October 24, 2021, https://twitter.com/thehill/status/1452351159604334599.

28. Erica York, "Summary of the Latest Federal Income Tax Data," Tax Foundation, January 20, 2022, https://taxfoundation.org/publications/latest-federal-income-tax-data/.

29. Rosalsky, "If a Wealth Tax Is Such a Good Idea, Why Did Europe Kill Theirs?"

30. Eisen and Tergesen, "Older Americans Stockpiled a Record $35 Trillion."

31. Ibid.

Chapter 11: Own Everything

1. "Accredited Investor," US Securities and Exchange Commission, https://www.sec.gov/education/capitalraising/building-blocks/accredited-investor.

2. Eddie Spence, "Bank of Russia Resumes Gold Buying After Two-Year Pause," Bloomberg, February 27, 2022, https://www.bloomberg.com/news/articles/2022-02-27/bank-of-russia-resumes-gold-buying-after-two-years-on-sidelines.

3. Jim Rickards, video interview, August 26, 2022; " Gold Is a Reserve of Safety—ECB President," GoldCore, October 18, 2013, https://news.goldcore.com/gold-is-a-reserve-of-safety-ecb-president/.

4. Jeff Thomas, "The Danger of Paper Gold," Doug Casey's International Man, https://internationalman.com/articles/the-danger-of-paper-gold/.

5. Lauren Foster, "Proposed Legislation Promises to Empower Investors. What to Know," *Barron's*, June 14, 2022, https://www.barrons.com/articles/proposed-legislation-promises-to-empower-investors-what-to-know-51655172926.

6. "29 CFR Part 2550: Prudence and Loyalty in Selecting Plan Investments and Exercising Shareholder Rights."

7. Glenn Gow, "The AI Bill of Rights: Protecting Americans from the Dangers of Artificial Intelligence," *Forbes*, January 9, 2022, https://www.forbes.com/sites/glenngow/2022/01/09/the-ai-bill-of-rights-protecting-americans-from-the-dangers-of-artificial-intelligence/?sh=126f88ea7173.

8. "Ron Coleman," Dhillon Law Group, https://www.dhillonlaw.com/team-showcase/ron-coleman/.

9. Ron Coleman, video interview, August 26, 2022.

10. "Larry G. Salzman," Pacific Legal Foundation, https://pacificlegal.org/staff/larry-salzman/.

11. Larry Salzman, video interview, August 23, 2022.

12. *Knick v. Township of Scott, Pennsylvania, et al.*, Supreme Court of the United States, argued October 3, 2018, reargued January 16, 2019, decided June 21, 2019, https://www.supremecourt.gov/opinions/18pdf/17-647_m648.pdf.

13. Tiffany Justice, video interview, August 22, 2022.

14. Ibid.

15. Ashlea Ebeling, "Farm Like a Billionaire—Harvest Tax Breaks," *Forbes*, June 6, 2012, https://www.forbes.com/sites/ashleaebeling/2012/06/06/farm-like-a-billionaire-harvest-tax-breaks/?sh=2aaec79b5777; Guido van der Hoeven, "Deducting Farm Expenses: An Overview," Iowa State University, Center for Agricultural Law and Taxation, April 3, 2020, https://www.calt.iastate.edu/article/deducting-farm-expenses-overview.

16. Jim Rickards, video interview, August 26, 2022.

17. Will Parker and Nicole Friedman, "Homeowner Groups Seek to Stop Investors from Buying Houses to Rent," *Wall Street Journal*, April 18, 2022, https://www.wsj.com/articles/homeowner-groups-seek-to-stop-investors-from-buying-houses-to-rent-11650274203.

18. Ibid.

19. Larry Salzman, video interview, August 23, 2022.

20. Andrew Egan, video interview, August 17, 2022.

21. Spencer Lindquist, "Here's How to Fight Back Against America's Emergent Social Credit System," Federalist, September 9, 2021, https://thefederalist.com/2021/09/09/heres-how-to-fight-back-against-americas-emergent-social-credit-system/.

22. @JesseKellyDC, Twitter, various, https://www.google.com/search?q=Jesse+Kelly+balkanize&client=firefox-b-1-d&sxsrf=ALiCzsZrdpHf7IR-wp5C2Or_br8Zl9lMBw:1660602643511&source=lnms&tbm=isch&sa=X&ved=2ahUKEwiRvbf18sn5AhUQGFkFHQZbB70Q_AUoAnoECAEQBA&biw=1536&bih=711&dpr=1.25#imgrc=TUim4byF3C-KAM.

23. Lindquist, "Here's How to Fight Back."

24. Clay Halton, "K-Percent Rule," Investopedia, updated September 14, 2021, https://www.investopedia.com/terms/k/k-percent-rule.asp.

25. Ines Ferré, "Bitcoin Bulls vs Bears: A Look at the Big Names Backing and Shunning Crypto," Yahoo, August 17, 2021, https://news.yahoo.com/bitcoins-bulls-vs-bears-184024406.html.

26. "Gold Demand Trends Full Year 2022," World Gold Council, January 31, 2023, https://www.gold.org/goldhub/research/gold-demand-trends/gold-demand-trends-full-year-2022/central-banks.

27. Ibid.

28. Tracy Alloway, "Crypto Critic Nouriel Roubini Is Working on a Tokenized Dollar Replacement," Bloomberg, May 9, 2022, https://www.bloomberg.com/news/articles/2022-05-09/crypto-critic-nouriel-roubini-is-working-on-a-tokenized-dollar-replacement?sref=hmG4mtJl.

29. Theron Mohamed, "Charlie Munger Says Buying Crypto Is Investing in Nothing—and He Avoids It Like a Dirty Sewer," Insider, July 12, 2022, https://markets.businessinsider.com/news/currencies/charlie-munger-crypto-bitcoin-warren-buffett-berkshire-hathaway-inflation-stocks-2022-7.

30. Nicolas Vega, "Warren Buffett Wouldn't Buy 'All of the Bitcoin in the World' for $25: 'It Doesn't Produce Anything,'" CNBC, May 2, 2022, https://www.cnbc.com/2022/05/02/warren-buffett-wouldnt-spend-25-on-all-of-the-bitcoin-in-the-world.html.

31. Tristan Bove, "Years after Calling Bitcoin 'Rat Poison,' Warren Buffett Just Invested $1 Billion in a Crypto-Friendly Bank," *Fortune*, February 16, 2022, https://fortune.com/2022/02/16/warren-buffett-invested-1-billion-crypto-bank/.

32. Ron Coleman, video interview, August 26, 2022.

INDEX

ABOUT THE AUTHOR

CAROL ROTH is a "recovering" investment banker; entrepreneur; TV pundit and host; speaker; economic, business, and financial commentator; content developer; and *New York Times* bestselling author. Her books include *The Entrepreneur Equation* and *The War on Small Business.*

Carol has worked in a variety of capacities across industries, including currently as an outsourced chief customer officer (CCO), as a director on public and private company boards, and as a strategic advisor and C-level consigliere.

Carol connects the dots on financial, business, and economic issues for novice and pro audiences alike.

She is also the creator of the Future File legacy planning system and software (FutureFile.com).

Carol advocates for small business, small government, and big hair. Coming from a blue-collar family, Carol has worked hard to seize the American Dream, and is fighting to preserve that opportunity for all Americans.

For more information or to connect with Carol, visit CarolRoth.com.